Walter Clark, Series Editor

Nor-tec Rifa!
Electronic Dance Music from Tijuana to the World
Alejandro L. Madrid

From Serra to Sancho:
Music and Pageantry in the California Missions
Craig H. Russell

Colonial Counterpoint:
Music in Early Modern Manila
D. R. M. Irving

Embodying Mexico:
Tourism, Nationalism, & Performance
Ruth Hellier-Tinoco

Silent Music:
Medieval Song and the Construction of History in Eighteenth-Century Spain
Susan Boynton

Whose Spain?
Negotiating "Spanish Music" in Paris, 1908-1929
Samuel Llano

Federico Moreno Torroba:
A Musical Life in Three Acts
Walter Aaron Clark and William Craig Krause

Representing the Good Neighbor:
Music, Difference, and the Pan American Dream
Carol A. Hess

Federico Moreno Torroba

A Musical Life in Three Acts

WALTER AARON CLARK
WILLIAM CRAIG KRAUSE

OXFORD
UNIVERSITY PRESS

OXFORD
UNIVERSITY PRESS

Oxford University Press is a department of the University of Oxford.
It furthers the University's objective of excellence in research, scholarship,
and education by publishing worldwide.

Oxford   New York
Auckland   Cape Town   Dar es Salaam   Hong Kong   Karachi
Kuala Lumpur   Madrid   Melbourne   Mexico City   Nairobi
New Delhi   Shanghai   Taipei   Toronto

With offices in
Argentina   Austria   Brazil   Chile   Czech Republic   France   Greece
Guatemala   Hungary   Italy   Japan   Poland   Portugal   Singapore
South Korea   Switzerland   Thailand   Turkey   Ukraine   Vietnam

Oxford is a registered trade mark of Oxford University Press
in the UK and certain other countries.

Published in the United States of America by
Oxford University Press
198 Madison Avenue, New York, NY 10016

Library of Congress Cataloging-in-Publication Data
Clark, Walter Aaron. Krause, William Craig.
Federico Moreno Torroba : a musical life in three acts /
Walter Aaron Clark, William Craig Krause.
p.   m.—(Currents in Latin American and Iberian music)
Includes bibliographical references and index.
ISBN 978-0-19-531370-3 (hardcover : alk. paper); 978-0-19-062846-8 (paperback : alk. paper)
1. Moreno Torroba, Federico, 1891–1982.   2. Composers—Spain—Biography.
3. Moreno Torroba, Federico, 1891–1982—Criticism and interpretation.
I. Clark, Walter, 1952– Krause, William, 1953–   II. Title.
ML410.M7776C53 2012
780.92—dc23[B]   2012019913

Publication of this book was supported in part by the John Daverio Endowment
of the American Musicological Society.

For Judith Cline and Carlin Miguel Krause

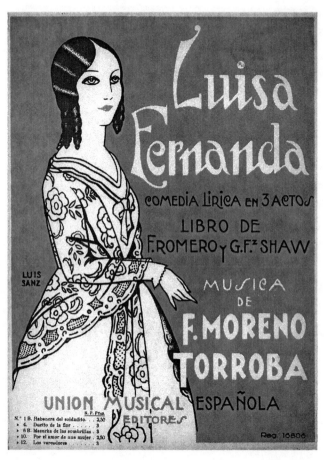

Cover art for the vocal score of Torroba's 1932 masterpiece *Luisa Fernanda*.
Courtesy of Unión Musical Ediciones

Federico Moreno Torroba As We Knew Him

It was a morning at the Hotel Suecia in Madrid. Our family was in the lobby after having breakfast when the great composer walked in looking for us. Upon meeting him, he ordered some tapas, and we immediately sealed a friendship that is eternal. It seemed surrealistic to us that the great genius of immortal melodies was embodied in such a friendly, totally personable, unassuming, humble man.

He soon took out a small pad and wrote down all of the ideas, thoughts, and wishes each of us had. He wanted to know and understand all of us. The result of this unforgettable meeting was the tremendously fruitful collaboration we were to have until the end of his life. Everything he wrote in that little pad became part of a masterpiece, as the readers will find out in this biography. The great composer wrote for each of us individually, and for the quartet he wrote many works that crowned his later years with glory.

In a perfect parallel with our musical collaboration was an intimate friendship of our two families. Torroba, with his daughter Mariana and his son Fede, would visit us for extended periods in our Del Mar, California, house. As well, we spent long stays in his Madrid home and his summer residence in Santesteban.

Torroba was the embodiment of the spirit of Spain. He was deeply touched by all that was around him and, through his gigantic poetic soul and his profound knowledge of his craft, he was constantly transforming his everyday experiences into music that glorified Spain and humanity. Torroba lived for the beauty of the moment and always exhibited a balance between his sweet, beautiful, loving spirit and his magnificent mind. He was a problem-solver, giving himself completely to the task at hand with the goal of bringing comfort and joy to all. And with his presence he brought harmony, happiness, and peace.

Celín, Pepe, and Ángel Romero

TABLE OF CONTENTS

ACKNOWLEDGMENTS

The Buddhist doctrine of dependent origination, *pratītyasamutpāda*, states that the history of our universe cannot be traced back to an Aristotelian (or Thomist) "uncaused cause." Rather, everything results from the interaction of preexisting forces, and there is no ultimate, autonomous source of all. In the Buddhist view, then, there can be no creator spirit—or any immaculately conceived books, for that matter. Although we are not Buddhists and cannot vouch for the cosmic truth of *pratītyasamutpāda*, we are certain that every biography, in particular, requires contributions from a small army of people—family, friends, scholars, publishers, librarians, archivists—stretching out in time and space. And every biographer knows from repeated personal experience that without that small army, no amount of individual insight or inspiration can prevail in producing much of lasting value. We therefore freely and cheerfully admit the dependence of this book's origination on the many people and organizations cited below, who gave so generously of their time and materials to make the first-ever biography of Federico Moreno Torroba possible. To all of them we offer a sincere "mil gracias."

Indispensable assistance came from the composer's son, Federico Moreno-Torroba Larregla. He has made the family archive in Navarra available and has provided counsel, guidance, personal recollections, and encouragement, as well as contacts with important people and copyright permission to use scores and photos in his collection. Without his help, we could never have written this book and would not even have tried. Several other individuals played important roles in this research. Guitarist Pepe Romero provided information about Torroba's music, photographs in his collection, and served as an early liaison between the authors and Torroba's family. In addition to Pepe, Celín and Ángel Romero had many useful and fascinating anecdotes to offer about the composer; moreover, we are extremely grateful for the eloquent Foreword all three brothers contributed. A friend and colleague of Torroba's for over twenty years, Santos Martín Pancorbo, was very helpful in clarifying issues of detail and context. Mrs. Andrés Segovia, widow of the guitarist, shared quotations from letters between her late husband and Torroba, while Alberto López Poveda, archivist for the Segovia estate, initially supplied important biographical information to Bill and later generously assisted guitarist Javier Riba in securing additional documentation at the Museo Andrés Segovia, in Linares, Spain. We also benefited from correspondence with the maestro's son, Carlos Segovia. Additional useful input came from guitarists David Grimes and Angelo Gilardino.

Interviews with musicologists Juan José Carerras, Tomás Marco, and Emilio Casares were very productive. Another Spanish musicologist, Leopoldo Neri, generously shared his groundbreaking research on guitarist Regino Sainz de la Maza with us. Antoni Pizà, director of the Foundation for Iberian Music at CUNY Graduate Center, also gave us valuable suggestions. We offer profuse thanks to Alfonso Pérez, a Mexican musicologist who was working on his doctorate at the Complutense in Madrid at the same time we were researching this book, for his selfless investigations on the authors' behalf, especially into matters of genealogy. We are very grateful for support and encouragement from our university colleagues past and present, including Michael Beckerman, whose insights inform several passages in this book.

We extend gratitude to our colleagues in Buenos Aires, musicologist Carlos Manso, Luciano Marra de la Fuente, Adriana María Costa of the Teatro Colón, and guitarist Irma Costanzo, for their help with gaining access to archival and other biographical materials and for permission to use photos from their collections. Special thanks are in order to José María Grillo Torres and Ricardo Formica of the Center for Cross Cultural Studies, Seville, for their guidance as we delved into questions concerning cultural life under Franco. We thank Claudia Flores de Franko and Ada Lis Jimena for their assistance in transcribing, and in some cases deciphering, garbled recorded interviews, as well as music theorist Barbara Mackin for her insights in musical analysis and Jay Batzner for typesetting musical examples.

Organizations worthy of mention include the Instituto Complutense de Ciencias Musicales, especially Emilio Casares Rodicio, director of ICCMU, and María Luz González Peña, director of the Centro de Documentación y Archivo. Many of the composer's manuscripts are located at the Sociedad General de Autores y Editores, as well as most of his publications, and we are indebted to the staff there, especially Antonio Gil, for their research assistance and copyright permission. The Unión Musical Ediciones (formerly Unión Musical Española), which published and retains rights to Torroba's zarzuela scores, also merits thanks for copyright permissions, as does the Museo de Historia in Madrid for permission to publish photos in their archive. We are grateful to the Archivo Ernesto Halffter, especially the composer's son Manuel Halffter, who manages the archive and provided photographs of Torroba and his father for our use. We shall not forget to thank the Iglesia Parroquia San José in Madrid, especially Pedro Pablo Colino, for timely archival support; the Archivo Militar in Segovia, especially José Ignacio Vázquez Montón, for their customarily gracious and highly efficient assistance; Jesús Cañadilla, groundskeeper at the sacramental San Justo, for guidance in locating the composer's grave; and the ever-professional staffs at the Biblioteca

Nacional, Hemeroteca Municipal, Archivo de la Administración in Alcalá de Henares, and library of the Real Conservatorio in Madrid for their unfailing assistance.

Naturally, we are thankful to Oxford University Press, especially music editor Suzanne Ryan, for agreeing to publish this book and waiting patiently for its completion. Funding for our research came from several sources, particularly the Program for Cultural Cooperation between United States Universities and Spain's Ministry of Culture, as well as our respective institutions (Bill's and Walter's): Hollins University in Roanoke, Virginia, and the University of California, Riverside. Most welcome was the publication subvention provided by the John Daverio Endowment of the American Musicological Society.

Special gratitude is reserved for musicologist Hugh Macdonald, who said upon Bill's completion of his dissertation in 1993, "Bill, this really ought to be a book someday." Now it is. Of course, without steady support and encouragement from our families, it would still not be. Bill's late mother, Anna Stregger, provided inspiration throughout his career, while his wife, Judith Cline, and son, Carlin Miguel, and Walter's wife, Nancy, and son, Robert, have contributed more than they know to the successful completion of this work.

Murrieta, California
Roanoke, Virginia
2012

LIST OF MUSICAL EXAMPLES

LIST OF PLATES

Frontispiece: Cover art for the vocal score of *Luisa Fernanda*
Courtesy of Unión Musical Ediciones

ABOUT THE COMPANION WEBSITE

www.oup.com/us/federicomorenotorroba

Oxford has created a password-protected Web site to accompany *Federico Moreno Torroba: A Musical Life in Three Acts*. This Web site presents a groundbreaking documentary exploring Torroba's relationship with the guitar through interviews with and performances by leading musicologists and guitarists. It features the authors of this book, Walter Aaron Clark and William Craig Krause, as well as the legendary guitarist Pepe Romero and the gifted young virtuosa Ana Vidovic. Produced by Stephen and Sheila Halpern (SMHmusicllc.com), it is the perfect complement to the biography and will be enjoyed by lovers of this composer's music and of the classical guitar.

Access with username Music4 and the password Book2497.

Federico Moreno Torroba

Introduction

"The Eternal Tradition"

Introduction:1a–g: Seven melodies

What do all these themes have in common?[1] For one thing, they were all composed in the 1900s, which is remarkable insofar as that was the century that witnessed the rise of atonality and ametricality in Western art music. These melodies,

[1] The melodies in order come from the *Sonatina*, 3rd mvmt. (1923), *Luisa Fernanda*, Act III (1932), *La Caramba*, Act I (1942), *Sonata-Fantasía*, 2nd mvmt. (1953), *Castillos de España*, "Turegano" (1968), *Concierto ibérico*, 1st mvmt. (1976), and a *seguidillas* melody that Torroba sketched on his deathbed (1982). Much will be said of these works in subsequent chapters.

all taken from that same classical repertoire, are resolutely tonal and metric. Moreover, though something in their modality and rhythmic character suggests an origin in folk music, not a single one of them is a quotation or even paraphrase of a preexisting or recognizable tune. That is to say that they comprise fundamentally folkloric elements in melody and rhythm, but these coalesce into lyric statements yielding no precise account of their origin. In short, they are utterly characteristic yet completely original at the same time.

In fact, their most salient commonality is that they were all written by the same composer; however, they span a period of over sixty years, each representing a different decade in the composer's prodigious output, from the 1920s to the 1980s. This makes the consistency among them nothing short of astonishing. In a century that prized artistic innovation, change, and "progress," often disdaining tradition in the process, these apparently innocuous but in reality artfully constructed themes stand out in their stubborn resistance to the new aesthetic currents that swirled around their genesis.

The creator of these melodies, a Castilian by the name of Federico Moreno Torroba (henceforth referred to simply as Torroba), enjoyed one of the greatest advantages a composer can hope for: he lived a long time. Born in 1891, the year in which Johannes Brahms composed his Clarinet Quintet in B Minor, op. 115, Torroba died a year before the 1983 premiere of Philip Glass's opera *Akhnaten*. His life thus spanned some of the most important developments in music—late Romanticism, Impressionism, Expressionism, Serialism, Neoclassicism, and Minimalism—as well as some of the most tumultuous decades in human history, characterized by unprecedented violence and destruction in tribal, civil, and world wars, with their attendant terror, aerial, and atomic bombings. Fascism, Capitalism, Socialism, Communism, and Anarchism—not to mention Catholicism, Protestantism, Existentialism, Atheism, and Nihilism—all competed for influence and control, their competition fueled by immemorial ethnic and racial feuds, national rivalries, mytho-history, pseudo-science, superstition, propaganda, and, on occasion, apparent mass hysteria. Tragically, Torroba's native Spain became the arena in which much of this ideological contest played out. As Antony Beevor aptly noted, "The incompatibility of 'Eternal Spain' with these new political movements developed into the clash which later tore the country apart."[2]

And yet, Torroba himself was, by all accounts, an amiable, gentle, kind, and generous man, one devoted to his family and possessing a charmingly self-deprecating sense of humor. Guitarist Pepe Romero was a close friend of the composer and states that "it was incredibly comfortable to be around him. He was very non-judgmental, and I was never nervous to play anything for him. But he was also hardworking and serious. He didn't talk a lot, but he was very observant. He occa-

---

[2] Antony Beevor, *The Battle for Spain: The Spanish Civil War 1936–1939*, rev. ed. (London: Penguin Books, 2006), 9.

sionally took a drink but never got drunk."[3] Ángel Romero confirmed that Torroba was not a talker, though when he spoke, the things he had to say "were like jewels." Moreover, he was "like a father, a grandfather, or an uncle—or the one you wanted to have."[4]

Catholic and loyal to the Spanish crown, Torroba nonetheless kept his distance from politics and political movements, never publicly declaring his opposition to or support for any ruler or regime, whether a constitutional monarchy, republic, or right-wing dictatorship. In fact, he wanted nothing so much as the peace and freedom to compose music, to commit to paper the resistless stream of lyric inspiration that flowed steadily from him, whether at the keyboard or the breakfast table. He was one of the dominant figures in Spanish music of the twentieth century, a composer best known for his zarzuelas (Spanish operettas) and guitar works but who was also active as an impresario and conductor and who played a crucial role in cultural administration as president of the Sociedad General de Autores de España (General Society of Spanish Authors) and director of the Real Academia de Bellas Artes de San Fernando (Royal Academy of Fine Arts of San Fernando).

Still, the fact remains that nationalist ferment and the philosophical roots of Torroba's music were intermingled in complex, at times ambiguous, but nonetheless undeniable ways. Though he was by no means a religious fanatic or political reactionary, no biographer could be excused for neglecting to interrogate the political posture of a person so closely situated to the *Sturm und Drang* of his own time and place. As George Orwell observed in his 1946 essay *Why I Write*, being apolitical in the name of art is in itself a political stance. Nonetheless, our interrogation will disappoint those looking to attach a precise political label to Torroba: it will lead neither to black nor white but rather to various shades of ideological gray.

Just as we refuse to attach political labels to Torroba, neither is it our purpose to determine the validity of earlier philosophical concepts regarding history, tradition, nation, and race that are interwoven with his art. Our age is quite different from the one in which Torroba came to maturity, for, after bitter experience, we have rightly come to disparage the notion that any country or group of people can or should be essentialized. After all, once you have reduced a polity or population to its imagined essence, exalting, exploiting, or even eradicating it is temptingly easy to justify. But neither can we dismiss the notion of such national or racial essences in our study of Torroba. Their actual existence is ultimately not the issue. What matters is that Torroba and other influential people *believed* that they were real and acted in decisive and enduring ways on those beliefs. That Spaniards are essentially different from all other peoples is beyond our ability to prove or disprove, though DNA research suggests that whatever genomic variations may exist between Spaniards and other

---

[3] Interview with Walter Clark, January 6, 2011.
[4] Interview with Walter Clark, September 20, 2011.

members of our species, they are in any case infinitesimal to the point of insignifi-
cance. Indeed, one suspects that genetic variation *within* the Iberian Peninsula is
greater than that between Iberia and many other regions of the world.[5]

Be that as it may, the music that arose from a belief in the essential differences
between Spaniards and everyone else—the uniqueness, though not necessarily
superiority, of Spanish culture—is anything but inconsiderable. Both the music
and the beliefs that animated it merit serious consideration, for Torroba was a
leading musical exponent in the twentieth century of the view, first articulated by
philosopher Miguel de Unamuno (1864–1936) in 1895, that there was an "eternal
tradition," a timeless, immutable essence of the Spanish people that emanated
from their folklore and daily life.[6] This is what Torroba consistently sought to
capture in his compositions. He is the logical and most attractive focus of any
study seeking to explore Unamuno's theory of an "eternal tradition" relative to
Spanish music. That is not our only purpose here, to be sure, but it is an important
purpose just the same (see Act II, Scene ii, for an in-depth treatment of this
subject).

So, why is this biography the first ever to be written of Torroba? Why are
serious scholarly publications devoted to this man and his music so few in
number?[7] Almost all the information in this book specific to Torroba was gleaned
instead from oral history, contemporary periodicals, and materials in the family
archive, not secondary sources of an academic provenance. And why is this volume
appearing fully thirty years after Torroba died? Is this an idea whose time is long
overdue in coming, or simply a bad idea?

When I mentioned to a fellow musicologist, an eminent and learned Hispanist,
a few years ago that Bill and I were working on this book, his immediate and
almost breathless reaction was, "*Torroba*? Wasn't he that . . . ?" I knew the words he

---

[5] For corroboration of these observations, see the American Anthropological Association's
statement on race at http://www.aaanet.org/issues/policy-advocacy/AAA-Statement-on-Race.cfm
(accessed August 1, 2010). Anthropologist Yolanda Moses describes race in definitive terms: "Most
people think biological race is real. [It is] not. Human variation is real. And the social construction of
race is real. Anthropologists and other biological scientists will tell you there is only one biological
race, because we are all the same species, *Homo sapiens sapiens*." See "Riverside Metropolitan Museum
Welcomes RACE Exhibit June 3," *Black Voice News* (online edition), June 2, 2010.

[6] Miguel de Unamuno, *En torno al casticismo*, ed. Jean-Claude Rabaté (Madrid: Cátedra, 2005), in
the chapter entitled "La tradición eterna."

[7] The principal published sources on Torroba's life are: Roger Alier and Xosé Aviñoa, *El libro de la
zarzuela* (Madrid: Ediciones Damien, 1982); Higínio Anglés, *Diccionario de la música* (Madrid: Ediciones
Labor, 1954); Antonio Olano, ed., *Homenaje a Federico Moreno Torroba* (Madrid: Sociedad General de
Autores de España, 1982); Enrique Pardo Canalis, "Necrologia del Excmo. Sr. D. Federico Moreno
Torroba," *Boletín de la Real Academia de Bellas Artes de San Fernando* (Madrid: Real Academia de Bellas
Artes de San Fernando, 1982); and an excellent entry by Javier Suárez-Pajares on him in the *Diccionario
de la zarzuela: España e Hispanoamérica*, ed. Emilio Casares Rodicio (Madrid: ICCMU, 2002). Periodicals
such as *El País, ABC,* and *Cambio 16* published lengthy obituaries. Interviews given by Torroba
throughout his life are also informative.

intended but hesitated to say: "composer associated with the Franco regime?" This is certainly part of the problem. It appears that Torroba was and continues to be viewed by some—imprecisely but persistently—as having been a fellow traveler with Franco. Pepe Romero, for one, contemptuously dismisses this notion: "He was the furthest thing from a fascist that you can imagine."[8] His brother Ángel wholeheartedly agrees, saying that "it is wrong to pass judgment on Torroba and others in the past."

Indeed, many eminent composers and artists made their peace with the Franco regime and flourished in Spain during the dictatorship, including not only Joaquín Rodrigo and Joaquín Turina, but also such stalwarts of the artistic avant-garde as Salvador Dalí and Joan Miró.[9] As Jorge Luis Marzo observed, during the depths of the dictatorship, in the 1940s and 50s, "many artists collaborated with prominent political and cultural figures of the regime in order to gain resources, visibility, and international projection."[10] Yet their reputations have not suffered. So, why tar and feather Torroba?

Perhaps it is because he was Catholic and a monarchist. But millions of his fellow Spaniards were the same, and that did not automatically make them suspect. Like many of them, Torroba was religiously and politically moderate and simply made the best he could of a potentially dangerous situation. Perhaps it is because of the conservative character of his nationalist aesthetic, which was anchored in nineteenth-century Romanticism. But his musical style remained unchanged throughout several different regimes, as we demonstrated at the outset here; it was in no way *intended by him* as a response to or affirmation of Francoism, though it may inadvertently have served that purpose at times. Perhaps it is because he moved with such ease in official circles, occupying prominent cultural posts that he could not have held without Franco's approval. But this aspect of his career can just as easily be explained by his innate capacity for administration and his affable temperament, which allowed him to get along well with colleagues of widely varying dispositions.

Let us be clear from the outset: Torroba *was* a conservative traditionalist, and some of his musical activities in the years during and immediately after the Civil War merit close scrutiny. But he was not a fascist composer, much less Franco's *Kapellmeister*. In fact, there is another explanation for the neglect to which he has been consigned that has not so much to do with politics as with class, if one may separate the two. Torroba was unapologetically bourgeois, and he cultivated a

---

[8] Interview with Walter Clark, January 6, 2011.

[9] Juan Pablo Fusi, *Un siglo de España, la cultura* (Madrid: Marcial Pons, Ediciones de Historia, 1999), 108, notes that Dalí got a free pass because he was Catholic and occasionally painted religious works, such as *El Cristo de San Juan de la Cruz* of 1951.

[10] Jorge Luis Marzo, *Art modern i franquisme: els orígens conservadors de l'avantguarda i de la política artística a l'estat espanyol (Arte moderno y franquismo: Los orígenes conservadores de la vanguardia y de la política artística en España)* (Girona : Fundació Espais d'Art Contemporani, 2007), 102.

style of music that he intended to be marketable, to please the audience, at a time when the avant-garde strove mightily to stick its collective thumb in the eye of that same bourgeois public (which nonetheless continued to support it, and ask for more!).[11] He specialized in composing pleasing guitar miniatures and zarzuela, forms of entertainment that required considerable craft, skill, and, yes, genius to bring forth, but which cultural elites disdained as inferior to symphony and opera—specifically, to German music. His stylistic disconnection from Expressionism, Impressionism, and Neoclassicism, i.e., from Schoenberg, Debussy, and Stravinsky, set him outside the parameters of the aesthetic debate that dominated Spanish music in the 1920s and 30s, between rival camps loyal either to Austro-German or Franco-Russian schools.[12] From a traditional musicological point of view, then, this has condemned him to a marginal position. Since Spanish music itself generally occupies the "suburbs" of musicological discourse, Torroba exists on the margin of a margin. This is no secret to Spaniards themselves.

Indeed, one must never underestimate the Spanish capacity for self-deprecation in regards to their classical music and those who composed it. The eminent Spanish musicologist Antonio Martín Moreno perceives a collective "inferiority complex" in regards to classical music.[13] The view prevails among even the musically literate populace that Spain has never produced composers to compare with its geniuses in art and literature, e.g., Goya and Cervantes, or to rival composers like Beethoven and Wagner. As Carol Hess notes, this is part of a pattern over the centuries, one in which Spain's ambivalent feelings about foreign influence took the form of "envy or defensiveness."[14]

Because Torroba was so overt in his promotion of the "eternal tradition" and remained wedded to an anachronistic nationalist aesthetic until his dying day, he made a conspicuous target for those who thought Spain's only hope as a musical presence in Europe was to imitate what France, Italy, and especially Germany were doing, e.g., to embrace the postwar avant-garde: atonality, serialism, and electronic music. Of course, Torroba would have none of this whatsoever. He did not even think that electronic music was actually, well, music![15] His son, Federico, Jr., artic-

---

[11] "The idea that the *avant-garde* and the bourgeoisie were natural enemies is one of the least useful myths of modernism," observed Robert Hughes in his *The Shock of the New* (New York: Alfred A. Knopf, 1996), 373.

[12] For an in-depth treatment of these trends in Spanish music between the two world wars, see Emilio Casares Rodicio, "La música española hasta 1939, o la restauración musical," in *España en la música de Occidente: Actas del Congreso Internacional celebrado en Salamanca 29 de octubre—5 de noviembre de 1985*, 2 vols., ed. Emilio Casares Rodicio, Ismael Fernández de la Cuesta, and José López-Calo (Madrid: Ministerio de Cultura, 1987), 261–321.

[13] Conversation with Walter Clark, August 19, 2010.

[14] Carol A. Hess, *Manuel de Falla and Modernism in Spain, 1898–1936* (Chicago: University of Chicago Press, 2001), 5.

[15] See Torroba's own remarks in Augusto Valera, "Federico Moreno Torroba: 'Luisa Fernanda,'" *El Noticiero Universal*, June 8, 1972, 21. "Electronic music is something that has nothing to do with

ulated Torroba's relationship with atonality in unmistakable terms: "It loses all its nationalism and thus its personality. Without a national identity, it could be from any country."[16] Is it necessarily a bad thing for music not to have a "national identity"? Of course not, but for a nationalist composer, it is the kiss of artistic death. This attitude is what led Luis de Pablo (1930–), leader of the Spanish avant-garde, to offer a rather qualified eulogy of the composer upon his death:

> The music of maestro Moreno-Torroba is the opposite of my own, of what I strive to create. It is the incarnation of a musical Spain from which I feel completely alienated. But that does not prevent me from lamenting his death, and from afar, I feel respect for him as a musical figure.[17]

In short, Spain's internal political struggles between nationalists and internationalists, between *españolistas* and *modernistas*, have migrated into the realm of musical historiography, and Torroba has gotten lost in the scrum.[18]

However, experience teaches that scholarly neglect in relation to Spanish music is more general. Walter's recent biographies of Albéniz and Granados, two respected major composers of enduring and renowned masterworks, were the first to appear in the English language, and remain among the few in any language.[19] We continue to lack a single monograph in English on any zarzuela composer (except the present volume), or even on a figure as eminent as Joaquín Turina.

Thus, Torroba's case remains unusual in the amount of neglect, but not extraordinary. After all, his major accomplishment was to write some of the most popular zarzuelas of all time. He was the last of the great *zarzueleros*, and his *Luisa Fernanda* (1932) is among the most successful and celebrated works in that genre. And yet, the zarzuela is now essentially moribund and a museum piece. No one in Spain

---

music; it is an experience in sound. As you know, music is harmony, melody, and rhythm." Of course, electronic music is quite capable of exhibiting these parameters as well, a distinction Torroba overlooks here. He did not think much of contemporary symphonic music, either. When asked where he thought that genre was headed, he was dismissive in his response: "In my opinion, nowhere. I don't believe in what they call 'contemporary music,' and because I don't believe in it, I don't compose it. I am convinced that it is a passing fashion." See Luis Sagi-Vela, "Moreno Torroba, nonagenario, trabaja diez horas diarias," *Ya Dominical*, November 15, 1981, 23.

[16] William Craig Krause, interview with Federico Moreno Torroba, Jr., Madrid, July 18, 1988. His full name is Federico Moreno-Torroba Larregla, but we will henceforth refer to him simply as Federico, Jr.

[17] Pablo's remarks appear in "Moreno-Torroba será enterrado hoy en la sacramental de San Justo," *ABC*, September 13, 1982, 39; reprinted in *Autores: Revista de información de la S.G.A.E.*, n3 (October 1982): 32.

[18] For the most insightful examination in English of this ideological and aesthetic debate in Spain during the first decades of the twentieth century, see Hess, *Modernism*.

[19] Walter Aaron Clark, *Isaac Albéniz: Portrait of a Romantic* (Oxford: Oxford University Press, 1999/2002) and *Enrique Granados: Poet of the Piano* (New York: Oxford University Press, 2006/2011).

composes zarzuelas anymore.[20] So, we might reasonably expect less than feverish interest in the composer of a genre that has literally gone the way of the horse and buggy. Beyond that, the zarzuela is an art form that has never gained much currency outside the Spanish-speaking world. It retains some popularity in Latin America and even parts of the US where there is a large Hispanic population,[21] but its repertoire, comprising hundreds of works, remains largely uncelebrated elsewhere. The lack of scholarly interest in Torroba outside of Spain can partly be explained by the simple lack of name recognition—or accomplishment recognition, as the case may be.[22] True, his guitar music is internationally renowned, but from a publisher's point of view, not to mention a musicologist's, its overall music-historical impact has been too limited to merit serious book-length investigation.

Why have not Spanish musicologists written books on him that would appeal to zarzuela aficionados in Spanish-speaking lands? The final nail in the coffin of neglect is precisely this: as will become clear in succeeding chapters, Spanish intellectuals have often taken a dim view of the zarzuela as a form of popular entertainment unworthy of serious musicological investigation. That attitude is now changing, but the net effect has been to retard our understanding of this extremely important aspect of Spanish culture and the artists who created it, artists like Federico Moreno Torroba.

When Spanish journalist Joaquim Zueras Navarro heard that two *norteamericanos* were researching this book in Navarra in 2006, he commented ruefully that it was unlikely to appear in Spanish translation, "given the scant interest that our nation shows in its composers."[23] This may initially strike one as a rather dire assessment, but it does seem to be the case that, traditionally, there has not been much of a market in Spain for scholarly books on classical music, particularly biographies—at least of Spanish composers. This view is embraced by, among

[20] As Janet Sturman, *Zarzuela: Spanish Operetta, American Stage* (Urbana and Chicago: University of Illinois Press, 2000), 25–26, observes, "It seems that audiences need to travel to Latin America or the United States for the rare opportunity to hear a freshly composed zarzuela, such as the Argentine production of *Viva la Verbena*, by Luis Aguile, or the New York production of *Los Jíbaros Progresistas* by Puerto Rican-born composer Manuel Fernández."

[21] For an excellent survey of its impact in the US, see Sturman, op. cit. *Luisa Fernanda* was revived in the US in 2004 by the Washington National Opera in DC, starring Plácido Domingo. This same production made its way to the stage of the Los Angeles Opera in 2007. Two other lovely L.A. productions, organized by Carlos Oliva and the Pacific Lyric Association, took place in 2009 and 2010. This group performed concert selections from *La chulapona* in March 2011.

[22] This was well understood by Torroba himself, who observed that "[In Spain] and South America, I am considered a lyric author; but in the rest of the world, I am better known as a composer for the guitar than for the theater." He made this disclosure in Lola Aguado, "Homenaje a Moreno Torroba," *Diario 16*, May 27, 1978. *Music Week* (Great Britain), December 6, 1980, observed that "Though not so well-known in this country as his compatriot Rodrigo, Torroba is immensely popular in Spain, with over 70 stage works."

[23] Joaquim Zueras Navarro, "Al respecto de Moreno Torroba," *OpusMusica*, n12 (February 2007). http://www.opusmusica.com/012/moreno.html.

others, Emilio Casares Rodicio, former head of the Instituto Complutense de Ciencias Musicales in Madrid and certainly in a position to know.[24] A curious reverse chauvinism dictates that the biographies people will buy are of composers like Beethoven and Wagner—and then in translation from non-Spanish originals.[25] Walter was once told by an editor at a leading publishing house in Madrid that biography in general was not a literary genre in which Spaniards specialized or excelled. The editor buttressed her argument by citing the case of Ian Gibson, the Irish scholar who has written the definitive biography of Federico García Lorca.[26] Now, that editor's perception may or may not correspond to reality, but it is worth noting nonetheless. Her observation, along with those by Martín Moreno, Casares Rodicio, and Zueras Navarro, is smoke suggesting the presence of fire. That this biography of Torroba has been written by two *anglosajones estadounidenses* and published by an Anglo-American publisher is not mere coincidence.

In 2003, Bill invited Walter to join him in writing the first-ever book on Torroba, using as a basis and guide Bill's own groundbreaking 1993 dissertation.[27] Of course, much additional research has been necessary, because new primary and secondary sources have surfaced over the intervening years. Yet, in a very real sense, this book is Bill's. Though Walter undertook the principal responsibility for writing it, to give it a consistent authorial voice, let there be no doubt: without Bill's pioneering writings and indispensable contributions as the principal researcher for this book, our biography of Torroba would not exist. And it appears that no one else would be taking up the resulting slack, for reasons that at this point should be blindingly obvious.

A final word, concerning the organization of this book. The use of acts and scenes may at first seem a gimmick. And yet, the reader will not be long in discovering that Torroba was, first and foremost, a man of the theater, a composer possessing not only a rare lyric gift but also a real love of drama, as well as a deep understanding and appreciation of his native Castilian language and literature. And it so happens that his life and work break down rather conveniently into the three-act format so typical of the *zarzuela grande* in which he specialized, beginning and ending with the traditional introduction and finale. Each act consists of three scenes: the first lays out the general historical and music-historical context; the second delves into biographical issues; and the third explores in depth selected compositions for the stage and the guitar. One could think of these as the scenic

---

[24] Conversation with Walter Clark, August 18, 2010.

[25] In all fairness, and modesty, Walter notes a happy exception to this general rule: the Spanish edition of his Albéniz biography, *Isaac Albéniz: Retrato de un romántico* (Madrid: Turner, 2002), which continues to sell several years after its appearance.

[26] Ian Gibson, *Federico García Lorca: A Life* (London and Boston: Faber & Faber, 1989).

[27] William Craig Krause, "The Life and Works of Federico Moreno Torroba" (PhD diss., Washington University, St. Louis, Missouri, 1993).

backdrop, dialogue narrative to advance the action, and lyric outpouring in response to that action. The historical scenes do not attempt to present a comprehensive, *Wikipedia*-style overview but rather focus on those events and developments that are crucial to understanding Torroba's world and worldview. Those already well versed in the history of Spain and Spanish music may choose to go directly to the biographical scenes.

This is the manner the authors have chosen to tell the story of Torroba's exceptionally long and productive life, and they hope it will facilitate the reader's study and appreciation of his particular humanity and genius. *¡Que así sea!*

Editorial policy: all quotations of Spanish-language source material appear in English translation only. Since the vast majority of sources for this book are in Spanish, providing the original along with the translation would take up too much space. All of these sources are in modern (mostly journalistic) prose and pose few difficulties in translation. Many of the secondary sources we relied on consist of press clippings in the family archive, in Navarra [Na]. Very often, these lack page numbers, authors, or even titles. Despite attempts to establish this information independently, a few citations remain incomplete. Because this is a jointly authored book, occasional use of the first-person personal pronoun, singular for Walter's voice and plural for both authors, is necessary in order to make clear who is speaking. That procedure will prevail for the remainder of the book. Finally, works whose titles appear in boldface on first mention are treated in greater depth in the third scene of each act.

ACT I

1891–1932

Back then, I fluttered like a mere sparrow; today, my wings long to soar like a golden eagle!

[Entonces yo volaba como un mísero pardal, ¡y hoy mis alas ambicionan vuelos de aguila caudal!]

Luisa Fernanda, Act I

ACT I
Scene i
1898
The End

"I saw this" is the caption to one of the many unsettling images of barbarity in Francisco Goya's unforgettable collection of etchings entitled "Disasters of War." It depicts villagers hastily fleeing French troops, a father urging his wife and daughter to hurry along, while a priest clutches a bag full of money.[1] There would be a lot more Spanish families fleeing violence in the decades to come, but this particular war resulted from Napoleon's invasion of the Iberian Peninsula in 1808 and the installation of his brother, Joseph, on the Spanish throne. It would take over five years and the intervention of the British, but the Spaniards eventually threw out the hated invader. Few conflicts in human history have provided more chilling examples of man's inhumanity to man. For it presented not only the set-piece battles typical of warfare in the previous century but also the savagery of guerilla war, the remorseless struggle between partisans and regular troops that took place in the shadows of "civilized" combat and scarred the psyche of a people for generations to come.[2]

The Spain that Napoleon invaded and sought to control was essentially a Castilian empire, mired in a late-feudal socioeconomic system that was autocratic and highly centralized. Beevor colorfully describes Spain as having had "the unbending pride of

[1] The print's Spanish title is "Yo lo vi" and is plate 44 in the collection *Desastres de la Guerra: Fatales consequencias de la sangrienta guerra en España con Buonaparte. Y otros caprichos enfáticos* (Fatal consequences of the bloody war against Bonaparte in Spain. And other emphatic caprices), created between 1810 and 1815. Robert Hughes, for one, is doubtful that Goya actually witnessed this occurrence, but the image of helpless innocents fleeing death and destruction is an apt one for much of the nineteenth and twentieth centuries in Spain. See Robert Hughes, *Goya* (New York: Alfred A. Knopf, 2003), 272–74, for more on this print and others in the series.

[2] For an excellent overview of this war, see Gregory Fremont-Barnes, *The Napoleonic Wars: The Peninsular War 1807–1814*, series: Essential Histories, ed. Robert O'Neill (Oxford: Osprey, 2002).

a newly impoverished nobleman, who refuses to notice the cobwebs and decay in his great house and resolutely continues to visualize the grandeur of his youth."[3] Indeed, a 1788 census revealed that fully half the adult Spanish males did no productive work. As the saying went, "one half of Spain eats but does not work, while the other half works but does not eat."[4] In short, the nobility, army, and Church were parasites supported by the starving rural proletariat. Such gross inequality prompted serious soul-searching and considerable unrest once the colonial curtain was rung down by events ultimately beyond the monarchy's control.

Why the Spanish empire crumbled in the 1800s is not the most relevant question to ask; rather, we might ponder why it did not disintegrate much earlier. The answer is that the collapse was a far more gradual process than the precipitous end in the early 1800s would suggest. In fact, as Hugh Thomas has observed, "For almost three centuries before 1808, Spain had been the most untroubled of European countries."[5] Yet, major steps on the road to ruin were taken at the defeat of the Spanish Armada (1588), the Thirty Years War (1618–48), and the War of the Spanish Succession (1701–14). Contributing to Spain's ruinous trajectory were pervasive religious bigotry and persecution, resulting in the expulsion of the Jews (1492), including some of the country's best minds; imperviousness to the more salubrious aspects of the Reformation; and the toxic influence of the Inquisition. In short, the heavy hand of the Church on the country's educational system and intellectual life retarded its progress and limited the Peninsular impact of the Enlightenment.

Yet, the Napoleonic war, or the *Guerra de Independencia*, as the Spaniards refer to it, was a bracket framing only one side of the nineteenth century. The other bracket fell into place nine decades later, in a war involving another rising imperial power, the United States. The contest was brief but produced no less devastating an effect. Spain's remaining possessions in the western hemisphere, Cuba and Puerto Rico, forever departed its embrace, as did the Philippines and other islands in the Pacific, including Guam and Wake Island (thus setting the strategic stage for the United States' war with another empire on the make, Japan).

In between these brackets, the calamities did not cease. Napoleon's invasion weakened Spain at precisely the time it was losing its colonial grip in the western hemisphere. All of its colonies in North, Central, and South America took the opportunity handed to them by Napoleon to assert their independence, to free themselves from centuries of Spanish imperial rule. By the 1820s, it was all gone, or nearly so, and Spain would now have to turn its attention within, simply to hold itself together. The expulsion of the French in 1814 brought the reactionary and highly unpopular despot Fernando VII to the throne, whom the French propped up in 1823 by means of another invasion. His death in 1833 would have been a relief had it not initiated a series of civil wars collectively known as the

---

[3] Beevor, *Battle for Spain*, 5.
[4] Ibid., 6.
[5] Hugh Thomas, The *Spanish Civil War* (New York: Simon & Schuster, 1994), 12.

Carlist Wars (1833–40; 1846–49; 1872–76). Fernando's young daughter Isabel II (1830–1904) ascended to the throne, with her mother, María Cristina (1806–78), serving as regent. This antagonized those loyal to the king's brother Carlos, whom they felt should have inherited the crown. But this was less a struggle between personalities and more a conflict over the nation's character and future. Carlism was basically an ultraconservative, agrarian, and very Catholic movement with deep roots in the Basque Country, Navarra, and Catalonia, regions in which separatist sentiment was intense. Navarra in particular made common cause with the other two regions in defense of its traditional *fueros*, or rights.

As if this were not enough, during the sixty years after France's exit in 1814 there were numerous attempted coups, some of which were successful.[6] The most significant of these was the *golpe de estado* of 1868, led by General Juan Prim. This banished Isabel II to Paris and eventually resulted in the First Republic (Prim himself was assassinated in 1870). The Republic had a short life, however, and the Bourbon monarchy returned to the Spanish throne in late 1874, under the leadership of King Alfonso XII. Just as the Carlist wars drew to a close and Spain began to achieve some measure of political stability and economic growth, however, anarchism descended on the country, especially in Catalonia. Anarchists were prone to setting off bombs in public places and assassinating government officials, as they sought to destabilize society in preparation for the radical restructuring they thought necessary for the utopia they envisioned.

Thus, the nineteenth was very possibly the worst century Spain had experienced since the Moorish invasion eleven centuries earlier. Much of this was due to fundamental political instability, exacerbated by the glaring inequalities in the socioeconomic structure of the country noted above. And these inequalities found expression in social unrest and attempts at repression. For, whatever the *Empereur*'s motivations in doing so might have been (including to protect the southern flank of his empire should Spain's alliance with him falter), the forceful introduction of French revolutionary ideas into the mainstream of Spanish society and thought initiated an ongoing conflict within the country between two diametrically opposed conceptions of Spain: a reactionary longing to return to the *ancien régime*, to a golden past haloed in Catholicism, absolutism, and the imperial splendor made possible by conquest and colonialism; and an opposing ambition to curtail the privileges and prerogatives of the Church, landowners, and nobility so that Spain could enter the ranks of modern liberal democracies, or at least constitutional monarchies, as a unified nation state under secular rule.

By the end of the nineteenth century, Spain was faced with difficult choices. The conservative faction clung to Catholicism, classical education, the monarchy, centralized government, and the prestige of the armed forces. The liberal faction favored a separation of church and state, secular and scientific education, regional autonomy, and universal suffrage. Finding common ground and reaching

---

[6] Beevor, *Battle for Spain*, 8.

compromise did not carry the day. The Restoration of 1874 was accompanied by the emergence of two powerful political parties in the Cortes (parliament) that controlled the government until the turn of the century. These parties, Liberal and Conservative, governed in rotation, at the pleasure of the monarchy. This "peaceful rotation," or *turno pacífico*, brought about a greater stability than Spain had experienced in seventy-five years, but it corrupted the constitutional guarantee of a representational Cortes. An extensive system of party operatives, or *caciques* (a Caribbean term for chieftain), ensured that the outcome of elections would perpetuate the *turno*. The two charismatic leaders who had kept extremism in check had no effective successors: Antonio Cánovas del Castillo (b. 1828), of the Conservatives, was assassinated in 1897, and Práxedes Mateo Sagasta y Escolar (b. 1825), of the Liberals, was assassinated in 1903, leaving a power vacuum. This was filled by the youthful King Alfonso XIII, who reached majority in 1902.

This situation tended to stifle innovation and harden attitudes favorable to the ruling elite. Their source of wealth and power was to be found in land—agriculture and natural resources—and in the bureaucracy itself, rather than in industry, science, or commerce. Without a large industrial or commercial base, Spain would continue to lag far behind the rest of western Europe, a fact not lost on the country's intellectuals and progressive politicians. In describing this era, Joseph Harrison memorably indicted "the motley assortment of parasites who dominated Restoration society: corrupt politicians, sterile bureaucrats, pious bishops, pedantic academics and incompetent generals [who were] responsible for the nation's decline."[7] In this environment of a weak aristocracy and corrupt political machine, any other outcome than the one that resulted from the Spanish-American War of 1898 is hard to imagine. This is how Spain entered the twentieth century, in which even worse calamities awaited.

In truth, the disastrous war with the United States actually did Spain little material harm. It did not cause an economic recession or jeopardize the monarchy. The textile sector was hardest hit, but only for a few years. In fact, the war freed the nation of burdensome colonial possessions, and it did not result in much domestic unrest. Still, Spain had been demoted to third-class status as a European power, one of virtually negligible influence and prestige. Even as France, Britain, Germany, Russia, and Italy were expanding their imperial domains, Spain's colonial cupboard was nearly bare.[8] All that remained was some real estate in Morocco, which would prove more of a burden than a boon.

---

[7] See Joseph Harrison, "Tackling National Decadence: Economic Regenerationism in Spain after the Colonial Débâcle," in *Spain's 1898 Crisis: Regenerationism, Modernism, Post-colonialism*, ed. Joseph Harrison and Alan Hoyle (Manchester: Manchester University Press, 2000), 56.

[8] See José Álvarez Junco, "History, Politics, and Culture, 1875–1936," in *The Cambridge Companion to Modern Spanish Culture*, ed. David T. Gies (Cambridge: Cambridge University Press, 1999), 73. He notes that "Spain had become a third-rate power some eighty years before, during Fernando VII's reign, when the vast majority of the American empire had been lost. From then on, all the rhetoric about imperial grandeur was empty. What the 1898 defeat did was to expose the rhetoric for what it was."

No, it was not so much material or political damage that required control, but rather psychological. In the words of Álvarez Junco, "if there was no real crisis, there was a very acute *consciousness* of crisis [italics added]. Contemporary Spaniards called these events "el Desastre," *the* disaster *par excellence*."[9] Spain had so long identified itself as a Great Power (even after it no longer was), that its diminished status in the world set intellectuals to pondering what had gone wrong and how to make things right again. What was Spain's place in the modern world, and how to achieve it? A group of writers collectively referred to as the Generation of 98 grappled with this dilemma. In novels, poetry, plays, and philosophical essays, these authors examined Spain's dilemma from a cultural standpoint.[10] British historian Raymond Carr viewed this group's motivation as "primarily the protest of a literary minority against the conformism, emptiness, rhetoric, and ignorance of the existing educational and literary establishment, which, in its turn, reflected the 'organized corruption' of the structure created by the Restoration statesmen."[11] There are differences of opinion concerning which authors to include in the Generation of 98, but in any case, they did not have a coherent program or manifesto of any kind. Still, the 98 consisted of some notable literary figures, including novelist Vicente Blasco Ibáñez, journalist Francisco Martínez Ruiz (known as Azorín), poet Antonio Machado, and philosopher Miguel de Unamuno. The redefinition—or reaffirmation—of Spanish identity was one of the principal tasks of these writers, and though they devoted little attention to music, composers would play a major role in the process of defining what it meant to be Spanish in the modern age.

Within the loosely knit group were two major currents of thought that paralleled the political developments of the time. The traditionalists believed that by resurrecting the past heroes of Spanish history and literature, they might somehow recover the glories of the *Siglo de Oro*. This group tended to be conservative and suspicious of foreign influences. For them, it was the overwhelming influence of France and Italy during the past two centuries that had contributed to the decay of authentic Spanish culture. The more liberal element felt that Spain's salvation lay in imitating Europe. These writers studied major European philosophies and political systems and sought ways to apply them to the Spanish situation. In any case, both groups were seeking a basis for action and were not interested in speculation.[12] Writing was regarded "as a method of investigating man's existential

---

[9] Ibid., 74.

[10] The 98 writers were part of a larger renascence in Spanish literature. In the opinion of John Butt, *Writers and Politics of Modern Spain* (New York: Holmes and Meier Publishers, 1978), 15, around 1900 there emerged "five major writers (Unamuno, Valle-Inclán, Juan Ramón Jimeenez, Gabriel Miró, Antonio Machado) whose best work, though often poorly translated or not translated at all, is an important contribution to European literature." A central figure during this era is certainly José Ortega y Gasset. His classic *Invertebrate Spain*, trans. Mildred Adams (New York: W. W. Norton and Co., 1937), is a deeply insightful commentary on Spain's condition and place in the modern world.

[11] Raymond Carr, *Spain: 1808–1975*, 2d ed. (Oxford: Clarendon Press, 1982), 528.

[12] Donald Shaw, *The Generation of 98* (New York: Barnes and Noble, 1975), 14.

situation"[13] in general, and finding a solution to Spain's faltering identity in particular.

Unamuno devoted much of his work to recapturing the essence of what it meant to be Spanish; for our purposes, he is the central figure in this development. It is important to understand, however, that his views underwent a fundamental transformation in 1897, in response to a personal crisis. In his 1895 essays entitled *En torno al casticismo* (On Genuine Spanishness),[14] Unamuno held that the old Castilian spirit survived beneath the "dead, reactionary traditionalism of his own day, mistakenly thought to be *castizo* [pure]."[15] The recent succession of regimes had done more to perpetuate the negative aspects of the Spanish character than to preserve its glory. Their xenophobia had taken Spain out of the international arena and deprived the country of its place among the great nations of the world. Spain would have to open up to developments in the rest of Europe and at the same time hold on to its uniqueness, which was found in the "eternal tradition" of the common people. True *casticismo,* then, is fidelity to this noble *tradición eterna,* which persists despite decadence. (More will be said of these concepts in Act II, Scene ii.)

However, after 1897, Unamuno turned away from Europeanization and instead promoted the idea of *hispanidad,* the distinctive traits that united people of the Hispanic world, in contradistinction to the rest of Europe. This rejection of Europe was accompanied by an increasingly interiorized spirituality.[16] From this point on, the words Spanish and European became incompatible, and the attempt of the Spaniard to see himself as essentially European resulted in a hopeless hybrid. The Spanish soul was something other than the sum of its parts. While its ancestors had come from Africa, Asia, and Europe, the Spaniard was ultimately a unique cultural entity.

Yet, despite all such philosophical ruminations, there really were serious problems in the social, political, and economic structure of Spain as it entered the twentieth century, and these were not merely "psychological" in nature. Persistent poverty drove a half million Spaniards (almost 4 percent of the population) to resettle in the Americas during the first decade. Life expectancy was the same as it

[13] Ibid.

[14] These appeared in the Madrid periodical *La España moderna* in 1895 and only later appeared in book form (1902). The first essay, published in the February issue (vol. 7, no. 74), was entitled "La tradición eterna," and that will remain the focus of our attention. We rely on the most recent edition of it, i.e., *En torno al casticismo,* ed. Jean-Claude Rabaté, 127–55. As Rabaté points out in his introduction (p. 14), the year before he began publishing these essays, Unamuno joined the Partido Socialista Obrero and contributed to the Bilbao socialist weekly *La Lucha de Clases* (Class Struggle).

[15] Shaw, *The Generation of 98,* 45.

[16] See Amy A. Oliver, "The Construction of a Philosophy of History and Life in the Major Essays of Miguel de Unamuno and Leopoldo Zea" (PhD diss., University of Massachusetts, 1987), 106. Also see Clark, *Granados,* 110–12, for more on Unamuno and *casticismo* in the context of Granados's *estilo goyesco.*

had been four centuries earlier, about thirty-five years. Literacy varied from one region to the next, but overall, one-third of the population could neither read nor write. Two-thirds of Spanish workers were employed in agriculture.[17] True, the First World War created a demand for neutral Spain's manufactured goods, agricultural produce, and raw materials, and this generated a sharp spike in its economic vitality and prosperity; banks, mining, iron, steel, paper, textiles, shipbuilding, and agriculture all benefitted. And there was a corresponding improvement in working conditions, reduction of illiteracy, increase in the number of students enrolled at universities, and in the number of periodicals, from 1,890 to 2,289.[18]

However, when the war ended, stagnation returned with a vengeance. Meanwhile, political and legal corruption made genuine reform difficult, if not impossible. The ruling elite, mainly powerful business interests and landowners, ensured that elections and courts were rigged to produce the desired results, "right down to the village tribunals.[19] Socialism, anarchism, and communism gained momentum in response to these problems and were, by their very nature, inimical to the old order, especially the Church, which they regarded as a medieval institution that colluded with the aforementioned elites in exploiting the lower classes.[20] The anarchists staged repeated terrorist attacks and assassination attempts, some successful. In addition to the assassinations of Cánovas and Sagasta, these included the bombing of the Teatre Liceu in Barcelona (1893), as well as the attempted assassinations of General Martínez Campos (1893) and Alfonso XIII (1906). To protest conscription for the war in Morocco, socialist forces rose up during the so-called "Tragic Week" in Barcelona in July 1909, burning seventy convents and bringing the city to its knees. More labor unrest ensued as a result of the economic contractions of the postwar period, and during the years 1918–20, there were uprisings in Andalusia and strife in Barcelona, giving this interlude the sobriquet the "three years of bolshevism."[21] To top that off, the following year witnessed the founding of the Spanish Communist Party.

The fundamental instability of Spanish society made the country exquisitely difficult—perhaps even impossible—to govern effectively, and on top of everything else, Alfonso XIII (reigned 1902–1931) proved to be a highly ineffective monarch. Rather than finding a way to defuse tensions, he instead became increasingly autocratic, and the legitimacy of the central government in Madrid steadily eroded. The worst crisis of his turbulent reign came in July 1921, when local tribesmen under the leadership of Abd el-Krim wiped out an entire division of the

---

[17] Beevor, *Battle for Spain*, 9.

[18] Casares, *Actas*, 278.

[19] Beevor, *Battle for Spain*, 9.

[20] Or as Beevor, *Battle for Spain*, 13, put it, "Much of the teaching of the Spanish Catholic Church sounded appropriate to the Dark Ages and this mental repression, together with the political role played by ecclesiastical authorities, made the Church rank with the civil guard as the first target of an uprising."

[21] Cited in ibid., 15.

Spanish army in Morocco. The king had egged the military on to battle, hoping for a victory to celebrate on the feast day of St. James. Instead, he had precipitated a disaster, and in a now time-honored Spanish tradition, the army soon rose up in revolt. Miguel Primo de Rivera (1870–1930), captain-general of Catalonia, issued a *pronunciamiento* on September 16, 1923, and assumed the role of dictator, reducing Alfonso XIII to the status of a mere figurehead.

At first, this dramatic change satisfied society's need for stability and order, and business interests in particular welcomed military rule; in fact, they were joined by some prominent intellectuals, like José Ortega y Gasset. And as dictators go, Primo de Rivera was relatively benign. As Thomas notes, "Though he used officers to run the municipal governments for three years, imprisoned or exiled those who opposed him, and banned political parties, there were no political executions during his six and a half years of power."[22] Indeed, he evenhandedly brought the leftist labor leader Francisco Largo Caballero into his government. Moreover, his rule "witnessed the spread of new forms of mass entertainment such as cinema and sport, together with the burgeoning of various avant-garde artistic movements, giving rise to the so-called 'Silver Age' of Spanish culture."[23] Add to this several public-works projects, expanding dams, roads, railways, and rural access to electricity, and he might even qualify as the sort of enlightened despot celebrated in many an eighteenth-century opera.[24] In fact, Primo de Rivera was not a fascist in the modern sense but rather an old fashioned *caudillo* (protector, chief of state). He had assumed power to protect Spain from itself, and he clung to the notion that individual rights were a form of national suicide, "the arabesques of unemployed intellectuals."[25]

Yet, he had an Achilles heel, and that was political naiveté combined with incompetence; thus, he soon wore out his welcome. As Beevor notes:

> Bankers and industrialists hated his intervention in matters he did not understand. The middle classes started to react when he interfered with the universities. Alfonso began to fear for his throne, and Caballero came to regret having signed on. Primo presented his resignation to the king on 28 January 1930 and went into exile. He died in Paris a few weeks later.[26]

[22] Thomas, *Spanish Civil War*, 25.

[23] "Cultural Policy in Spain" (Madrid: Real Instituto Elcano de Estudios Internacionales y Estratégicos, 2004), 3.

[24] As Thomas, *Spanish Civil War*, 26, observes, Primo de Rivera was "patriotic, magnanimous, sympathetic, and tolerant, while his physical and his moral courage, in Cuba, the Philippines and Morocco, were well-attested." But his autocratic instincts did not serve him at all well, and he tended to take the law into his own hands. When Miguel de Unamuno criticized his governing style, the dictator exiled him to the Canary Islands.

[25] Carr, *Spain: 1808–1975*, 566.

[26] Beevor, *Battle for Spain*, 18.

With the death of Primo de Rivera, the king's own grip on what power he had left quickly loosened, and a Republican alliance was formed in August 1930, determined to end Spanish monarchy once and for all. Strikes and general upheaval followed in the wake of these developments, and elections in April 1931 gave the socialists and Republicans victory. The Second Spanish Republic became a reality on April 14, 1931.[27] Niceto Alcalá Zamora, a Cordovan landowner and Catholic, faced daunting problems as the first president of Republican Spain. The military was not happy, especially with the prospect of reductions in their forces, particularly among the bloated officer corps; separatist movements in the Basque country and Catalonia now smelled blood in the water and pressed their demands; and the relationship between Church and state had to be defined anew. International banking and business interests were suspicious of the leftist regime's intentions.[28]

It did not take long for these simmering feuds to boil over into violent conflict. In particular, the burning of churches by mobs in Madrid and elsewhere prompted only a lukewarm response from the revolutionary government, which quickly moved to ban the Jesuit order, nationalize its property, end state subsidies to the Church, and secularize education—first of all by removing crucifixes from classrooms. One usually thinks of Spain as one of the great bastions of Roman Catholicism, so it comes as a bit of a shock to learn that even in the 1930s, less than 20 percent of Spaniards attended mass on anything like a regular basis, and in some areas, especially the south, the figure was a fraction of that. In fact, religious attendance was lower in Spain than in any other Christian country. None of this prevented Cardinal Pedro Segura y Saénz (1880–1957) from asserting that, in Spain, at least, one was "either a Catholic, or nothing at all."[29] Many Spaniards obviously chose to be nullities rather than heed the good Cardinal's summons to piety. The Church and its right-wing allies perceived Spain's problems in simplistic terms, blaming a coalition of Jews, Freemasons, and communists for the unrest. Only a year after the birth of the Second Republic, General José Sanjuro launched a failed coup attempt. This was a fell harbinger of things to come.

The Musical Parallel

The history of Spanish music during the 1800s is one of general decline followed by florescent renewal. The decline reached its nadir in the first half of the century

---

[27] Ironically, the Republicans had the initial support of General Francisco Franco and other like-minded military leaders. Their sympathies would prove short-lived. Torroba's most-admired politician, Romanones, however, remained loyal to the old regime, even asking the Civil Guard to intervene in preventing a Republican takeover. See Beevor, *Battle for Spain*, 19.

[28] Beevor, *Battle for Spain*, 21.

[29] See ibid., 23–26, for more on the status of the Church in Spain during this period.

and was in large measure the consequence of the disasters summarized above.[30] Economic growth and increasing political stability in the last half of the century, however, made possible a corresponding enlargement of cultural life, with the advent of nationalist composers who commanded international attention and the rise of homegrown musical theater. Cultural infrastructure, in the form of music schools, choral societies, symphony orchestras, and opera companies, also increased in quantity and quality, mainly through the patronage of an expanding bourgeoisie with enough time and money to devote to the finer things in life. This renascence was especially pronounced in Barcelona, an industrial powerhouse intent on transforming itself into a cultural capital.[31] Madrid would also play a central role in this rebirth.

Nationalism

The underlying motivation for the late-century florescence of Spanish music was a spirit of nationalism, partly in response to the turmoil and uncertainty Spain was facing, in an attempt to affirm its identity and relevance in the modern world, and partly as a response to the general current of nationalism pervading Europe in the nineteenth century, a current that was swiftly carrying the continent toward cataclysms of civil and world wars in the twentieth. The patriarchal figure in the history of Spanish nationalism is certainly Felipe Pedrell (1841–1922), composer, musicologist, and pedagogue. Pedrell urged Spanish composers to use the historical music and folklore of Spain as the inspiration and foundation for their works, rather than aping foreign styles or standing passively by as Spain was defined by foreign composers. While he was a prolific composer, with over three hundred opus numbers, his main contribution was in the areas of musicology and ethnology. As editor of collections of works by Renaissance masters such as Victoria, Guerrero, and Cabezón, he brought the past glories of Spanish music to the forefront. His historical investigations gave coherence to the continuity of Spanish music, and decades of research culminated in his four-volume *Cancionero popular español* (1919–20), the most ambitious collection of Spanish folk music of its day.[32]

However, Pedrell's thorough knowledge of Spanish music brought him to the disturbing conclusion that there was a sort of identity crisis in Spanish culture. As

---

[30] See Walter Aaron Clark, "The Iberian World: The Philippines, Latin America, and Spain," in *Nineteenth-century Choral Music*, ed. Donna M. Di Grazia, series: Studies in Musical Genres, ed. R. Larry Todd (New York: Routledge, 2012). According to Casares, *Actas*, 268, during the 1830s, Prime Minister Juan Álvarez Mendizábal drastically reduced spending for music. In particular, orchestral music was not supported or cultivated in Madrid, which lagged behind even small cities in Germany and Belgium in this regard.

[31] See Clark, *Enrique Granados*, 76–80, for more on Barcelona's transformation.

[32] See the entry on Pedrell in the *New Grove Online*, by Walter Aaron Clark. Among the leading scholars in this field is the Catalan musicologist Francesc Cortès, who has been responsible for reviving several of Pedrell's operas.

an introduction to his opera *Els Pirineus* (1891), he wrote the essay *Por nuestra música*, in which he rejected slavish imitation of foreign models and argued for the creation of a national opera based on Spanish folk song. In Casares's view, Pedrell's multifaceted activities dovetail ideologically with the Generation of 98: recovering Spain's musical past, increasing the intellectual sophistication of contemporary Spanish music through better preparation of Spanish musicians, and engaging with mainstream trends in the rest of Europe. But it would not be Pedrell or his fellow travelers who would advance Spanish music itself. That would be the job of the composers who followed his advice, including Isaac Albéniz, Enrique Granados, Conrado del Campo, Manuel de Falla, Joaquín Turina, and several others.[33]

If one were to characterize the status of Spanish musical nationalism in the decades just before and after 1900, one could say that it had two main facets: international and domestic. There were Spanish composers and performers active throughout Europe whose works and interpretations disseminated an autochthonous profile of Spanish musical culture, instead of one invented by inspired foreigners (as indelible and convincing as those foreign works may often be). Certainly the music of these internationalists had a domestic following, but the overwhelmingly dominant genre of Spanish music *in Spain* during this period was not instrumental but rather theatrical, i.e., zarzuela. In other words, Spain asserted its musical identity abroad through media and genres that were not bound up with the Spanish language and were thus exportable, in the form of solo-instrumental and orchestral music, and occasionally (though never very successfully) opera—and then in foreign translation. On the home front, Spanish nationalism asserted itself principally in the only kind of entertainment that attracted a mass audience—not opera, least of all Spanish opera, or chamber music or symphonies, but rather zarzuela.[34] Any composer seeking fame and fortune in Spain by writing music of a Spanish character—affirming what was distinctive about Spanish culture, customs, language, and folklore—wrote zarzuela. To provide some idea of the incredible popularity and potential profitability of the zarzuela, some ten thousand of them were composed during its golden age, from 1850 to 1950—on average, about one new zarzuela every eighty-eight hours, for a hundred years.[35]

---

[33] See Casares, *Actas*, 266.

[34] Symphonic organizations were slow to develop in Spain, but by the early 1900s, they existed. Although they did perform works by Spanish composers like Campo, there was not a sufficient public for such music to provide composers with a reliable livelihood. Casares, *Actas*, 270, points to the creation of the Sociedad Nacional de Música, the Orquesta Sinfónica de Madrid (1905), directed by Arbós, the Filarmónica of Pérez Casas, and the Orquesta Sinfónica de Barcelona (1910) of Lamote de Grignon. These groups were important in promoting orchestral music, especially symphonic poems, concertos, and suites, but not symphonies. Spaniards in the latter half of the nineteenth century took scant interest in composing symphonies, which audiences regarded as a German genre, not a local one.

[35] See Christopher Webber, *The Zarzuela Companion*, foreword by Plácido Domingo (Lanham, Maryland: Scarecrow Press, 2002), 5.

Those musicians having an international impact wrote for the instruments on which they performed. They would provide the foundation for the advent of composers in the twentieth century with greater range and technique. The most prominent of these pioneers were undoubtedly Albéniz (1860–1909) and Granados (1867–1916). Later composers like Falla (1876–1946), Turina (1882–1949), Joaquín Rodrigo (1901–99), and Torroba all followed, to one extent or another, in the footsteps of these two trailblazers, who basically defined the sound of Spanish music—as composed by Spaniards—in the modern era.

Albéniz and Granados were complementary figures. Albéniz had an international career as a touring virtuoso in Britain, France, and Germany, and he acquired fame through his suites of pianistic miniatures, evoking the various regions and regional folklore of Spain. Feeling disaffected from what he regarded to be the cultural, political, and religious backwardness of his homeland, he spent the last nineteen years of his life as an expatriate, first in London (1890–93) and then Paris (1894–1909). His crowning achievement is *Iberia*, a collection of twelve extended and difficult pieces for solo piano. This represented an extraordinary evolution in the nationalist aesthetic through its combination of his characteristic *españolismo* with highly complex formal and harmonic structures. In particular, it bears the imprimatur of contemporary Parisian Impressionism, especially of Debussy. It was this fusion that pointed the way for Falla and Turina, who extended their compositional reach into other media and genres, including ballet and symphonic works.

Granados and Albéniz were close friends, and both hailed from Catalonia. Both studied with and were deeply influenced by the teachings (if not the music) of Pedrell. Unlike Albéniz, however, Granados remained in Barcelona almost his entire life, aside from two years of piano study in Paris as a young man (1887–89). He was active as a performer and conductor, but he chiefly made a living as a teacher, establishing a music academy bearing his name. His devotion to music pedagogy also differentiates him from Albéniz, who took no such interest.

Granados had a more conservative musical temperament than Albéniz and did not come under the spell of French Impressionism.[36] However, he would also have an impact on Spanish music through his *Goyescas* suite for piano. This set of six highly original works drew its inspiration not from Andalusian towns, songs, and dances, as did *Iberia*, but rather from Madrid in the time of Goya. Goya's colorful depictions of streetwise bohemians known as *majos/as* were the touchstone for Granados's musical evocations of that earlier time and place. Although his musical language was thoroughly grounded in late Romanticism, in the piano works of his

---

[36] Granados was more conservative in several respects. Whereas Albéniz made no secret of his socialist leanings and atheism, Granados abjured politics and remained Catholic. Albéniz's father was a customs official and a Freemason, while Granados's father was an army officer and came from a family with a history of military service. Though born in Catalonia, Granados was ethnically Castilian, whereas Albéniz had Basque and Catalan ancestry.

idols Chopin, Schumann, and Liszt, he blended these currents with the urban folklore popular around 1800. Granados's *Twelve Spanish Dances* from the early 1890s and his *Goyescas* from 1911 brought him international renown, so much so that the operatic version of *Goyescas* premiered at the Metropolitan Opera in New York in 1916.[37] If Albéniz's *Iberia* heralded a Franco-Andalusian dimension of twentieth-century Spanish nationalism, Granados's fixation on Goya and Madrid was a vital precursor to Spanish neoclassicism, a crucial shift away from Romantic evocations of Andalusia toward an emphasis on Castile as the true nexus of Spanish history and identity, timeless and universal. Torroba would manifest a similar fascination with Goya, one no doubt indebted to Granados's example.

Like Albéniz, Falla and Turina resided for an extended period in Paris and were influenced by Debussy. They returned to Spain at the outbreak of the First World War but remained closely connected with foreign artists and composers. Falla inherited Albéniz's mantle as the leading innovator with his Impressionistic *Noches en los jardines de España* for piano and orchestra and his ballets *El amor brujo* and *El sombrero de tres picos*, all dating from the 1910s. This final work is transitional toward the neoclassicism of the 1920s, in which Falla's guiding star was no longer Debussy but rather Stravinsky. As Hess observed, "Falla saw Stravinsky as a model to Spanish composers."[38] Falla's contemporaries and successors, composers and critics alike, hailed him and his example as the best that Spanish music had to offer, though he was a polarizing figure as well because of his affiliation with Picasso and Stravinsky, whom conservatives considered corrupting influences in Spanish culture.[39]

In works such as *El retablo de Maese Pedro* (1923), for marionettes, singers, and chamber ensemble, and *Concierto para clavicembalo* (1926), Falla employed neoclassical bitonality, in which the juxtaposition of keys and the instrumentation allude to the interweaving of times past and present, as also found in the poetry of Rubén Darío.[40] While Falla employed compositional techniques of non-Hispanic composers such as Stravinsky in these works, the spirit of his native music remained clearly evident. *El retablo de Maese Pedro* recounts episodes from *Don Quijote*, while the Concerto recalls music of the eighteenth-century Spanish court by alluding to the keyboard styles of Domenico Scarlatti and Antonio Soler. It also draws on themes from the sixteenth century, especially Juan Vásquez's song "De los álamos vengo, madre." Later composers, especially Rodrigo and Ernesto Halffter, would combine Falla's neoclassical musical procedures with the flamenco touches that characterized his style from the 1910s. This became the standard

---

[37] The composer assisted in the production but perished on his return voyage when the ship on which he was sailing was attacked by a German submarine. Albéniz, by contrast, died in his bed from nephritis. Both died at the same age, just short of their 49th birthdays.

[38] Hess, *Modernism*, 101.

[39] For a thorough treatment of this phenomenon, see ibid., 161–79.

[40] Ann Livermore, *A Short History of Spanish Music* (New York: Vienna House, 1972), 196.

musical aesthetic of the post-Civil War period, the one that foreign audiences would come to identify as characteristically Spanish.

Turina arrived in Paris in 1905, and he studied at the Schola Cantorum with Vincent d'Indy. His works show a stronger influence of the French school, especially the innovations of Debussy.[41] His works were by no means lacking in evocative Hispanicism, however, and Albéniz inspired him to compose music grounded in his native culture.[42] Thus, nearly all of his compositions bear programmatic titles referring to Spanish customs and localities, and incorporate traits of folk music—particularly that of Andalusia. Turina's style remained tied to Franco-Andalusianism, featuring elegant and subtle evocations of his native Seville in the *Sinfonia sevillana* and *Canto a Sevilla*.

These composers represent the musical parallel to the literary Generation of 98,[43] whose influence continued to be felt throughout the first decades of the twentieth century. They were active later than their literary counterparts and lived well into the twentieth century, long enough to see the consequences of the cultural and political revolution that had begun in the late nineteenth century. In contrast to the cooperative spirit prevalent among Spanish intellectuals in the 1920s and 30s, the writers of the Generation of 98 seldom collaborated with musicians of the same period.[44] It was the following generation of writers, led by García Lorca, who made common cause with Falla and younger composers. To the Spanish intellectual at the turn of the century, the word "culture" designated literature and philosophy, while "art" referred to the plastic arts. Music was not part of this scheme. This attitude can be traced to the eighteenth century and persisted well into the twentieth.[45] The parallel to be drawn between the Generation of 98 and its musical contemporaries is their common goal to revitalize Spanish culture and respond to foreign ideas from a position of self-assurance rather than dependence.[46]

The First World War solidified certain divisions within Spanish cultural spheres, between the *aliadófilos* and *germanófilos*. Liberals sympathized with the French, while conservatives and Catholics sided with the Germans. Those composers with close connections to Paris, like Falla and Turina, aligned themselves with the

[41] See Isabelle Laspeyres, "Joaquín Turina à Paris," *Revue internationale de musique française* 9/26 (June 1988): 61–84.

[42] Turina wrote that "Albéniz showed us the road we had to follow," in "Sobre Granados," *Revista musical hispano-americana* 3 (April 30, 1916): 7.

[43] Tomás Marco, *Historia de la música española: siglo XX* (Madrid: Editorial Alianza, 1983), 40.

[44] According to Marco, *Historia*, 18, literary members of the Generation of 27 were in much closer contact with their musical counterparts than were the members of the Generation of 98, which was more interested in literature and the plastic arts. "It is certain that the literary figures of the 98 were, in general, absolutely indifferent to music."

[45] Marco, ibid., notes that music was dropped from the university curriculum in the eighteenth century.

[46] Marco, ibid., 40.

French. Others, especially Conrado del Campo, sympathized with Germany. On balance, French influence prevailed in the 1920s.[47]

Criticism

Crucial during the early decades of the twentieth century was the rise of music criticism in Spain. Casares describes the first almost forty years of the century as a kind of golden age of music criticism, and the periodicals and newspapers of the time—especially *El Liberal, El Periódico, El Debate, El Imparcial, La Voz, El Sol*—provided information about premieres, performers, concerts, reviews, writings, manifestos, and economic conditions. Criticism of the time focused on musical theater, and most of the writings were either for or against Wagner, whose operas were linked with symphonic works as the ultimate expressions of German music. During the 1920s, however, the pendulum began to swing in favor of the French. *La Voz* and *El Sol* were supportive of the French avant-garde, while *ABC, Debate,* and *Liberal* were less so.[48]

The leading figure in this development was Adolfo Salazar (1890–1958), who wrote for *El Sol*. He was a reliable defender and promoter of modernism, Europeanization, and the avant-garde. Salazar championed the new music of Falla, Debussy, Stravinsky, and Ravel, and encouraged the evolution of Spanish music in the early twentieth century as it advanced from progressive nationalism to Impressionism and then to neoclassicism.[49] Not surprisingly, Salazar was opposed to regionalism as a "depressive" force that resisted national unity, with Madrid as the national center of power. Though regionalism may have played an important role in preserving and promoting local styles of music and dance, it belonged to the Romantic age, not the modern, and was anachronistic.[50]

As Casares observes, "the confrontation between new and old in music gives the 1920s and 30s the impression of simultaneous anachronism, of traditionalism and modernity, a process between regeneration and restoration...a ferocious battle, an authentic crusade, with a grand protagonist, Adolfo Salazar."[51] No less a figure than Rodrigo praised Salazar's writings in *El Sol* for opening a window on musical life in Madrid and for expanding local vistas toward Europe.[52]

With the advent of the Second Republic, Salazar called for the creation of a Dirección de Música y Teatro Lírico Nacional, a permanent organization that "would escape from the political waves of influence, which will be invigorated to

---

[47] See Casares, *Actas*, 288–90.

[48] Ibid., 277–80.

[49] Ibid., 285.

[50] Ibid., 286–88.

[51] Ibid., 304.

[52] Cited in Emilio Casares Rodicio, "Música y músicos de la Generación del 27," in *La Música en Generación 27: Homenaje a Lorca, 1915–1939,* ed. Emilio Casares Rodicio (Madrid: Ministerio de Cultura, 1986), 22.

the point it is thought indispensable." Although Salazar disapproved a prominent role for *zarzuelistas*, he had no problem with composer Amadeo Vives (1871–1932): "the clear intelligence of the gifted and friendly author of zarzuelas presents no danger." But he was convinced it was unwise to bring in others who may be musically as gifted but "do not have his general or good sense." Was this a shot across Torroba's bow? He makes his targets clear enough in the following:

> Though the author of the trendy foxtrot or tango or *cuplé* or latest national hymn may think he has the same rights to be consulted, the leaders of the Republic do not have to permit the predilections of Caligula. Spain is a country where music culture does not have a tradition or roots, and therefore, it will always be relegated to a subaltern position in relation to the plastic arts and the administration of the artistic treasures of Spain, with its cathedrals, museums, altars, and monuments.[53]

In the eternal debate between Europeanization and *casticismo*, between universalization and isolation, Salazar and other progressives looked to Falla to point the way ahead, not necessarily in the precise style of his music but by his progressive example.[54]

During the 1920s and 30s, many new composers came to the fore. As with the those analogous to the Generation of 98, these composers are identified by their literary contemporaries.[55] The Generation of 27 was comprised of writers active in the years immediately preceding and during the Second Republic (1931–36), especially Federico García Lorca (1898–1936). The corresponding musicians of this period were active in Madrid and Barcelona. In the capital city were Ernesto (1905–89) and Rodolfo Halffter (1900–87), Gustavo Pittaluga (1906–75), Rosa García Ascot (1902–2002), Salvador Bacarisse (1898–1963), Julián Bautista (1901–1961), Fernando Remacha (1898–1980), and Juan José Mantecón (1897–1964). Collectively they were known as the Grupo de los Ocho, or "Group of Eight," in imitation of *Les Six* in Paris. They issued their manifesto in 1930 at the Residencia de Estudiantes in Madrid, declaring their mutual predilection for "Pure music. Without literature, philosophy, strokes of fate, physics or metaphysics."[56]

---

[53] All of the above appears in Aldolfo Salazar, "La reorganización del teatro lírico nacional y de los conciertos sinfónicos," *El Sol*, April 14, 1931.

[54] See Casares, *Actas*, 303, and "Música y músicos," 22.

[55] See Casares, "Música y músicos," 20–34, for more on the Connection between music and literature.

[56] Cited in Ruth Piquer Sanclemente, *Clasicismo moderno, neoclasicismo y retornos en el pensamiento musical español (1915–1939)* (Sevilla: Editorial Doble J, 2010), 156. For an in-depth examination of the relationship between *Les Six* and its Spanish epigones, see Elena Torres Clemente, "Interrelaciones personales y artísticas entre 'Les Six' y el Grupo de los Ocho de Madrid," in *Cruces de caminos: Intercambios musicales y artísticos en la Europa de la primera mitad del siglo XX*, ed. Gemma Pérez Zalduondo and María Isabel Cabrera García (Granada: Editorial Universidad de Granada, 2010), 167–213.

Those active in Barcelona included Federico Mompou (1893–1987), Roberto Gerhard (1896–1970), Manuel Blancafort (1928–), Ricardo Lamote de Grignon (1899–1982), and Eduardo Toldrá (1895–1962).

The Parisian musical scene was a Mecca-like antipode to German Romanticism and its metaphysical, autobiographical, subjective approach to composition. The Generation of 27 sought to free itself completely from such literary and philosophical pretensions in music. Among Spanish writers, Ortega y Gasset, Eugenio d'Ors, and Antonio Machado shared this anti-Romantic view. Instead, the neoclassical aesthetic in particular conceived of music "as a merely playful act of diversion, considering it as a mental and intellectual discipline and thereby a type of participation in the culture of the moment. A consequence of this was the preference for symphonic music rather than musical theater."[57]

Wagner did not rate highly among this Generation, but neither did zarzuela, especially of the kind Torroba wrote, anchored as it was in Puccini and late Romanticism. As Casares memorably expressed it, "The music of the 27 is anti-Romantic, anti-rhetorical, anti-plebian, and anti-pathetic, pro-cinema, sport, circus, happiness, purity, mathematics, pro-forma, pro-French, and anti-German."[58] Beyond this, Falla's neoclassical phase served to redefine Spanish identity, establishing Castile as the source of national essence and renewal, rather than Andalusia. This was perfectly in keeping with the sentiments of the Generation of 98, for Unamuno and Azorín, in particular, had affirmed "the historical originality of Castile as the unifying force of the peninsula and the creator of its culture."[59] But this idea now found expression in a musical language of the European avant-garde, en rapport with the Generation of 27. As Julián Bautista described Falla's aesthetic in *El retablo* and the Harpsichord Concerto:

> And it is curious that Falla, in order to universalize himself, finds his authentic Spanish personality and then Castilianizes his style: it is recti-linear, dry, geometric. His Andalusian side disappears. It is presented denuded of sensualism. Because the essential characteristic of Castile is not the sensual nor the exuberant, nor the nostalgic: it is the severe, muscular, and sober.[60]

Another influential critic, tending toward the other end of the ideological spectrum from Salazar and Falla, was Rogelio Villar (1875–1937). He was a strong proponent of nationalism, which he broke down into three basic types: 1) that in which one finds direct citations of folklore, in the context of a highly developed style; 2) another kind in which such citations are not accompanied by a cultivated

---

[57] Casares, "Música y músicos," 23–25.
[58] Ibid., 30.
[59] E. Inman Fox, "Spain as Castile: Nationalism and National Identity," 32.
[60] Cited in ibid., 31.

style, which predominates in Spain, particularly the zarzuela and regional music; and 3) a final one in which references to folklore, scales, modes, rhythms, etc., are stylized and lend themselves to the avant-garde, like *The Rite of Spring*.[61] In his *El sentimiento nacional en la música española*, Villar declared that "To universalize our music should be the ideal of the Spanish school...not just writing about the songs of the people but creating them, inventing them."[62] He proposed Albéniz, Ruperto Chapí, and Tomás Bretón as models of composers who composed folklore rather than simply transcribing or mimicking it. Although he does not mention Torroba, our composer's approach to nationalism was of the kind Villar approved; however, they differed on the subject of French music. Torroba was a great admirer of Ravel, while Villar was an antimodernist who regarded Impressionism as "an avalanche of vulgarity and barbarism that comes from the north and is invading our art of fidelity; a gross sensuality of technique for the sake of technique."[63] Villar extolled Wagner and Richard Strauss, saying in his essay *Músicos españoles* that "it is not possible to become a composer without following the royal road that is the German tradition, because all music that does not have an intimate connection with the German classics is destined to live but a short time."[64]

The Second Republic greatly concerned itself with culture and promotion of the arts, as a form of social upliftment as well as an affirmation of Spain's modern identity. Its principal aims in regard to music were several:

1. Give music a social function;
2. Incorporate music into contemporary intellectual life;
3. Stimulate musical creation;
4. Decentralize music in response to regionalist sentiments;
5. Revive musicological investigation;
6. Reform music education;
7. Change the conception and organization of orchestras, choral groups, opera and zarzuela companies;
8. Promote folklore.[65]

Moreover, the government issued a decree already on July 21, 1931, creating the Junta Nacional de Música y Teatros Líricos (National Committee for Music and Lyric Theater).[66] In addition to Salazar as secretary, it consisted of the following:

---

[61] Casares, *Actas*, 306.

[62] Cited in ibid., 307.

[63] From Villar's *Sentimiento*, cited in Casares, "Música y músicos," 28.

[64] Cited in Casares, *Actas*, 289.

[65] Casares, *Actas*, 315.

[66] For information about this decree and the Junta, see "Disposiciones legales," *La Música en la Generación del 27: Homenaje a Lorca, 1915–1939*, ed. Emilio Casares Rodicio (Madrid: Ministerio de Cultura, 1986), 256.

President: Óscar Esplá

Vice President: Amadeo Vives

Members: Manuel de Falla, Conrado del Campo, Joaquín Turina, Ernesto Halffter, Salvador Bacarisse, Facundo de la Viña, Enrique F. Arbós, Bartolomé Pérez Casas, Arturo Saco del Valle, Eduardo Marquina, Jesús Guridi

Even a casual glance at this list reveals a preponderance of the avant-garde, modernist wing of Spanish music. This would change when the elections of 1933 brought the conservatives to power and the Committee was reorganized by 1935. Thus, the members of the original Junta never had enough time in which to realize their ambitious program for the revitalization (as they saw it) of Spanish music; nonetheless, their brief tenure represents a defining moment, one never to be repeated.

The domestic scene was dominated by a different cast of musical characters. For though the music of Albéniz, Granados, Falla, Turina, and others certainly figured prominently in the concert life of Spain, the majority of people who went to theaters for entertainment went to see zarzuela, not concert music. The zarzuela had by far the greatest impact in Spain among Spanish types of music, and its composers gained considerable fame, while remaining virtually unknown outside the Spanish-speaking world, even to this day. Whereas international audiences are familiar with Albéniz, Falla, and the others, they do not recognize at all names like Barbieri, Chueca, Caballero, Bretón, Giménez, or Vives. Yet, these men occupy the same revered niches in the pantheon of Spanish music as Gershwin, Porter, Rodgers, Loewe, Bernstein, and Sondheim do in American musical theater.[67] A brief overview of the zarzuela's history is necessary here if we are to situate Torroba in the proper musical lineage.

Zarzuela

The zarzuela is the only type of musical theater whose name derives from a plant. It gets its unusual designation from the venue where it was born, the Palacio de la Zarzuela, outside Madrid, which itself was named after the bramble bushes, or *zarzas*, growing around it. The first zarzuela was *El laurel de Apolo*, with a text by Pedro Calderón de la Barca and music by Juan Hidalgo. It premiered in 1657, during the reign of Felipe IV, and exhibited two traits that would come to characterize the genre. First, its use of spoken dialogue in alternation with musical numbers set it apart from opera, which featured continuous singing throughout, either in arias or recitative. In this respect, it resembled other national genres such as German *Singspiel* and French *opéra comique*. Unlike Italy, Spain had a strong tradition of theater, and audiences preferred hearing dialogue in their native

---

[67] An indispensable collection of essays about the Broadway musical is William A. Everett and Paul R. Laird, eds., *The Cambridge Companion to the Musical*, 2d ed. (New York: Cambridge University Press, 2008).

tongue delivered through speaking rather than recitative.[68] Second was its use of music and dance grounded in Spanish folklore. For instance, *El laurel de Apolo* features a shepherdess singing a *seguidilla*, a type of song and dance with stanzas of four to seven lines in a quick 6/8 meter. The emphasis in zarzuela on musical numbers, especially of a popular character, has meant that throughout its history and even today, "most contemporary devotees would argue that the music is by far the most memorable component of the zarzuelas they know."[69] In that respect, it strongly resembles Broadway musicals. Indeed, without a succession of spirited songs and dances like "I'll Go Home with Bonnie Jean," it is unlikely *Brigadoon* would have attracted much of an audience with its dialogue and drama alone, well crafted though they are. The same is true of the musical's Spanish cousin.

During the eighteenth century, zarzuelas became increasingly Italianate, reflecting the enormous popularity and dominance of Italian opera. Not surprisingly, there was a reaction against this dominance, which resulted in the cultivation of new genres related to the zarzuela, the *sainete* and *tonadilla escénica*. Both were lighthearted skits set in contemporary society and featuring equally accessible music of a popular character. They often appeared in between the acts of a more substantial dramatic work. The chief difference between them was in their structure, as the *tonadilla escénica* featured an introduction, main section, and musical finale in contrast to the *sainete*'s simpler layout. The word *sainete* comes from *saín*, fatty parts of a kill given to hunting dogs. Thus, *sainete* means literally a kind of treat or delicacy (in cooking, it means seasoning or sauce). The leading figure in the cultivation of these immensely popular genres was Ramón de la Cruz (1731–94), whose more than 400 *sainetes* portray in delightful detail everyday life in the Madrid of that epoch. Those familiar with the contemporary conflict in Paris between proponents of French and Italian operatic styles, the so-called Quarrel of the Comic Actors, will see some similarity in the desire of Spanish composers and audiences to push back against Italian domination of the stage.

The upshot of all of this, however, was that the zarzuela gradually faded from view, squeezed out of favor by Italian opera on one side and these lighter domestic genres on the other. By the early 1800s, zarzuela was dormant. However, like Sleeping Beauty, it would be awakened from its slumber by the kiss of a composer capable of providing it with new life: Francisco Barbieri (1823–94). In 1851, Barbieri's *Jugar con fuego* (Playing with Fire) introduced a new generation to the charms of zarzuela, alternating spoken dialogue with set numbers. However, part of the reason for this work's success was the obvious debt its music owed to the ever-popular operas of Rossini.[70] In some respects, the history of the modern zarzuela did not really begin until 1874, with the premiere of Barbieri's other big

---

[68] See Louise Stein, *Songs of Mortals, Dialogues of the Gods: Music and Theatre in Seventeenth-century Spain* (Oxford: Clarendon Press, 1993).

[69] See Sturman, *Zarzuela*, 18.

[70] Donald P. Thompson, "*Doña Francisquita*, A Zarzuela by Amadeo Vives" (PhD diss., University of Iowa, 1970), i, 131–40.

hit, *El barberillo de Lavapiés*. There is an obvious reference to the *Barber of Seville* in the title, though Lavapiés is a neighborhood in Madrid and far removed from Andalusia; the diminutive *barberillo*, or "little barber," is another variation. But the most significant departure from Rossini's work is the extensive use of popular Spanish songs and dances in the score. The characters talk, sing, and dance in a manner typical of the lower classes.

El barberillo de Lavapiés became the prototype for almost all zarzuelas to follow, including Torroba's. Although Madrid is most often the setting for zarzuelas during the genre's ensuing golden age, several feature regional settings, e.g., Aragon (*Gigantes y cabezudos* by Caballero), Andalusia (*La tempranica* by Giménez), Murcia (*La parranda* by Alonso), and Toledo (*El huésped del sevillano* by Guerrero).[71] Some notable dramas even take place outside Spain, e.g., Italy (*La canción del olvido* by Serrano), the Middle East (*El asombro de Damasco* by Luna), Mexico (*Don Gil de Alcalá* by Penella), and Russia (*Katiuska* by Sorozábal). But most deal with Spain, and these rely so heavily on cultural and linguistic nuance that they are difficult to export to non-Spanish-speaking countries.[72]

Yet, there is a bifurcation in the zarzuela's evolution at this point, in the emergence of two principal varieties: the *género grande* (large variety) and the *género chico* (light variety). The *zarzuelas grandes* were in three acts and often featured historical subjects, especially those set in the courts of the Spanish nobility. Barbieri's *El barberillo de Lavapiés* is an example of this kind of work, as its action takes place in the Madrid of Carlos III, in the eighteenth century. The stylistic distance from *grande* to opera was not at all great, and the only substantive difference was the continued reliance on spoken dialogue in the former. An early experiment in creating modern *opera española* was carried out by Emilio Arrieta (1821–94), who converted his 1855 *zarzuela grande Marina* into an opera by substituting recitatives for the spoken dialogue. Yet, in whatever form, the debt zarzuela owed to Italian prototypes, especially Rossini, was obvious in its emphasis on numbers, subordinate accompaniments, and vocal *fioritura*.[73]

It is in no way surprising that Barbieri believed Wagner an inappropriate model for Spanish opera composers to follow. Instead, he preferred Italian opera, as did Torroba, and he buttressed his argument by stating that "The most philosophical and perfect musical composition will produce indifference and even hostility if a clear and expressive melody does not prevail in it. . . . I am opposed to those composers who drown the melody in a lot of dissonant modulations."[74] But he need

---

[71] Volker Klotz, "Aspectos nacionales y estéticos de la zarzuela," *La Chulapona*, program notes for the production at the Teatro de la Zarzuela, Madrid, September 14–October 1 and October 11–30, 1988 (Madrid: Teatro de la Zarzuela, 1988), 35–36.

[72] Josef Öhrlein, "La zarzuela y el casticismo madrileño," *La Chulapona*, program notes for the production at the Teatro de la Zarzuela, Madrid, September 14–October 1 and October 11–30, 1988 (Madrid: Teatro de la Zarzuela, 1988), 23.

[73] See Hess, *Modernism*, 26.

[74] Cited in Casares, *Actas*, 272.

not have worried. Although a few prominent composers strove mightily to fulfill the dream of launching *ópera española*, the movement never really got off the ground. Salazar, for one, thought it a doomed enterprise, citing the general indifference to it not only on behalf of the public and government but also the critics, performers, and most composers. With the closing of Madrid's Teatro Real in 1925 (as we will see, Torroba's *La virgen de mayo* was the final production), the Teatre Liceu in Barcelona was the only stable opera theater in Spain.[75]

Instead, musical theater was dominated by the comic one-act music dramas of the *género chico*, which harkened back to the *sainetes* of an earlier epoch;[76] in fact, sometimes composers continued to use that same name for them. In contrast to the historical settings of the *grande*, the *chico* featured Madrid itself—"her people, her buildings and streets, and her traditions"—as their central theme.[77] As Webber points out:

> The great *sainete* composers, such as Chueca, wrote simply and directly, utilizing the forms of popular urban dances such as the *chotis* (schottische), mazurka, *pasodoble* and, from further afield, the Spanish American tango and habanera. Some versatile musicians such as Ruperto Chapí (1851–1909) and Manuel Fernández Caballero (1835–1906) were able to keep a foot in both camps, producing *chico* and *grande* zarzuelas as occasion demanded.[78]

The plots themselves revolved around the joys, fears, and foibles of the people, i.e., workers, officials, police, bartenders, artists, and organ grinders. The middle and lower classes who attended these unpretentious productions could readily recognize their world in them. Whatever irony or satire the dramas contained was there to provide light social commentary, to create the illusion that they had some political influence.[79] Perhaps the most popular and enduring example of the *chico* genre is Tomás Bretón's *La verbena de la paloma* (Festival of the dove), of 1894, which he labeled a *sainete lírico*.

However, *La verbena de la paloma* brings to the fore the problem of nomenclature surrounding the zarzuela during its revival, and that is the wide variety of designations composers used to categorize their works. As Sturman aptly notes,

> The term zarzuela has always been a fairly elastic designation, but after 1880 it became even more so. Depending on the circumstances of

[75] Casares, *Actas*, 274–75.

[76] Adolfo Salazar, in *La música de España: La música en la cultura española* (Buenos Aires: Espasa-Calpe, 1953), 282, states that the *género chico* is an example of the kind of drama that has existed "throughout history: Plautus, Terence, and others."

[77] Patricia Bentivegna, "A Study of Three Zarzuelas Madrileñas Together with a Historical Outline of the Zarzuela" (master's thesis, Columbia University, 1955), 59.

[78] Webber, *Zarzuela Companion*, 5.

[79] Öhrlein, *La Chulapona*, program notes, 1988, 24.

performance and plot, designations such as *juguete, revista, sainete, parodia, humorada, apropósito, écloga, pasatiempo,* and others were applied to various types of theatrical presentation featuring music. All these forms were considered to be close relatives to zarzuela, and examples of them were frequently billed as such, despite the composers' labels.[80]

Indeed, as Hess points out, even Breton's *sainete lírico* "includes accompanied recitative and melodrama."[81] The chief distinction between zarzuela and its related forms is that they rely on spoken dialogue to advance the action, whereas operas depend on recitative to do this (though both genres may include melodrama, like Beethoven's *Fidelio*.) We will see that Torroba also used a wide variety of labels in designating his theatrical works.

In any event, both the *grande* and *chico* genres were soon facing stiff competition from one of the variants mentioned above, the *revista*, an adaptation of the Parisian music-hall revue. Subsequent writers have coined the pejorative term *género ínfimo*,[82] "the most inferior genre," to describe the *revista*. Its immense popularity derived more from its "feminine revelations" than its dramatic or musical quality.[83] These works served as a conduit for mild political satire and lighthearted commentary on social norms, and Torroba could not resist public demand for them, even late in his career. In fact, his penultimate zarzuela, *El fabuloso mundo del music-hall* (1966), bears the subtitle *revista espectáculo*.

The forty-year plunge from *zarzuela grande* to *ínfima* was of concern to composers during the first decades of the twentieth century. Old Madrid, the backdrop for so much of the zarzuela's development, was becoming a modern city. By 1920, many theaters had been converted into motion-picture houses, and automobiles filled the streets. By the 1930s, there were only seven venues dedicated to zarzuela: the Calderón, Coliseum, Fuencarral, Ideal, Latina, Rialto, and Teatro de la Zarzuela. These continued the practice of offering several works every day. For instance, on July 12, 1934, the Latina featured *Gigantes y cabezudos* at 6:45 p.m., *La reina mora* at 8, and *Pepe Botella* at 10:45. On the 28th of that same month, *Los de Aragón* was at 4:15 p.m., *El dúo de la Africana* at 5:30, *La calesera* at 7, and *Doña Francisquita* at 11! Such late-night entertainment suited the *madrileño* temperament, and the best performers typically made their appearances in the day's final production. And yet, in that same year of 1934, in

---

[80] Sturman, *Zarzuela*, 22. On the following page, she points out that Vives's *Maruxa* (1913) bears the designation *écloga lírica*, though it features continuous singing in the manner of opera.

[81] Hess, *Modernism*, 27.

[82] Thompson, "Doña Francisquita," i, 131–40.

[83] Ibid. See Emilio Casares Rodicio, *Historia gráfica de la zarzuela* (Madrid: ICCMU, 2002), 165–66, for a discussion of these genres. He states that their "worst feature was undoubtedly the libretto."

contrast with 21 zarzuelas, no fewer than 138 plays were produced in the city's 14 theatrical venues.[84]

The zarzuela faced the challenge of adapting to modern times, and in the second decade of the twentieth century, many composers were content to mimic Viennese operetta and French *revue*, as these enjoyed favor with the public. As Webber observes,

> The literary focus of zarzuela again changed, as the influence of mainstream European and especially Viennese operetta with its exotic settings and situations pervaded the *madrileño género chico* and *zarzuela grande* alike. Longer libretti became the norm, the role of dance was expanded, new zarzuelas became more lavish scenically and musically, in contrast to the increasingly risque *revistas* which were quickly written and performed to popular audiences without much thought as to artistic integrity.[85]

The authentic zarzuela tradition was sustained by a small group of composers led by José Serrano (1873–1941) and Amadeo Vives. Their works combined sentimental plots with a musical style clearly indebted to Puccini. A native of Valencia, Serrano became a disciple of Bretón and Chapí in Madrid. But unlike those of his mentors, Serrano's fifty zarzuelas depart from *madrileño* stereotypes. Many of his works were set in provincial Spain, including Alicante, Andalusia, and Aragon. Adapting the folk music and dance of these regions, Serrano helped transform the zarzuela into a genre embracing the whole country. Vives is credited with reviving the *zarzuela grande*. The works of these composers encompassed a wide range of plots and locales; through them, Spain was represented as a country that was full of diversity and yet essentially unified as a culture. Although progressive intellectuals continued to look askance at the zarzuela, Vives earned the respect and praise of Salazar. Casares concurs, characterizing Vives as a "great intellectual."[86] For his part, Torroba followed in the footsteps of Vives and Serrano to create the zarzuela's final florescence.

Librettists Federico Romero (1886–1976) and Guillermo Fernández Shaw (1893–1965) wrote for both Vives and Torroba, demonstrating "advanced literary and theatrical craft, plus an awareness of the great traditions from which they had emerged."[87] Federico Romero was from Oviedo in Asturias. He was a skilled engineer who worked for the telegraph and later helped to found the Spanish

[84] María Victoria Jiménez de Parga, "La zarzuela en Madrid en 1934," *La Chulapona*, program notes for the production at the Teatro de la Zarzuela, Madrid, September 14–October 1 and October 11–30, 1988 (Madrid: Teatro de la Zarzuela, 1988), 31–34.

[85] Webber, *Zarzuela Companion*, 5–6.

[86] Casares, *Actas*, 295, singles out *Sofía* (1923) as a Vives work that earned special approbation.

[87] Webber, *Zarzuela Companion*, 6.

telephone system, or Telefónica, in 1917. He gave all this up to become a writer. Fernández Shaw's background was quite different. He was born in Cádiz but had Scottish and Irish ancestry. He later became a *madrileño* journalist and editor of *La Época*, as well as contributing poetry to *Blanco y Negro*. He eventually became director of the Sociedad de Autores, a position Torroba would one day occupy. He inherited this literary gift from his father, Carlos Fernández Shaw, who had written the libretto for many a successful zarzuela, including Chapí's *La revoltosa*; he also wrote the book for Falla's first opera, *La vida breve*. Guillermo Fernández Shaw was a notable poet, while Romero had a profound knowledge of classics.[88] Their partnership was a fruitful one and lasted until 1948.[89]

Romero and Fernández Shaw were to supply the books for two of the greatest zarzuelas of all time, Vives's *Doña Fransciquita*, based on Lope de Vega's *La discreta enamorada*, and Torroba's *Luisa Fernanda*, which "self-consciously evoke both the older *madrileño género chico*, with its pasodobles and habaneras, and the broad scope and aristocratic fandangos of the old *zarzuela grande*."[90] Particularly with the stability of the regime of Primo de Rivera (1923–30), it was again possible to mount such lavish, large-scale zarzuelas. These works provide the link between the large romantic and comic zarzuelas of the nineteenth century and the last flowering of the zarzuela during the 1930s.

It is useful to understand, however, that intellectuals and those who valorized classical music often looked askance at the zarzuela, as cheap entertainment reflecting the low taste of the masses. Gómez Amat noted that "the enemies of the zarzuela... have used every kind of argument against it, one of these being that it is an anachronism of the nineteenth century. But it is no more anachronistic than Rachmaninov."[91] Cultural elites, such as Pedrell, Rafael Mitjana, and Luis Villalba, were prone to viewing the *género chico* in particular as "a kind of 'national disgrace,'" accusing it of "triviality, frivolity, and of not reflecting the reality of Spanish society." Yet, if they had looked and listened a bit more closely, they would have perceived strains of sociopolitical criticism and protest, as well as considerable musical substance, along with smiles and laughter.[92]

---

[88] F. Hernández Girbal, "Federico Romero y Guillermo Fernández-Shaw," *La Chulapona*, program notes for the production at the Teatro de la Zarzuela, Madrid, September 14–October 1 and October 11–30, 1988 (Madrid: Teatro de la Zarzuela, 1988), 16–18.

[89] Julian García León, "'La Chulapona', alegoría y homenaje a la zarzuela decimonónica," *La Chulapona*, program notes for the production at the Teatro de la Zarzuela, Madrid, February 6 to March 7, 2004 (Madrid: Teatro de la Zarzuela, 2003), 13.

[90] Ibid.

[91] Carlos Gómez Amat, "*La Chulapona* en su momento," *La Chulapona*, program notes for the production at the Teatro de la Zarzuela, Madrid, September 14–October 1 and October 11–30, 1988 (Madrid: Teatro de la Zarzuela, 1988), 20–21.

[92] See Enrique Encabo, *Música y nacionalismos en España* (Barcelona: Erasmus Ediciones, 2007), 20. Catalan modernists like Joan Maragall also took a dim view of the *género chico*. See Clark, *Granados*, 80.

In any case, as Enrique Encabo points out, the zarzuela represented a process of receiving and giving: composers received the people's contribution of popular song and dance, and they returned this "treasure" of melodies in rhythms within the zarzuela.[93] That was a fair exchange, and the public recognized it as such.

Guitar

It would be wrong to suggest that the early 1800s in Spain have nothing of musical value to offer us. Even during the worst years, some Spanish musicians were leaving an indelible mark in composition and performance. Chief among these was no doubt Manuel García (1775–1832), the famed tenor, composer, and pedagogue whose impact on nineteenth-century opera and singing was enormous.[94] The Spanish Basque composer Juan Crisóstomo Arriaga (1806–26), sometimes referred to as the "Spanish Mozart," is another figure worthy of mention, an astoundingly gifted musician who composed sacred music as well as symphonies. Unfortunately, this composer's promising career was cut short by a fatal illness.

However, one name in particular is germane to our subject here: the Catalan Josep Ferran Sorts i Muntades (1778–1839), universally known as Fernando Sor. A guitar virtuoso, he established an international reputation as a composer and pedagogue, leaving Spain in 1813 to reside in Paris, London, Moscow, and again Paris, where he died. Sor was a very literate musician, thoroughly grounded in Viennese classicism, and unlike so many of his predecessors in the realm of guitar performance and composition, he had considerable range as a composer and was not restricted to writing for his own instrument. Indeed, Sor composed opera, orchestral works, and even a lovely *O Crux* for SATB chorus.[95] Of course, his reputation rests on his guitar works, which include variation sets, sonatas, and various character pieces (waltzes and minuets). His pedagogical works are foundational, especially his many etudes, later edited and popularized by Andrés Segovia (1893–1987).[96]

With the passing of Sor, however, there was no immediate successor in Spain to inherit his mantle and carry on his work. To be sure, there were some outstanding guitarists who also wrote and made arrangements for the guitar. Chief among

[93] Ibid., 23.

[94] See James Radomski, *Manuel García (1775–1832): Chronicle of the Life of a* bel canto *Tenor at the Dawn of Romanticism* (New York: Oxford University Press, 2000).

[95] This work has been edited by Michael Fink and published by Tecla Editions (1980). See Clark, "The Iberian World," for a discussion of it.

[96] For more on Sor's pedagogical works and the sources of their stylistic inspiration, see Walter Aaron Clark, "Fernando Sor's Guitar Studies, Lessons, and Exercises (Opp. 6, 29, 31 & 35) and the London Pianoforte School," in *Estudios sobre Fernando Sor/Sor Studies*, ed. Luis Gásser, 359–72 (Barcelona: Instituto Complutense de Ciencias Musicales, 2003). This collection of essays is indispensable for the study of every aspect of Sor's life and work.

these were Trinidad Huerta (1800–74)[97] and Julián Arcas (1832–82). But neither Huerta nor Arcas achieved Sor's stature. That feat awaited the advent of Francisco Tárrega (1852–1909), who studied with Arcas. Tárrega was a native of the province of Valencia but spent most of his career in Barcelona. He was to the Romantic period what Sor was to the Classical, i.e., the chief exponent on the guitar.[98]

Tárrega composed numerous character pieces for the guitar, many of which are central to the standard repertoire. The most famous and popular guitar solo of all time is certainly Tárrega's tremolo study *Recuerdos de la Alhambra* (1899). Already in his early adolescence, Segovia was deeply inspired by the music of Tárrega, of whose Preludes he later wrote: "I felt like crying, laughing, even like kissing the hands of a man who could draw such beautiful sounds from the guitar. My passion for music seemed to explode into flames."[99] Born in Linares, in Andalusia, Segovia never studied with Tárrega, though he undoubtedly learned much from Tárrega's leading pupil, Miquel Llobet (1878–1938), with whom he became friends while living in Barcelona. Still, Segovia had an ambivalent relationship with the Tárrega "school" because he felt they were too timid in asserting what he thought was the guitar's rightful place on the concert stage, in the same league as the piano and violin. Building on the foundation laid by Tárrega and Llobet, Segovia determinedly and successfully developed the repertory and technique of, as well as public interest in, the classical guitar.

Falla wrote one of the first works for the modern classical guitar. He had agreed to compose a piece for Llobet, a promise fulfilled with the *Hommage pour le Tombeau de Debussy*, published in the *Revue Musicale* in 1920. Although Torroba was the first nonguitarist to collaborate with Segovia, Falla's *Hommage* is now considered an early milestone in the development of guitar music. In collaboration with Segovia, composers both Spanish and foreign began to write new works for his extensive concert tours. Within the decade, Segovia was concertizing throughout Europe and the Americas programming works by Turina, Heitor Villa-Lobos, Mario Castelnuovo-Tedesco, Manuel Ponce, Torroba, and Rodrigo. Segovia's achievement was of major importance to the evolution of Spanish music, as he inspired many of the country's most prominent composers to write for their national instrument and provided a worldwide audience for their works.

Segovia would break the historical mold of the guitarist-composer, however, as he would compose relatively little music of his own, instead aggressively urging nonguitarist composers to write for the instrument. By virtue of his relentless

---

[97] For a recent study of Huerta's career, see Robert Coldwell and Javier Suárez-Pajares, *A. T. Huerta: Life and Works* (San Antonio, TX: Digital Guitar Archive Editions, 2006).

[98] Two important biographies of Tárrega are Wolf Moser, *Francisco Tárrega y la guitarra en España entre 1830 y 1960*, 2d ed. (Valencia: Piles Editorial, 2009) and Adrián Rius, *Francisco Tárrega (1852–1909): Biography* (Valencia: Piles, 2006).

[99] Taken from Segovia's autobiography and cited in David Tanenbaum, "Perspectives on the Classical Guitar in the Twentieth Century," in *The Cambridge Companion to the Guitar*, ed. Victor Anand Coelho (Cambridge: Cambridge University Press, 2003), 183.

concert tours, composers knew that their works would gain global recognition. That alone was a powerful incentive to write for him, and over 500 original works bear a dedication to Segovia.[100] The only truly controversial aspect of his single-handed expansion of the guitar's limited repertoire has to do with his very conservative taste. He was not interested in avant-garde music, i.e., works that were highly dissonant, atonal, or serial, and as a consequence, he passed up opportunities to elicit works from such leading composers as Schoenberg, Stravinsky, and Bartók.

Even Frank Martin's relatively tame *Quatre Pièces Breves* (1933) were too modernistic for Segovia, and though they were composed for him, he refused to play them. As he once remarked,

> I am too old to accept this terribly dissonant music.... While the tuning of the guitar continues to be the same, it is an instrument for consonant music. That doesn't mean that delicious dissonance cannot be played, [and] there are many composers today that have used that. But not the cacophony.[101]

Therefore, Segovia solicited works from composers who shared his late-Romantic predilection for tonal, metrical music, often grounded in folk and popular styles. Torroba was his man.

Though the beauty of the works these men composed for Segovia is undeniable and enduring, the judgment of many critics is that he condemned guitar literature to second-rate status. Later guitarists would pursue a different tack, but they would not be able to retrieve the opportunities Segovia had passed up. In studying the dozens of pieces that Torroba composed for his friend Segovia, this is the context we must keep in mind. As much as Torroba's reputation as a composer benefited from his large output of pieces for the guitar, some observers continue to feel that the guitar itself did not benefit in equal measure. We do not hold that view, but it persists. Julian Bream is one guitarist who, rather than cursing the darkness, simply decided to light a candle by commissioning works from composers whose style was beyond the Spanish pale so typical of the guitar's repertoire up to the mid-twentieth century. In particular, his 1967 album *20th Century Guitar*, with works by Reginald Smith Brindle, Hans Werner Henze, Frank Martin, and Benjamin Britten, charted a new course for the instrument, one fundamentally at odds with the Segovia aesthetic.[102]

At this remove in time, there is no rational reason to take sides anymore, as the dialectic between Romantic nationalism and modernist internationalism has lost most of its steam. Both approaches produced masterpieces from which we derive legitimate pleasure today.

---

[100] Tanenbaum, "Perspectives," 184.

[101] Cited in Graham Wade, ed., *Maestro Segovia* (London: Robson Books, 1986), 73.

[102] See Taylor J. Greene, "Julian Bream's *20th Century Guitar*: An Album's Influence on the Modern Guitar Repertoire" (master's thesis, University of California, Riverside, 2011).

2

ACT I
Scene ii
Madrileño
1891–1932

What is a *madrileño*? In simplest terms, it is someone who hails from Madrid. Yet, clearly the word connotes more than that. Someone who just moved from Barcelona to Madrid yesterday would not suddenly metamorphose, in Kafkaesque fashion, into a *madrileño*. Not now, perhaps never. To be a *madrileño* is to be a product of, or at least significantly reflect in one's life and work, the *culture* of Madrid.

To the casual tourist, that culture may now seem submerged under a tidal wave of immigration; however, the city was always a magnet for immigrants in search of a better life. And many of these became true *madrileños*. In fact, one of the enduring ironies of the city is that so many of the famous writers and musicians working in it during Torroba's life came from the provinces, including Azorín (Valencia), Fernández Shaw (Cádiz), Chapí (Alicante), Bretón (Salamanca), Vives (Barcelona), Guerrero (Toledo), Serrano (Valencia), Sorozábal (San Sebastián), Giménez (Seville), Luna (Alhama de Aragón, Zaragoza), Arrieta (Puente la Reina, Navarra), and Fernández Caballero (Murcia). Chueca and Torroba stand out as exceptions to the rule, at least among composers and librettists, thus burnishing their *madrileño* credentials.[1] In this respect, Madrid somewhat resembles Vienna, which received as many famous musicians (Mozart, Beethoven, Brahms, Bruckner, Mahler) as it produced (Schubert, Johann Strauss, Jr., Schoenberg, and Berg).

Pepe Romero, an Andalusian, believes that *madrileños* have a particular manner, "a certain charm and proud sense of humor, i.e., a penchant for insulting others in

---

[1] During an interview with a certain A.C. that appeared in "Federico Moreno Torroba, gloria musical de España," *La Voz de Áviles*, November 24, 1976, Torroba described himself as a "madrileño por los cuatro costados, como castizamente se dice." This translates roughly as: "I am a *madrileño* on both sides [literally, four flanks, or grandparents] of the family, as one says in the *castizo* fashion."

a mocking way. They also have a sense of honor and duty."[2] No doubt there is truth to this, but in the end, the best way to define the word is not to rely on origins or anecdotes but rather to examine the life of one who was universally regarded as a quintessential *madrileño*. Federico Moreno Torroba was one such person. Over and over again in the periodical literature, commentators depicted him as a *madrileño castizo*—of pure caste. This is certainly how he viewed himself. [3] Madrid made him what he was, and in turn he added greatly to the cultural legacy of the Spanish capital and enhanced its stature as an urban center *sui generis*. It was the place where he was born and died, the home he would never have considered abandoning except under duress, and then only temporarily.

We have much to reveal here regarding Torroba's long association with Madrid, but we begin with an interview he gave only a few years before his death, one in which the questions he was asked and the answers he provided shed much light on the nature of the *madrileño*, as represented by him. The rest of this biography will help us to understand how he came to answer these questions in the way that he did.

The Man

In late 1975, Torroba sat down for perhaps the most probing interview ever to appear in the press. His interlocutor was a well-known and respected journalist, Julián Cortés-Cavanillas, who worked for the Madrid daily *ABC*. Much of this interview appears below, followed by some commentary to guide our exploration of Torroba the man, and of the time and place that made him what he became.[4]

***

How would you define yourself musically?
My style responds to traditional Hispanic roots, which are clearly reflected in my zarzuelas and guitar works.
What is your favorite opera?
Carmen, *without forgetting* La Bohème. *Remember that I am essentially a melodist.*

---

[2] Interview with Walter Clark, January 6, 2011.

[3] In an article entitled "Moreno Torroba: un siglo de música española," *Música clásica*, February 27, 1991, 4, Juan José Alonso Millán is quoted as saying that Torroba was a *madrileño* "right down to the marrow of his bones." See also Concha Gil de la Vega, "Federico Moreno Torroba: un madrileño castizo," *Autores: Revista de información de la S.G.A.E.*, n3 (October 1982): 11–12. Indeed, Torroba more than once referred to himself this way, for example in Gabriel Imbuluzqueta, "El compositor Federico Moreno Torroba será homenajeado el viernes en el Teatro Real, en Madrid," *Diario de Navarra*, November 11, 1981: "I was always a very *castizo madrileño*."

[4] Julián Cortés-Cavanillas, "El maestro Moreno Torroba, 85 años de juventud," *ABC*, October 12, 1975, 46–48.

How many times have you fallen in love?

Only once. And I had only one girlfriend, Pilar, who is now my wife, thanks to God.

What constitutes a man's success?

In that he is recognized for his goodwill, equanimity, and generosity.

And of a woman?

For me, that she resemble my wife.

Describe your character.

I believe my character is temperate. My nerves are given to impatience. My fits of anger do not last. And I am more frequently angry with myself than with others.

Are you vain?

I don't think so, but I may be.

Does popularity attract you?

It doesn't repel me, but it does fatigue me. I want people to take me into account without annoying me.

What kind of eulogy most bothers you?

When people congratulate me on a work I know is not good.

Are you capricious?

No. I adapt to everything and conform with everything, except uncomfortable travel.

What is your greatest virtue?

Friends say that it is my good tact.

And your major character liability?

I am too trusting.

What is your religious disposition?

I always strive to comply with the duties I was taught.

What topic annoys you the most?

How well I am doing after 85 years! That really gives me a hunchback and makes me unwell.

Are you afraid of death?

Before, yes. Now, no, perhaps because I am better prepared to receive it.

Would you draft your own epitaph?

It would seem to me excessively vain to put even my own name on my tombstone beforehand.

Do you dream a lot?

At night I have anxious dreams, e.g., that I have missed a train or flight, things of that nature.

And by day?

I dream of things that cannot be.

Do you go to bullfights?

These days very little, but I used to go a lot. In the time of Bombita and Machaquito, Joselito was my favorite.

Do you go often to the theater?

Now, seldom. I used to go to all the premieres. But I have become convinced that opening nights are a farce, where nobody says the truth about their feelings. Instead, I go more to the movies, though if you ask me the names of the actors, I know none except Charlot [Charlie Chaplin].

What do you like to read?

I prefer history and novels. I really enjoy Galdós and, earlier, Gironella.

And poetry?

There are so many poets who delight me that, in order to avoid making a long list, I will cite only one: Rafael Alberti.

Which three painters can you give me as models?

Goya, Sorolla, and Picasso.

Who are three extraordinary people you have known?

As a musician, Ravel. As a politician, Romanones. Beyond music and politics, my father.

Which historical figure do you admire?

Charles V.

Whom would you defend in The Court of Universal Justice?

Martin Luther, who has already been vindicated at that level.

Which cities of the world do you like the most?

In Europe, Vienna. In Latin America, Buenos Aires. And in Chaos, New York, which, with all its defects, is the capital that renders the greatest tribute to the theater. [The reference to *Chaos* is an example of Torroba's sense of humor.]

What most amazes you about human progress?

The absurd fact of thinking more about the moon than the Earth and to spend money on going there that could be put to better use here.

In which century would you like to have lived?

The current century is not too bad, despite all the bad in it.

Looking back, for which epoch in Spanish history do you feel the greatest nostalgia?

Madrid in the 1910s. In 1911, my first serious premiere, La mesonera de Tordesillas, *took place in the Teatro de la Zarzuela. It was the age of the tertulias, with Ramos Carrión, Benavente, Valle-Inclán, Lhardy, Mancinelli, Pepita La Morena, etc.*

Do you like to dress well?

Definitely. Nothing disturbs me more than a poorly made suit—or an ensemble out of tune.

What do you want for Spain?

Stability, serenity, and peace as a consequence.

What do you hope for in the future?
To live right, without putting limits on Providence, as Leo XIII said.

***

Torroba was, if we attach any importance at all to his answers, a man of sobriety, humor, restraint, and diplomacy. His answers are generally terse and to the point. There is no evasion, but neither is there anything sensational or offensive. One perceives a hint of Don Quixote in his dreams of things that cannot be. It is understandable that a man carrying his responsibilities and perpetually on the go would have bad dreams about missing travel connections. Yet, his reply suggests a certain detachment or nonchalance about the real-life nightmares all about him in the world, even in his own past, during the Civil War. As we will see, he might well have dreamed of facing a firing squad, as that nearly happened. His resort to humor in such responses reflects a certain determination not to dwell on ugly political or social realities; however, it does not suggest he never thought about them. Quite the opposite impression emerges, especially in what he wishes for Spain.

His musical tastes were remarkably conservative. His two favorite operas are warhorses of the Romantic repertoire, famed for their lyric character. He himself was a melodist who planted the seeds of his musical inspiration in the rich soil of Spanish folklore. He has savored local culture, including bullfights, theater, socializing in *cafés*, and, now, cinema. His love of literature and affinity for leading literary figures is also apparent. Yet, though he was thoroughly grounded in his own culture, he was no xenophobe and kept an open mind toward foreign styles and trends, whether or not he incorporated them into his own music. His love of New York was connected with Broadway, as we shall later see, and his undying devotion to musical theater; though he does not articulate his attraction to Vienna, it may have been for similar reasons, i.e., the operettas of Johann Strauss, Jr., and others—and perhaps the historic connection between Habsburg Spain and Austria. This would dovetail with his admiration for Emperor Charles V. Interestingly, he does not, as many of his compatriots did, resent French characterization of Spanish culture, as in *Carmen*.[5]

Indeed, Torroba cites Ravel as the most impressive musician he had known. We will see that he admired Ravel's *Alborada del gracioso*; no doubt *Rapsodie espagnole* was a favorite, too. In fact, when once asked if there was a work by someone else he wished were his own, he cited *La Valse*.[6] Nonetheless, his admiration for Bach and Wagner exhibits considerable respect for the German masters as well, something he acquired from his organist father and Wagner-devotee composition teacher, Conrado del Campo. In other words, he had a balanced relationship with the antipodes of twentieth-century classical music, the French and the German.

---

[5] For more on this fascinating topic, see Michael Christoforidis and Elizabeth Kertesz, *Carmen and the staging of Spain: Bizet's Opera and Theatrical Entertainments in the Belle Époque* (New York: Oxford University Press, forthcoming).

[6] He also mentioned Franck's Symphony in D Minor. This is in Imbuluzqueta, "El compositor Federico Moreno Torroba."

In the period just before the Civil War, composers and critics in Spain tended to ally themselves with one or the other, but rarely both. We conclude from this that urbanity and cosmopolitanism seem to suit our *madrileño* well, despite the city's geographical isolation in the middle of a peninsula separated from the rest of Europe by mountains and water.

Given his attraction to French culture, it is not as surprising that he would list among his favorite artists Joaquín Sorolla (1863–1923), a Madrid painter whose shimmering canvases often depict scenes of Spanish life using brush strokes clearly indebted to French Impressionism. Yet, intriguing anomalies emerge. Francisco Goya (1746–1828) is famous for his trenchant visual commentaries on the cruelty, absurdity, and foibles of the society he observed around him. For Goya, the sleep of reason produced nightmares, and not about missed flights. Of course, though born in Aragon, he was a *madrileño* par excellence, and so much of his art was inspired by the culture of his adopted city, especially the colorful bohemians known as *majos* and *majas*. This alone could account for the attraction, were it not for other indications here of encrypted nonconformity.

One conspicuous example of this is the invocation of Pablo Picasso (1881–1973) as one of his "model" artists. Picasso was fascinated with bullfighting, as was Torroba (and Goya), but he was also the polar opposite of Torroba politically and anything but the model of monogamy Torroba proudly claimed to be.[7] And his art was revolutionary, cubism and abstraction representing the visual equivalent of the breakdown of tonality, which held no fascination for Torroba the composer. Torroba was anything but a musical revolutionary in the manner of a Picasso, whose canvas *Guernica* is one of the greatest protests against war since Goya's series of prints entitled *Desastres de la guerra*. Torroba protested nothing, preferring instead to "adapt and conform with everything."[8]

Was his admiration for Picasso an expression of latent sympathy with the Republican cause? After all, Torroba's favorite poet, Rafael Alberti, was an avant-garde author of the Generation of 27 (to which Lorca also belonged). He became a Marxist during the Second Republic and fled Spain after the war. Torroba's favorite politician, Álvaro Figueroa, First Count of Romanones (1860–

---

[7] To be sure, Torroba later contradicted his claim that Pilar was his only love. When asked about other women in his life (before or after her), he coyly said, "In all these years, there have been a few. But they never caused me problems worth mentioning. Okay, there was once...a rival who challenged me to a duel. Thank God no blood was spilled."

See Hebrero San Martín, "Federico Moreno Torroba, 90 años de vida y de música," unknown periodical, between March 3, 1981, and March 2, 1982. This clipping is in the Torroba family archive in Navarra, henceforth indicated by [Na].

[8] As Tomás Marco observed in "Un músico integral," *Autores: Revista de información de la S.G.A.E.*, n3 (October 1982): 33 [reprint of an article in *Diario 16*, September 13, 1982, 16]: "The music of Moreno Toroba was always in a popular vein and was based on Spain's diverse folklore, on which he impressed a *casticista* character....He was not and never aspired to be a revolutionary, but he was a composer of great professionalism, with a very personal melodic style, and he knew how to appeal to the public without devoting himself to popular music."

1953), was a leading member of the liberal party and consistently fought for social justice and progress. He was also a Francophile who sided with the allies during the First World War, in apparent violation of Spain's official neutrality. He fled to France during the Civil War, and upon his return retired from politics. The novelist Pérez Benitez Galdós (1843–1920) was another liberal.[9] These are odd heroes for a conservative like Torroba to revere; unthinkable ones for a Francoist, had he been one, which obviously he was not.

However, not all of Torroba's heroes were of a liberal stripe. That same Romanones was a minister in Alfonso XIII's government and was not an early supporter of the Republic; he was cozy with General Primo de Rivera, a military dictator Torroba admired. Torroba's other favorite writer, José María Gironella (1917–2003), fought on the side of the nationalists and later penned a trilogy about the Civil War, the first volume of which is written from a Catholic perspective. Gironella was himself Catholic and educated at a seminary. And there are other quirky responses here that invite scrutiny, especially in regard to religion.

On the one hand, he is clearly comfortable with such authoritarians as Charles V and Leo XIII. Charles V (1500–58) presided over the Spanish empire during its rapid expansion in the Western hemisphere. Did Torroba approve of colonialism, or was he simply proud of Spain's accomplishments during the apex of its global power and influence? Certainly Charles V was one of the Right's heroes during the Franco era, the official propaganda of which exalted the sixteenth century, its Catholicism and conquest.[10] Leo XIII (1810–1903) was pope when Torroba was born, and in that same year of 1891 issued his landmark encyclical *Rerum Novarum*, in which he sought to engage the modern world in a disquisition on the relationship between capital and labor, offering sympathy with the plight of the working class. However, this work delivered a stern warning against socialism and made clear the Church's belief in private property (especially its own). Torroba's evident admiration for Leo XIII may tell us something not only of his distrust of socialism but also his possession of a social conscience, something characteristic of the bourgeoisie around 1900 and of importance to Torroba, whose family was one of modest means and not far above the ranks of the working poor that swelled in Spain during the early twentieth century.[11] Indeed, guitarist Pepe Romero avers that Torroba "was against any violation of human rights."[12]

---

[9] In another interview, however, he made the following admission: "I read a lot during my youth, and I really liked the stories of Galdós.... Now, I don't read at all." See Manuel Gómez Ortiz, Manuel, "Moreno Torroba o la zarzuela viva," *Ya*, April 4, 1976, 15.

[10] As Juan Pablo Fusi, *Un siglo de España, la cultura* (Madrid: Marcial Pons, Ediciones de Historia, 1999), 106, notes, "Historiography of the 1940s promoted the exaltation of the official past: the Catholic kings,...the discovery and colonization of America, the Counter-Reformation, Carlos V, Felipe II. Catholic kings served as symbol of united Spain."

[11] And focusing on the lives of the underclass was a characteristic of nineteenth-century realism, outstanding examples of which are the operas *Carmen* and *La Bohème*.

[12] Interview with Walter Clark, January 6, 2011.

That Torroba was a sincere Catholic is not in doubt; yet, his terse treatment of religion strikes an unusual chord, as he apparently viewed it as a kind of bottom-line contract in which one's rewards were commensurate with doing one's duties. He offers no hint of devotion, or if he did feel devotion, he did not feel that this interview was the place to express it. He makes no mention of faith in Church teachings, and thus it comes as less of a surprise that sacred music figures hardly at all in his overall output.[13] Moreover, his anticipation of death displays acceptance and resignation, but he makes no mention of salvation and heavenly rewards. Astonishingly, he goes on to cite Martin Luther as someone who has been vindicated in The Court of Universal Justice! Martin Luther was a burr under the saddle of that same Charles V, whom Luther openly defied at the Diet of Worms in 1521, and of every pope since 1517. Like Picasso, Luther was the exact opposite of Torroba—or perhaps there was a skeptical side to Torroba's relations with Catholicism that found expression in this remark. In fact, Torroba's slight caginess and poker playing—"tact"—were maneuvers that helped him to survive Civil War and dictatorship, not to mention his administrative work. They are on display here.

It is possible but far from easy to wrest some philosophical coherence from his admiration for Romanones, Picasso, Charles V, Goya, Sorolla, Ravel, Alberti, Gironella, Galdós, Luther, and Leo III. In the famous words of F. Scott Fitzgerald, "The test of a first-rate intelligence is the ability to hold two opposed ideas in mind at the same time and still retain the ability to function."[14] What we can definitely take away from these quotes, if they were offered with even a particle of sincerity, is that Torroba was in possession of a first-rate intelligence. It would be difficult to argue otherwise, and pointless. We will have occasion to observe later, however, that he was quite capable of self-contradiction—which is not always the same thing as dishonesty—as well as diplomatic fence-sitting. That certainly offers a plausible explanation for some of this. We will also note that his memory was not always accurate. For instance, his "first serious premiere," La mesonera de Tordesillas, did not take place in 1911 but rather in 1925. The work he might have been thinking of was Las decididas, but that premiered in 1912.

In any case, our madrileño was neither a linear thinker nor predictable, but the seeming incongruities in his thought and personality were only a matter of appearances. To him, if not to us, it all made perfect sense. As Torroba once

---

[13] He did write a set of Cuadros (1919), one of which was inspired by religious subjects in the art of Velásquez. He also wrote villancicos for Christmas and several ballets with biblical themes (more will be said of the ballets in Act III, Scene ii). However, compared to the hundreds of works he wrote for the guitar and the stage, this output is very limited and simply constitutes the exception that proves the rule.

[14] From his 1936 essay "The Crack-Up." Though this passage is well known, one rarely encounters the rest of this quote: "One should, for example, be able to see that things are hopeless and yet be determined to make them otherwise." This would also apply to our composer.

observed, "To those who know my habits,...my life may seem disordered; however, I cannot say that, because to me it seems pure order."[15]

What does *not* emerge from these responses is a complex intellectual, a rebel, an *artiste*, or a visionary. His values are those of the bourgeoisie: reverence for his parents and devotion to his wife and family; a desire for domestic tranquility in the country as a whole, without which neither business nor art can prosper; conformity to social conventions and religious injunctions, without which there can be no tranquility; adaptability and a corresponding abhorrence of fanaticism; and respect for tradition, from which everything of lasting value comes. His remarks reveal a man thoroughly grounded in his present reality, without a hint of lunar otherworldliness. He is sure of himself and his opinions, without being dogmatic or doctrinaire.

In short, then, our *madrileño* is first and foremost someone steeped in and loyal to Madrid, its history, culture, and traditions. This grounding in local culture is leavened by an urbanity and awareness of the world outside the Castilian plain, an awareness that leads, however, neither to excessive fears of inadequacy nor to chauvinistic assertions of superiority. He possesses faith in himself, without narcissism. Indeed, he is unmoved by flattery, but nonetheless appreciative of respect. This *madrileño* is a pragmatic realist, dreaming of things he simultaneously knows "cannot be." He focuses on the here and now, on the reality with which he must contend, though this can paradoxically lead to sentimental nostalgia for an earlier time.

Though our *madrileño* respects royal and ecclesiastical authority and conforms to its dictates, there is a concomitant recognition that authority is not always correct or just, and that rebellion is occasionally necessary to redress grievances. Torroba himself, however, preferred the sidelines to the hurly-burly of politics and revolution. His political convictions were muted and circumspect, in recognition of the fact that, throughout most of Spanish history, speaking out on politics and religion was dangerous; apathy and equivocation were the safer alternative, since few imagined that fundamental change could be brought about by peaceful political means. This no doubt explains why Francesc Cambó (1876–1947), leader of the Catalan conservatives (Lliga Catalana), observed that

> During a whole century, Spain has lived under the appearance of a constitutional democratic regime, without the people having ever, directly or indirectly, had the least share in the Government....Who does not remember elections in which the Civil Governors used the police to steal

---

[15] Marino Gómez-Santos, "Federico Moreno Torroba," *Tribuna médica*, May 28, 1971. Specifically, they might think his life disordered because they would occasionally see him at the theater. But he insisted that for him to go to the theater was as "logical for me as it is for you [as a journalist] to read a newspaper." He went on to observe that the "order" in his life consisted of working every morning. Among his many attributes, one would have to include a healthy appetite for unrelenting work.

the voting urns or in which the counts of votes were falsified in the very rooms in which justice is administered.[16]

Yet, Torroba never lapses into cynicism or despair here, and that is noteworthy. If not a cynic, he was something of a stoic, content to work within constraints he could not change, though he admired others, like Martin Luther, who were not content to do so. What most impresses is his obvious passion for order and stability. He had learned from painful personal experience that radical change would lead to upheavals inimical to commerce and to his art—and *his* art in particular was a form of commerce—though one suspects that the political, regional, and ethnic tensions within Spain were in many respects the mainspring of its creative vitality. At all events, they were the more or less inevitable consequence of his nation's great cultural diversity, diversity that Torroba exploited in almost all of his works.

This was the man, by turns ordinary and enigmatic, straightforward and contradictory, self-assured and self-deprecating, who wrote some of the greatest zarzuelas of all times, and whose guitar music forms one of the essential pillars of that instrument's modern repertoire. How did such a man come to be and to do what he did?

Madrid

Castile (*Castilla*) gets its name from the thousands of castles (*castillos*) located within it, each bearing mute testimony to the struggles waged between Christian and Muslim forces during the medieval *reconquista* to control this militarily and economically important region. The Manzanares River flows through the arid expanse of the Castilian plain and has made possible agriculture, animal husbandry, and human habitation since prehistoric times.[17] The Romans established villas here, which benefited from their proximity to the settlement at Complutum (now Alcalá de Henares). However, the city's actual founding took place in the late ninth century, during the Muslim occupation. The Muslims named it Mayrit, "place of life-giving water," referring to the nearby river, and built a small fortress there. Their principal interest in this locale was to create a defensive perimeter against Christian forces attempting to penetrate farther south during the *reconquista*. But the Muslims could only delay, not prevent, their own expulsion from this region.

---

[16] Cited in Gerald Brenan, *The Spanish Labyrinth: An Account of the Social and Political Background of the Civil War*, reprint ed. (Cambridge: Cambridge University Press, 2001), 6, fn 2.

[17] Much of the following discussion of Madrid's history is indebted to Carlos González Esteban, *Madrid: Sinopsis de su evolución urbana* (Madrid: Ediciones La Librería, 2001). This is a very useful one-volume introduction to the subject. The magnum opus in this field remains Federico Morata Bravo's multi-volume *Historia de Madrid* (Madrid: Fenicia, 1986).

Christian forces under Alfonso VI of Castile occupied the area in 1083–85, during their campaign to seize Toledo. Over time, the name of the village underwent further modification, evolving to the Mozarabic Matrit and, finally, Madrid.[18] It achieved some prominence as a residence for Castilian kings and, in 1309, the occasional meeting place of the Cortes, or parliament. In the sixteenth century, Philip II established Madrid as the permanent Spanish capital and the principal residence of the royal family, which it remains to this day. There is no documentation indicating exactly why he did this, but certainly one reason was Madrid's central location, and its relative lack of "great noble families and ecclesiastical authorities who could obstruct the creation of the new political order planned by Philip II."[19] In the late Middle Ages, Madrid had a population of about twenty thousand, but as a direct result of this transformation under Philip II, its population had trebled by the year 1600.

Madrid now became the administrative nerve center of what was essentially a Castilian empire, encompassing the entire Peninsula except for Portugal (and even that from 1580 to 1640) and stretching around the globe. But strong centrifugal forces persisted in opposing Madrid's centripetal pull. The outlying regions of the country, especially the Basque country and Catalonia, had a strong sense of their distinctive identities, in language, customs, and culture, and agitated for greater autonomy, or even outright independence, from Castile. It would require repeated affirmation of Madrid's centrality and supremacy to hold the country together, and such affirmations would not only be political and military but also cultural in nature.[20]

For here lived some of Spain's greatest writers, artists, and musicians, including Cervantes, Victoria, Velásquez, Lope de Vega, Calderón de la Barca, and Goya. Monuments such as the Palacio Real, Museo del Prado, Conservatorio Real, Biblioteca Nacional, and Teatro Real would become potent symbols of Madrid's— and by extension, Castile's—preeminent status among Spanish cities and regions. Indeed, many commentators would later come to view Madrid as the "real" Spain, which, tucked away in the deepest interior of the country, preserved what was best and most genuine—*castizo*—about the nation and its people. It was, as Azorín put it, "that most glorious part of Spain to which we owe our soul."[21] And

---

[18] There are other theories regarding this etymology, but this is the most recent and compelling. It has nothing to do with "Madre," as much as votaries of the Beata Virgine Maria might wish.

[19] See González Esteban, *Madrid*, 27.

[20] The Bourbons established Royal Academies, the Royal Library, and the Royal Theater. "They were inspired by the conviction that education and culture would promote social and economic progress." See "Cultural Policy in Spain," 3.

[21] Cited in Gayana Jurkevich, *In Pursuit of the Natural Sign: Azorín and the Poetics of Ekphrasis* (London: Associated University Presses, 1999), 32. Azorín was the pen name of journalist José Martínez Ruiz (1873–1967), one of a seminal group of writers in the early twentieth century to address the issue of Spain's regeneration and Castile's central importance to it.

it was not only the source of Spanish tradition but also of the nation's postimperial revival, of its destiny in the twentieth century and beyond.

Madrid in the late nineteenth century was a rapidly expanding city of over a half million people, but one in which tradition and the old ways persisted in the face of modernization. As Gómez Labad colorfully put it, with more than a touch of nostalgia:

> It is the Madrid of strolling musicians,... of the *schottische*, mazurka, *pasacalle*, and polka, [and] of dances and feasts in open-air cafés. It is the Madrid of the barrel organ, that instrument made to cause women to look out of windows and from balconies as it fills the air with zarzuela music. However, it is also the Madrid of tears shed over revolutions, *pronunciamientos*, dethronements, wars in Cuba or Africa, and of hunger. Hunger for peace, for well-being, for progress in securing our daily bread, which was very easy for some and very difficult for others.[22]

It was, in many respects, a big *pueblo*, "so uncomfortable that international travelers did not offer excessive compliments to it," to say the least.[23]

The Puerta del Sol, or Gate of the Sun, lies at the center of Madrid and is the hub around which much of the city's commerce revolves.[24] In the 1800s, it was, by one description, "a small universe" presenting the best and worst, the newest and oldest that Madrid had to offer, "the good life and the struggle for survival."[25] By 1890 this had become the heart of the city, serving as the "great distributor in which the principal arteries of the city flowed together and apart."[26]

The calle de la Montera cuts a diagonal swath through the center of Madrid, flowing southward from the Gran Vía into the Puerta del Sol. According to one tradition, Montera street was named after the wife of a sixteenth-century mountaineer (*montero*), whose house stood there before the street was established.[27] His hunting expeditions in the mountains were evidently organized from that place, and the wife became legendary for dispensing her favors while her husband was away. She would supposedly stand on her balcony, fanning herself seductively.

---

[22] José M. Gómez Labad, *El Madrid de la zarzuela: Visión regocijada de un pasado en cantables* (Madrid: Juan Piñero G., 1983), 11–12. *Pronunciamientos* were the "pronouncements" of military officers that they were rising up in revolt against the government.

[23] Cayetano Luca de Tena, "Pequeña historia del año 1891," *Blanco y negro* 79 (November 1, 1969): 35.

[24] In "Moreno Torroba, Mucha música en muchos años," *Diario de Mallorca* (Palma de Mallorca), December 10, 1976, an anonymous journalist claimed that it was still one of Madrid's most popular streets.

[25] Ángel del Río López, *Los viejos cafés de Madrid*, 2d ed. (Madrid: Ediciones La Librería, 2009), 21.

[26] See González Esteban, *Madrid*, 58.

[27] This charming, if apocryphal, legend is found in Federico Bravo Morata, *Los nombres de las calles de Madrid*, 2d ed. (Madrid: Fenicia, 1984), 374.

In any case, of greater interest to us is the street's proximity to major cultural attractions, rather than the nearby Guadarrama Mountains. The Museo del Prado is a fifteen-minute walk to the southeast, while the Palacio and Teatro Real are but twelve minutes by foot due west; the Plaza Mayor, historic center of the old city, takes less than that to reach.[28] Here and there the urban landscape sports lovely *madroños*, a Mediterranean citrus tree that, along with a bear eating from it on hind legs, serves as the city's emblem. Numerous *puertas*, not so much gates as triumphal arches, demarcate thoroughfares leading in and out of the city, often bearing the names of the places to which the roads led: Puerta de Alcalá, Puerta de Toledo, etc. The buildings in which Goya and Cervantes lived are close by, as is the Monasterio de la Descalzas Reales, where the great Renaissance composer Tomás Luis de Victoria worked. Most of the city's theaters were near here, especially the Calderón and Apolo, among the chief venues for zarzuela. Those preferring their musical dramas to be sung throughout could attend opera at the Teatro Real. In 1891, there were plenty of zarzuelas for devotees to choose from, including Francisco Barbieri's final work, *El señor Luis el tumbón o Despacho de huevos frescos* at the Apolo, and Ruperto Chapí's *El rey que rabió* at the Teatro de la Zarzuela. Most theaters featured several different shows each day, one after the other, so great was the demand for this type of entertainment. And there were other diversions.

In addition to the city's monuments, theaters, and art museums, *verbenas* (fiestas) and *romerías* (religious pilgrimages) provided welcome relief from the daily routine and strengthened the communal bond among *madrileños*. A special institution was the *tertulia*, informal gatherings in cafés to discuss politics, the arts, and philosophy. These flourished in Madrid around 1900, and though cafés had been around since the eighteenth century, already by the middle of the 1800s there were no fewer than seventy of them in the capital. In one historian's opinion, "Madrid has been the most 'caféd' city in the world," and the café "achieved the level of an actual institution."[29] This was due not only to demand for coffee and comestibles but also for intelligent conversation—sometimes heated. The great writer Ramón María Valle-Inclán (1866–1936) got into an altercation with journalist Manuel Bueno at the Café de la Montaña one night, and the wound he sustained required the amputation of his left arm. Cafés tended to specialize in particular kinds of *tertulias*. Writers went one place, politicians another. Revolutionaries met at the Lorenzini, which presumably made them rather too easy for the police to find![30] Most featured music and even dance, often of a high caliber. For instance, Albéniz and violinist/conductor Enrique Fernández Arbós

---

[28] These timings are based on the perambulations of an aging musicologist. Younger, more vigorous *homines sapientes* may require less time.

[29] Río López, *Los viejos cafés de Madrid*, 37.

[30] Ibid., 41.

(1863–1939) sometimes performed at the Platerías,[31] while patrons of the Café de Zaragoza were treated to Pablo de Sarasate's displays of violin virtuosity.[32] In any case, the Puerta del Sol offered many cafés to choose from, all within a short walking distance from number 3, calle de la Montera.

On March 3, 1891, in a small apartment at that address, the cries of a newborn baby were added to the sounds of horse-drawn carriages, vendors, and passers-by emanating from the street outside and the nearby Puerta del Sol. This baby received the name Federico Moreno Torroba.[33] The boy's father, José Moreno Ballesteros (1861–1956), was a professor of organ at the Real Conservatorio de Música y Declamación (henceforth called the Real Conservatorio) and church organist at La Concepción, on calle Goya, as well as at the church of San Millán y San Cayetano, on calle de Embajadores.[34] He also had a local reputation as a composer, and wrote several light stage works as well as an *Oficio de difuntos* (Office for the Dead). In addition to his responsibilities as professor and church musician, he served as the music director and pianist at the Teatro Lara for three decades, where he led a sextet that played selections from zarzuelas before and after productions and during intermissions.[35] Federico's mother, Rosa Torroba López (1870–1940), was also a gifted musician and came from a musical family. Federico's two surnames are sometimes hyphenated, but not necessarily so, and not here. Normally, he would be known by his father's name, i.e., Federico Moreno, rather than his mother's. However, the composer himself preferred the matronymic Torroba because it was far less common in Spanish society, and hence more distinctive, than Moreno. For similar reasons, we know Pablo as Picasso, not Ruiz, and Federico as Lorca, not García.[36]

By his own account, Torroba had a happy childhood, spent among the engrossing sights and sounds of the city and in a family that, though far from wealthy, always had enough to eat and provided him with all the love and attention he needed. No

---

[31] These tidbits about Valle-Inclán and Albéniz are in Río López, *Los viejos cafés de Madrid*, 9–10. This author informs us that one of the most "musical" establishments in the early 1900s was the Café de Viena, in the calle de Luisa Fernanda. It attracted a clientele of students and intellectuals, who formed their own *tertulia*.

[32] According to Víctor Ruiz Albéniz, "Aquel Madrid," in *Albéniz y su tiempo*, ed. Enrique Franco (Madrid: Fundación Isaac Albéniz, 1990), 18.

[33] According to Pedro Pablo Colino, archivist at the Iglesia Parroquia San José, Torroba's baptismal certificate would have been located at a parish church that went up in flames during the Civil War. It is now lost.

[34] Records of his appointment as professor of organ survive in the archive of the Real Conservatorio. The certificate of his appointment as acting professor of organ (Profesor interino de la enseñanza de órgano) is signed by Tomás Bretón and dated January 1, 1904 (p. 17). He was reappointed on January 2, 1911 (p. 53), and yet again on April 1, 1914 (p. 81).

[35] Torroba's son, Federico, Jr., fleshes out much of this family history in an interview by María Antonia Estévez, "Federico Moreno Torroba: Entre los recuerdos de su padre y de su abuelo, el maestro Larregla," *Diario de Navarra*, February 27, 1994, 40.

[36] According to Pepe Romero, in a conversation with Walter Clark, September 6, 2011.

tales of abuse, neglect, or privation surface in his recollections, which he conveyed in some detail to journalist Manuel Vicent less than a year before his death.[37]

Among his happiest memories were those of excursions to a country house in Carabanchel (a southwestern suburb of Madrid), which was owned by a relative who worked as an inspector for the Banco de España. They would travel there by horse-drawn carriage and pass the summer enjoying bucolic splendor and relief from the stifling heat of the city. It was here that Torroba's passionate love of the theater first surfaced, at the tender age of four:

> It was a lot of fun for me because there was a theater nearby, owned by a businessman, where [zarzuelas] were produced, for example, *La canción de la Lola* and *El barquillero*. . . . Keep in mind that I am talking of the year 1895, in a Spain still governed by Cánovas del Castillo, in which Lagartijo was a toreador, and the disaster in Cuba had not yet happened.[38]

Of course, Madrid around 1900 had its own attractions, which Torroba fondly recalled with astonishing detail even late in life. In the Puerta del Sol he observed ordinary people dancing to the music of the accordion and tambourine, while more elegant society sipped tea in equally elegant salons from the era of Isabel II (i.e., 1840s–60s). Organ grinders entertained pedestrians while vendors sold honey, flowers, fruit, clothes, and all manner of commodities. People gathered in small groups and held informal *tertulias* on the street; in fact, one such casual *tertulia* took place some mornings in the Puerta del Sol, consisting of the *maestro de capilla* (chapelmaster) of the Cathedral, *zarzueleros* Tomas Bretón and Federico Chueca, and Torroba's father. Bretón, a young professor at the Conservatorio recently arrived from Navarra, quickly established a close friendship with the young organ professor named Ballesteros.[39]

They would remain there chatting until bells on the large clock of a nearby government building (now the administrative building of the President of the Comunidad de Madrid) summoned them to the midday meal. Sometimes they would run into Chapí, who lived nearby in the calle del Arenal. Torroba's father organized a more regular *tertulia* at the Café Comercial, in the glorieta de Bilbao. This included not only Bretón and sometimes Federico Chueca but also *zarzuelista* Gerónimo Giménez.

Predictably, some memories were not so pleasant, as the cruel realities of the world he inhabited intruded on his awareness.

---

[37] From an interview with the composer in Manuel Vicent, "El pentagrama de Federico Moreno Torroba," *El País*, November 14, 1981, 13.

[38] Although *La canción de la Lola* was a zarzuela from 1880, with music by Chueca and Valverde, Chapí's zazuela *El barquillero* did not premiere until 1900.

[39] Estévez, "Federico Moreno Torroba," 41.

At age 7, I was a witness to a great historical event, covered with blood:
the wedding of King Alfonso XIII and the assassination attempt while
the royal retinue passed. I was standing on a balcony on the calle del
Arenal, and the attack took place in the calle Mayor. I heard the bomb
blast, and immediately thereafter the shouting of the people. A festive
atmosphere changed to one of terror in a matter of seconds. Everyone
was running. I was really frightened. That day I understood a few things
for the first time.[40]

One can only speculate what his cryptic reference to understanding "a few
things" meant. The horrors of political violence? The amorality and treachery of
the anarchists in particular? The fundamental instability of Spanish society? We
do not know. One thing is certain, and that is that his memory did not serve him
well here. The attack, by anarchist Mateu Morral, took place on May 31, 1906,
when Torroba was already fifteen years old, not seven. Still, there is no denying
the imprint it left on his memory and his nervous system. However, worse horrors
than this awaited him and his fellow *madrileños* thirty years on.

To be sure, there were other, more benign disruptions to his daily life. Torroba's
mother had a fondness for variety, which led to occasional changes of residence.[41]
Thus, at some point they moved from calle de la Montera to calle de Carretas, 7.
His grandfather, who was a tailor and made clothes for the local nobility, lived ten
doors up the street. "Imagine how much less noise there was back then, that I was
able to stand on our balcony and shout to my grandmother, 'Mama Pilar!' And she
was able to answer me from her house."[42] One familiar with the Spanish capital
today can easily imagine that Madrid was a quieter place in those days, before the
proliferation of *motocicletas*, whose deafening roar now reverberates along the
narrow streets from that earlier time. Indeed, "in those days you could cross the
street without looking because you could actually hear the hooves of the horses
pulling the streetcars. When we later moved to calle de Santa Engracia, we would
take the last streetcar at midnight in order to go visit the grandparents," a journey
of about twenty minutes. And he recalled meditating on more mundane attractions, including cauldrons of molten asphalt, which was being used to pave the
Puerta del Sol. Other memories were warm in a different kind of way:

I can see myself at my grandfather's house eating *buñuelos* [a kind of
dumpling] when I was just 3 or 4 years old. He bought them from a

---

[40] San Martín, "Federico Moreno Torroba."

[41] In Ismael Fuente, "Concedida la Medalla de Oro de Madrid a Moreno Torroba en el cincuentenario del estreno de 'Luisa Fernanda,'" *El País*, March 28, 1982, Torroba uses the word "mudancitis"—
changeitis—to characterize his mother's penchant for moving. He states that they lived in three
different apartments (*pisos*) in the Santa Engracia district, on calles Fuencarral, Goya, and Lagasca.

[42] Vicent, "El pentagrama," 13.

churros vendor on calle de la Montera, 100 of them for just one peseta! They were made the way God intended.[43]

The Student

It was during these halcyon years that Torroba began his formal education. He learned to read and write at Santo Ángel de la Guarda, in the Plaza del Ángel. After that, he attended school at the Escolapios de San Antón, and at eleven years of age, the Liceo Francés, on calle de Jacometrezo, where he learned mathematics and prepared for college study.[44]

Torroba also began music studies at this time. He claimed that he learned his first notes at age eight and that by sixteen he had determined to be a musician.[45] He obviously grew up in a musical environment, imbibing from an early age the sounds of classical music, church music, urban folklore, and theater music, for all of these formed the sum and substance of his father's profession, his mother's avocation, and the soundscape he inhabited. He attended opera at the Teatro Real, as well as zarzuelas there and at the Alhambra, Apolo, Eslava, Cómico, Novedades, and Buen Retiro theaters.[46] His general education was thus supplemented by the rich cultural surroundings of the capital, with the aforementioned monuments being part of his everyday experience. The keenly observant Federico would absorb all of these stimuli into his later works, for both the stage and the guitar.

Something of a prodigy, he enrolled in the Real Conservatorio when he was only eleven years old, taking solfège. According to the extant records in the Conservatorio's archives, the young boy acquitted himself admirably, demonstrating obvious musical talent.[47] However, curiously enough, his musical education there terminated a short while later. Perhaps he had already learned at home all that he really needed to know, or maybe he simply tired of the numbing routine of formal study. As he later recalled, it was his father who "taught me harmony, and I still affectionately recall how devotedly he taught me those very strict rules

---

[43] San Martín, "Federico Moreno Torroba."

[44] Cortés-Cavanillas, "El maestro Moreno Torroba," 47.

[45] "Moreno Torroba, el más famoso compositor actual de zarzuela, pasó por Montevideo," *El Día* (Montevideo), June 17, 1975. Torroba was interviewed for this piece on his way to Spain, returning from Buenos Aires and a production of *Luisa Fernanda* at the Teatro Colón.

[46] The list of theaters he attended appeared in an interview with Gómez-Santos in "Federico Moreno Torroba."

[47] The records are for the years 1901–02 and 1902–03. His name appears only in these two classes, so he took no other courses at the conservatory. In any case, his final evaluation, on September 26, 1902, describes his ability as *sobresaliente*, or "outstanding." He was not the youngest enrollee, as there were students as young as nine. Most were in their teens, however.

that today are thrown overboard and forgotten."[48] In any case, he began writing music when he was about fourteen years old.[49] One day he composed a waltz—"the fashion in those days"—and this was soon premiered at a theatrical gala by a *cupletista*, a singer of *cuplés*, light, satiric songs of a frequently suggestive nature. This may well have been the very first piece he composed, but it has not survived.[50]

Ironically, his father now decided to nip young Torroba's musical career in the bud. The elder Moreno "did not want me to become a composer and have to endure the struggles he endured."[51] However proud he may have been of his son's talent and promise, he was also dismayed by his determination to make a living as a musician and urged him to find a more remunerative career, one less subject to the vicissitudes of fortune, if not outright penury. As the composer recalled on another occasion in later years, "[My father] did not want me to become a musician. 'Find yourself a career with more of a future,' he told me."[52]

So, despite his early efforts in composition and after completing his basic education at the Liceo Francés, Torroba commenced studying for a position in the civil service, in the customs department, "which is what young men did in those days."[53] However, his apathy regarding this unpalatable curriculum is not hard to comprehend, and neither are the resulting poor grades that earned him suspension from the program. A contributing factor may have been his penchant for making the rounds of cafés and *tertulias*, rather than hitting the books.[54] By his own admission,

> In my early years I passed my time going from *tertulia* to *tertulia*, at the Teatro Real, where my father was organist, . . . and at the home of maestro Arbós every Wednesday. There I had occasion to meet many great musicians of the century, including Richard Strauss.[55]
>
> Just imagine, in those days you would spend the day passing from one *tertulia* to the next, crossing the calle de Alcalá without looking both ways. First you would go to the café de Levante, . . . which was frequented

[48] Sagi-Vela, "Moreno Torroba, nonagenario," 22.

[49] In "Moreno Torroba nombrado director de la Academia de Bellas Artes," *El País*, May 9, 1978, 35.

[50] Sagi-Vela, "Moreno Torroba, nonagenario," 22. However, Blanca Berasategui, "Moreno Torroba, más que noventa años de zarzuela," *ABC*, November 14, 1981, viii, stated that he composed this waltz at age 12.

[51] Vicent, "El pentagrama," 13.

[52] Sagi-Vela, "Moreno Torroba, nonagenario," 22.

[53] His studies at the Liceo are mentioned in "Moreno-Torroba será enterrado," 38.

[54] Fuente, "Concedida la Medalla de Oro," states that the young man preferred "palling around" (*compadreo*) to studying, and that he frequented *tertulias* at the Oriental, Alhambra, and Levante cafés before finding his calling as a *zarzuelero*. Río López, *Los viejos cafés de Madrid*, 52, tells us that the Oriental, founded in 1861, could accommodate fifteen hundred customers!

[55] Marisol Colmenero, "Lírico Moreno Torroba," *La Hora Leonesa*, August 4, 1979.

by politicians, singers, and writers. Later you could go to the café de Puerto Rico, and meet the painters. Then I would take a stroll on the calle de Sevilla with the *toreros*. Bombita, Machaquito, Vicente Pastor, Fuentes, and Bejarano were all my friends. I also fought bulls once, one day at El Escorial. As you can see, I've done it all![56]

There were, in fact, less mundane reasons for his being at the Escorial. Undeterred by Torroba's failure as a budding civil servant, his father now directed him to study mining at the Universidad de María Cristina there. Not surprisingly, Torroba also failed that unappetizing course of study. At this time, his father was giving music lessons to the director of the army band at the *alcázar* in Toledo. According to Torroba, his father's exposure to military life inspired him to guide his son's faltering footsteps toward becoming an army officer. So, in 1912, at the age of 21, Torroba commenced his service, though without ever being called up for the fruitless fiascos in Morocco that wasted so much Spanish blood and treasure in the early decades of the twentieth century—only to prolong the inevitable final end of Spain's imperial history and provide a staging area to Franco and the army in their 1936 coup. Torroba later said that he must have been the first "*quinta de cuota*," a new system under which his father paid the government 500 *pesetas* in exchange for his son's advancement from private to corporal to sergeant and finally to the rank of lieutenant ("teniente de cuota"), all within six months, and subsequent honorable discharge, in 1913.[57] Another reason he proffered for this short-lived military career was his difficulties with trigonometry.[58] He claimed that this contributed to his early departure from the ranks, despite the army's need for soldiers during the Moroccan war. In any case, enough was enough, and Torroba's father finally bowed to the inevitable, a sagacious capitulation that changed the course of Spanish music history.

This is the account given by Torroba and the only one available until now. In fact, the extant records of Torroba's military service compel a reevaluation of Torroba's military autobiography.[59] For it turns out that Torroba was in the army for eighteen years, though most of that time was spent in the reserves. He began

---

[56] Vicent, "El pentagrama," 13. Río López, *Los viejos cafés de Madrid*, 41, reports that the Levante hosted several prestigious *tertulias*, including "Los hombres de buena fe" and "los Periodistas." It was adorned with paintings by *madrileño* painter Leonardo Alenza (1807–45) and attracted such literary luminaries as Valle-Inclán and Galdós. Painters patronized not only the Puerto Rico but also, perhaps, the ladies of the night who plied their trade at that café.

[57] Vicent, "El pentagrama," 13.

[58] See Roberto Rioja, "Federico Moreno Torroba: Ochenta y una gloriosas primaveras," *Hilo mundial* (January 1973): 27, for Torroba's recollections of his military "career." He appears always to have had difficulties with mathematics, and in later years admitted that he did not have a head for numbers. He made this admission while guessing that he had made fifteen million pesetas from the rights to *Luisa Fernanda*. "...though I don't have a head for numbers."

[59] The records of his military service are located in the Archivo Militar in Segovia.

his infantry training on August 1, 1912, in Madrid, and entered active service on March 6 of the following year. Promotions did follow in fairly rapid succession: corporal by July 1, 1913, and sergeant by May 1, 1915. However, he obtained this rank in the army reserve, in which he became a second lieutenant on February 1, 1916. His honorable discharge took place on July 31, 1930, after exactly eighteen years in the army. His service records state that his conduct was consistently "good" ("*buena*"), as was his knowledge of tactics and ordinances. Moreover, we learn that his height was one meter, 682 millimeters (about five and a half feet). No mention is made of difficulties with trigonometry, of being the beneficiary of any quota system, or of receiving an early discharge for either reason. Conveniently enough, he was stationed in Madrid the whole time and never sent into action. (Thus, the records state that his valor was simply "supposed," in the absence of actual demonstration in combat.) The service could not have been too onerous, as it does not seem to have interfered much with his music career. While on active duty, he published his first piano work in 1913, a "One and Two Step" entitled *À petits pas*, and *El mate*, a "Tango argentino," two years later.[60] As we will see, in 1915 he even participated in the premiere of an important work by Falla, an unlikely turn of events had he not already been an active musician with a solid reputation at the time.

It also seems unlikely that he actually enlisted, as a conscription law was passed on February 27, 1912, that would have required him to receive some military training, and to remain eligible for mobilization for eighteen years. That coincides precisely with the length of his service, something that cannot be mere coincidence. As for benefiting from the quota system, it is hard to interpret with precision Torroba's account. The amount required was not 500 pesetas but rather 1,500 (for release after twelve months) or 2,000 (after six).[61] His statements about his father's small income and mother's exacting economies (see below) make it unlikely that they could have afforded such sums. Yet, it is also doubtful that his account is a fabrication. A possible explanation is that some sort of less costly transaction occurred within the *cuota* system that resulted not in a formal discharge or release, but in seven months of training followed by circumstances that allowed Torroba to pursue music while technically remaining on active duty. Such a scenario accommodates Torroba's recollection of a short military stint and documented musical activities at the time, as well as the conscription law and official record.

The Musician

In the absence of any aspirations to make a career of the army, Torroba arrived at the gates of adulthood without a clear idea of where he was going. "So, I asked

---

[60] Both with Madrid publishers, i.e., Casa Dotesio and Unión Musical Española, respectively.

[61] See Carolyn Boyd's excellent article on the sociopolitical circumstances of the Spanish army in the early twentieth century at http://libro.uca.edu/boyd/chapter2.htm (accessed November 12, 2010).

myself, what will I do, what will become of me?"[62] Thanks to his musical training, an answer to this existential dilemma was at hand. He assisted his father playing the organ in churches, and thereby began to earn a little money. This was indeed fortuitous, because the family's finances were in a perpetually precarious state, and only hard work and thrift would see them through.

> My father earned a ridiculously low salary, but in those days one could live on it. In the evenings he put one *duro* [five *pesetas*, roughly five cents] on the table, and with that we could all eat. I helped him play the organ during mass and enjoyed improvising. At baptisms they paid me six *reales* to amuse myself at the organ while they sprinkled the baby with water and the people passed by.[63]

His mother's exacting management of the household finances was an important factor in their survival:

> I recall my mother keeping accounts. She had one *duro* for her daily shopping. And she would say to herself, "1.15 for meat, 20 for milk, 15 for bread, 1 *real* for a filet." [Thus], despite my father's modest salary, we ate well and lived without problems.[64]

It is not hard to imagine that this early example of successful money management served Torroba well in later years, when he undertook responsibilities as an impresario and as president of the Sociedad General de Autores de España, where he was dealing with millions of *pesetas* instead of a few *duros*. The basic principle of living within one's means proved to be the same in both instances.

Torroba not only found work playing organ at various churches in Madrid but also providing light entertainment on the piano in the lobby of the Teatro Lara, alongside his father.[65] He later said that he earned his first 1,000 *pesetas* at the Lara, on December 28, 1911. He did this by organizing a concert of well-known singers of musical comedy on that evening of the *Día de los Inocentes* (a day commemorating the Slaughter of the Innocents related in Matthew 2:16).[66] In fact,

---

[62] Vicent, "El pentagrama," 13. At the end of his life, when asked what he would like to be if he were not already a composer, he answered without hesitation: "A dealer in excellent cattle...and also an architect—or better yet, an architect who owns a herd of excellent cattle!" This speaks to nothing except his sense of humor. See Sagi-Vela, "Moreno Torroba, nonagenario," 23.

[63] Vicent, "El pentagrama," 13.

[64] San Martín, "Federico Moreno Torroba."

[65] According to Federico, Jr., in an interview with William Krause, July 19, 1988. Torroba once said that although he played the piano well enough, his organ playing was a "joke." See Gómez Ortiz, "Moreno Torroba."

[66] Cortés-Cavanillas, "El maestro Moreno Torroba," 47. In another article, he incorrectly recalled this as taking place in 1909. The significance of the misrecollection is that he tied it into the political events of that year, headlined by the Tragic Week in Barcelona. See Vicent, "El pentagrama," 13.

his father had actually composed a number of zarzuelas for production there. These were of the *género chico* variety, each with one act and two scenes. They utilized librettos by local literary figure Tomás Rodríguez Alenza, who had also collaborated with major *zarzueleros* such as Emilio Arrieta. The zarzuelas he wrote with Ballesteros featured such intriguing titles as *¡Bruto!* (Brutus!, 1902) and *El sueño de la princesa* (The Princess's Dream, 1907). Young Federico made his very first mark in the theater collaborating with his father and Alenza on a similar work entitled *Las decididas* (The Determined Ones), subtitled a "lyric fantasia in one act with two scenes."[67] This premiered at the Lara on May 27, 1912, and initiated Torroba's eventual composition of approximately seventy works for the stage.

Certainly an important part of Torroba's early musical education came from meeting leading musicians through the agency of his father's numerous professional connections, as well as soirées at the home of conductor and violinist Enrique Fernández Arbós, who became a good friend.[68] His expanding circle of acquaintances came to include Rubinstein, Picasso, Stravinsky, and Manuel de Falla. Of this latter figure Torroba said:

> His *Noches en los jardines de España* contains the essence of Spanish music. He is undoubtedly the greatest Spanish musician of the twentieth century, with a great distance separating him from all others.[69]

It was on April 15, 1915, that Torroba first had the opportunity to meet his idol, as father and son participated in the premiere of Falla's ballet *El amor brujo* at the Lara. Ballesteros conducted the fourteen-member chamber orchestra in which Torroba played the piano.[70] Torroba was not an original member of the ensemble, but its pianist, José Media-Villa, fell ill on the morning of the premiere. Torroba would have to fill in, and with only hours to acquire the notes, he faced something of a crisis.

> "Muchacho," my father told me, "you have to play the piano tonight. Here's the score. Start practicing it now." I didn't really understand, but I knew my father wasn't joking. So I sat myself down at the piano and began to bang out the notes. That evening, though feeling timorous and full of self-doubt, I was able to fulfill with flying colors the responsibility I'd been given. My father felt very proud of his son, and

---

[67] Performance program, Teatro Lara, Madrid, May 27, 1912.

[68] Sagi-Vela, "Moreno Torroba, nonagenario," 22.

[69] Daniel Stéfani, "Federico Moreno Torroba: La juventud de un compositor de 89 años," *El Día* (Montevideo), October 24, 1980.

[70] The ensemble for the first performances of *El amor brujo* was a small chamber orchestra. Later versions were scored for a large orchestra.

Manuel de Falla, fully satisfied and indulgent, came over to congratulate me.[71]

This occasion marked Torroba's debut as a concert performer.[72]

The Composer

It was about this time that Torroba began studies in composition with Conrado del Campo (1878–1953).[73] A violinist and later conductor, Campo was one of Spain's leading music pedagogues and a nationally important composer. He was, moreover, a devotee of Wagner, championed the works of Richard Strauss, and wrote in a late-Romantic style. This put him at odds with an emerging avant-garde that looked to Paris rather than Germany and Austria for its musical cues. This Frenchified avant-garde began with Albéniz and was in full flower with the works of Falla and Turina. Still, as Javier Suárez-Pajares has noted, although Campo was one of the *guardia vieja* (old guard), in the role of teacher he contributed greatly to the renovation of Spanish music in the 1920s and 30s; in fact, most of the progressive young composers of that epoch studied with him. He imparted more than just technique to his students: he inculcated in them "the necessary discipline and also encouraged them to create freely." A key element of his personality was his "ability to position himself to best advantage among his professional colleagues."[74] This final observation could also be made of Torroba.

Campos's conservative musical nature had a decided impact on the young Torroba, whose first important compositions owed an obvious debt to German masters such as Strauss. Following the example of his teacher, Torroba's first orchestral work was a symphonic poem, which was awarded second prize in the Conservatorio's "concurso del Maestro Benedito." Based on contemporary author Gustavo Bécquer's story of the same name, *La ajorca de oro* (The Golden Bracelet) was given its 1918 premiere by the Orquesta Sinfónica de Madrid under the direction of Arbós.[75]

---

[71] "'La zarzuela está vivita y coleando,'" *Revista 7 Días* (Argentina), July 18, 1975, 56. Evidence of his sometimes faulty memory appears here, as he recalls the year of this premiere as 1904, when he was only thirteen years old.

[72] See Antonio Gallego, *Manuel de Falla y* El amor brujo (Madrid: Alianza Música, 1990), 287, for more details on the premiere. A detailed summary of its critical reception appears on pp. 46–51. The ballet's run at the Lara was a good one, lasting for thirty performances. The lead role of Candelas was interpreted by Pastora Imperio.

[73] Although one occasionally reads that he studied with Campo at the Conservatorio, a thorough search of the records there indicates that he never reenrolled. The studies with Campo were private.

[74] Javier Suárez-Pajares, "Moreno Torroba, Federico," *Diccionario de la zarzuela: España e Hispanoamérica*, ed. Emilio Casares Rodicio (Madrid: ICCMU, 2002).

[75] *Ajorcas* are rings that Moorish women wear around their wrists and ankles.

The following year, on December 19 at the Teatro Price, another composition, *Cuadros*, received its premiere by the Orquesta Filarmónica under the direction of Pérez Casas. This four-movement work comprised reflections on four famous paintings: *La Era* (Goya); *El baile en San Antonio de la Florida* (Goya); *Nuestro Señor Crucificado* (Velásquez); and *Ninfas de Diana sorprendidas por los sátiros* (Rubens). The paintings were reproduced in the program at the premiere.[76] It appears that, to some extent, Torroba was not truly dedicated to following in his teacher's footsteps, and he soon abandoned symphonic composition for the theater. There were also practical reasons for this decision, however.

In those days, there was simply not much of a living to be made writing symphonic music. Torroba truly believed that "all musicians are born with the intention of dedicating themselves to symphonic music, to serious music."[77] Though he also dreamed of writing symphonic music, "I had to make a living, so I dedicated myself to the zarzuela. And I certainly can't complain about the small amount of glory that it has given me."[78] Indeed, the real money was in zarzuela. As his son, Federico, Jr., remarked, he made this transition because,

> at that time the theater formed part of the daily life of the people, espe-cially in the big cities. The zarzuela was an integral part of the culture of the time, and people talked about premieres with the same fervor that they talk about major cultural events today. In Madrid alone there were five or six theaters presenting zarzuelas daily.[79]

This is corroborated by journalist Eduardo Haro Tecglen, who observed that,

> In the early years of Torroba's career, the theater could be very lucrative. For a librettist or composer, it could provide the money that in a country with our lack of culture dedication to "pure art" almost never yields. Moreno Torroba has lost money. Someone has said that a man of theater shows what he's made of when he loses money—like a gambler. Moreno Torroba, who could have made a lot of money simply off of the rights to his works, which continue to be performed, instead lost money in becoming an impresario and taking his own company to America.[80]

During this same period, Torroba occasionally traveled with his father to Paris. Though he did not pursue formal music studies there, either at the Conservatoire or Schola Cantorum, he nonetheless learned a great deal from the music he heard

[76] A program for this concert is in the Navarra archive.

[77] Colmenero, "Lírico Moreno Torroba."

[78] "Moreno Torroba, el más famoso compositor."

[79] Estévez, "Federico Moreno Torroba," 41.

[80] Eduardo Haro Tecglen, "Un personaje del Madrid de Chueca," *El País*, September 13, 1982, 22.

and the people he met, including some of the leading musical figures at that time.[81] When asked about influences, Torroba responded, "When I was young, [I was influenced by] Wagner, as were all of the musicians of my era. Besides, my teacher, Conrado del Campo, was very Wagnerian. Later, [I was influenced by] Debussy and Ravel, and still later, Bela Bartók."[82] On other occasions, Torroba also cited César Franck as an influence.[83] We recall that, late in life, Torroba said Ravel was among the extraordinary men he had known and that Stravinsky and Picasso had been among his friends, but no further details about these acquaintances have surfaced.[84]

It is clear from evidence in the Navarra archive that Torroba's acquaintance with Joaquín Turina began during his formative years, for five of Turina's printed piano works are located there, each with regards and signed by the composer.[85] These salutations are dated between 1923 and 1927, during Turina's long residence in the capital city. In addition, handwritten and signed scores of two of Turina's works for organ are found in the archive. These pieces date from the period 1914–15, raising the possibility that Turina and Torroba were acquainted as early as 1914, shortly after Turina's return from Paris and when Torroba was only twenty-three years of age. Based on this evidence and stylistic similarities, it is quite possible that Turina played a role in Torroba's early development, perhaps encouraging his nationalist orientation.

The region of Navarra played an important part in Torroba's life as well. María del Pilar Larregla y Nogueras, the daughter of the Navarrese composer Joaquín Larregla (1865–1945), became Torroba's wife in 1926. He was now thirty-five years old, and she was thirty-three. It was her family's estate in Santesteban, Navarra, that became their refuge during the Civil War and summer home for the rest of their lives. The couple had two children: Mariana (1928–1990) and Federico, Jr. (b. 1933). Federico, Jr., called José Grandpa "Pepe" and Larregla Grandpa "Quin," both of whom had originally become friends without suspecting that one day they would be in the same family. Larregla had three sons, one of whom became a famous graphic artist for *Blanco y Negro* (by coincidence founded in the same year Torroba was born). Federico, Jr., recalled that his mother

> was singing in the chorus at San Manuel y San Benito in Lagasca street, and it was there that she met the son of the organist, Torroba, who occasionally came along to help his father and exchange glances with the *chicas* in the chorus.[86]

[81] Federico Moreno Torroba, Jr., interview with William Krause, July 20, 1988.
[82] Sagi-Vela, "Moreno Torroba, nonagenario," 23.
[83] In "'La zarzuela está vivita y coleando,'" *Revista 7 Días* (Argentina), July 24, 1975.
[84] *Baleares* (Palma de Mallorca), April 23, 1982, and *El Día* (Montevideo), October 24, 1980.
[85] These scores are in the Navarra archive.
[86] Estévez, "Federico Moreno Torroba," 41.

Torroba himself said the same, adding that they both performed on Eucharistic Thursdays, and that he not only played the organ but also composed motets. Asked at what point Cupid fired his dart, our witty composer replied, "When I said to her, 'You are singing out of tune, señorita!'"[87] They were married on July 21 in the parochial church of San José, across from the Gran Vía. A splendid Baroque edifice, it was erected in 1732 on the site of a convent of Carmelite nuns originally founded in the 1500s by St. John of the Cross.[88]

An important turning point in Torroba's career was his acquaintance with Segovia.[89] In his autobiography, Segovia states that he and Torroba met shortly after Arbós's premiere of one of Torroba's orchestral works.[90] It is very possible that this work was *La ajorca de oro*, from 1918. Furthermore, Segovia states that the orchestra's first violinist, Julio Francés, introduced Torroba to him.

> It did not take us long to become friends, nor for him to accede to my suggestion: Would he compose something for the guitar? In a few weeks he came up with a slight but truly beautiful Dance in E Major [*Danza*]. In spite of his scant knowledge of the guitar's complex technique, he approached it accurately by sheer instinct, and to my joy the work remained in the repertoire. The abovementioned Dance in E Major in time became part of Torroba's *Suite castellana*, joining the other components of the suite, the Fandanguillo and the Arada. These last two Torroba composed after my return from South America.[91]

Torroba remembered the sequence of events somewhat differently, putting the composition of his first guitar music *after* Segovia's return:

> Oh, many years ago, after returning from one of his innumerable tours in Latin America, the artist expressed to don Ernesto Quesada, director and owner of the unforgettable organization "Conciertos Daniel," his idea of obtaining works written directly for the guitar. And it was he who

[87] Cortés-Cavanillas, "El maestro Moreno Torroba," 47.

[88] A record of their nuptials is located in the archive of this church, in Libro número 25, Folio 310. According to this document, Pilar's father was from Lumbier, Navarra, while her mother, Mariana, was from Cárdenas, Cuba.

[89] There are some sixty pieces of correspondence from Torroba to Segovia preserved in the Fundación-Museo Andrés Segovia in Linares. These include postcards, letters, and manuscripts, the majority of them signed and dated. The earliest is dated June 17, 1946, and the last, April 17, 1982. A listing of the manuscripts is available in Luigi Attademo, "El repertorio de Andrés Segovia y las novedades de su archivo," *Roseta*, n1 (October 2008): 69–100.

[90] Andrés Segovia, *An Autobiography of the Early Years 1893–1920*, trans. W. F. O'Brien (New York: Macmillan, 1976), 194.

[91] Ibid.

proposed to present me to Segovia in order to initiate my collaboration with that brilliant guitarist.[92]

Given the uncertainty of the circumstances under which they first met, it is not surprising that the date of their meeting is also unknown. Alberto López Poveda, the director of the Fundación-Museo Andrés Segovia in Linares and biographer of the guitarist, believes they met in Madrid in either 1916 or 1917.[93] Torroba's own statements on the subject are contradictory, putting the date anywhere between the late 1910s and 1926.[94] It is certain that they met before 1920, based on the evidence of Torroba's first guitar works.

In any case, when asked, decades later, which performer fascinated him most, Torroba cited Segovia: "All eulogies to him pale into inadequacy."[95] When Segovia was admitted to the Real Academia de Bellas Artes de San Fernando in 1978, Torroba prepared remarks in response to Segovia's acceptance speech. In these he expatiated on the nature of their relationship, characterizing it as a

fraternal friendship, always enlivened by a growing admiration for his art. And [it was] a friendship that awakened within me the instant attraction that I felt towards the magic of his guitar, with its universality [as] one of the most human instruments that music possesses for creating immediate and intimate communication with the feelings of its listeners.[96]

The friendship between Segovia and Torroba was to have a major impact on both of their careers. As we know, acting on Segovia's suggestion, Torroba composed *Danza* for solo guitar in the first months of 1920. Segovia recognized this piece as a breakthrough in the development of the classical guitar as well as one that would affect his own career. In his autobiography, Segovia states that this was "the first time a composer who was not a guitarist wrote for the guitar."[97] According to López Poveda, Segovia premiered it at the Teatro Odeón in Buenos Aires on June

---

[92] Andrés Segovia, "La guitarra y yo," discurso leído por el Excmo. Sr. Don Andrés Segovia Torres con motivo de su recepción pública el día 8 de enero de 1978, y contestación del Excmo. Sr. Don Federico Moreno Torroba" (Madrid: Real Academia de Bellas Artes de San Fernando, 1978), 27.

[93] Alberto López Poveda, letter to William Krause, July 7, 1990.

[94] People who knew Torroba during his later years agree that his recollection of specific dates pertaining to his early career was often inaccurate. For instance, in an interview published in *Brújula* (Madrid) on January 3, 1976, he stated that he met Segovia in 1922. However in Colmenero, "Lírico Moreno Torroba," he said the year was 1926.

[95] Cortés-Cavanillas, "El maestro Moreno Torroba," 48.

[96] Segovia, "La guitarra y yo," 27.

[97] Segovia, *Autobiography*, 194. Sticklers for historical detail will cite Luigi Boccherini (1743–1805) as a nonguitarist who wrote for the instrument, though in the context of string quintets and not solos. Others might cite Paganini, but he played the guitar as well as the violin. He wrote duets for violin and guitar, as well as solos.

11, 1921. He gave the Madrid premiere on April 4, 1922, at the Teatro de la Comedia.[98] This work became a part of Segovia's concert repertoire and "prompted Falla to compose his very beautiful *Homenaje*, and Turina his splendid *Sevillana*."[99] Torroba's own statement supports that of Segovia: "I was the first [non-guitarist] to write for the guitar. Maestro Falla followed my path somewhat later."[100] Concerning this first work, the composer stated that his twin inspirations in writing it were "Segovia's art as well as by a cadence with a typically Castilian flavor."[101]

The arrangement was more than a matter of mutual convenience, however. Torroba and Segovia had similar tastes in music, which is to say that both were confirmed Romantics and had little use for "modern" music. Indeed, as Suárez-Pajares notes,

> [Torroba] never involved himself in the experiments of the younger com-
> posers of the Generation of '27, and neither did he join their associa-
> tions....he opposed the musical avant-garde in Madrid. The
> avant-gardists, *Los Ocho*, wrote for [Regino] Sainz de la Maza, while
> Torroba wrote for Segovia, who was likewise opposed to modernism and
> resided musically in the late Romantic.[102]

Again dedicated to Segovia, **Sonatina** (1923) was Torroba's next guitar work. Segovia described this three-movement composition as "another jewel in our repertoire,"[103] and he premiered the work at the Teatro de Comedia de Madrid on December 17, 1923. In 1926 Segovia played the *Sonatina* for Ravel, who was impressed with Torroba's talent.[104] This work has remained one of Torroba's most widely performed and recorded guitar compositions. In fact, Torroba actually met Ravel and presented him with a copy of the music. Federico, Jr., later fleshed out some details:

[98] Alberto López Poveda, *Andrés Segovia: vida y obra*, 2 vols. (Jaén: Universidad de Jaén, 2009), ii, 1036.

[99] Ibid., 195.

[100] Mengual, "Federico Moreno Torroba: 'El género de zarzuela está enfermo,'" *Levante*, June 6, 1981.

[101] Letter from Federico Moreno Torroba to Alberto López Poveda, dated July 12, 1972, and cited in a letter from Poveda to William Krause dated Linares (Jaén), July 7, 1990. Poveda believes the *Sonatina* was inspired by "placid visions and noble songs of Castile."

[102] Suárez-Pajares, "Moreno Torroba, Federico," *Diccionario de la zarzuela: España e Hispanoamérica*. However, in a strange irony, Sainz de la Maza was later a member of the Falange and an admirer of Nazi cultural policy. See Gemma Pérez Zalduondo, "La música en los intercambios culturales entre España y Alemania (1938–1942)," *Cruces de caminos: Intercambios musicales y artísticos en la Europa de la primera mitad del siglo XX*, ed. Gemma Pérez Zalduondo and María Isabel Cabrera García (Granada: Editorial Universidad de Granada, 2010), 419–20.

[103] Segovia, *Autobiography*, 195.

[104] "Hoy, entierro del maestro Moreno Torroba," *Ya, Hoja del Lunes*, September 13, 1982.

The Hotel Paris in the Puerta del Sol accommodated Ravel whenever he visited Spain, and one day Andrés Segovia organized a meeting between the French Basque composer and my father, because he wanted Ravel to write a piece for guitar. He hoped to overcome Ravel's reluctance because of his unfamiliarity with the instrument by introducing him to a Spanish composer who had dared to do so. My father gave him the score for the *Sonatina* as a gift. Ravel said he would study it, but he died the following year without producing anything.[105]

According to Segovia himself, Ravel was impressed not only by the composition but by the composer. Upon later hearing the *Sonatina*, in a private performance that Segovia gave at the Paris home of Henri Prunière, Ravel said of Torroba, "Except for the relative dimensions of the works, it could be said of him...what Spontini said of Rossini concerning his *Barber of Seville*, which is that to compose such a graceful *Sonatina* not only does one have to possess talent but one also has to be young."[106]

Late in life, Torroba gave a slightly different account of his first works for Segovia. In 1980 he said, "I wrote a prelude for him, and he liked my style so much that he asked me to write something more important for him. Accordingly, I wrote a *Sonatina*."[107] The prelude may have been *Danza*; otherwise, the *Danza* remains unaccounted for in this chronology. Torroba did write a *Prelude* during the early years, which was published in 1928. Considering the many discrepancies in statements made by Torroba in his later years, one is more inclined to accept Segovia's account.

In any case, not all critics received this work kindly, despite its proven durability in the repertoire. Progressive critic Adolfo Salazar, for instance, had decidedly mixed feelings about Torroba's accessible aesthetic, as revealed in the *Sonatina*:

> We only feel it our duty to warn Sr. Torroba of the dangerous proximity of these little pieces to the genre of lovely embellishment, of music for young ladies. And I believe that that is certainly not the most favorable orientation for a serious musician.[108]

[105] Estévez, "Federico Moreno Torroba," 41.

[106] Segovia offered this recollection in his remarks at Torroba's funeral, reported in "Moreno-Torroba será enterrado," 39. See also his printed recollection of this encounter in "Breves palabras sobre Torroba," *Academia: Boletín de la Real Academia de Bellas Artes de San Fernando*, n55 (second semester 1982): 27.

[107] Stéfani, "Federico Moreno Torroba."

[108] In Adolfo Salazar, "El nuevo arte de la guitarra y Andrés Segovia. Obras españolas. El primer concierto del Real. Brahms y Von Holst," *El Sol*, December 20, 1923, 6. Cited in Leopoldo Neri de Caso, "La guitarra en el ideario musical de Adolfo Salazar (1915–1939)," in *Música y cultura en la Edad de Plata, 1915–1939*, ed. María Nagore, Leticia Sánchez de Andrés, and Elena Torres (Madrid: ICCMU,

In 1926 Torroba published the **Suite castellana** as well as *Nocturno*. These enchanting essays quickly reached a wide audience during Segovia's regular concert tours throughout Europe. All were written in a nationalistic spirit. The *Suite* includes *Fandanguillo*, *Arada* (a song pertaining to the plowing of fields), and ends with the earlier *Danza*. Segovia had already premiered the *Fandanguillo* and *Arada* in Madrid on May 10, 1922; he performed the entire *Suite* for the first time in Granada ten days later, at the Centro Artístico.[109] *Nocturno*, though more abstract, makes use of the modality and phrase structure of Andalusian folk music (more will be said of the *Suite castellana* in Scene iii).[110] The importance to Torroba's career of these publications—and the recordings of Torroba's pieces that Segovia made for La Voz de su Amo (His Master's Voice) starting in 1927—cannot be exaggerated, as they provided not only substantial income but an international reputation, too. As Graham Wade points out, they were

> among the first editions of Schott's Segovia Guitar Archive Series....This series was one of the most important publishing events in the guitar's history. At first, sales were sparse but in time to come the financial returns would be remarkable as works from the series began to be studied in academies by all students of the guitar and recitalists played them many times in concert. Recording royalties alone would ultimately prove phenomenal.[111]

The collaboration between Segovia and Torroba contributed significantly to the renaissance that took place in the guitar world during the 1920s. At this time, many critics were still skeptical of the legitimacy of the guitar in the concert hall. With the help of Torroba and others, Segovia was able to present music of high quality that was undeniably appropriate to the instrument. Other pioneering works produced for the guitar during this time were: Falla's only guitar work, *Hommage, pour le Tombeau de Claude Debussy* (1920);[112] Turina's initial efforts,

---

2009), 306. To be sure, Salazar esteemed other guitar pieces by Torroba, especially the *Danza*. Franco reports that the famous critic praised its proximity to the kind of popular music that was "natural" to the guitar. See Enrique Franco, "Moreno Torroba o la supervivencia del casticismo," *La Chulapona*, program notes for the production at the Teatro de la Zarzuela, Madrid, September 14–October 1 and October 11–30, 1988 (Madrid: Teatro de la Zarzuela, 1988), 9. In *La música de España: La música en la cultura española*, 286, he lauded Torroba's many "fine pages" written for Segovia.

[109] López Poveda, *Andrés Segovia*, ii, 1037.

[110] See Josep Crivillí i Bargalló, *Historia de la música española: el folklore musical* (Madrid: Alianza Música, 1983), chap. 7.

[111] Graham Wade, *Segovia: A Celebration of the Man and His Music* (London: Allison & Busby, 1983), 63. "Torroba's Burgalesa, Preludio, and Serenata Burlesca followed into print in 1928 and the ever popular Pièces caratéristiques appeared in 1931."

[112] As Piquer Sanclemente points out in *Clasicismo moderno, neoclasicismo y retornos en el pensamiento musical español (1915–1939)*, 324, from a purely aesthetic standpoint, the guitar comported perfectly with the modernist aesthetic of Falla, given its frequent evocation in the cubist works of Picasso, Braque, and Gris, as well as with "an austere vision of Castile."

Sevillana and *Fandanguillo* (1926); Manuel Ponce's first guitar works, *Sonata mexi-cana*, *Sonata clásica*, *Sonata III* (1928–29); Alexandré Tansman's premier guitar piece, *Mazurka* (1928); and Heitor Villa-Lobos' *Douze Études* (composed 1929, pub. 1953). Interest in the guitar was also evident among composers who were not members of the Segovia orbit. Arnold Schoenberg and Anton Webern wrote their only works that included the guitar during this period, op. 24 (1923) and opp. 18 and 19 (1926), respectively; however, they did so without any encourage-ment from Segovia.

The Impresario

In 1925 and 1926, Torroba produced the works that would establish his reputa-tion as an important young impresario and composer of zarzuela. In the tradi-tion and style of Vives and Serrano, Torroba wrote *La mesonera de Tordesillas* in 1925 and *La pastorela* in 1926. Torroba recalled that he earned ten *duros* per act for *La mesonera de Tordesillas*, 300 *pesetas* in all. He was up against stiff competi-tion, as Vives, Giménez, Lleo, and Chapí were all in full career.[113] So, he was off to a good start.

As impresario, he directed a resident company at Madrid's Teatro Centro throughout the decade.[114] Torroba was among few successful *zarzueleros* of his epoch who also became impresarios. What were the reasons for this unconven-tional career move? Chief among them was a desire to gain more artistic control over the production of his own works. He noted that one of his zarzuelas was done in Barcelona (he could not remember exactly which), and "I was shocked that on the day of the premiere no one knew what they were supposed to do on stage. I later learned that the cast had only received their parts the day before the premiere!"[115] He clarified that he did not undertake the job out of sheer egoistic ambition but rather because, in order for the author to prevail in the zarzuela, it is necessary to be the impresario. "The music counts for nothing if it is badly sung or poorly played by the orchestra."[116]

Of course, remuneration was another incentive. As Haro Tecglen later noted:

> Why does a composer want to be an impresario? The simple answer is money. An author suffers greatly when another person gets rich off a work that is the product of his own talent; ... However, there is another reason beyond simply money: an author always feels that the impresario

---

[113] Vicent, "El pentagrama," 13.

[114] Colmenero, "Lirico Moreno Torroba."

[115] Ibid.

[116] Félix Centeno, "Moreno Torroba espera dejar una fortuna a sus hijos," *Pueblo*, before June 15, 1966.

has not given to his work all that it deserves, that he has not paid the cast well enough, gotten a good enough orchestra or the best sets. So, one becomes an impresario in order to care for his own works the way he thinks they deserve.[117]

Torroba himself made his reasons clear enough: "I did it because I want my works to have a good cast, and the only way to get that is to pay them myself."[118]

Thanks to his decision to become an impresario, "all my works have premiered with very good casts, with singers chosen by me." Being an astute diplomat, he was able to avoid major problems with the artists, such as a singer becoming angry and stalking off the stage, requiring a last-minute substitution. Of course, there were economic ups and downs, as sometimes he made a lot of money, and sometimes not. "But I have survived."[119] Of course, though he had made a lot of money from the zarzuela, he had also invested a lot of his funds in his three companies, promoting singers, traveling, etc.[120]

Years later, he described in an interview the ordeals he endured as both composer and impresario.[121] He first deals directly with his income and thoughts on music as a business:

> Now, the work is enormous. You have to sow a lot of seeds just to reap a small harvest. Not all works are successful and in fact most achieve much less. People remember the successes but forget the failures, which are much more numerous. I consider a work successful if it receives a thousand performances. Otherwise, it is not worth the effort to be a composer.

Obviously, he found his work to be very difficult:

> However, it pleases and inspires me; but I recognize that it is overwhelming. A score represents an immense amount of work: hundreds and hundreds of hours devoted to the task at hand. And later, if the work fails, the work of many months is undone in a single evening. Jiménez put it very graphically: In order to say "sí," the librettist need only write two letters and he is done. But for this single syllable on the lips of the character, the composer has to write thirty-two signs in music notation,

---

[117] Haro Tecglen, "Un personaje del Madrid."

[118] Albino Mallo, "Los noventa jovenes años de Moreno Torroba," *Heraldo de Aragón*, December 21, 1980.

[119] Lola Aguado, "Lo que dice el maestro Torroba," *Ya*, 1980 (interview with FMT shortly before premiere of *El Poeta* on June 19, 1980) [undated clipping in Na].

[120] Serafín Alonso, "Homenaje en el Ayuntamiento al maestro Moreno Torroba," Murcia newspaper of unknown title, March 21, 1981, 3 [Na].

[121] Centeno, "Moreno Torroba."

so that each of the members of the orchestra will play his or her own note.

Of course, it was all a matter of business, and that meant that money eventually drove every other consideration.

> In my hands, money is a relative thing, because in addition to being the author, I am the impresario of my own works and of others'. That is to say that I manage a large amount of capital, but with a lot of risk, because the budget of a zarzuela is so great that, given the normal twists and turns in the course of business, the deficit can run up to thousands of *duros* and spell ruin.

When asked if he had the necessary *sangre froid* for that sort of thing, he responded, "That's the question. But, yes, I have it.... I have faith."

A couple of incidents from this formative period in his career not only shed further light on his decision to get control of his works by becoming an impresario but also reveal a deeply engrained trait in his personality: humility, and the ability to make fun of himself. These incidents also provide us with some insight into the backstage realities of the zarzuela, its risks and intrigues.

He was engaged to compose the music for a two-act zarzuela entitled *La caravana de ambrosio*, with a text by García Álvarez (whom Torroba described as a *descuidado*, or a bit of a slob). The plot dealt with a caravan that goes in search of Atlantis only to get lost in the desert, a suitable metaphor for the production itself. The author completed his libretto in a single day, and Torroba, the music in a single night. The hastily prepared work premiered May 11, 1925; though it was supposed to have opened on May 9, this was delayed two days to allow for more rehearsal. Still, while conducting his own score, Torroba got lost among the thicket of notes, and the orchestra quickly dissolved in confusion. The curtain had to be lowered while everyone strove to get the show back on track. "Behind me I could hear the insults and shouts of the public, like a pack of wild animals," Torroba remarked. Despite this fracas, the unassuming work ran for fifty nights, to packed houses. "The people were laughing and stamping their feet. It was incredible!" And the critics found the music to be "delicious," the jokes "very graceful," and the presentation "sumptuous."[122]

The impresario who presided over the production of **La marchenera** was a "very good friend" of Torroba's, or so he thought. He soon proposed a business deal to the young composer:

> "Listen, you are a great musician, and instead of 300 pesetas a night, I'm going to pay you 400, as God is my witness." ... Time passed, and it finally

[122] Vicent, "El pentagrama," 14; Sagi-Vela, "Moreno Torroba, non agenario," 23; García Carretero, *Historia del Teatro de la Zarzuela*, ii, 102.

turned out that he was a counterfeiter.... He was paying me with fake *pesetas*! I had given him my best, and he gave me his worst.... He wound up in jail, but I spent all that money without knowing it was counterfeit, and nothing ever happened to me.[123]

Despite any and all such vicissitudes, his one-act opera **La virgen de mayo** opened in Madrid at the Teatro Real on February 14, 1925, with great fanfare and expectation. The drama is set in Andalusia and features passion, jealousy, and violence, concluding in tragedy. Torroba's masterful use of local color clearly derives from popular culture, and no doubt *Carmen* served him as an instructive prototype in this regard.[124] The opera was warmly received, but the work could not overcome the public's longstanding ambivalence toward Spanish opera. It has never been revived.

In his review of *La virgen de mayo*, Adolfo Salazar was not so much hostile toward Torroba's music as doubtful of the future of Spanish opera.[125] Torroba himself was not entirely satisfied with the performance. Years later he would recount that the cast was mediocre and unrehearsed, and the sets were undistinguished.[126] *La virgen de mayo* was the last opera to premiere at the Teatro Real, which traditionally had been Madrid's main opera house (opened November 19, 1850). Its closing the same year was a devastating blow to Spanish composers interested in opera, and Torroba did not bring out another major opera until *El poeta* in 1980. Torroba later joked that *La virgen de mayo* had the longest run of any opera in the history of the Teatro Real, because the posters for it remained attached to the walls of the theater for years after it had already closed![127] And the premiere was memorable for another reason, which the composer recalled with relish.

On the day of the premiere of *La virgen de mayo*, at the Teatro Real, King Alfonso XIII was in attendance and invited me to his box. He offered me a long cigarette with a golden mouthpiece, of the kind that high-class people smoke. Holding it in my hands, I didn't know what to do with it. Clearly, I wasn't a smoker, and I hesitated. But Luis Paris, scenic director, nudged me with his elbow and said, "Light the cigarette quickly so he doesn't think you're spurning it; otherwise, you'll piss him off." That was

---

[123] Torroba relates this incident in Vicent, "El pentagrama," 14.

[124] Enrique Franco had particularly high praise for the literary and musical quality of this work. See his "Moreno Torroba o la supervivencia del casticismo," *La Chulapona*, program notes, 1988, 9.

[125] Adolfo Salazar, *El Sol*, February 16, 1925 [review of *La virgen de mayo*].

[126] Untitled newspaper clipping in *ABC Reportaje*, May 2, 1980.

[127] Related in Gómez-Santos, "Federico Moreno Torroba."

the only cigarette that I smoked in my life, not counting the cigar that I smoked in the bathroom of my school when I was 8 years old.[128]

Torroba met musical royalty as well, in the form of Richard Strauss, at a social function at the Teatro Real in February of 1925. Strauss did not arrive in Spain until February 17, three days after the premiere of *La virgen de mayo*.[129] It is quite possible that Strauss heard one of the four subsequent performances, since he gave Torroba a handwritten note and photograph, dated June 8, 1925, congratulating him on the opera's premiere.[130]

The failure of indigenous opera in Spain was not an obstacle for Torroba. Having already found success in nationally oriented tone poems and guitar works, Torroba had not tied his career to the elusive dream of Spanish opera and had never been convinced that the foreign genre of opera could become truly national. The zarzuela, on the other hand, was uniquely national in character. Torroba and much of the Spanish public realized that the zarzuela had its own legacy and need not be compared to or compete with opera. He seized the moment and turned his attention to the zarzuela in the spring of 1925, cultivating that genre for the next four decades.

The *Zarzuelero*

As mentioned earlier, Torroba's first major success in the field of zarzuela was *La mesonera de Tordesillas* (The innkeeper of Tordesillas), set during the epoch of Felipe IV (reigned 1621–65). It premiered on October 30, 1925, at the Teatro de la Zarzuela in Madrid. In *El Sol*, Madrid's leading newspaper, the response was extremely favorable.[131] The reviewer, identified only as R.H.B, placed *La mesonera de Tordesillas* in the top rank of modern zarzuelas. The work was very popular with Madrid audiences and was performed regularly at the Teatro de la Zarzuela until mid-January 1926. It was revived there later that year, on November 22, and again at the Teatro Pardiñas on September 5 of the following year.[132] However, it does not remain in the standard repertoire.

Hard on the heels of that success came *La pastorela*, a collaboration with Pablo Luna, which opened at the Teatro Novedades on November 10, 1926. Though it escaped the notice of critics, the zarzuela was very successful, running until late January of the following year. Other zarzuelas produced during this period were

---

[128] Vicent, "El pentagrama," 13.

[129] Kurt Wilhelm, *Richard Strauss* (New York: Rizzoli, 1989), 193.

[130] This photograph is now in the Madrid home of Torroba's grandson.

[131] *El Sol*, October 31, 1925.

[132] See García Carretero, *Historia del Teatro de la Zarzuela*, ii, 103. Another critic praised its "very original score."

Mari-Blanca, on March 3, 1926, and *Colasín, el chico de la cola*, on May 9, 1926. Of the three, *Mari-Blanca* received the most favorable response, and it was revived the following year in Valencia.[133]

La marchenera was Moreno Torroba's next major success. Though he would later write his biggest hit, **Luisa Fernanda**, in less than a month, he spent fully ten months laboring over *La marchenera*, which despite its inferior libretto, offers some of his finest musical inspirations.[134] It opened on April 7, 1928, at the Teatro de la Zarzuela and was presented by a recently formed company, the Teatro Lírico Nacional. Despite lukewarm response from the press, *La marchenera* was the most popular zarzuela of the season, playing until mid-June.[135] On May 25th, a banquet was held in the composer's honor at the Teatro de la Zarzuela. The evening's festivities also included the performance of his symphonic poem *Estampa aragonesa* and excerpts from *La marchenera* (more will be said this zarzuela in Scene iii).

It is with this work that Torroba first emerges as the *zarzuelero* par excellence, one of whom Enrique Franco would later write:

> Torroba possessed the innate condition of the *madrileño* composer: a certain romantic flight, love of the zarzuela based in popular culture, and the will to communicate with the public at large, through a simple language, direct and elegant. [His music is remarkable for its] melodic grace, popular air, suitable instrumentation, and fluid spontaneity. However, one cannot accuse his cordial pages of cultivating the *pandereta* [tambourine; a reference to kitschy evocations of folk music]. Amidst a confluence of influences bearing a French stamp, such as one finds in the works of Falla and Turina, or of a German character, as in Conrado del Campo, Federico Moreno Torroba knew how to be *that which he was*.[136]

Not all conditions in Madrid favored the zarzuela. As elsewhere, the motion picture was becoming an irresistible force in urban Spain. Articles about Hollywood and actors such as Rudolph Valentino dominated the entertainment pages of newspapers, sometimes relegating theater and zarzuela to the sports or financial pages. Many theaters once devoted exclusively to live performances succumbed to the rising tide of film. Even the Teatro de la Zarzuela began to show films in 1930.

---

[133] *El Sol*, March 5, 1926.

[134] Suárez-Pajares, "Moreno Torroba, Federico," *Diccionario de la zarzuela: España e Hispanoamérica*.

[135] According to Víctor Sánchez Sánchez, "Moreno Torroba y la nostalgia de un Madrid idealizado," *La Chulapona*, program notes for the production at the Teatro de la Zarzuela, Madrid, February 6 to March 7, 2004 (Madrid: Teatro de la Zarzuela, 2003), 20, the critics found too great an abundance of musical inspiration in the work. This reminds us that for all their love of the zarzuela's music, critics and the public alike preferred equilibrium between text and music, neither dominating at the expense of the other.

[136] Enrique Franco, "Una figura del nacionalismo musical," *Autores* (October 1982): 34 (reprint of an article that first appeared in *El País*).

On September 24, 1928, the Teatro Novedades burned to the ground, ending a theatrical tradition that had begun in 1857. The loss of the Novedades further limited opportunities for composers and dramatists alike. But help was on the way.

Through the assistance of Primo de Rivera, Torroba and Pablo Luna had become the impresarios at the Teatro de la Zarzuela in about 1925.[137] In fact, the background of this development reveals that Torroba was on good terms with generals in, well, general, as we learn from his recollections of this period, particularly concerning Primo de Rivera.

> General Pepe Ungria...was a companion of mine at the *tertulia* at the Palace Café. Where the Iberia stands today there was at that time a tremendous café with a small theater, where I premiered a little work entitled *Cuidado con la pintura*. That was a very unassuming work. General Primo de Rivera went there often to play billiards.
>
> ...I have a very grateful memory of the general, because thanks to him, Pablo Luna and I came to direct the Teatro de la Zarzuela. I was then a critic for *Informaciones*. Luna and I requested an audience with the dictator in August, during terrible heat. His secretary, Monis, told us: "He is taking a nap, but wait here and he will receive you."...We were waiting in the antechamber for him to wake up when in walked Calvo Sotelo,[138] in a bright grey suit, exhibiting extreme impatience to meet with the dictator right away about something very urgent. He anxiously paced back and forth, looking nervously at his watch. Soon Monis invited Pablo and me in, ahead of Sotelo, whose grim countenance I still remember. We went in and asked for the Teatro de la Zarzuela, which belonged to the state. And the dictator responded right away: "I will give it to you at no cost, as long as you end performances before midnight." That man was very accessible....I used to see him often at the Teatro Martín, always accompanied by his friend, the impresario Paco Torres.[139]

Though this rapport with army generals may raise questions about Torroba's political leanings, he himself was unequivocal on this point:

> I have always kept my affairs in order. And I have never meddled in politics. I don't know, but I believe I could be as much of a communist as anyone, if they let me organize it in my own way.[140]

---

[137] See notice in *ABC Reportaje*, November 14, 1981.

[138] José Calvo Sotelo was a right-wing Spanish politician during the dictatorship and Second Republic. His assassination by left-wing elements in July 1936 helped to precipitate the Civil War.

[139] Vicent, "El pentagrama," 14.

[140] Ibid.

In fact, Torroba's definition of having "never meddled in politics" was quite narrow. He had numerous friends and acquaintances who were politicians, and throughout his career he served on music-related governmental commissions. However, he himself was never an office holder in the manner of those whom he considered politicians. In the years ahead, we will see that he continued to walk an exceedingly fine line in this regard. Still, in his own mind, at least, he was making an accurate statement. In addition, when we recall that during this period, and throughout the Rivera *dictadura*, Torroba was still an officer in the army reserve, his admiration for generals and affinity for Primo de Rivera in particular are less difficult to understand. Yet, Torroba's gratitude does not clarify our understanding of his views concerning Rivera's political ideology as much as it reflects his enthusiasm for a regime that supported his musical endeavors.

One hastens to add here that Torroba did not approve every action that Primo de Rivera took, and he even openly objected on one occasion. As Francesc Cortés reports, in 1925 the dictatorship closed down both the Barcelona soccer club and the Orfeó Català choral group because of Catalan-nationalist sentiments expressed on their behalf by Miquel Utrillo. The cultural establishment in Madrid was quick to protest this heavy-handed response, and Torroba joined José Subirá and others in defending the Orfeó, one of Spain's leading cultural institutions.[141]

In any case, the partnership of Torroba and Luna not only sustained the quality of programming at the Teatro de la Zarzuela but also produced at least five co-authored zarzuelas that premiered in various Madrid theaters between 1926 and 1929. It also resulted in the establishment of the Teatro Lírico Nacional during the 1926–27 season, whose purpose was to promote native musical theater. Luis París and Luis Pascal Frutos joined Torroba and Luna in directing this effort.[142] However, along with this monopoly came an obligation to their benefactor: the Teatro de la Zarzuela not only produced zarzuelas but propaganda spectacles as well, such as the "Homenaje a Primo de Rivera" and "Unión Patriótica," which convened on September 15–16, 1928.[143] Does this constitute meddling in politics, or just scratching the back of someone who scratched yours? Is it possible to separate the two completely? In any case, as director of the theater, there is no indication that Torroba resisted its use for the nationalistic and self-serving propaganda of a *caudillo*.

With Rivera's precipitous fall from power in 1930, Torroba and Luna lost their monopoly, and the programming at the Teatro de la Zarzuela subsequently took a different course. The production of zarzuelas was becoming erratic, competing

---

[141] Francesc Cortés, "Reflejos, imagenes y distorsiones en la recepción de las vanguardias musicales en Barcelona (1914–1936)," in *Música y cultura en la Edad de Plata, 1915–1939*, ed. María Nagore, Leticia Sánchez de Andrés, and Elena Torres (Madrid: ICCMU, 2009), 484.

[142] See Emilio García Carretero, *Historia del Teatro de la Zarzuela de Madrid. Tomo Segundo: 1913–1955* (Madrid: Fundación de la Zarzuela Española, 2004), 122.

[143] *El Sol*, September 15, 16, 1928.

with dance troupes, opera adaptations, recitals, and eventually films. Perhaps due to the lack of commitment to zarzuela at the Teatro de la Zarzuela at this juncture, Torroba severed his ties with that theater and became impresario and artistic director of the Teatro Calderón in 1930. Torroba's departure from the Teatro de la Zarzuela also coincided with the end of the short-lived residence of his troupe there, the Teatro Lírico Nacional.

Again, although Torroba claimed he "absolutely never" became involved in politics,[144] we have seen that he enjoyed a special rapport with influential public figures—which proved to be professionally advantageous. Indeed, his arrival at the Calderón was due to another personal favor. The Calderón was financed by Joaquín de Arteaga y Echagüe (1870–1947), the XVII duque del Infantado. It began life in 1917 as the Teatro del Odeón and later the Teatro del Centro. The Duke acquired it in 1927 and renamed it after the famous playwright. Though it could accommodate two thousand people, it had a small stage.[145] Torroba recounted, "I had the luck to win his confidence. He put the theater at my disposal with a generous contract." It was, in his opinion, "an excellent theater for zarzuela.[146]

The Calderón became a safe haven for traditional *zarzuela grande*. Its management was deliberate and unfaltering in championing the zarzuela in the face of competition both indigenous and foreign. During its first season, in 1930, singers Felisa Herrero and Emilio Sagi-Barba revived many of the best-known zarzuelas, such as Vives's *Doña Francisquita* (1923), Usandizaga's *Las golondrinas* (1914), which Sagi-Barba had originally premiered, and Barbieri's classic *Jugar con fuego* (1851).

Torroba's position at the Calderón was ideal for the furthering of his own aspirations as a composer. During the next six years, he premiered nearly all of his zarzuelas there, as well as numerous works by other composers. The first, on June 6, 1930, was Gerónimo Giménez's hit *La tempranica* (1900), converted by Torroba into an opera for the occasion at the request of his descendents.[147] As Enrique Franco has observed, along with the zarzuelas of Bretón, Barbieri, Giménez, and Chueca, this zarzuela in particular is one of the antecedents to Torroba's own works. It was ultimately his immense admiration for Giménez that motivated Torroba's operatic transformation, *María la tempranica*. "That it recalls the final scenes of *Luisa Fernanda* demonstrates the proximity in musical substance between the one composer and the other."[148] This was followed by

---

[144] Vicent, "El pentagrama," 14.

[145] Víctor Sánchez Sánchez, "Un zarzuelista en la Junta Nacional de Música. *Talismán* de Vives, como modelo para el Teatro Lírico Nacional," in *Música y cultura en la Edad de Plata, 1915–1939*, 533.

[146] Berasategui, "Moreno Torroba," ix.

[147] A historic recording of Torroba's revision has been reissued on the Blue Moon label, 7544, with Torroba conducting. See Joaquim Zueras Navarro, "Sus obras menos conocidas: Más sobre Moreno Torroba," *OpusMusica*, n30 (November 2008), http://www.opusmusica.com/030/torroba.html.

[148] Enrique Franco, "Una figura del nacionalismo musical, *Autores* (October 1982), 34 (reprint of an article that first appeared in *El País*).

Baturra del temple, which premiered on August 26 and received very favorable reviews.[149] During the same year, he also revived one of his own zarzuelas, *La marchenera*, this time performed by the Calderón's resident company.

The year 1930 ended with a short opera season at the Calderón. The Nied-Oester-Stadtbund-Oper of Vienna presented Mozart's *Don Giovanni* and *Le nozze di Figaro*, and a Russian company from Paris performed Mussorgsky's *Khovantchina* and *Boris Godunov*, as well as Rimsky-Korsakov's *Snegourochka*. As if in response to the foreign operas and performers at the Calderón, in January 1931 Torroba produced a Spanish opera, Arrieta's *Marina*, followed by three of his own zarzuelas and one by Vives.

Even in the midst of all this theatrical activity, Torroba continued to write music for the guitar as his friendship with Segovia deepened. In 1931, Torroba's *Piezas características* were published. A suite of six movements, this work became a regular feature on Segovia's programs throughout the rest of his career. A work rich in variety, it includes thematic relationships between movements, folkloric references, subtle dissonances, and fugal writing. While the inner movements are lyrical and folkloric, the outer movements of this work are probably as close as Torroba would come to exhibiting French influences (this work is also discussed in Scene iii).

On April 14, 1931, the Second Republic of Spain was declared. Eight days later, the first in a series of four articles by Adolfo Salazar appeared in *El Sol*.[150] The leading music critic of his day, Salazar was to become very influential in shaping the new government's policies toward the arts. Salazar argued that music should be granted equal footing with the other fine arts, and therefore eligible for financial assistance from the state. He proposed a ministry that would oversee the plastic arts, theater, and music. Within the musical division, the Junta Nacional de Música y Teatros Líricos, there would be the following subdivisions: Teatro Lírico Nacional; Orquesta Nacional de Conciertos; Concursos (contests); and Edición Nacional de Música. All of Salazar's recommendations were adopted by the new government within the year. While these proposals were intended to be broad guidelines, they suggested that, as a leading zarzuela composer and impresario, Torroba would play a central role in promoting native musical theater.[151]

Salazar's proposals had a strong nationalist bias. Beyond general administration and financial support, the responsibilities of the Junta Nacional de Música y Teatros Líricos included the promotion of Spanish music abroad and of folkloric festivals within Spain, the creation of performance opportunities for lesser-known Spanish composers, and the sponsorship of competitions to seek out such com-

[149] *El Sol*, August 27, 1930.

[150] Emilio Casares, ed., *La Música en la Generación de 27: Homenaje a Lorca, 1915–1939* (Madrid: Mercantil-Asturias 1986), 256.

[151] Tomás Marco, *Historia de la música española, siglo XX* (Madrid: Alianza Música, 1983), 156.

posers. The curriculum at the Real Conservatorio Superior de Música was revised to include a course of study in Spanish folklore. Perhaps most indicative of the nationalist bias was the requirement that all foreign operas performed in Spain be translated into Spanish. Salazar's grand design was innovative and widely supported but difficult to implement during the chaotic years of the Second Republic. Consequently, it was never meaningfully implemented and was doomed with the Republic's fall.[152]

Salazar was among the liberal intellectuals who formed the first government of the Second Republic, and as we noted earlier, he served as secretary of the first Junta Nacional de Música y Teatros Líricos, established by governmental decree on July 21, 1931. Though Torroba was by now a leading musician in Spain, he was not in the cultural orbit represented on the Junta. This probably did not disturb his sleep very much, as he was lukewarm toward the Republic; in fact, if one reads between the lines of his sarcastic assessment below, one detects a certain hostility toward, or least dubiousness about, the entire democratic enterprise:

> The proclamation of the Republic left me feeling neither hot nor cold. With the advent of a libertine atmosphere there were very picturesque scenes, with the women dedicating themselves to their tasks on the street.[153]

Despite all this, Torroba flourished during the Second Republic. The Teatro Calderón became the new residence of the revived Teatro Lírico Nacional. The stress laid on national music in intellectual circles served to support Torroba's sensibilities as an impresario and composer. The 1932 season put an even greater emphasis on Spanish composers, with the staging of *La Dolores* (Bretón), *Balada de carnaval* (Vives), *Las golondrinas*, and *Marina*. While the 1930 season had featured opera companies from Vienna and Russia performing works of Mozart and Rimsky-Korsakov, the only foreign operas staged at the Calderón in 1932 were Rossini's *Il barbiere di Siviglia* and Bizet's *Carmen*—works based on Spanish themes and likely to have been performed in translation.

Among the zarzuelas staged at the Calderón in 1932 was Torroba's most famous composition, *Luisa Fernanda*. Torroba claimed that he wrote *Luisa Fernanda* in

---

[152] Santos Martín Pancorbo, interview with William Krause, Madrid, July 12, 1990.

[153] Vicent, "El pentagrama," 14. This is an allusion on his part to a supposed increase in prostitution and loose morals that attended Republican reforms. Beevor, *Battle for Spain*, 46, states that "On 4 May José Antonio [Primo de Rivera] delivered a diatribe from prison against the Popular Front. He claimed that it was directed by Moscow, fomented prostitution and undermined the family. 'Have you not heard the cry of Spanish girls today: "Children, yes! Husbands, no!"'" Torroba's offhand remark about women on the streets illustrates the concerns he shared with the Church and Falange concerning declining moral standards.

twenty days because of his "enthusiasm for the work and my close friendship with the libretto's authors, Federico Romero and Guillermo Fernández-Shaw."[154]

This *zarzuela grande* received over two hundred consecutive performances after its premiere on March 26, 1932. After it closed at the Calderón, other theaters revived it with almost continuous performances in Madrid for the next two years. Within a year of its premiere, it was already being performed in the Philippines. Since 1932, the remarkable appeal of this work has become increasingly evident: it has been performed over fifteen thousand times world-wide.[155] Romero and Fernández Shaw became important collaborators over the next twenty-five years and contributed to some of Torroba's greatest successes. Torroba estimated that this zarzuela alone had earned him a million pesetas. By contrast, his first work, *Las decididas*, netted him a mere 12.5 *pesetas* each day, for two or three months. The author's rights were five *duros* (about twenty-five *pesetas*), which he had to share with the librettist, Tomás Alenza.[156]

As we noted earlier in the chapter, except for Chueca, Torroba was the only *madrileño* among the zarzuelists. The rest were from the provinces. This may help explain why he was so effective depicting the Madrid of that bygone era. Reviewing a production of *Luisa Fernanda* seventy-one years after its premiere, Miguel Ángel Nepomuceno found enduring inspiration in the score, inspiration of a nationalist-patriotic tenor:

> This is Spanish zarzuela, grandchild of the Spanish romance, of Juan de la Encina, Gil Vicente, Lope de Vega, Ramón de la Cruz, the eighteenth-century *tonadilla escénica*, nineteenth-century Italian opera, and our best traditions. It speaks of the Spanish people's struggle to represent them-selves, musically speaking, at least, singing their picaresque despair, their labor, feelings, and desires.[157]

Most composers did not see the zarzuela as a vehicle for political expression. But there were exceptions, such as Francisco Alonso's popular *La calesera* (1925). Portraying liberals rebelling against the absolutist monarchy of 1832, the chorus sings, "slaves of the earth shall rise, shouting 'War!' ... demanding liberty."[158] This

---

[154] Roberto Rioja, "Federico Moreno Torroba: Ochenta y una gloriosas primaveras," *Hilo mundial* (January 1973), 27–28. He later confirmed this in an interview with García, "'Lo único que no se repite es la música'": "I really liked the libretto, so much so that I had the work ready in twenty days, which is not to say that everything went that fast." He was able to beat that record a few years later with *Sor Navarra*, which he penned in two weeks and "nothing more."

[155] "Las 15 mil representaciones de la zarzuela 'Luisa Fernanda,'" *El Comercio* (Buenos Aires), February 1, 1981. Obviously, this number is higher now, though an exact total is unknown.

[156] Centeno, "Moreno Torroba."

[157] Miguel Ángel Nepomuceno, "Amor, guerra y ambición," *Diario de León*, May 30, 2003, 73.

[158] Donald Thompson, "Doña Francisquita, a Zarzuela by Amadeo Vives" (PhD diss., University of Iowa, 1970), 141.

was a particularly bold statement to make under the dictatorship of Primo de Rivera. By the time Moreno Torroba premiered *Luisa Fernanda* in 1932, the dictatorship had given way to the more tolerant Second Republic. While the libretto is not overtly political, its subject is the fall of Isabella II in 1868 and the proclamation of the First Republic. Characters in the story sided with either the Crown or the First Republic. At the time *Luisa Fernanda* opened, the Second Republic was less than one year old, and the same conflicting loyalties divided the populace. Both Republicans and Monarchists in the audience easily identified with the sentiments of the zarzuela's characters (see Scene iii for an analysis of this work).

Despite its immediate and enduring popularity, *Luisa Fernanda* was not Torroba's favorite zarzuela; he repeatedly cited *La chulapona* (1934) and especially *Monte Carmelo* (1939) as his best stage works. We will see in Act II that he was not alone in feeling this way. However, *Luisa Fernanda* is by far and away his most successful and enduring stage work. When asked many years later whether he had any inkling at the outset of its career that *Luisa Fernanda* would enjoy such great success, Torroba did not hesitate in answering,

> On this occasion, yes. It got off to a very good start. After just a few days, people were singing some of the melodies in the streets. After the premiere, it had a run of 800 successive performances.[159]

Thus, *Luisa Fernanda* became the perennial updraft that sustained his musico-theatrical flight for the remaining fifty years of his life, providing him with a dependable and sizable income. Indeed, it is one of the most beloved—if not *the* most beloved—zarzuelas of all time. Had he composed nothing else, *Luisa Fernanda* alone would secure Torroba's place in the annals of music history. It merits closer study in the next Scene.

[159] Albino Mallo, "Los noventa jovenes años de Moreno Torroba," *Heraldo de Aragón*, December 21, 1980. This number seems to include performances at other theaters after its Calderón production.

3

ACT I
Scene iii
Major Works of the Period 1920–32

Torroba was committed in every facet of his musical being to the composition and promotion of music that he believed to be identifiably and distinctively Spanish. That much we have clearly established in everything he said and wrote about himself. Yet, a profile of the Spanish songs and dances that inform his music for the stage and the guitar is surprisingly difficult to sketch, precisely because the understanding of Spanish music that most foreigners (and many Spaniards themselves) bring to Torroba's works does not necessarily correspond with the composer's own perception of the musical heritage he had inherited and strove to preserve and pass on.

To be precise, the prevailing foreign characterization of Spanish music has generally been Andalusian in character, utilizing certain rhythmic and melodic clichés that, no matter how fetching or familiar, do not even begin to present the totality of the Spanish soundscape with which our composer was on intimate terms. Now, there are Andalusian allusions aplenty in his works, including use of the descending minor tetrachord, the so-called E mode, hemiola rhythms, references to and use of the guitar, and suggestions of flamenco singing, with its soulful melismatic outbursts. But they exist side by side with evocations of the rural and urban folklore of Castile, Asturias, Extremadura, and Navarra, among others. In short, Torroba had a more extensive and nuanced comprehension of Spanish music than that possessed by foreign audiences subsisting on a diet of "Spanish" capriccios, souvenirs, rhapsodies, and other exoticizing works, not to mention *Carmen*. We delight in such *espagnolades* as much as anyone, and *Carmen* was one of Torroba's very favorite operas. But this music does not fully equip one to understand the zarzuela repertoire in general and Torroba's works in particular, which were written, so to speak, "from the inside out."

Complicating this profile is the fact that much of what became fixtures of urban folklore in Spain were in fact imported from elsewhere. Traditional folk dances, such as the *fandango, seguidilla, zapateado,* and *jota,*[1] as well as urban folklore including the *pasacalle* and *pasodoble,* frequently shared the zarzuela stage with the habanera, a song and dance that resulted from the intermingling of African, French, and Spanish traditions in Cuba and gained currency in Spain only during the latter half of the 1800s. The waltz, mazurka, and schottische (or *chotis*) were in no way autochthonous, but their assimilation into the zarzuela was complete by the time Torroba started composing for the stage. Such foreign genres were standard fare in the urban, middle-class dance halls of Madrid ca. 1900 and added considerable popular appeal to any stage works that deployed them. Of course, going far enough back in time, it could be argued that a lot of Spanish music and dance had its origins elsewhere.[2] Torroba himself was quite convinced that most Spanish folk music came from the Arabs, who forcibly transplanted their culture in the Iberian Peninsula during the Middle Ages. We will explore and contest that idea in Act II, Scene ii, but we are not so much concerned with determining what is "authentically" Spanish as with identifying the elements of Spanish folklore, in all its variety and whatever its pedigree, that are crucial to Torroba's nationalist style.

In addition to foreign songs and dances that insinuated themselves into the Spanish musical world and subsequently into Torroba's works, there are two other features of his style that we must bear in mind, features that owe nothing to his homeland. First is the profound influence of Puccini on his style of vocal writing, e.g., doubling the voice in the orchestra (*violinata*), and even the way he structured his music dramas. As Roger Alier observed about *Luisa Fernanda,* "the musical numbers do not prevent the dialogue from moving the action forward. . . . In this way, the piece moves smoothly at the same time keeping the 'closed forms' which appealed to the public for this kind of traditional theatre."[3] If this procedure seems reminiscent of *La bohème,* for instance, we would do well to recall that that was another of Torroba's favorite operas. The intensely lyrical and emotional character of Italian *verismo* operas from the 1890s exerted a pronounced influence on Spanish

---

[1] The *fandango* is a time-honored Spanish dance in triple meter and is related to the *malagueña, granadina,* and *rondeña.* Typical of all of them is use of the so-called E mode, which can begin on any note but is essentially the Phrygian mode with a raised third degree ascending, creating an augmented-second interval between the second and third degrees of the mode. The corresponding chord progression is a tetrachord moving from A minor to G major to F major and cadencing on E major. The *seguidilla,* from central and southern Spain, is a dance in quick triple meter. The *zapateado* is danced, not sung, and features, as its name suggests, fancy foot- and legwork. The meter of a *zapateado* is always 6/8, with use of hemiola (3/4). The *jota* is danced throughout Spain in various forms, and is also in a quick triple meter, alternating with rhythmically freer sung passages, or *coplas.*

[2] Ascertaining the "true" origins of Spanish folk music is a complex undertaking. For instance, imitations of rural and urban folklore in the zarzuela are often so persuasive that ethnomusicologists have found cases in Latin America and Spain in which popular dances and songs are actually fragments of zarzuelas. See Miguel A. Palacios Garóz, *Introducción a la música popular castellana y leonesa* (Madrid: Artes Gráficas Santiago Rodríguez, 1984), 85.

[3] Roger Alier, "*Luisa Fernanda*: A Graceful Score," liner notes for *Luisa Fernanda* (Auvidis Valois, V 4759, 1995), 26.

composers of musical theater during that decade and well into the twentieth century. Torroba's concern for realism manifests in the use of sounds from everyday life, such as the *organillo* (barrel organ) or the cries of street vendors (*pregoneros*), as well as the use of dramatic settings, in taverns, cafés, or out of doors, featuring musicians and dancers performing Spanish music of various kinds.

The second point to make about foreign influences in Torroba's style is this: although it is difficult to overstate the conservative nature of Torroba's musical aesthetic, he was no troglodyte. As we survey his works for the guitar in particular, it will become ever clearer that they are products of the century in which he composed them, regardless of their fundamentally nationalistic, tonal, and metrical character. Torroba stated on several occasions that he deeply admired Ravel, and though Torroba's music does not sound like Ravel's, the harmonic language in his guitar works exhibits flourishes revealing an awareness of innovations from north of the Pyrenees—and across the Atlantic. Indeed, another influence on Torroba's harmony came from jazz, assimilated through the Broadway musicals he loved so much.

The difference in style between his zarzuelas, on the one hand, and his guitar pieces, on the other, owes to the fact that, in the case of the zarzuela, he was continuing along a path already broken for him by preceding generations of inno-vative and successful composers, from Barbieri to Vives. Carlos Gómez Amat found in *Luisa Fernanda*, for instance, "Caballero's melodic elegance, Bretón and Chapí's rich invention, Chueca's malicious humour or Giménez's gracefulness, not forgetting Barbieri's unfailing mastery."[4]

In the case of the guitar, however, there were no such footsteps in which to follow. Most of the works of Tárrega look backward to Chopin and Schumann, though some are rather clichéd orientalist evocations, such as *Capricho árabe* and *Danza mora*. These are all lovely and understandably popular works, but they offered little in the way of a model for Torroba to copy. Segovia essentially pre-sented Torroba with a blank slate, as far as the guitar's repertoire was concerned, and Torroba wrote on that slate in ways that are both personal and modern. Of course, the zarzuela appealed to one audience, classical-guitar music to another. If Torroba's zarzuelas are more derivative in nature, it is not only because of his absorption in the tradition he inherited, but also because of the tastes and expec-tations of his audience, habituated to that same decades-old repertoire. In other words, the bourgeois public for which he wrote embraced the zarzuela as a genre that was immediately intelligible and familiar.[5] Continuity was of paramount

---

[4] Carlos Gómez Amat, "*Luisa Fernanda* and Its Time," liner notes for *Luisa Fernanda* (Auvidis Valois, V 4759, 1995), 24.

[5] This point is made in Ramón Barce, "La ópera y la zarzuela en el siglo XIX," in *España en la música de Occidente: Actas del Congreso Internacional celebrado en Salamanca 29 de octubre–5 de noviembre de 1985*, 2 vols., ed. Emilio Casares Rodicio, Ismael Fernández de la Cuesta, and José López-Calo (Madrid: Ministerio de Cultura, 1987), 150; also see Barce's "El folklore urbano y la música de los sainetes líricos del último cuarto del siglo XIX: La explicitación escénica de los bailes," *Actas del XV Congreso de la Sociedad Internacional de Musicología*, in *Revista de Musicología* 16/6 (1993): 3217–25.

importance to them; in fact, that attitude persists today. In the opinion of baritone Antonio Lagar, "it's very difficult to present new compositions because the audience doesn't want to listen to unknown music."[6] By contrast, Torroba crafted his guitar pieces for a concert setting in which the audience would have a different background and set of expectations. He could afford to be somewhat more experimental in that arena, and he was, especially in his later works.

In other ways, however, Torroba's guitar works exhibit two prominent traits in common with his zarzuelas. First, he preferred writing collections of short, evocative pieces rather than individual, stand-alone compositions of greater length and complexity. The average length of his solo pieces or movements is about two and a half minutes: some are less than a minute (e.g., "Coplilla" from *Aires de La Mancha*), and rarely if ever do they exceed four minutes. These short essays often derive their inspiration from places and objects that suggest a scenic or even dramatic idea, whether trees (*madroños*), castles (*castillos*), gates (*puertas*), or a "dialogue" between an orchestra and a solo guitar. Pepe Romero, who knows the entire corpus of Torroba's guitar music intimately, sees in it a "strong sense of drama."[7] Thus, deploying a potpourri of short, lyric, often dancelike, and enticingly allusive pieces for guitar was not so different an exercise after all from writing a series of lyric or instrumental numbers separated by spoken dialogue, which was what composing a zarzuela essentially entailed.

The second similarity is this: Torroba's unfailing lyric gift shines through as much in his guitar writing as in his zarzuelas. He was, as he described himself, first and foremost a "melodist." The ceaseless flow of melodic inspiration in all of his music is the principal reason for its enduring popularity. Added to this is his love of Spanish-dance rhythms, which are central to both types of works. In short, Torroba was basically a sort of song-and-dance man. That was his great gift—to us.

Stage Works

La virgen de mayo

It is a strange irony in Torroba's career on the stage that, dedicated to the zarzuela as he was and skeptical about the prospects for *ópera española*, his first major scenic work was an opera, as was his final stage work, *El poeta*. These are the only two large-scale operas he ever composed, yet they form the bookends between which we examine his vastly more numerous (and renowned) zarzuelas.[8]

---

[6] María Dolores Travesedo concurs, saying that "the public is afraid to go and see the unknown." Both Lagar and Travesedo were interviewed by William Krause, Madrid, June 6–11, 2010.

[7] Pepe Romero related this to Walter Clark in a conversation on January 6, 2011.

[8] Torroba also composed a one-act "chamber opera," *Bromas y veras de Andalucía*, with a libretto by Rafael Gil. It premiered in April 1956 at the Ateneo in Madrid.

La virgen de mayo (The Virgin of May) is an adaptation by Fernando Luque of a book by Paul Max. Like Prosper Merimée, whose 1845 *novela* *Carmen* served as the inspiration for Bizet's opera (and the similarity to *Carmen* gives us a clue as to Torroba's attraction to this work), Max found in Andalusia a "dramatic vision of loves and lovers, which outsiders feel with the intensity of its azure skies and the fire of its sun."[9] The protagonist in this drama is a seductive woman, who hides her shameful past from the honorable man she loves and who intends to marry her. However, she cannot escape the fate local Gypsies have predicted for her. Accompanied by her *prometido* (fiancé), she attends a spring religious festival and seeks salvation in prayer. As she privately invokes divine forgiveness and blessings, her fiancé goes to offer flowers to the image of the Virgin of May; however, at precisely this moment, her former lover, a criminal who has been hiding in the countryside, returns to torment her. He promises to leave her in peace in exchange for a final kiss, but in his arms she finds only the freedom of death. Not content with this cruel outrage, he confronts the stunned and hapless fiancé to tell him of her past. But at just that moment, his escape is blocked by the image of the Virgin of May being carried in a procession of adoring multitudes. His own fate is now sealed.

The one-act opera's action takes place during a religious festival and features low-class characters and a shocking murder. In other words, it is obviously indebted to Italian *verismo*, particularly *Cavalleria rusticana*. And the interest in realism extends to the music as well. The Andalusian setting was reason enough to stock the work with a supply of flamenco numbers, and the southern flavor Torroba imparted to his score won the accolades of critics and public alike. One of the best numbers is the "Bulerías," a *palo* or genre of flamenco characterized by a rapid tempo and a *compás* (meter) consisting of twelve beats, with accents on 12, 3, 6, 8, 10. This, at least, is how *flamenquistas* count it. The rest of us would be tempted to say this is a hemiola meter (*sesquiáltera*, in Spanish) alternating 6/8 and 3/4 (see ex. I:iii:1).

Ex. I:iii:1 *La virgen de mayo*, "Bulerías," mm. 12–16

[9] Ángel María Castell, "Informaciones y noticias teatrales: 'La virgen de mayo'. 'El carillón mágico,'" *ABC*, February 15, 1925, 35.

La marchenera

La marchenera (The girl from Marchena) is a *zarzuela grande* in three acts and utilizes a prose libretto by Ricardo González del Toro and Fernando Luque. It is set
in the Andalusian town of Marchena, about thirty miles east of Sevilla, in 1842.
The complex plot, complete with political intrigue, jealousy, and duels, is reminiscent of Alonso's *La calesera*. As with *Luisa Fernanda*, the drama is situated during a time of struggle between the aristocracy and the restless lower classes. The
action begins in a *ventorro* (tavern) belonging to Sra. Jeroma. The Count of
Hinojares is seeking recruits to help him launch a movement to end political
oppression and give to the people a constitution that will meet their needs. A
certain Félix de Samaniego arrives from court, preceded by his reputation as a
womanizer. In fact, he has come to visit Paloma, cousin of Sra. Jeroma and *la
marchenera* of the drama. As her name metaphorically suggests, she is a bird in a
cage seeking to fly from the unhappiness that has been her lot in life. She does
not hesitate to express her feelings about Don Félix's appeal to members of the
opposite sex, including Valentina, daughter of the Count. Though Félix intends
to marry Paloma, it is clear that Valentina is something of a rival. Things get
more complex when Félix hears a baseless rumor that Paloma is the Count's lover.
In fact, Paloma was an orphan whom the Count kindly adopted. Félix now directs
his attentions to Valentina, with the intention of abducting her; he and the
Count fight a duel, in which Félix is injured. His conspiracy having been revealed,
the Count flees to Gibraltar in exile. La marchenera finds no relief from her sufferings in this tale.

The very opening of this work is one of Torroba's more striking conceptions,
featuring a dissonant major seventh above a major triad on B-flat, whose atten-
tion-grabbing stridency is enhanced by brass, strings, and percussion, including
triangle and castanets. From the standpoint of orchestration, it is one of the most
distinctive and arresting orchestral numbers in the zarzuela repertoire. The lively
triple-meter rhythm is reminiscent of the *sevillanas* (see ex. I:iii:2).

In fact, the score is replete with popular songs and dances, such as Valentina's
petenera "Tres horas antes del día" (Three hours before day) (Act I, no. 5), a *zapateado* (Act II, no. 7), and a *malagueña* (Act III, no. 12, preludio). One of the loveliest
habaneras Torroba ever composed is certainly that sung by a forlorn Paloma (Act I,
no. 4), in which she declares, "Yo soy Paloma marchenera bravia que ha aprendido
a volar y hasta el cielo llegar con audaz valentía" (I am the brave dove of Marchena,
who has learned to fly to the heavens with audacious courage). The dramatic
upward sweep of an octave at the outset of her song establishes something of her
character, though the relentless downward course of the harmony through a
descending minor tetrachord in the Andalusian E mode gives us a feeling for the
pathos of her situation (see ex. I:iii:3).

A moving evocation of flamenco *cante jondo* (deep song) occurs at the
outset of no. 6, the finale of Act I, in which Felix sings, "¿A que presumir de

Ex. I:iii:2 La marchenera, Act I, no. 1, Introducción, mm. 1–9

brava? si hay paloma marchenera que cuando llega la noche es paloma volan-
dera" (Who would presume to boast, if there is a dove from Marchena who,
when night arrives, is a dove in flight?). The opening strokes in the orchestra
clearly mimic the strumming of guitars in introduction of the *copla*. Of special interest here is the harmony in m. 3, which represents the superimposi-
tion of the chord on the second degree of the Andalusian mode, here an E-flat
chord, over a D pedal in the bass. This imitates a guitarist's shift from E to F,
while leaving the bottom and top E strings open. Such a movement is not
functional but rather performative, i.e., it is a chord progression idiomatic to
flamenco guitar. Reducing it to roman numerals would miss the point.
Moreover, it is very reminiscent of Falla's *El amor brujo*, a work Torroba knew
well, or the Miller's *farruca* in *El sombrero de tres picos*. The subsequent scalar
flourish imitates a fast *picado* (scale) on the guitar. When Felix enters, the
rhythmic freedom of his melodic line, its use of repeated notes, rhythmic
flourishes at cadence points, and its gradual downward contour through the
pitches D, C, B-flat, and A (rising dramatically back to D via F and E-flat) mark
it as a conspicuous specimen of flamenco singing. What impresses most here,
however, is not Torroba's mastery of clichés but rather his ability to impart
genuine emotion to such moments, compelling our attention and sympathy
(see ex. I:iii:4).

Ex. I:iii:3 *La marchenera*, Act I, no. 4, "Yo soy Paloma," rehearsal 1

The absence of *La marchenera* from the standard zarzuela repertoire is regrettable. Whatever the merits of the drama, we consider this score to be among the composer's finest, whether he esteemed it as such or not.[10]

Luisa Fernanda

Here we are dealing not only with Torroba's single most celebrated composition, but also with one of the greatest zarzuelas in the entire repertoire. The reason for this is at once simple and complex: it represents the confluence of a masterful

---

[10] María Dolores Travesedo, a renowned soprano who often sang the lead role under Toroba's direction, believes that "The music was beautiful but the script was a disaster." That is probably the main reason for its absence from the stage. Interview with William Krause, Madrid, June 6–11, 2010.

Ex. I:iii:4 *La marchenera*, Act I, no. 6, "¿A que presumir de brava?" mm. 1–16

libretto with music that captures our attention from the very first measure and matches the text stride for stride in emotional intensity, nuance of characterization, and dramatic pacing. Considering that Torroba wrote this work in about three weeks, it is clear that, as he himself said, the libretto fired his imagination and brought forth some of his finest inspirations. It is often the case that works written rapidly, in the white heat of inspiration, will either be very good or very bad; for instance, we recall that he wrote his unexceptional *La caravana de ambrosio* in a single day. In the case of *Luisa Fernanda*, however, both the story and the music are consistently compelling.

The first thing to note is that this is a *zarzuela grande*, a substantial three-act work set during a tumultuous period in Spanish history that some elderly members of the audience at the 1932 premiere might well have recalled. In turn, the work has had a lasting impact of its own. Gómez Amat noted that, as late as the 1990s, the music of *Luisa Fernanda* was still "deeply rooted . . . in the memory of all Spaniards. Several of the phrases, such as "Caballero del alto plumero," have become part of everyday language and, when heard, automatically call to mind the corresponding tunes."[11]

One reason the score is so memorable is that it approaches the level of opera in the demands it makes on the singers; moreover, the orchestral writing approaches symphonic music in its richness and complexity.[12] And yet, what stands out is Torroba's ability to evoke that epoch through his employment of urban folklore, especially the *pasodoble* and habanera, as well as evocations of the folklore of Extremadura in the final act. The "Marzurka de las sombrillas" (Mazurka of the parasols) is one of the most memorable numbers from *Luisa Fernanda*. When we view the genre of zarzuela from a structural perspective, then, it often resembles nothing so much as a suite of dances, both indigenous and foreign.[13] This is certainly the case in *Luisa Fernanda* and something we should bear in mind. Audiences expected wonderful dance numbers in addition to beautiful singing.

Luisa Fernanda is essentially a love story using a time-honored formulaic plot. Luisa Fernanda (soprano) is in love with Javier Moreno (tenor), a colonel in the royal guard, who has left her to pursue Duchess Carolina (soprano). Vidal Hernando (baritone), a handsome and wealthy gentleman from Extremadura (southwestern Spain) appears on the scene and falls in love with Luisa. Believing Javier will stay with the duchess, Luisa turns to Vidal and agrees to marry him. Javier is captured by revolutionaries and rescued by Luisa. Seeing this, Vidal suspects Luisa to be still in love with Javier. When Javier arrives at the wedding to confess his love to Luisa, Vidal releases Luisa to return to Javier, which she does.

The story of *Luisa Fernanda* is set during the political crisis in Spain between 1868 and 1873. The struggle between the monarchy and Republicans resulted in the First Republic in 1873; however, the Republic was doomed by the end of 1874, when the Bourbons were restored to the throne. The authors of the libretto, Federico Romero and Guillermo Fernández-Shaw, made clear their intention to use these historic

---

[11] Gómez Amat, "*Luisa Fernanda* and Its Time," 24.

[12] A point made by Federico, Jr., in the introduction to his recent critical edition of the score (Madrid: ICCMU, 2011).

[13] Ramón Barce, "El folklore urbano y la música de los sainetes líricos del último cuarto del siglo XIX," 3217.

events as background, not foreground, for their drama.[14] As tempting as it is for us now to read some encoded political message into the plot, they disavowed any such intention. As far as they were concerned, the Revolution of 1868 was simply "*ambiente*," or atmosphere, not the vehicle for commenting on the situation in Spain during the nascent Second Republic. True, the name of the title character was suggested by a historical figure, María Luisa Fernanda, the duchess of Montpensier and sister of Queen Isabel II. She was actually a potential successor to the throne, but the libretto makes no attempt to represent the historical Luisa Fernanda. The zarzuela's protagonist is not of royal birth, and her preoccupation is clearly with love, not politics. The authors themselves insisted that the characters are nothing more or less than standard types, e.g., the ambitious soldier of fortune (Javier), the noble romantic (Vidal), the scheming and manipulative noblewoman (Carolina), and the embodiment of feminine charm and virtue, poor in material goods but "opulent in graces and sentiments" (Luisa). Carolina serves as the perfect foil for Luisa, and though they represent two different kinds of female, they both suffer, in Ángeles Maso's notable phrase, the "consequences of political avatars" during that era.[15]

A reviewer for *ABC* confirmed after the premiere that the drama was "absolutely devoid of political opportunism."[16] Perhaps. But if we want to find any political message here, we will have to do so without the assistance of the librettists and the composer—not to mention the critics. Mere speculation on this point would reveal more about *our* political agenda than that of the authors and composer, and we have no such purpose in mind.

Act I opens with a lively orchestral overture (Introducción, no. 1-A) resembling a *rondeña*, a southern Spanish dance related to the *fandango* and *malagueña*, especially in its alternation of 6/8 and 3/4. It also bears a certain resemblance to the *jota* that opens Act III (see ex. I:iii:5).[17]

There follows a lyrical dialogue, which is sung and accompanied but not as static as recitative, in which Carolina and several characters are introduced. The character Saboyano (tenor) and the chorus sing "El Saboyano" (no. 1-B), a *habanera* which speaks of a soldier whose beloved waits behind, unaware of his fate.

After a recitative between Javier and a minor character, Mariana, the first important aria of the work begins (no. 2). This is in a ternary form, ABA' coda. In the first theme of the A section, Javier recalls his youth and his longing for perfect love (see ex. I:iii:6).

---

[14] For these and other insights into their drama, see Federico Romero and Guillermo Fernández-Shaw, "'Luisa Fernanda,'" *ABC*, March 26, 1932, 16.

[15] Ángeles Masó, "Teatro Victoria: Presentación de 'Luisa Fernanda' en la temporada de zarzuela," *La Vanguardia*, June 10, 1972.

[16] "Calderón, 'Luisa Fernanda,'" *ABC*, March 27, 1932, 33.

[17] In cases where Torroba actually called a piece a *jota*, the meter is 3/8. This is also the case with Albéniz, Larregla, and Falla. Likewise, the opening of the *jota* in Liszt's *Rhapsodie espagnole* is also in 3/8, but the rhythmic pattern is otherwise essentially the same as the introduction of *Luisa Fernanda*. Torroba may have scored the piece in 6/8 not to distinguish it from a *jota* but rather only to facilitate the transition to 3/4 later in the piece. In any case, the *fandango, rondeña, malagueña,* and *jota* are all related.

Ex. I:iii:5 *Luisa Fernanda*, Act I, no. 1-A, Introducción, mm. 1–4

Ex. I:iii:6 *Luisa Fernanda*, Act I, no. 2, Javier's Romanza, A theme, mm. 48–51

Ex. I:iii:7 *Luisa Fernanda*, Act I, no. 2, Javier's Romanza, B theme, mm. 82–86

The brief B section is a martial-sounding *bolero*, in which Javier declares that fortune is his companion and that on its wings he is swept away to his fate. His is the path of a lonely but idealistic soldier. This theme will return throughout the zarzuela as a musical reminder of Javier's temperament and aspirations (see ex. I:iii:7). The A' section paraphrases the first two themes, followed by a coda that quotes the *bolero* in the closing measures.

Torroba's use of recurring themes to unify the score reveals a capacity not only for developing melodic ideas in response to the drama but also a sophisticated conception of musical drama itself, of zarzuela as a play through music and not merely a mechanical alternation of spoken dialogue and self-contained numbers. This is on display in the ensuing material as well.

In the following two duets (no. 3), Vidal and Luisa reveal their affection for one another. Although Luisa says that they can never be united, Vidal insists they will someday be together. The first duet between Luisa and Vidal is in a sort of bar

Ex. I:iii:8 *Luisa Fernanda*, Act I, no. 4, Duet between Carolina and Javier, A section, mm. 4–10

form, AA'B. The A sections share a common theme, sung first by Vidal and then Luisa, suggesting their possible union. The B section consists of short exchanges between these characters. Without a pause, Vidal begins another duet, this time in ABA form, one in which the B section employs material from the A section and is set as a duet with Luisa. Hemiola is prominent in this piece, suggesting perhaps a *guajira*, a Spanish-Cuban dance alternating 6/8 and 3/4. One should note that this is not a duet in a strict sense, since the characters seldom sing simultaneously, but rather converse by means of alternating phrases or entire sections. This is a common feature throughout *Luisa Fernanda*, and the simultaneous continuity of interest in both the drama and the music reflects the influence of Puccini, not to mention Wagner.

Attention now focuses on Carolina and Javier, who provide another in this series of duets. Their exchange (no. 4) is in binary form, ABA'B', and contains important thematic material, which will recur in later on in the zarzuela. The melody of the A section has a slightly Spanish flavor, accentuated by the shift between major and minor modalities and ornamented descending lines. However, no obvious rhythmic reference to traditional Spanish dance is present. Rather, it seems more like a *pasacalle*, an urban street song sung by young men below the window of their maiden (see ex. I:iii:8). As elsewhere in the work, both A and B sections are shared by both characters, not assigned to one person to sing an entire section. In this case, Carolina begins both sections but defers to Javier to close each passage.

The theme of the B section will come to represent Carolina and Javier's relationship (see ex. I:iii:9). The passage is romantic, light, and lyrical. Carolina drops a rose at Javier's feet saying, "This flower fell from my heart." Accepting the rose, Javier says that with the rose begins the story of their love.

When the A and B sections are repeated, Javier and Carolina exchange melodies and are united through shared themes. In the short coda, Carolina warns Javier that the rose is not an invitation to play with love, but Javier comments only on the rose's fragrance. Carolina now warns that the fragrance could be fatal, but Javier ignores her, enraptured by the beauty of the flower. Overall, the gently rocking rhythm and graceful melodic ornamentation in this duet artfully convey this flirtatious encounter between Carolina and Javier.

The finale of Act I (No. 5) strengthens the listener's suspicion that there is something fundamentally unstable about the relationships between Luisa and Vidal, on the one hand, and Carolina and Javier, on the other. The finale closes with Carolina and Javier obliviously singing their theme, but as they conclude, Luisa, with her eye on Javier, repeats Carolina's line, while Vidal coolly observes that in one's heart there may be room for another rose.

Act II does not immediately continue to develop the deepening tension of the previous act. Instead, the opening choral number, "En la Romería de San Antonio de la Florida" (no. 6-A), or the Pilgrimage of San Antonio de la Florida, is a *habanera*, danced by a crowd of "damiselas, pollos elegantes, músicos y vendores" (young women, elegant young men, musicians, and vendors), who share the stage with Carolina and Javier. Such outdoor scenes are typical of the zarzuela, particularly in the second act.[18] This portion of the scene ends with an instrumental recall of the second theme of Javier's first aria and the opening *habanera*. The scene then continues with the celebrated "Mazurca de las sombrillas" (Mazurka of the parasols) (no. 6-B), danced with parasols (see ex. I:iii:10).

It may seem somewhat ironic that the text, which refers to the festival of San Antonio and the fact that the singers are truly Spanish, is set to a mazurka,

---

[18] Alier, "*Luisa Fernanda*: A Graceful Score," 26.

Ex. I:iii:9 *Luisa Fernanda*, Act I, no. 4, Duet between Carolina and Javier, B section, mm. 26–30

especially given the nature of the text at this point. The *Pollos* insist, "I am a Spanish gentleman," and the *Damiselas* affirm that "I am no foreigner." However, given the popularity of the mazurka in Spain during the period in which the drama takes place, the audience was not likely to see this as a lapse in Torroba's sense of decorum. In fact, this carefree song and dance remains one of the most popular numbers in the entire work.

Vidal and Carolina's friendship is established in a recitative and a light, playful duet, "Para comprar a un hombre" (In order to buy a man). This levity is interrupted by the entrance of Luisa, Javier, and various minor characters. In an accompanied recitative followed by a trio with Javier and Vidal, Luisa accepts Vidal as her *novio* (fiancé) to spite Javier. As was the case in the duets, the singers rarely sing simultaneously. Instead, the piece is in effect a dialogue in ternary form, supported by a brisk *bolero*.

As a means of raising tithes in honor of the pilgrimage of San Antonio, the duchess, Carolina, proposes to dance with whoever makes the largest gift. She claims that this is a custom in her native Granada, and she does so by singing a *tirana*, an Andalusian song characterized by a moderate triple meter and an ornament on the second beat of every third measure, with the third beat of that measure tied to the first beat of each fourth measure (see ex. I:iii:11).

Javier offers one ounce of silver for the honor, but Vidal humiliates him by giving her fifty ounces and then offering Javier the right to dance with Carolina as

Ex. I:iii:10 Luisa Fernanda, Act II, no. 6-B, "Mazurca de la sombrillas," mm. 22–30

Ex. I:iii:11 Luisa Fernanda, Act II, no. 8, "En mi tierra de Granada," mm. 182–85

a gift. Javier challenges his adversary, throwing his glove at Vidal's feet. Though furious and vowing revenge, Javier dances a waltz with Carolina, bringing this tumultuous scene to a peaceful conclusion.

Spoken dialogue is a distinguishing trait of the zarzuela. In the next scene, marked "recitado sobre música interna" (recited over internal music), there occurs a short melodrama preceding the dramatic scene in which a chorus of revolutionaries sings of liberty. But Vidal sets himself apart with an aria (No. 10) that says, "my fight is for my heart" and "the ideal of my ambition is the love of the woman I adore." This aria is of central importance. Through it, Vidal contrasts himself with Javier and asserts that he is more pure of heart. Appearing between two dramatic scenes with full choruses, the aria's importance lies in its placement and text: while a violent revolution swirls around him, Vidal does not share the concerns of the *madrileños* and cares only about capturing Luisa's heart.

The closing scene of Act II (No. 11) is of particular interest, since it represents the culmination of conflicts on many levels: Javier is now a captive of the revolutionaries, who threaten to execute him. At the moment when Luisa intervenes to save him, their affection for one another is obvious to all, though apparently hopeless. The revolution is crushed and its leader, Nogales, is arrested. Javier and Vidal are reconciled.

The scene opens with a melodrama and continues through a series of choruses and solo passages. It begins with a group of women, including Luisa, who realize that Javier is about to be executed. The approaching crowd is singing "A él, muera!" ("Kill him!"). Luisa and Javier can be heard over the frenzied excitement, Luisa pleading for his life and Javier defiantly addressing the mob and proclaiming his loyalty to the crown. The passage ends with Javier and Luisa rekindling their affection and Vidal entering to return Javier's glove. This scene is skillfully erected on various vocal lines over recurring layered motives in the orchestra and is one of the composer's most remarkable musico-dramatic conceptions.

The continuous quarter-note ostinato in the bass, F—G-flat—F—A-flat, within a key signature of five flats, and the ensuing ascending sequence of chords create a dramatic backdrop for dialogue. When the chorus enters, singing " Muera! A él, muera!" (m. 18), the ascending motive is reharmonized with less dissonance and reaches a crescendo in B-flat minor (m. 22), before returning to the initial quarter-note motive. The chorus returns over the ascending motive (m. 26), singing "death to the prisoner, death without pity." Propelled by increasing dynamic levels, the passage reaches double forte with the word "Muera!" (m. 30). At this dramatic moment (m. 37), Javier makes his case to the crowd. Musically, this serves as a contrasting section, but with renewed fury the chorus returns to condemn him, accompanied by the diminished harmonies of the initial second motive (m. 52). His damning question to the lynch mob, "Is this your idea of liberty?" no doubt struck a resonant chord among many in the audience of the Second Spanish Republic.

However, on balance, Torroba adroitly sidestepped contemporary political rivalries by making Vidal and Luisa, who have no allegiances, the most sympathetic characters of the story. Even as Javier derides the mob's notion of liberty, the orchestra is moving toward a third theme, suggesting that the mob has the upper hand in the struggle. This third theme (m. 56) appears as the tonality moves momentarily to the dominant, which is reinforced by the V of V. This accompanies the text "You will not escape our grip!" Luisa enters to defend Javier (m. 58), placing herself between him and the mob. Also in contrast to the chorus, her theme is derived from Javier's. Javier, through a new theme (m. 80), expresses his affection and gratitude to Luisa. Out of respect for Luisa's bravery, the crowd relents.

On stage, another group of revolutionaries arrives to announce the failure of the revolt. Vidal accompanies this group and approaches Javier to return his glove, ending their feud. The remaining passages are a mixture of recitative, melodrama, and short duets. At the end of Act II, only one conflict remains unresolved: even though Luisa has saved Javier from the gallows, he ends the scene with Carolina, singing their duet from Act I. Vidal and Luisa remain together, evidently still planning to marry, and leave the stage with an excerpt of their theme, also from Act I.

Act III is shorter than the preceding two and is divided into five sections:

1. Orchestral introduction, *tirana/jota* (No. 11);
2. Vidal's aria (No. 12);
3. Luisa and Javier's duet (No. 13);
4. *Tirana/jota* (No. 14, Finale), first sung by the chorus, then as the background for dialogue and sung once more;
5. The concluding melodrama and thematic excerpts.

The spirited introduction of Act III contains elements of both the Andalusian dance/song *tirana* and the *jota,* of which there are several variants throughout Spain (see ex. I:iii:12).

In 3/8 meter, a characteristic rhythmic formula of the *tirana* is found in various forms in this piece. It also strongly resembles other pieces written by Torroba, such as *San Fermín* and *Jota levantina,* which he specifically designated as *jotas.* A short B section of twenty measures presents a new idea, also in 3/8, but employing drum and oboe over a drone in imitation of a kind of folk music associated with the countryside. It is worth noting that bagpipes and double-reed instruments, in tandem with drums, are common in Spanish folklore (see ex. I:iii:13).

Ex. I:iii:12 *Luisa Fernanda*, Act III, no. 11-B, Introducción, A section, mm. 1–4

Ex. I:iii:13 *Luisa Fernanda*, Act III, no. 11-B, Introducción, B section, mm. 44–47

A chorus of *vareadores*, or peasant workers, introduces Vidal's famous aria about Luisa, "Mi morena clara" ("My Fair Brunette"). In the opinion of Alier, this is "one of the most refined baritone solos in the zarzuela repertory. It is beautifully orchestrated."[19] The chorus foretells the impending ruin of Vidal's anticipated marriage to Luisa in one of its first lines, "Without *mi morena*, I am no longer good for anything." The pastoral background of the *vareadores* is represented by an interlude including open fifths as a drone in the bass, a simple melody in which the third can be both raised or lowered, and a drum accompaniment. This interlude reminds us that Vidal, though wealthy, is not a *madrileño*. He comes from the remote and rural province of Extremadura, and this music helps establish the rustic side of his character.

However, having no reason to doubt the future, Vidal begins his aria with "For all of my life, my companion will be *mi morena*." Like many zarzuela arias, this piece is strophic, alluding to folk or popular influences rather than aristocratic tastes. The phrases of "Mi morena clara" are symmetrical, lie within an octave, and are based on simple harmonic and rhythmic schemes (see ex. I:iii:14).

Luisa and Javier's duet (No. 13) is in three parts. It begins as a plaintive aria acknowledging their insoluble dilemma: it is too late to challenge the forces of destiny. Luisa will marry Vidal, despite her love for Javier. The phrases are characteristic of Spanish folklore, with repeated notes (like reciting tones) followed by descending melodic lines and ornaments on penultimate beats. The theme from Javier's aria in Act I (No. 2) is heard briefly before the recitative section begins. This theme, and the text about isolation and loneliness, reinforces Javier's character and makes it seem all the more likely that he and Luisa will indeed remain forever apart. In the following recitative, this is confirmed by their resolve to go their separate ways. The last lyrical passage, "Subir, subir," speaks of climbing only to fall in the end.

The *tirana/jota* returns as a chorus for the peasants attending the wedding of Vidal and Luisa. This is an occasion to fill the stage with dancers and serves as a temporary relief from the unhappy circumstances of the plot. Also, within this section is some spoken text accompanied by oboe, clarinet, and drum, creating a

---

[19] Alier, "*Luisa Fernanda*: A Graceful Score," 27.

Ex. I:iii:14 *Luisa Fernanda*, Act III, no. 12, "Mi morena clara," mm. 87–94

rustic backdrop. As the dancing concludes, Luisa, Vidal, and Javier finally resolve their differences in a melodramatic passage. Vidal recognizes that Luisa belongs with Javier and persuades her to go with him. This is the most important moment in the zarzuela, yet the characters do not sing. The chorus enters with a phrase from "Mi morena clara," and Vidal sings the response. Now resigning himself to a future without Luisa, he sings the line with which the chorus had introduced his aria, "Without *mi morena* I am no longer good for anything." Vidal is ultimately alone on the stage, clearly the most tragic and sympathetic character. But in a clever allusion, Torroba ends the work with an orchestral reminiscence of Javier's theme—Javier the victor.

The success of *Luisa Fernanda* may be attributed to at least three factors. First and foremost is the strength of Torroba's score. The music was well suited to the middle class of Madrid in 1932, projecting both tradition and modernity. The *boleros, jotas,* and *tiranas* reminded the audience of the unique flavor of Spain's folk and aristocratic inheritance, while the waltzes, mazurkas, and simple love songs evoked a sense of stylishness, linking the listener to the popular culture of the dance hall.

Second, the *zarzuela grande* was in decline during the first decades of the twentieth century, facing stiff competition from the *revista* and motion pictures. Serrano and Vives were among the few zarzuelists active and successful in this environment. Thus, they literally set the stage for Torroba, who inherited an audience that was beginning to lament the loss of the late-nineteenth-century zarzuela and to yearn for its revival. He, along with Sorozábal, became the principal composer of zarzuela during its last flowering in the 1930s and 40s.

A third contributing factor was likely to be the social and political climate in 1932. Although the Second Republic had replaced the monarchy, it by no means had won the hearts and minds of all Spaniards. Throughout the short life of the Republic, conservative forces feared that Spanish culture would be corrupted by emulating modern Europe, and they sought to undermine the government. Harkening back to the First Republic of sixty years before, *Luisa Fernanda* was comfortably detached from this crisis. Yet, regardless of their individual political persuasions, everyone in the audience found a hero in the cast: Javier the loyalist, Vidal the apolitical romantic, and Nogales the revolutionary. One is free to read into it any meaning or message one wants. But it remains above all else a moving story of love and self-sacrifice, a story that appeals to people in times and places far beyond those of the drama or the zarzuela's premiere. It is rivaled perhaps only by Vives's *Doña Francisquita* as the most popular of zarzuelas, and by Rodrigo's *Concierto de Aranjuez* as one of the monuments of Spanish music in the modern era. In fact, Rodrigo's wife, Vicki, once expressed to her husband that Torroba had never written an *Aranjuez*. Rodrigo's immediate rejoinder was that he himself had never composed a *Luisa Fernanda*.[20] True on both counts, though Torroba unquestionably wrote more memorably for the guitar than Rodrigo did for the stage.

Guitar Works

The eminent guitarist David Tanenbaum is of the opinion that Torroba's guitar works are "both difficult to play and musically simple. Despite a limited harmonic vocabulary and choice of keys, his guitar pieces display a keen melodic sense and gentle nationalistic flavor that have found them a secure place in the repertoire."[21] There is considerable truth to this observation, though it strikes us as a bit dismissive. Tanenbaum is an outstanding interpreter of contemporary music, and it is easy to see why he would feel this way. However, as historians, we cannot afford the luxury of judging the past by the standards of the present. We must look at this music in the stylistic context of the period in which it was composed. From that perspective, Torroba's guitar music does not seem quite so simple after all.

As mentioned earlier, Torroba was not a guitarist and had no real understanding of the guitar's idiomatic technique before he began to write for it in the 1920s. He was clearly dependent on Segovia to show him how to compose effectively for the instrument. Aside from studying guitar music and observing Segovia perform, one assumes that Torroba depended on Segovia's editorial services,

---

[20] Pepe Romero, conversation with Walter Clark, January 6, 2011. Rodrigo apparently also admired how fast Torroba could compose and how much music he wrote.

[21] Tanenbaum, "Perspectives on the Classical Guitar in the Twentieth Century," 186.

revising a piece to make it playable and adding fingerings for the left and right hands. Segovia thus played an important role in the composition of these early works, though Torroba was a quick study and eventually needed less assistance (except for the fingerings). Even at the end of his life, however, we will see that he preferred to have a guitarist play back to him what he had written, to make sure it produced the desired effect.

We have chosen three works to illustrate these features in Torroba's guitar music from the period under review: *Suite castellana* (1920), *Sonatina* (1923), and selections from the *Piezas características* (1931). Rather than presenting a blow-by-blow description, we focus on those aspects of the music, its harmony, texture, and rhythm, that characterize Torroba's style and identify whatever folkloric roots it has, if any.

Suite castellana

This suite contains Torroba's first-ever composition for the guitar, the "Danza"; he composed the "Fandanguillo" and "Arada" later, and combined them into a "Castilian suite." The individual numbers are of diminutive dimensions: the outer two movements last about two and a half minutes, while the slow middle movement clocks in at about three. There is considerable repetition of material, and simple part forms characterize the three works. Yet, these disclaimers do not diminish the originality and freshness of this suite, which has remained in the repertoire since its appearance.

The "Fandanguillo" is marked "Allegro, tempo di Fandango." The fandango is a triple-meter song and dance found in various regions in Spain; its earliest evocations appear in the keyboard sonatas of Domenico Scarlatti, who resided for many years in Madrid.[22] A *fandanguillo* is a variant of the fandango, featuring a slightly faster tempo. Like so many Spanish songs and dances, it alternates sections in which either dancing or singing (*copla*) predominate. It is important to understand that the fandango is just as Castilian as it is Andalusian, and that it is not, strictly speaking, flamenco. It was absorbed into the flamenco repertoire in the nineteenth century, and certain Andalusian manifestations, particularly the *fandango de Huelva*, are mainstays in the flamenco repertoire. But Torroba is not evoking that here.

A striking feature of this piece is that it starts out monophonically, presenting a very brief *copla* in E minor, the tonality of the work. This little incipit introduces a vital concept in Spanish music: the octosyllabic rhythm. *Coplas* frequently feature eight-syllable verses, and the music obligingly mimics this rhythm in a syllabic setting, concluding with a short melisma in the form of a rapid embellishment— for example, a triplet followed by a concluding longer note. The little song-like introduction here presents a paradigm of this octosyllabic rhythm (see ex. I:iii:15).

---

[22] See Luisa Morales, "Dances in Eighteenth-century Spanish Keyboard Music," *Diagonal: Journal of the Center for Iberian and Latin American Music* 1 (2005), http://cilam.ucr.edu/diagonal/issues/2005/morales.html.

Ex. I:iii:15 *Suite castellana*, "Fandanguillo," mm. 1–3

We can use an actual line from a traditional *copla* to make this clear: "El a-mor es un ple-i-to" (Love is a quarrel).[23] Better yet are words that Torroba himself attached. The "Fandango castellano" is one of seven songs he published in the first set of his *Canciones españolas* (1956), and it is an arrangement for piano and voice of this "Fandanguillo." One line of text corresponding to this opening gambit is "No te mi-res en mis o-jos" (Don't look at yourself in my eyes). Any guitarist learning this work would do well to consult the song, to form a more accurate idea of Torroba's intentions.[24]

The ensuing main theme is very idiomatic on the guitar and features arpeggios passing through a descending minor tetrachord of D major, C major, B minor, and A minor, all over an E pedal in the bass. (E is the lowest open string, making this a logical choice.) This chord progression is a virtual cliché of Spanish music, but it did not originate there. It was already common in the early Baroque period and frequently formed the basis for variation sets, especially *chaconas*. The practice of improvising over such a bass line or chord progression persisted, and persists, among Spanish guitarists accompanying a wide assortment of songs and dances.

This idea is repeated and then followed by a song-like B section that elaborates on the *copla* idea presented as an introduction, though now in the parallel major, accentuating a Phrygian feeling through modal mixture, i.e., use of C major. A sort of retransition mimics the scalar *falseta* (solo passage) of a guitarist and brings us to the A section, which concludes with a brief coda.

What captures one's attention here is that the guitar is, in a sense, imitating itself. That is to say that a classical guitar is pretending to be its folkish cousin. To be sure, there are evocations of folk and flamenco guitar in the keyboard literature, starting with Scarlatti and continuing through Albéniz, Granados, and Falla. But this is a conspicuous instance, and perhaps the first, where a nonguitarist sought to imitate the guitar on the guitar itself. It is too easy to overlook such an obvious detail now, given how familiar we are with Torroba's music. In the 1920s, however, this was a novel approach, one soon adopted by Turina and Rodrigo. Much of this has to do with the fact that in the late 1800s, the guitar was not a concert instrument in the same league as the piano or violin. Most thought it was too intimate and its repertoire too limited. In the hands of Segovia, however, the general concert

---

[23] Taken from Antonio Machado y Álvarez, *Cantes flamencos*, 4th ed. (Madrid: Espasa-Calpe, 1985), 96. The first edition appeared in 1947.

[24] In 1984, Federico, Jr., gave the Romeros the composer's manuscript sketch in pencil of this song, as a gift in memory of the late maestro. We thank them for sharing it with us.

Ex. I:iii:16 *Suite castellana,* "Arada," mm. 1–2

public's attitude toward it had begun to change. But the guitar's association with flamenco and regional folklore was so powerful that it exerted a kind of gravitational pull on the style of the music composers provided for it, effectively blurring the distinctions between classical and vernacular guitar musics.[25]

An *arada* is traditionally a work song associated with plowing fields. The tonality here is A, and again Torroba makes use of the open A string as a pedal note. Over this he moves through the dominant, V/V of IV, and IV chords, producing some poignant dissonances (see ex. I:iii:16).

This reliance on pedals in the first two movements merits some scrutiny. First, the use of pedal notes to produce these expressive harmonic contrasts was especially characteristic of the French composers, like Ravel, whom he admired. Coincidentally, it is also typical of folk accompaniments realized on the guitar. There is a performative aspect here, because the guitar is rather limited in the number of keys in which it can effectively perform. In order to maintain the instrument's resonance, a composer is well advised to write in a key that will utilize at least one of the open strings. Not surprisingly, then, the majority of successful guitar pieces are in E, A, D, G, or B (major or minor). Few employ more than three flats or five sharps. In these rookie essays, Torroba wisely chose tonalities that would utilize the open bass strings, i.e., E and A. Employing them as pedals generated not only attractive harmonic contrasts but also increased the resonance of the instrument itself.

"Arada" is also in ABA form, and the relatively expansive middle section makes imaginative use of natural and artificial harmonics, as well as striking exploration of the instrument's potential for chromaticism and modulation. In fact, the middle section is not so much contrasting as it is a development of the principal theme. There are some impressionistic touches in this piece as well, including planing of seventh chords in mm. 6–7 and 18, as well as whole-tone intimations in the retransition, mm. 21–22. The work ends reassuringly in A major, despite a

---

[25] To be sure, there were guitarist-composers in the 1800s who wrote pieces in imitation of vernacular styles. According to Wolf Moser, "The literature for guitar has followed, at a certain distance, the advancement of flamenco and popular music of Andalusia. There is one solitary *fandango* among Aguado's works, as a representative of the oldest form, while there are some *seguidillas* among Antonio Cano's works, and *malagueñas, panaderos, soleares* and *zapateados* in those of [Tomás] Damas, possibly under the influence of the success obtained by Arcas." See Wolf Moser, *Francisco Tárrega y la guitarra en España entre 1830 y 1960,* 2d ed. (Valencia: Piles Editorial, 2009), 25.

Ex. I:iii:17 *Suite castellana,* "Danza," mm. 1–12

key signature without flats or sharps. It is safe to say that this is one of the most harmonically adventurous pieces anyone had written for solo guitar up to that time, tame though it may be in comparison with contemporary works of the Second Viennese School.

As we already know, the "Danza" was the first piece written by a nonguitarist, and it is quite unlike anything in the repertoire up to that point. It is marked "Vivo," and the A section evinces a lively triple meter; thus, this piece logically serves as the suite's vivacious finale. In E major, it commences with the now-customary procedure of establishing the tonal center through use of a tonic pedal, though here the pedal appears in the middle and upper registers rather than in the bass (see ex. I:iii:17).

The phrasing is in symmetrical four-bar units, and Torroba gets additional mileage out of his attractive theme by sequencing it through the subdominant and dominant key areas. The brief B section features a lovely *copla*-like passage, marked "Lento espressivo." A dominant retransition returns us to a verbatim restatement of the A section and a cursory coda.

Torroba's formal procedures in the *Suite castellana* are rudimentary but not the result of technical inability. Rather, they serve as simple, sturdy frames in which to present attractively lyric vignettes. The composer never made any secret of his intention to please the audience rather than cultural elites. He was true to his own self, as Polonius adjured his son Laertes to be, and as a result, there is never anything pretentious or affected in his music.[26] Few of his compositions display this genuineness to better effect than the *Sonatina.*

Sonatina

In fact, Tanenbaum goes on to opine that "Torroba's Sonatina in A, with its beautiful middle movement and bright outer movements, is perhaps his most captivating piece."[27] The Romeros certainly concur with this assessment, Pepe saying of the

---

[26] See *Hamlet,* Act I, scene 3. "This above all: to thine own self be true, and it must follow, as the night the day, thou canst not then be false to any man."

[27] Tanenbaum, "Perspectives on the Classical Guitar in the Twentieth Century," 186.

Sonatina that "not only are the melodies beautiful but also the way Torroba weaves them." However, Pepe is quick to note that though Torroba was prolific in composing melodies, "he did not develop them symphonically the way Rodrigo did." In Pepe's opinion, "Rodrigo could have written ten concertos with all the themes that Torroba packed into the *Sonatina*." Pepe's critique has merit, but the relative lack of extensive development in his music does not necessarily reflect a lack of compositional technique. Since he did not specialize in writing piano sonatas, string quartets, or symphonies—did not feel they would be a productive or remunerative use of his time as a composer in Spain—he did not have many opportunities to display the capacity for developing thematic material. Nonetheless, it is true that here and there in his guitar music, and very often in his zarzuelas, particularly *Luisa Fernanda*, he exhibits the ability to extract from melodic ideas their inner potential for development. This is one such case. Still, we must point out that the dedicatee of this work, Segovia, had reservations about its inherent musical quality. In a letter to Manuel Ponce dated August 31, 1930, he urged the Mexican composer to write a guitar sonatina with a "distinctly Spanish character. . . . I want you to write it very much, [as] I am certain you would write something as graceful as the one by Torroba, and of much more musical substance."[28] In any event, however one may assess its "musical substance," Celín insists that the *Sonatina* is "more difficult than it sounds. It is very tricky. People hear it and don't realize how difficult it is."[29]

The first movement of the *Sonatina* is in a classical sonata form, and it provides ample evidence of Torroba's ability to manage structures more complex than simple part forms. It also exhibits remarkable symmetry in its form and phrasing, which is grounded in a steady tonic-dominant harmonic motion. These traits suggest the influence of neoclassicism. Torroba was certainly aware of larger trends in European music, particularly in relation to recent works by Falla and Falla's idol, Stravinsky. But we hasten to note that, regardless of its "classical" traits, there is nothing here of the irony, satire, and sardonic detachment, i.e., no bitonality or "wrong" notes, so characteristic of neoclassicism. In the final analysis, Torroba's *Sonatina* exudes a lyric warmth and dancelike vivacity indebted to the late-Romantic nationalism of Albéniz, Granados, and early Falla.

The exposition, development, and recapitulation in this sonata form are each approximately thirty measures in length and are followed by a ten-measure coda. After a textbook repetition of the exposition, Torroba focuses his developmental attention on the opening motive, within a kaleidoscopic shifting of tonal emphasis. The tonality of A major dominates the movement, but Torroba exhibits a fondness

---

[28] Miguel Alcázar, ed., *The Segovia-Ponce Letters*, trans. Peter Segal (Columbus, Ohio: Editions Orphée, 1989), 80. In September of that same year, he complained to Ponce that "it is useless to ask Torroba to be more caring and tasteful in choosing the harmonies, development, and rhythmic grace that has [*sic*] been until recently characteristic of his talent. He has given himself up completely to the light music of the zarzuela and is losing his artistic honor." Ibid., 85.

[29] Pepe and Celín shared these insights with Walter Clark on January 6, 2011.

Ex. I:iii:18 Sonatina, 1st mvmt., mm. 1–4

for excursions to the parallel minor, particularly in tandem with use of the lowered sixth degree of the minor scale, lending a Spanish flavor to the harmony. The rhythm suggests the Castilian *seguidillas* (see ex. I:iii:18), and the irrepressible rhythmic motive of an eighth followed by two sixteenths initiates and pervades the movement, propelling it forward.

The middle movement, in D major, features one of the most lushly sensual melodies in the guitar repertoire. This is in part the result of the *scordatura* tuning of the low E string down to D, which gives the guitar added resonance in the bass as the theme sings out in the upper register. But it also results from expressive use of the parallel minor mode. The appearance at the outset of C-natural and B-flat softens the tonic-dominant angularity of the previous movement and establishes a deliciously languorous affect. Also effective is the sinuous, meandering quality of the melodic line, with its lyrical embellishments (see ex. I:iii:19).

The ternary structure, AABA, is typical not only of sonata middle movements but also opera arias—here a soprano aria, to be sure. Torroba's exploration of the upper register of the instrument in this piece is complemented by skillful use of harmonics, evidence of his growing confidence in writing idiomatically for the guitar.

The final movement is a brisk Allegro driven by a dancelike motive featuring four sixteenths followed by an eighth note in 3/8 meter; the rhythm bears some resemblance to the "Bulerías" from *La virgen de mayo*, but without the hemiola (see ex. I:iii:20). Though in A major, E-mode coloring on the dominant by means of modal mixture (C-natural, G-natural, and F-natural) lends a Spanish flavor to the harmony in the second half of the main theme (mm. 13–15).

Ex. I:iii:19 Sonatina, 2nd mvmt., mm. 1–4

Ex. I:iii:20 Sonatina, 3rd mvmt., mm. 1–9

The structure of this finale is a clear-cut case of sonata-rondo form, with a developmental C section: ABAC(develop.)ABAcoda. This architecture is skillfully handled and reveals again a genuine capacity for the development of motivically incisive themes and modulation by means of a rich harmonic palette.

Sonatina is an evergreen favorite among performers and audiences around the world, and careful consideration of its detailed workmanship in harmony, form, and melody deepens our appreciation for Torroba's compositional craft at this stage in his career. And he would proceed from strength to strength in ensuing works.

Piezas características

Piezas características often exploits techniques found in *Sonatina* and *Nocturno* (1926). Moreover, this six-movement work is unified by the repetition of thematic material in the sixth and final movement, "Panorama." As the title implies, "Panorama" offers an overview of the suite as a whole through the integration of themes from the preceding movements. This procedure lends a cyclic character to the suite and is a novel procedure in the guitar literature up to that time.

Piezas características taken as a whole, and "Panorama" in particular, represent a summary of Torroba's style before the Civil War. In this work, three of the six movements are inspired by folk models. "Los mayos" recalls secular Castilian folk songs that are sung on the last night of April to celebrate the coming of May and spring. "Albada," with variants throughout Spain, is a song sung by a young man to his beloved at dawn. "Oliveras" refers to the olive orchards that cover entire mountainsides in southern Spain. Though not folkloric in character, *Melodía* was the finest tremolo study to that time after Tarrega's *Recuerdos de la Alhambra* (1899) and was no doubt modeled on it.[30] "Panorama" combines references to the

---

[30] The tremolo technique involves playing rapid repeated notes with two or more fingers over a bass pattern played by the thumb. Later contributions to the tremolo repertoire include Eduardo Sainz de la Maza's *Campanas del alba*, Rodrigo's *Junto al Generalife*, and Torroba's own "Zafra" from *Castillos de España*.

French school, neoclassicism, and folk music. It also provides another insight into the use of the dominant in close proximity to the flat-VI chord, to provide a Spanish-style Phrygian tinge to the harmony.

Panorama begins with a repetition of the opening eight measures of the first movement, *Preámbulo*. Measures 9–62 are based on the two main themes of the second movement, *Oliveras*. The first theme appears in A minor and the second, in E major. Still in E major, the opening measures of the fourth movement, *Los mayos*, are stated at m. 63. But reference to *Los mayos* merely sets the stage for a 97-measure fugue, whose subject is based on the second theme of *Oliveras*. At m. 167, the theme from *Los mayos* returns, now to prepare the final cadence to E major, at m. 198.

The opening passage of *Panorama*, mm. 1–8, and its more expanded version in the first movement, is among the closest references to the French school to be found in Torroba's music (see ex. I:iii:21).

The languid major-major seventh sonority on C (i.e., a major chord, here in first inversion, with a major seventh above the root) with which he begins is identical to that with which *La marchenera* commences. This may be mere coincidence, but both instances reveal a penchant for colorful added-note sonorities that trace their patrilineage to Chopin, Liszt, Albéniz, Ravel, and other composers he admired. Supporting a pentatonic melody in the opening measures are chromatic harmonies that vaguely suggest E minor through the prominence of the pitches E and G; however, though E minor may be implied as the tonal center, the harmonies do not have clear functional relationships to that center. Nor do these opening eight harmonies derive from Spanish folk or popular sources. Moreover, the blurring of tonal cadences through avoidance of dominant-tonic progressions, even at the conclusion of the piece, is conspicuous. Thus, we should consider the nonfunctional and nonfolkloric character of his harmony and his blurring of tonality at cadence points to be just as much a style trait as any other procedure, and they belie characterizations of his guitar pieces as harmonically simplistic.

The fugue beginning at m. 69 is the only one Torroba ever composed for the guitar. In fact, there are very few examples of this device in post-Baroque fingerboard literature, largely because imitative counterpoint is the most difficult of

Ex. I:iii:21 Piezas características, "Panorama," mm. 1–8

textures to render on the guitar. This is due in part to its small number of strings and limited capacity for sustaining a truly independent bass line (as opposed to a Baroque lute, for example). The syncopated, fourteen-measure subject is answered at the fifth (m. 83); restated in a three-part texture (m. 97); and again answered at the fifth (m. 111). After an episodic passage (mm. 125–42) and fragmentations of the subject (mm. 143–66), the fugue gives way to a restatement of the theme from *Los mayos* (m. 167) before a pyrotechnic conclusion in E major.

In summary, the guitar works of the 1920s and 30s were not dependent on foreign models, nor were they necessarily based on precedents in Spanish guitar literature. Rather they reveal a skillful intermarriage of contemporary harmony with folkloric rhythms and harmonies, in tandem with an approach to the guitar that is both idiomatic and sufficiently challenging to represent an enlargement of the instrument's technical resources and a significant departure from the repertoire to that point. In this sense, Torroba was both conservative and innovative at the same time.

ACT II

1932–1960

"Her soldier boy does not answer, and she is sad, poor girl, for she fears that he is dead."

[El soldadito no la contesta . . . y ella está triste, la pobrecita, porque sospecha que se murió.]

Luisa Fernanda, Act II

4

ACT II
Scene i
1936
Anarchy

The Spanish Civil War and its attendant ideological conflicts continue to haunt Spain and, not infrequently, perplex the outside world. They are exquisitely complex. Moreover, the effects of that war are still palpable, as thousands of survivors and their offspring will attest. Antonio Moreno Juste aptly observes that the conflict split Spanish society into two groups, "conquerors and conquered," leaving a very deep wound that has been slow to heal.[1]

However, at least one impulse has united virtually all Spaniards since that terrible ordeal: a determination to avoid another such struggle at all costs. As one Spanish scholar has noted, "It was an experience so tragic and extensive, affecting nearly the entire population, that the Spaniards found any solution preferable to a new war."[2] This has been accomplished at least in part by the so-called *gran olvido*, or "great forgetting," in which the war and its many ramifications were either ignored or treated in gingerly fashion by laypersons and scholars alike. Post-war society has focused instead on building a "modern, tranquil, affluent society, [as] no one wanted to dwell on the painful memory of a bitter civil conflict."[3] It is ironic that such a forgetting would continue into a period of democratization and increasing openness, after the death of Franco, but as Jorge Luis Marzo noted in 1995, "An inability to deal with [the recent] past is a defining

[1] Antonio Moreno Juste, "La Guerra Civil (1936–1939)," in *Historia contemporánea de España, siglo XX*, ed. Javier Paredes (Barcelona: Editorial Ariel, 1998), 546.

[2] Julio Montero Díaz, "El Franquismo: Planteamiento general," in *Historia contemporánea de España, siglo XX*, 639.

[3] Frances Lannon, *The Spanish Civil War: 1936–1939*, series: Essential Histories, Robert O'Neill, series ed. (Oxford: Osprey Publishing, 2002), 89. Lannon adds that "The wilder dreams of both extremes—Fascist and Anarchist, reactionary and revolutionary—seemed very distant" by the 1980s, after democracy was firmly in place.

feature of the intellectual landscape of Spain's resurgent democracy, from the late seventies to the present."[4] One ought not to take this thesis too far, however; the Civil War has figured prominently in literature and cinema, as many artists and intellectuals grappled with its significance. Santos Juliá reminds us that

> the memoirs of Dionisio Ridruejo or Pedro Laín Entralgo, the novels of Juan Benet or Camilo José Cela, the theater of Antonio Buero Vallejo, or the cinema of José Luis Borau and Carlos Saura were full of constant references to the Civil War and the years immediately after it, evoking recollections of a time that many Spaniards had not experienced directly, but the effects of which they had suffered for a long time.[5]

Still, this took place during the transition to democracy in the 1960s and 70s and not the period we survey here. The fact remains that, as the journalist Luis María Anson put it, "the postwar generation was the generation of silence."[6]

In any case, the *gran olvido* is at last dissipating, and in the wake of the recent seventieth anniversary of the end of the Civil War, scholars are coming to grips with its legacy as never before. Nonetheless, we are acutely aware that many of the issues we raise here—issues one cannot avoid in examining Torroba's career—are of a sensitive nature. We hasten to point out, however, that we do not subscribe to the good guy/bad guy, gunfight-at-the-OK Corral treatment of the Spanish Civil War that prevails in superficial histories. The Republicans were not the Earps, and the rebels were not the Clantons—or vice versa. Neither side was all good or all bad (for that matter, neither were the Earps or Clantons), and there was plenty of blame to go around for the outbreak and conduct of the war. Moreno Juste also notes and disapproves a tendency to simplify the conflict, to view it as a struggle between two camps, the one "urban, progressive, secular humanist, democratic, republican," and the other "rural, conservative, authoritarian, monarchical, traditional, Catholic."[7] It was *not* that simple, and Torroba himself serves as an example of someone who fits into neither tidy category but combines elements of both. A substantial portion of the population was not firmly attached to either side. As Hess has noted, "Many Spaniards, however—including Falla—found themselves unable to declare allegiance to either camp, effectively forming a 'third Spain' that historians are just beginning to explore."[8]

Lest we seem hereby to lapse into a sort of wishy-washy relativism, we state for the record that neither of us believes in military dictatorship or theocracy as a

[4] Jorge Luis Marzo, "The Spectacle of Spain's Amnesia: Spanish Cultural Policy from the Dictatorship to Expo '92," trans. Ian Kennedy, *Alphabet City* 4–5 (1995): 92.

[5] Santos Juliá, "History, Politics, Culture, 1975–1996," in *The Cambridge Companion to Modern Spanish Culture*, ed. David T. Gies (Cambridge: Cambridge University Press, 1999), 112.

[6] Luis María Ansón, "La generación del silencio," *ABC*, March 1, 1973, Cited in Juan Pablo Fusi, *Un siglo de España, la cultura* (Madrid: Marcial Pons, Ediciones de Historia, 1999), 115.

[7] Moreno Juste, "La Guerra Civil (1936–1939)," 521.

[8] Hess, *Modernism*, 5.

viable solution to the economic and social ills of the modern world. Neither do we endorse equally calamitous utopian ideologies like Marxism or anarchism. History has rendered a resounding verdict of "guilty" on all of them. In fact, we step out of scholarly character here long enough to deplore the ideological rigidity and resort to violence that characterized the worst elements on both sides of the conflict. Indeed, this story has enduring relevance for us today, as it reveals what happens when political factions become so entrenched in their respective worldviews that constructive dialogue and compromise become impossible, leaving armed conflict as the only means of settling disputes. Spaniards are not uniquely susceptible to such impasses, and the Civil War has valuable lessons to teach us. As Spanish-American philosopher George Santayana famously noted, until we learn those lessons, we will have to repeat them.[9]

In any event, Spain reached its current state of relative felicity due to a certain sequence of historical events. There is no guarantee that similar or superior results would have ensued from a different causality skein. History does not reveal its alternatives, of course, but there is reason to believe that Franco and his followers unwittingly planted the seeds of their movement's demise in Spain through gradual cultivation of a large and stable middle class, a class sensible and informed enough to reject the religious fanaticism and anti-intellectualism of the dictatorship. Such a class of people invariably forms the indispensable foundation for democracy. It is safe to assume that the wholesale destruction of the bourgeoisie proposed by the radical leftists in the early 1930s would have produced its own brand of misery. This was already obvious to the Spanish socialist politician Indalecio de Prieto (1883–1962), who, writing from exile in Mexico in 1954, expressed the fervent hope that Spain would be able find an "option other than the two infernos [of Francoism and communism], which are equally horrific and abominable."[10]

Of course, Prieto was himself proof that Spain paid a steep cultural price for Franco's victory, as many of its leading intellectuals, writers, artists, and musicians died or went into permanent exile. The loss was devastating and irreparable. Again, however, there would have been an exodus of talent regardless of which side won—and our composer might well have been among those fleeing a communist Spain—but we can only assay the impact of the exodus that actually occurred, and that impact was disastrous.[11]

In any case, our sole purpose in examining this conflagration, which has already inspired an entire library of books and articles, is obviously not to take sides but

[9] "Those who cannot remember the past are condemned to repeat it." In *The Life of Reason*, vol. 1 (1905).

[10] Indalecio de Prieto, "Dos infiernos: franquismo y comunismo," *Siempre* (Mexico), September 29, 1954, and reproduced in Justino Sinova Garrido, ed., *Un siglo en 100 artículos* (Madrid: La Esfera de los Libros, 2002), 277.

[11] To get an accurate feeling for just how disastrous, consult Henry Kamen, *The Disinherited: Exile and the Making of Spanish Culture, 1492–1975* (New York: HarperCollins, 2007), 260–321.

rather to situate Torroba in a proper historical context, in order better to grasp the nature of his art and personality. We continue to believe that the process also works in reverse, i.e., that the better we understand figures like Torroba, the more we will learn about the overarching calamity in which he and millions of others found themselves unwilling captives.

Thus, we focus on those aspects of it that are relevant to our subject, that help us to understand how the conflict affected Torroba and the trajectory of his career, to understand why he reacted to it the way he did and took the side he apparently considered the lesser of two evils. Above and beyond all other considerations, we sincerely honor the memory of all those who sacrificed life and limb either to *restore* or to *elevate* Spain to what they passionately believed, for good or ill, was its rightful place in the modern world. As outsiders, we can do no more than this. We shall certainly do no less.

Recall from Act I, Scene ii, that, towards the end of his life, Torroba wished for his native land nothing so much as "stability, serenity, and peace." He understood the alternative all too well, and in 1936, it was the alternative that increasingly prevailed. José María Gil-Robles (1898–1980), leader of CEDA (Confederatión Española de Derechas Autónomas), the Catholic party formed in 1933, might well have been speaking for the composer himself when he declared in the Cortes on June 16 of that year:

> Let us not deceive ourselves. A country can live under a monarchy or a republic, with a parliamentary or a presidential system, under communism or fascism! But it cannot live in anarchy. Now, alas, Spain is in anarchy."[12]

It is difficult for us today, in a "safe, civilian environment of health and safety, and citizen's rights,"[13] to comprehend the hell through which Spain was going at that time, and the inferno that awaited it in the ensuing years. As Beevor observed, the Republic had moved too far too fast, attempting to accomplish in a few years what had taken decades elsewhere in Europe to achieve. And there were ludicrous and needlessly provocative excesses that did nothing to advance the Republican cause and did much to impede its progress. For instance,

> One priest in Andalusia [was] fined by a socialist magistrate for saying mass in his church whose roof had been destroyed by lightning: he had

---

[12] Quoted in Thomas, *The Spanish Civil War*, 5.

[13] In the words of Beevor, *The Battle for Spain*, xxvi, who goes on to speculate: "This, perhaps, is why it is unwise to try to judge the terrible conflict of seventy years ago with the liberal values and attitudes that we accept today as normal." At the time of this writing, Spain just concluded its first National Siesta Championship (October 24, 2010), with a prize of 1000 Euros going to the winner of a snoozing competition. Such a contest suggests increasing anxiety about the frenetic pace of life in Spain and the passing of cherished traditions, but 2010 is a far cry from 1936, even with an unemployment rate currently hovering around 20 percent.

been charged with making a public display of religion. Another priest was fined as a monarchist for alluding to the Kingship of God in the festival of Christ the King. In one parish, the tolling of bells was taxed, in another the wearing of crucifixes forbidden.[14]

Certainly one understands the antagonism that many people felt towards the Church, historic ally of Spanish autocracy and opponent of badly needed political and social reforms. Pope Pius IX had spent much of the nineteenth century inveighing against free speech and conscience, the separation of church and state, and democracy in general, enshrining these antimodern views in his infamous *Syllabus of Errors* (1864).[15] We have already noted that in the early 1900s, only 20 percent of Spaniards went to mass on a regular basis, and disenchantment with the Church and its policies was widespread. There was good reason for such apathy. But the Second Republic's actions simply elicited sympathy for the Church. Overall, one must confront the fact that "the left had often shown as little respect for the democratic process and the rule of law as the right."[16]

The slide into anarchy had accelerated after the elections of 1933, which brought the right wing to power. One of the ironies in the balloting on November 19 of that year was that though women went to the polls for the first time in Spanish history, thanks to the Republic's new constitution, many of them cast their ballots for center-right candidates. People want freedom, yes, but they also require stability and continuity, as Torroba himself made clear. In Thomas's opinion, "Azaña had frightened the middle class, without satisfying the workers."[17] That proved a fatal combination. Thus, Azaña was now succeeded as prime minister by Alejandro Lerroux (1864–1949). Ironically, Lerroux was a leading leftist and Republican; however, the president who appointed Lerroux, Niceto Alcalá-Zamora, found him preferable to the rightist alternative, Gil-Robles.

Despite Lerroux's appointment, the left's response to this reversal was not resignation in a spirit of compromise and determination to learn its lessons and do better two years hence. No, it immediately raised the specter of civil war, egged on by labor leader Largo Caballero, who bellowed, "If legality is no use to us, if it hinders our advance, then we shall bypass bourgeois democracy and proceed to the revolutionary conquest of power."[18]

[14] Thomas, *Spanish Civil War*, 101.

[15] See Geoffrey Robertson, *The Case of the Pope: Vatican Accountability for Human Rights Abuse* (London: Penguin, 2010), 68. This book provides an excellent, if disturbing, overview of the modern Papacy and the Vatican's implausible claims to statehood. Pius IX's declaration of Papal infallibility in faith and morals followed the 1864 *Syllabus of Errors* in 1870. Papal abuses prompted Lord Acton to utter his famous dictum, "Power tends to corrupt, and absolute power corrupts absolutely."

[16] Beevor, *The Battle for Spain*, xxvii.

[17] Thomas, *Spanish Civil War*, 102.

[18] Cited in ibid., 105.

On January 3, 1934, *El Socialista* defiantly declared: "Harmony? No! Class War! Hatred of the Criminal Bourgeoisie to the Death!"[19] So much for peaceful coexistence. Ten days later, the socialist executive committee charted a new course for the country. This included nationalizing all of the land, dissolving religious orders and confiscating their property, replacing the army with a "democratic militia" (think "People's Army"), and getting rid of the Guardia Civil. Lest anyone imagine that they were just blowing smoke in the heat of the moment, on February 3, a "revolutionary committee" began to plot the overthrow of the right-wing government, an insurrection that it said would depend for success on the "violence it produces."[20] Of course, cooler and wiser heads, like Ortega y Gasset, realized that such moves would simply give the army the pretext it needed to impose a dictatorship. And the middle classes, terrorized by the prospect of their annihilation, would ally themselves with the right. But, as the old saying goes, "if the facts do not conform to the theory, they must be discarded." These facts did not conform to socialist theory, and they were duly discarded.

On October 5, 1934, the left called for a general strike throughout the country. But others wanted more than a mere strike, and on that day leftist rebels in Asturias launched an assault on Civil Guard stations in various cities. Forty priests and wealthy citizens were promptly murdered, and with their murders, a real civil war had actually begun, though largely confined to the Asturias region. In another exquisite irony, the military forces sent in to quell the violence—by the Republican Lerroux—were under the command of none other than General Francisco Franco, who three years later on would teach the rebels a thing or two about how to stage a successful *golpe de estado*.

The revolt lasted a couple of weeks and claimed one thousand lives, in addition to causing a lot of property damage. The communists wasted no time in taking credit for the uprising, which confirmed many people's worst fears about them, and, in fulfillment of Ortega y Gasset's warnings, gave Franco the rationale he needed to claim that there was a "red conspiracy" afoot.[21] It was, as Beevor wrote, "a near fatal blow to democracy in Spain." Largo Caballero, always good for a memorable quote, made it clear that he and his followers wanted "a Republic without class war, but for that one class has to disappear."[22] The die was now effectively cast, and it was only a matter of time before a civil war would engulf the entire nation.

Elections were again held on February 16, 1936, and these were to be the last free elections in Spain for four decades. In truth, elections were unlikely to solve any problems, because, in Beevor's opinion, "The depth of feeling was too strong on either side to allow democracy to work."[23] Largo Caballero reliably left no doubt

---

[19] This discussion is indebted to Beevor, *Battle for Spain*, 27–29, in which *El Socialista* is quoted.

[20] Beevor, *Battle for Spain*, 28.

[21] Ibid., 31.

[22] Ibid., 33.

[23] Beevor, *Battle for Spain*, 34.

what would happen if his side lost the election: "open civil war."[24] The right consisted of the usual *compadres*, i.e., wealthy landowners, powerful business interests, and the Roman Catholic Church. Knowing full well which side of the political toast to butter, the Church proclaimed that "a vote for the right was a vote for Christ."[25] Perhaps it really was *easier* for a camel to pass through the eye of a needle than for a rich man to enter the kingdom of heaven,[26] but it was *impossible* for a communist to do so, and that was all that mattered. After all, the Republic had eliminated the state subsidy on which the Church depended, and the Church was now in desperate financial straits, especially since most of its thirty thousand priests were poor and poorly educated, unfit for other types of employment.[27] And if the Church needed any reminding whose side Christ was taking in the election, all it had to do was read *El Socialista*, which made no secret of its intention to "do in Spain what has been done in Russia. The plan of Spanish socialism and Russian communism is the same." This "plan" spelled doom for the middle class, corporations, and clerics, who now fled to the right in Spanish democracy's last gasp.

Interestingly, given the supercharged atmosphere in which the balloting took place, the elections went off without a hitch, unmarred by violence. And, the Savior's presumed political preferences notwithstanding, the left triumphed—but only by a narrow margin. This did not prevent the leftists from proceeding with sweeping changes, as if they possessed an overwhelming mandate, which they did not. As Álvarez Junco notes, "The winner of those elections, the Popular Front, again made the mistake of believing that they were the owners of the state and that their mission was to crush their political enemies."[28]

For its part, the Church was now quite convinced that it was facing a Judeo-Masonic-Bolshevik conspiracy of satanic proportions, one bent on the destruction of Christianity.[29] On July 1, forty-eight bishops publicly supported a military uprising, and "from this moment, the war was legitimized as a crusade in defense of religion."[30]

In truth, the Catholic cause was not without powerful allies of its own. These included not only the army but also the Falange Española (Spanish Phalanx), the Spanish fascist party founded in 1933 by the son of dictator Miguel Primo de Rivera, José Antonio. As Thomas described him,

> José Antonio was always ready to fight anyone who criticized his father, and his career was in some ways simply an attempt to vindicate the old dictator. From his father, he inherited a contempt for political parties, a

---

[24] Ibid.

[25] Ibid., 35.

[26] See Matthew 19:23–24, Mark 10:24–25, and Luke 18:24–25.

[27] Beevor, *Battle for Spain*, 35.

[28] Álvarez Junco, "History, Politics, and Culture, 1875–1936," 84.

[29] Ibid., 38.

[30] Moreno Juste, "La Guerra Civil (1936–1939)," 543.

belief, instinctive in the father, rationalized in the son, in 'intuition'—
the triumph of experience over intellect.[31]

The Falange attracted a wide assortment of malcontents united in their rejection
of the rapid and revolutionary changes taking place in Spanish society. Yet, it
would be a mistake to see the Falange as simply the Spanish version of Nazism.
German fascism under Hitler was, for all its evil, a form of utopian idealism, a
belief in the destiny of the German *Volk* to govern and perfect mankind in its role
as the master race. This kind of futuristic vision, albeit corrupt, was alien to
Falangism, which was fundamentally reactionary and backward looking. As Pérez
Zalduondo reminds us, "The fusion of religion and patriotism was one of the most
obvious differences between the Falange and Nazism."[32]

José Antonio in particular shared Franco's disdain for the Enlightenment, the
French Revolution, and liberalism in general. He made no secret of his contempt
for Liberté, Egalité, and Fraternité. The "atheistic" liberal state may have inscribed
that motto on the "façade of its temple," but, he declared, "beneath that sign none
of the three flourish." His ideal was *Unidad*: "to that unity all classes and individuals must pledge themselves."[33]

Thus, the ideal Falangist was "'half-monk, half soldier,'"[34] a sort of latter-day
Knight Templar, one who revered the fifteenth-century *Reyes Católicos* (Catholic
Kings), Ferdinand and Isabella, as model monarchs. This does not mean that José
Antonio and his followers were insensitive to the sufferings of the lower classes, just
that, in keeping with Leo XIII's encyclical *Rerum Novarum* (1891), they rejected
socialism as any sort of solution to the socioeconomic dilemmas inherent in
capitalism. And, in truth, they held the Church and monarchy at arm's length, recognizing their responsibility in bringing Spain to this pass. As Boyd has observed, the
Falange "was as unrelenting in its condemnation of monarchism, conservatism, and
capitalism as it was of liberalism and socialism.... its revolutionary message of stat-
ism, imperialism, and corporativist economic modernization was viewed with deep
suspicion by the anti-statist Catholic right and the monarchist agrarian elites."[35]

Despite all this, in the opinion of Moreno Juste, "Spanish fascism never derived
its power from below as a party of the masses but rather in all cases sought to gain
power from above."[36]

---

[31] Thomas, *Spanish Civil War*, 108.

[32] Pérez Zalduondo, "La música en los intercambios culturales," *Cruces de caminos*, 423.

[33] José Antonio Primo de Rivera, "Orientaciones hacia un nuevo Estado," *El Fascio* (Madrid),
March 16, 1933, and reproduced in Sinova Garrido, ed., *Un siglo en 100 artículos*, 168–69.

[34] Beevor, *Battle for Spain*, 41. The famed guitarist Pepe Romero once said to this author that a
Spaniard is a "cross between a monk and a pervert." It is not necessary for foreigners to essentialize
the Spanish people, as Spaniards are already quite keen to do the job themselves.

[35] Carolyn P. Boyd, "History, Politics, and Culture, 1936–1975," in *The Cambridge Companion to
Modern Spanish Culture*, ed. David T. Gies (Cambridge: Cambridge University Press, 1999), 91.

[36] Moreno Juste, "La Guerra Civil (1936–1939)," 543.

A more dependable, and older, ally of the Church was the Carlists. They dreamed of restoring Catholic supremacy in Spain. We recall that the Carlists had originally supported Carlos, brother of Ferdinand VII, for succession to the throne in 1833, rather than Isabel II, the deceased king's daughter. Carlist discontent fueled three civil wars in the nineteenth century and was about to add fuel to a fourth, in the twentieth. Carlism's power base was always in northern Spain, particularly the Basque country and Catalonia, though Navarra was its principal stronghold. This was a rural region without industry or much of a bourgeoisie; therefore, it was extremely conservative and Catholic. As Thomas has noted, "A journey to Navarre was still an expedition to the middle ages."[37] It had long since shed its sympathy with the separatist aspirations of the rest of the Basque country and Catalonia. It was Navarra, but it was also Spain, and content to remain that way. The soldiers from this region wore red berets and formed into paramilitary units called *requetés*. They were ferocious fighters and wasted no time choosing sides in the coming conflict. When the military uprising began on July 17, 1936, the *requetés* immediately rallied to Franco's banner and remained steadfast in support of the rebels. No wonder Torroba would spend much of the war in Navarra, on property owned by his wife's family, safe from turmoil and harm.

Provocations to insurrection were not in short supply. For instance, on May Day in 1936, the socialists orchestrated a massive parade through Madrid. Naturally, "conservatives watched in trepidation from their balconies or from behind shutters. They eyed with mounting alarm the red flags and banners and portraits of Lenin, Stalin and Largo Caballero."[38] And they were even more palpable reasons for worry. Gil-Robles reported that, since the election, numerous depredations had been committed against church property, with attendant injuries and murders, and that over 300 strikes had been called. Whether or not his figures were entirely accurate, it seemed to many that the country was teetering on the precipice of anarchy. Drastic action was needed, and it was not long in coming.

Students of the American Civil War may not immediately recognize a facsimile of that conflict in the Spanish version. Wanton murder of civilians was rare in the American Civil War.[39] During the Spanish Civil War, the torturing and slaughtering

---

[37] Thomas, *Spanish Civil War*, 94. Beevor, *The Battle for Spain*, 7, also noted Navarrese "religious fanaticism and ferocious rejection of modernity." The authors happily report that this thoroughly delightful region of Spain is now firmly ensconced in the twenty-first century, without any loss of its historic charm.

[38] Beevor, *Battle for Spain*, 46.

[39] It did happen, of course. In the summer of 1863, Quantrill's Confederate raiders shot down unarmed men in cold blood during a dastardly attack on the Union stronghold of Lawrence, Kansas; indeed, the border war in general had always been a brutal affair, stretching back to the Pottawattomie massacre in 1854 and the depredations committed by border ruffians on both sides leading up to and during the war. For a useful overview of this conflict, see Craig Miner, *Kansas: The History of the Sunflower State, 1854–2000* (Lawrence: University of Kansas Press, 2002), 49–93. Jubal Early's sacking

began immediately and continued after the war was over, as Franco sent thousands to the killing fields. The most notorious example of this mindless bloodlust was the murder of the 38-year-old poet and playwright Federico García Lorca, who was shot by a firing squad on August 19, 1936, and unceremoniously thrown into a mass grave, whose exact location remains unknown. For its part, the left gunned down priests and anyone else suspected of collusion with the rebels. The savagery Goya claimed to have witnessed during the war against Napoleon now made an encore appearance in a new century, and it immediately initiated a pervasive climate of suspicion and dread, hatred and reprisals.

It is important to understand this situation in order to comprehend why Torroba and others like him reacted the way they did: running to get as far away from danger as they could. As a bourgeois, Catholic, and monarchist, he was increasingly unsafe in Republican Spain and sought refuge in the northern areas firmly under Franco's control. This does not mean that he was a supporter of fascism in general or Franco's regime in particular, only that Franco's Spain was the lesser of two evils for a man of Torroba's background and sensibilities. We will see in the next scene that his fears were far from irrational, and he had plenty of company on the left in this regard. Years later, Gregorio Marañon reported that,

> Eighty-eight per cent of the university teachers of Madrid, Valencia and Barcelona have had to flee abroad, abandon Spain, escape in any way possible. And do you know why? Quite simply because they were afraid of being murdered by the Reds, even though many of the threatened intellectuals were known to be men of the left.[40]

The radicalization of the Spanish government, or Popular Front, quickly dominated by communists and anarchists in response to the uprising, gave people like Torroba little choice. Indeed, though histories often portray the Spanish Civil War as a conflict between democracy and fascism, we have already seen that such reductionism is misleading. Both sides vowed to rise up if they did not get their way at the ballot box. Once Franco and his forces made their move, the Spanish government lurched even further to the left. It soon seemed to many Spaniards, and no doubt to our composer, that they had two basic choices: a right-wing

---

of Chambersburg, Pennsylvania, in the summer of 1864 is another instance. But those cases are simply the exceptions that prove the rule: generally speaking, civilians were not singled out for murder, even during Sherman's March to the Sea. Property and economic assets were destroyed, of course, but civilians themselves were not slaughtered as a matter of policy or uncontrolled animus. As John F. Marszalek points out in *Sherman: A Soldier's Passion for Order* (New York: The Free Press, 1993), 317, Sherman believed that "an important military victory had been won with minimal human casualties though substantial property loss."

[40] Cited in Kamen, *The Disinherited*, 273. Among these refugees were Eugenio d'Ors, Juan Ramón Jiménez, Azorín, Antonio Machado, and Ortega y Gasset. Marañon himself fled with his family to Alicante and managed to escape on an English destroyer.

dictatorship modeled on fascist Italy or a left-wing dictatorship modeled on communist Russia. A Catholic like Torroba could only go one way.

This is not the place to present a military history of the Spanish Civil War. Suffice it to say that the government's only real hope was to crush the rebellion in its early stages, for once the rebels established a base of operations on the Peninsula, they would quickly gain strength and be hard to defeat. The military uprising began in Spanish Morocco and immediately spread to the mainland the following day, on the 18th. Hitler and Mussolini did not hesitate to aid Franco, transporting soliders across the Strait of Gibraltar and sending large amounts of war materiel along with thousands of troops. France and Britain did their best to remain aloof, fearing that the conflict would spread beyond Spain and start a second world war. Not surprisingly, Anglo-American business interests preferred a Franco victory and did their best to influence the outcome in the general's favor (Texaco sold oil to Franco's forces).

The Republic had only two dependable foreign allies, Mexico and the Soviet Union, which provided weapons and other material support. Various nations sent volunteers to fight, of course, including the famous Lincoln Brigade from the United States. Fighters for both sides also came from Ireland, England, and France. Yes, the Spanish Civil War was certainly a "rehearsal" for World War II, in which Germany in particular tried out new weapons and tactics and sought to give its fighting men combat experience. But it was also a pan-European civil war, one that exposed deep fault lines between left and right in several countries.

By October 1, the rebels were sufficiently in control of large parts of Spain so that Franco became not only supreme military commander but also head of a new nationalist government. Though Franco's forces failed in their attempt to seize Madrid early on, they made steady progress elsewhere. San Sebastián fell in September, Málaga in February of 1937, and Bilbao in May. By this time, the Germans, Italians, Soviets, and international brigades were all in the thick of it, and the Spanish Civil War had metamorphosed into an international conflict. The Republican government fled from Madrid, first to Valencia and then to Barcelona. Despite occasional Republican offensives, by late 1938, the end was in sight. The nationalists had reached the Mediterranean in April, cutting the Republic in twain, and on January 26, 1939, they entered Barcelona. A month later, France and Britain recognized Franco's government, and a month after that, Madrid was in Franco's possession. He announced the end of the Spanish Civil War on April 1.[41]

Who was this man who had risen from relative obscurity to the post of *caudillo*, supreme leader of his country? Francisco Franco Bahamonde (1892–1975) was an anti-intellectual who sincerely wished the nineteenth century, with its chaos and liberalism, had never happened. He wanted to turn the clock of Spanish history back to the age of the *ancien régime*. He was a thoroughgoing Catholic who intended to support and defend the Church against its enemies, to restore it as the principal

---

[41] An excellent chronology of the conflict is available in Lannon, *The Spanish Civil War*, 11–12.

foundation of Spanish society and culture. He had a "firm conviction that he had been chosen by God to save Spain from irreligion and the atheism that communism represented."[42]

Pragmatic and hardheaded, he was neither sophisticated nor especially articulate, and he did not possess the charisma of either Mussolini or Hitler. But, unlike them, he was a capable (if not brilliant) military leader who knew how to exercise discipline and keep his forces in line. As Boyd puts it, "Franco displayed great skill in balancing competing interests and in imposing a monolithic political and cultural structure that stood in dramatic counterpoint to the fragmentation in the Republican zone."[43]

If one had to identify a single attribute, then, that contributed to Franco's success (and Republican failure), cohesion (or the lack of it) would probably be it. For, by contrast, the leftists had soon come to blows with one another, especially in Barcelona in May 1937, as various factions spent most of their time fighting each other. This pathetic spectacle is the subject of George Orwell's classic *Homage to Catalonia*, based on his personal experiences in that place and time.[44] Franco's ability to hold together his forces was due to his own lack of a clear ideology, something that would have suggested a level of intellectual activity uncharacteristic of him. Thus, in the opinion of Montero Díaz, "Francoism should be understood less as an ideology and more as a manner of exercising political power, maintaining it in its hands without limitations"—but with the objective of holding back communism and its allies, not promoting anything positive.[45]

The Francoists wasted no time exerting their authority and settling scores. The middle class could not object to their ruthlessness, for fear of facing the same retribution and because they had narrowly escaped annihilation at the hands of the extreme left.[46] Estimates vary, but by Thomas's calculations, "Spain may be supposed to have lost nearly 800,000 people in the civil war, including the flower of the new generation, including 500,000 killed and executed during and after, as well as 300,000 emigrés who never returned."[47] These included some of Spain's best artists, writers, and musicians. In a country with a population of about 20 million or so, these losses were simply stunning. They exceeded, in sheer numbers

---

[42] Montero Díaz, "El Franquismo: Planteamiento general," 645.

[43] Boyd, "History, Politics, and Culture, 1936–1975," 91.

[44] George Orwell, *Homage to Catalonia*, intro. Lionel Trilling (Orlando, FL: Harcourt, 1980). However, Orwell states on p. 230 that though the war had left him with "memories that are mostly evil," the result of his experience was "not necessarily disillusionment and cynicism. Curiously enough the whole experience has left me with not less but more belief in the decency of human beings."

[45] Montero Díaz, "El Franquismo: Planteamiento general," 645.

[46] Thomas, *Spanish Civil War*, 898. This helps to explain why Torroba never had much to say about the depredations Franco's forces committed during and after the war.

[47] Ibid., 901. Moreno Juste, "La Guerra Civil (1936–1939)," 545–46, has somewhat different figures: 300,000 deaths; 500,000 exiles (165,000 permanently); 300,000 returnees spent time in jail or internment camps, and as late as 1950, 30,000 were still there.

and percentage of the population, losses resulting from the American Civil War, which lasted a year longer.

The sheer material devastation was also appalling. Eight percent of homes were damaged or destroyed, 40 percent of rolling stock, and 225,000 tons of merchant marine shipping. Industrial production fell 31 percent during the period 1935–39, agricultural production by 21 percent, and national wealth by 25.7 percent. Personal income fell 28.3 percent and would not return to pre-war levels until the early 1950s.[48] The Popular Front had sent Spain's gold reserves to Stalin to pay for weapons, and the loss of these further impoverished the country for years after the war. Of course, the available labor force shrank due to the large number of working-age men killed and maimed in the war. Moreover, a hungry and malnourished population proved highly susceptible to epidemics such as typhus, TB, and dysentery, from which about 200,000 people died in the years 1940-45. On top of everything else, people were cowed by the threat of reprisals. Executions continued long after the war, and at least 28,000 people perished between 1939 and 1945. Repression was especially strong against lawyers and journalists.[49] As Montero Diaz notes, "In reality, the war continued by means of repression."[50]

In yet another irony, the Second World War began just after the Spanish Civil War drew to its exhausted and increasingly inevitable conclusion. Franco, now in absolute control of the entire country, was deeply indebted, both figuratively and literally, to his fascist fellow travelers Mussolini and Hitler, and yet he was determined to travel just so far and no further with them. Though they pressured him to join the Axis, he placed a very high price on doing so: Spain would require Vichy France's colonial possessions in North Africa. Hitler would not accede to this demand, and Franco would not budge. There would be no formal alliance.

When Hitler invaded Russia, however, Franco authorized the formation of volunteer units to aid in fighting Bolshevism, which he perceived as the ultimate threat to Christian civilization. Although Spain sent thousands of soldiers to fight in the Wehrmacht, in which they formed the so-called *División Azúl* (Blue Division, after the blue shirts they wore), Franco placed strict rules of engagement on their participation. They were only to fight against the communists, on the eastern front, and never to be deployed against the Western allies, i.e., Britain and the United States. Obviously, he did not want to incite them to declare war on Spain. And Franco clearly recognized that Hitler's gambit might fail, in which case he

[48] These figures comes from Moreno Juste, "La Guerra Civil (1936–1939)," 546.

[49] Montero Díaz, "El Franquismo: Planteamiento general," 643.

[50] Ibid., 642. Boyd, "History, Politics, and Culture, 1936–1975," 95, points out that "a Law of Political Responsibilities of February 1939 specified a long list of political crimes and applied them retroactively to October 1934. By the end of the year political prisoners officially numbered 270,719. The following year a Law for the Suppression of Masonry and Communism extended the definition of political crimes to include sympathy for doctrines that Franco and his allies deemed incompatible with national values."

would have to treat with the victorious allies. In fact, once the war began to turn in favor of the allies, Franco distanced himself from Hitler and Mussolini, emphasizing his regime's Christian character, in opposition to the pagan nature of Nazism and the anti-clerical bent of Italian fascism.[51] Stalin would never be inclined to forgive and forget, but economic assistance might well come from the West. Better to hope for the best but plan for the worst. In any case, Spain was flat on its back after three years of devastating war, and Franco did not want his country needlessly dragged into an even greater conflict. For all these reasons, then, Franco frustrated Hitler with his repeated refusals to enter the war on the side of the Axis. Despite its obvious pro-Axis stance, Spain remained officially neutral.[52]

In the event, the worst happened, at least from the fascist perspective. During six years of world war, no help had been forthcoming to Spain from any quarter. But the Franco regime was nonetheless tainted by its relationship with Hitler and Mussolini and found itself in the position of international pariah after the war. The United Nations summarily rejected its bid for admission in 1946, and it would receive no share of funds from the Marshall Plan, starting in 1947. Neither was Spain invited to join the North Atlantic Treaty Organization at its founding in 1949—though dictator Salazar's Portugal was! Adding insult to injury, Britain's Foreign Secretary, Hector McNeil, declared that giving Franco weapons would be like "putting a pistol in the hands of a convicted assassin."[53] No wonder that Franco forced his own fascist party, the Falange, to the political margins. It had served its purpose and was no longer necessary; frankly, it was now an embarrassing liability.

In summary, during the 1940s Spain was broke, stagnant, and isolated. Franco had once dreamed of a Spain that was both self-contained and self-sufficient, uncontaminated by compromises with modernity and foreign influence. That dream bubble had now burst. In the postwar era, isolation of that kind spelled economic and political doom. Spain's only hope was to find a way back into the good graces of the West. Two words would prove its salvation: Cold War.

As the United States faced off against the Soviet Union—in a confrontation many feared would complete an unholy trinity of world wars—the enemy of one's enemy now became one's friend. The democracies were soon willing to overlook the nature of Franco's regime in light of his steadfast anticommunism. Spain was to become a valuable bulwark in a global effort to "contain" the "red rot." Nineteen hundred and fifty was a key year in Spain's rehabilitation, as the United States reestablished diplomatic relations and Congress approved $62.5 million in credit.

---

[51] Montero Díaz, "El Franquismo: Planteamiento general," 649.

[52] The best documentary film we have seen on this history is *Franco, Franco, Franco*, a production of Spanish Television (TVE) directed by Elías Andrés (Princeton, New Jersey: Films for the Humanities & Sciences, 2005).

[53] Cited in Marzo, *Art modern i franquisme*, 77.

The United Nations revoked sanctions against Spain in that year, thus paving the way for its integration into international organizations. Further economic assistance was forthcoming in 1953, in which year Spain and the United States cemented economic and military ties, resulting in the establishment of American military bases on Spanish soil the following year and the Eisenhower administration's official recognition of the Franco government in 1955. Spain finally gained admission to the United Nations that same year. Eisenhower made a state visit to Spain in 1959, and this new alliance with the United States opened the door to financial assistance from the International Monetary Fund, which soon poured $46 million into the Spanish economy. These resources made possible revitalization of the Spanish economy, under the guidance of Opus Dei technocrats.[54] Thus, as one historian has put it, "The history of postwar Spain is divided into two fundamental periods: autocracy and neocapitalist normalization."[55]

The 1960s would witness a Spanish-style *Wirtschaftswunder* as a result of these diplomatic and financial coups. Spain was out of the woods, and the emerald towers of Oz beckoned in the distance. It is in this context that we place Torroba's increasing love affair with the United States, especially his affection for Broadway.

Cultural Life under Franco

Franco was obsessed with foreign influence and sought to extirpate all corrupting strains of culture that had accumulated in Spain since the Golden Age. In fact, he was convinced that the history of the previous two centuries was "nothing but the result of a gigantic Masonic conspiracy," which continued to be, with communism, a vital threat to Spain's survival.[56] This may strike us as positively lunatic now, but insofar as Freemasonry was the Church's *bête noir*, and Franco was a devout Catholic, there is a certain logic to his obsession.

According to the stridently anti-intellectual *Caudillo* himself, "the spirit of criticism and reservation is a liberal thing that has no roots in the soil of our movement, and I repeat to you once again that its tone is military and monastic and to discipline and patriotism of the soldier must be added the faith and fervor of the man of religion."[57] Even the conservative writer José María Pemán observed that in Franco's discourses there never appeared so much as "a drop of literature,

---

[54] An excellent summary of these transformative developments is available in Marzo, *Art modern i franquisme*, 121–25.

[55] Manuel Vázquez Montalbán, *Cancionero general del franquismo: 1939–1975.* (Barcelona: Crítica, 2000), xiv.

[56] Fusi, *Un siglo de España*, 100.

[57] From Francisco Franco, *Palabras del Caudillo* (Madrid: Ediciones de la Vicesecretaría de Educación Popular, 1953), 317, and cited in Arango, *Spain: From Repression to Renewal*, 206.

quotation from an author, metaphor, figure of speech, or even a verbal tic." The *Generalísimo* believed that most intellectuals were leftists or communists.[58]

Franco reserved his most venomous diatribes for the nineteenth century, "a century of defeat and decadence [that demands] a revolution. . . . a revolution in the Spanish sense that will destroy an ignominious century of foreign-inspired doctrines that have caused our death. . . . In the name of liberty, fraternity, and equality and all such liberal trivia our churches have been burned and our history destroyed."[59] In short, the nineteenth century "is what we would like to eliminate from our history; it is the negation of the Spanish spirit."[60]

It is true that Torroba's music was not "intellectual" in the sense that it sought to break new ground or to challenge the sense and sensibility of his audiences. Critics like Salazar saw him as basically irrelevant in the movement towards the rejuvenation of Spanish music as they envisioned it, a rejuvenation that popular zarzuelas and lightweight guitar music could not sustain. However, the essentially nonintellectual character of Torroba's music does not make him a perfect fit with the bellicose anti-intellectualism of the Franco regime. It is good to recall that Torroba's entire aesthetic was rooted in the nineteenth century, of which some of his favorite works—*Carmen*, *La bohème*—were products. Moreover, Unamuno, who was to have a profound influence on Torroba's thinking, was also a product of the previous century. As Arango notes, "Unamuno the Hispanist represented for those suffocating in the orthodox, incensed air of Francoism everything that had been and that one might be again sublime in Spanish culture, in Ortega's words, 'the iridescent gem of the Spain that could be.'"[61]

Thus, we must be careful not to associate Torroba with Francoism. True, his conservative style was compatible with the nationalist ethos of the *Nuevo Estado* (New State). Francoism sought to glorify and exalt Spain's imperial past, e.g., the *Siglo de Oro*, El Escorial, Spanish mysticism, and to favor established cultural forms—landscapes and portraits, as well as conventional drama and traditional narrative idealizing Castile and the Castilian landscape. Musical Compositions like these, bearing picturesque titles, fitted hand-in-glove with that agenda, whether or not it was intentional.[62] However, in the final analysis, the roots of his style and its philosophical underpinnings were utterly alien to Franco's prejudices and predilections. This is a subtle but crucial distinction.

It comes as no surprise that the cultural preferences of the Franco regime and its censors were very conservative. What does surprise is that, over time, they became much more tolerant, not for aesthetic reasons but rather for political and economic

---

[58] Cited in Fusi, *Un siglo de España*, 100.

[59] From Franco, *Palabras del Caudillo*, 54, and cited in Arango, *Spain: From Repression to Renewal*, 206.

[60] From a speech delivered on June 21, 1950, and cited in Fusi, *Un siglo de España*, 107.

[61] Arango, *Spain: From Repression to Renewal*, 207–08.

[62] Fusi, *Un siglo de España*, 103.

aims on the international stage. The regime's principal concerns were that cultural manifestations not incite resistance to the regime and that they respect, at all times, the prerogatives and sensitivities of the Church. As one expert has summarized it:

> Academies and cultural institutions were purged, together with many of those scientists and artists who had not fled to exile abroad. The Press Act of 1938 imposed censorship and State monopoly control over information.... The official culture of Francoism combined fervent nationalism with equally fervent Catholicism. Its artistic predilection was for traditional styles.[63]

There was no question that Castile, meaning Madrid, was the incontestable center of the Spanish universe, and the regime actively suppressed local languages, like Catalan, Basque, and Galician, in order to take the wind out of separatist sails once and for all. What rose in the place of regional and high culture, former arenas for the expression of political dissidence, was "evasion culture," that is, "football, bullfighting, film, radio, popular fiction and gossip magazines."[64] These forms of cultural recreation were safe and noncontroversial, though the regime still sought to gain complete control of media access to them, especially radio, cinema, and, later, television.[65] Evasion culture also included zarzuela. Movies were the most popular form of public entertainment, especially Hollywood films, though these were censored and dubbed to control their content.[66]

One does not find in Francoism the notion of "degenerate art," or *enartete Kunst* (code for Jewish art), that preoccupied Hitler and the Nazis, or the "bourgeois decadence" and "formalism" that Stalinism demonized. Francoism eschewed the sort of social mobilization and militant culture of both Nazism and communism; thus, the ardent anti-intellectualism of Francoist culture "indirectly fomented tolerance through a type of forcibly acritical cultural production."[67] As a consequence, there was instead a conspicuous "lack of a definite and consistently applied music policy."[68] The dominant theme of the Francoist cultural project was cleansing and purification, of academic faculty, curricula, and libraries, through repression, censorship, and control. But, again, this was fundamentally negative and reactive. In truth, "Francoism did not initiate a new cultural period, as there was a continuity with the preceding period."[69] This is important to bear in mind

[63] "Cultural Policy in Spain," 4.

[64] Ibid.

[65] Vázquez Montalbán, *Cancionero general del franquismo*, xiv.

[66] Fusi, *Un siglo de España*, 109–10.

[67] Álvaro Ferrary and Antonio Moreno Juste, "La vida cultural: Limitaciones, condicionantes y desarrollo. El Franquismo," in *Historia contemporánea de España, siglo XX*, 856–57.

[68] Eva Moreda-Rodríguez, "Italian Musicians in Francoist Spain, 1939–1945: The Perspective of Music Critics," *Music & Politics* 2/1 (Winter 2008): 10.

[69] Ibid., 857.

when considering Torroba's music before and after the Civil War, because it helps to explain why the Franco regime had no effect on his style whatsoever. He continued to compose the same way he had before, as the regime neither suppressed nor encouraged his work—as long as it did not cast the Catholic religion in an unfavorable light. Torroba was not inclined to do any such thing, though as we will see, his zarzuela *Monte Carmelo* (1939) ran afoul of the censors. Indeed, as Tomás Marco has noted, Franco turned Spain into a sort of "confessional state," in which the Church and its teachings pervaded every aspect of its life. This resulted in an evasion of all "internal evolution" and the "absence of information from abroad." It bears repetition that, unlike the Nazi and Stalin regimes, the Franco regime "did not have an official ideology in regards to music…there was no official musical line."[70]

As part of the campaign to clean up education, the Ley Universitaria of 1943 placed the universities under the aegis of the Church. Ironically, it was in these same church-run universities that the seeds of sedition were planted. As Arango notes, "Some of the earliest dialogue that quietly and obliquely questioned the regime took place among progressive Catholic elite academics. They revered Teilhard de Chardin, one of the most celebrated living exponents of liberal Catholicism."[71] Universities became hotbeds not only of intellectual liberalization but also of social critique and democratization.[72] So-called Liberation Theology was also a product of this liberalization within the Church.

Moreover, what started in the universities soon spread to other sectors of Spanish culture. A spirit of protest and critique erupted in art in 1957 with the Madrid group El Paso, which promoted abstract art.[73] This paralleled developments in composition with the Generation of 51, led by Luis de Pablo, and the development of atonal, twelve-tone, and electronic music in Spain.

The Musical Parallel

With the return to power of the conservatives in 1933, the make-up of the Junta Nacional de Música y Teatros Líricos soon changed, much to the dismay of the avant-garde. The new prime minister, Filiberto Villalobos, began to roll back the reforms of the previous government, and the more progressive members of the previous Junta were replaced by Alberto Romea, Serafín Álvarez Quintero, Turina, and Torroba.[74] Salazar could not have been happy to see a *zarzuelero* (other than

[70] Tomás Marco, "Los años cuarenta," in *España en la música de Occidente*, 401.

[71] Arango, *Spain: From Repression to Renewal*, 209.

[72] Fusi, *Un siglo de España*, 126.

[73] Ibid., 128.

[74] Javier Suárez-Pajares, "El periodo de Entreguerras como ámbito de estudio de la música española," *Mundoclasico.com*, February 21, 2002.

Vives) on the Junta, as he distrusted the zarzuela in general and Torroba's music in particular as inimical to the modernist agenda for enriching and deepening musical life in Spain. The Junta ran throughout the Republic, until it was replaced by the Consejo Central de la Música in 1938. This entity included such prominent progressives as Salvador Bacarisse, Rodolfo Halffter, Julián Bautista, and Roberto Gerhard, but not Torroba, who had by this time had fled to Navarra.

It comes as no surprise that the dramatic events of this era had a decided impact on music. First and foremost, the Civil War forestalled indefinitely the reforms launched by the Republican government in 1931. With the outbreak of hostilities, the government's main concern was survival. Second, the conflict and its aftermath sent many of Spain's leading composers and critics into exile, either temporary or permanent. Predictably, most of these were progressives like Salazar and Rodolfo Halffter, people whose avant-garde aesthetics tracked otherwise liberal social and political attitudes. Among the leading lights in exile were Esplà, Bacarisse, Bautista, Pittaluga, María Rodrigo, Rosa Ascot, Casals, Enrique Casal Chapí, and Catalans Gerhard and Jaime Pahissa. This exodus resulted in what Fernández-Cid described as an "undeniable vacuum in composition" during the 1940s.[75] Tomás Marco viewed the evaporation of the Generation of 27 during the Civil War as "one of the greatest cataclysms in the history of Spanish music, and therefore left an indelible mark on the music composition in the 40s."[76]

Marco is further of the opinion that the 1940s were "one of the most sterile periods" in Spanish music.[77] That does not mean there were no notable achievements. After all, the year 1939 had witnessed the birth of one of the most popular and influential concertos of the twentieth century, Rodrigo's Concierto de Aranjuez for guitar and orchestra (composed in Paris). Rodrigo and several other nonexiled composers would remain productive during this period, even if the international resonance of their music would not come anywhere near the standard set by the Aranjuez. Composers active at this time included Turina, though his works from this decade said little that his earlier compositions had not revealed. A short list of notable works might include: Conrado del Campo's En la pradera; Jesús Guridi's Diez melodias vascas; Ernesto Halffter's Rapsodia portuguesa for piano; and Xavier Montsalvatge's Sinfonia mediterranea. Moreover, Joaquín Homs, the only disciple of serialist Roberto Gerhard, wrote chamber music in an avant-garde, atonal style. The advent of the Orquesta Nacional stimulated a public for symphonic music, which flowered in the concertos of Rodrigo for guitar, piano, and violin. By the mid-1960s, Casal Chapí, Pittaluga, Ascot, and Esplá returned to Spain.[78]

---

[75] Antonio Fernández-Cid, La década musical de los cuarenta. Discurso del académico electo ... el día 30 noviembre de 1980, con motivo de su recepción (Madrid: Real Academia de Bellas Artes de San Fernando, 1980), 10.

[76] Marco, "Los años cuarenta," 401.

[77] Ibid., 399.

[78] See Suárez-Pajares, "El periodo de Entreguerras."

Yet, worthy though these efforts may be, they are the exceptions that prove the rule. Though Falla's neoclassicism had been highly experimental in the 1920s and 30s, the musical vocabulary he utilized was now devoid of the spirit in which it originated. What prevailed during this period is what Marco calls "nationalism by archetypes," i.e., musical works informed by urban folklore, zarzuela, and "conventional *andalucismo*."[79] Thus, Spanish music was increasingly divorced not only from foreign trends but from the intellectual world altogether. This form of musical nationalism could easily be incorporated into the *Caudillo*'s broader vision of the New Spain—veneration of tradition, rejection of foreign elements, exaltation of folklore, and patriotism. Marco labels it *nacionalismo casticismo*, a sort of neoclassical nationalism, rather than avant-garde.[80]

Spain's musical isolation was reinforced and protracted by the nature of musical education under Franco. The clergy dominated music education at every level, and their tastes in music were very conservative. The regime's indifference to music meant that state support declined markedly over that provided by the Republic. In turn, this would produce a reduction in the musical public, a public of limited means that increasingly spent its meager disposable income on other forms of entertainment. And, as Marco notes, parents were not keen to see their children take up music as a profession, precisely because it was not remunerative.[81] (We already saw this attitude on display in Torroba's father's attempts to steer him away from a musical career.)

It does not follow, however, that those who remained behind were supporters of or necessarily sympathetic to the Franco regime, simply that they felt they had more to gain by staying than leaving. Neither does it follow that conservatives and Catholics all remained behind. One such, Manuel de Falla, decamped for Argentina at war's end and never returned.

The departure of the Spanish avant-garde and Spain's economic and diplomatic isolation in the wake of the Second World War meant that Spanish composers were largely disconnected from the European mainstream. As Casares points out, the advent of total serialism around 1948 was "irrelevant" in Spain.[82] This is not to say at all that music did not flourish during and after the war. In addition to renowned performers like Segovia, cellist Gaspar Cassadó, conductor Eduardo Toldrá, outstanding composers such as Federico Mompou, Xavier Montsalvatge, and Ernesto Halffter—not to mention Campo, Torroba, Rodrigo, and Turina—continued to create. And, in fact, both the right and the left had found music useful as a propaganda tool, and for maintaining some semblance of normalcy. Patriotic hymns were popular on both sides, and zarzuelas continued to be done as well.

---

[79] Marco, "Los años cuarenta," 404.

[80] Tomás Marco, *Spanish Music in the Twentieth Century*, 129–41, for a discussion of this idea.

[81] Marco, "Los años cuarenta," 410.

[82] Casares, "La música española hasta 1939," 264.

Indeed, though it is tempting to view the decline of the zarzuela as beginning in the 1940s, it continued to play a vital cultural role. As Plácido Domingo recalls,

> A great many zarzuelas were being written.... In those days zarzuela singers performed once or twice every weekday and twice or three times on Sundays. Many works were given a hundred or even two hundred performances and as soon as a company stopped performing one zarzuela, another was immediately mounted.[83]

As examples of new works composed after the war, one could cite not only Torroba's *Monte Carmelo* (1939) and *La Caramba* (1942) but also Sorozábal's *Black, el payaso* (1942) and *Don Manolito* (1943), as well as Pablo Luna's *Las Calatravas* (1941) and José Serrano's *La venta de los gatos* (1943).[84] Not everyone celebrates this fact, however. Marco in particular feels that the zarzuela's apparent rebirth was merely "artificial" and could not prevent its demise. This was not altogether a bad thing, in his view, because it had become "a true obstacle to the advancement of Spanish music.... [It] absorbed efforts of potential symphonists who could only make a living writing zarzuelas. It also impeded the development of Spanish opera."[85] Later commentators, such as Carlos Gómez Amat, have dismissed such derogations of the zarzuela as "nonsense." "One only wishes that opera, symphonic and chamber music had fulfilled the social and artistic function as well as the zarzuela managed to do in its golden years."[86] For his part, Torroba felt that only the zarzuela was truly autochthonous, truly Spanish. Symphonies and operas were not, and hence it was not necessary for Spanish composers to cultivate them.

That sort of dialectic remained strictly academic, however, as changing tastes, not ideological arguments, would determine the zarzuela's destiny. Even as the *cuplé* and *revista* had competed with the zarzuela in the prewar era, now the genre faced stiff competition from sporting events, cinema, and the television, so that "by 1951 reporters no longer noted new works and a flurry of zarzuela production but referred instead to 'a revival of zarzuela.'"

Another new technology, the long-playing record (LP), made possible the formation of a canon of zarzuela classics in the 1950s, on such labels as Montilla, Soria, Angel, London, and Columbia. In fact, this was not a matter of happenstance but rather one of official state policy, as the regime "tried to encourage the production of zarzuela and lent support to a series of zarzuela recordings devoted to documenting the genre. These efforts helped to turn a handful of works into

---

[83] Cited in Sturman, *Zarzuela*, 24.

[84] Fernández-Cid, *La década musical de los cuarenta*, 17.

[85] Marco, "Los años cuarenta," 400.

[86] Carlos Gómez Amat, "*Luisa Fernanda* and Its Time," liner notes for *Luisa Fernanda* (Auvidis Valois, V 4759, 1995), 23.

classics."[87] Of course, this process of canon formation attended the zarzuela's installation in the museum of cultural history, not as a living, thriving tradition but as an artifact of a bygone era, one increasingly associated by young people with the regime.

The available statistics bear out the gradual decline of live theater and the zarzuela in the face of cinematic competition. In 1908, for instance, when Madrid had a population of about a half million people, there were thirty-five theaters.[88] A decade later, there were twenty-four theaters (and 215 premieres).[89] In the week of July 18, 1936, there were offerings from eight theaters, four of them dedicated to zarzuela. By contrast, there were already forty-five movie theaters in Madrid. Clearly, the inroads made by cinema sounded the death knell for zarzuela. By the end of the Civil War, there were seventeen theaters for dramatic presentations, three for variety shows—and twenty-four for movies.[90]

During the Civil War, Zaragoza and San Sebastián were the chief centers in the nationalist zone for musical theater, while Madrid, Valencia, and Barcelona served that purpose for the Republicans. In spite of chaos and turmoil, symphonic music persisted as well. There were also numerous choral and instrumental ensembles in Madrid and Barcelona. Burgos, capital of the Francoists, was home to the Orquesta Sinfónica Patriótica de Zaragoza, though Fernández-Cid wryly opines that this was "more patriotic than symphonic."[91] In the opinion of Suárez-Pajares, one of the main reasons that both sides promoted music was that the "war resulted in a conception of the clearly political and social uses of music."[92]

The so-called culture of evasion featured popular songs, which assumed (or retained) great importance. Light song, disseminated on the radio, included *canciones andaluzas*, zarzuela numbers, boleros, *canciónes mexicanas*, as well as French, Italian, and Spanish romantic melodies.[93] A dominant tendency among the popular songs of the 1940s was "sentimentalism, based on the theme of love, friendship and solidarity, with a slow foxtrot or bolero rhythm."[94] In fact, the nationalist impetus sought to affirm Spanish uniqueness through song, to assert individualism in contradistinction to Marxist ideas about collectivism and communitarianism.[95]

---

[87] The quotes in this and the preceding paragraph are from Sturman, *Zarzuela*, 24.

[88] J. Francos Rodríguez, *El teatro en España. 1908* (Madrid, 1908), 229, and cited in Andrés Amorós, "Los espectáculos," *La Edad de Plata de la cultura española (1898–1936)*, vol. 2: *Letras, ciencia, arte, sociedad y culturas*, ed. Pedro Laín Entralgo (Madrid: Espasa Calpe, 1994), 783.

[89] Ricardo de la Fuente Ballesteros, *Introducción al teatro español del siglo XX (1900–1936)* (Aceña, Valladolid, 1987), 11, and cited in Amorós, "Los espectáculos," 783.

[90] Amorós, "Los espectáculos," 783–84.

[91] Fernández-Cid, *La década musical de los cuarenta*, 9.

[92] Casares, "La música española hasta 1939," 321.

[93] Fusi, *Un siglo de España*, 115.

[94] Vázquez Montalbán, *Cancionero general del franquismo*, xvi.

[95] Ibid., xix.

The eminent American Hispanist and musicologist Gilbert Chase offered some choice contemporary commentary on the conflict's impact on music, revealing his own decidedly right-wing views. These are useful in gauging how many people, both inside and outside of Spain, viewed the prospect of a Franco triumph.

> It is very probable that the revival of historical feeling and traditional sentiment inherent in the Nationalist movement will have an effect upon the creative artistic activity of Spain.

No doubt Chase believed that the effect would be positive, as he cited with approbation the fact that

> long before the conclusion of the war the Nationalist regime had shown its concern with musical culture by creating a Department of Musicology as an adjunct of the Ministry of the Interior. Selected to head this department was P[adre] Nemesio Otaño, prominent Basque composer and musicologist, editor of the review *Música Sacro-Hispana* from 1907 to 1922, and of the collection "Antología de Organistas Españoles." ... At the summer courses in Spanish history and culture held for foreign students in Santander last summer [i.e., 1938], an important place was accorded to musical subjects. [In addition to Higinio Anglés], other musicians who took part in the musical courses at Santander were Regino Sainz de la Maza [and] the composer Federico Moreno Torroba, best known for his pieces for guitar, who gave three lectures on contemporary Spanish music.

Chase further claimed to have received a published statement from Manuel de Falla approving the "Nationalist movement as a check to anti-religious activities and godless ideologies."[96] It is unlikely that Torroba's views, which he never made public, differed substantially from Falla's, at least as reported by Chase. His collaboration at Santander placed him firmly in the traditionalist camp, though his motivation for doing so was probably twofold: 1) a genuine interest in the subject of Spanish music and its traditional sources, and 2) a desire to go along to get along. We will see in Scene ii that non-cooperation was not an alternative. Not surprisingly, the study of Renaissance music in particular dovetailed with the regime's glorification of the *Siglo de Oro* and Spanish mysticism. As Pérez Zalduondo puts it, the regime "identified the music of the great polyphonists [like Victoria] with the Spanish tradition, the Spanish race with the Catholic faith, and

[96] All of these quotes appear in Gilbert Chase, "Spanish Musicians Since the Civil War." *The Musical Times* (July 1939): 499–500.

all of this with the imperial past."[97] Thus, musicology had an important role to play in affirming national greatness.

In any case, soon after the war, the regime created its answer to the Republican's Junta, i.e., the Comisaria de la Música, which included Jesuit conductor Padre Nemesio Otaño, pianist José Cubiles, and Turina. Though its aims were less ambitious and more conservative that those of the Republican Junta that preceded it, there was no slackening of effort or standards. It did not have much in the way of resources to work with, but it sought to restore musical life as best it could. Marco has noted the ironical fact that "many of the initiatives of the Comisaria coincided with the Plan Salazar."[98] Certainly its revival of the Orquesta Nacional and creation of the Agrupación Nacional de Música de Camara were consistent with the Republic's aims, though these goals were impeded by the loss of so many orchestral musicians, now in exile or in prisons, hospitals, and graves.

The 1950s represented a transitional period out of the relative doldrums for the revival of Spanish music, and the postwar avant-garde found a more or less permanent niche in the Spanish soundscape. We have seen already that there was an ongoing debate within musical circles about the relationship between Spanish musicians and intellectuals. Some, like Salazar, felt there was too great a disconnect between them. The general attitude was that, as Suárez-Pajares notes, the non-intellectuality of Spanish musicians resulted in a preference for zarzuela over symphony.[99] With the decline of the zarzuela and the growing market for symphonic music, however, there was a gradual shift in the musical winds. Most of the composers of the new generation were educated at institutions of higher learning. They were musicians as well as intellectuals, in a manner that many of their forebears found essential. As Rodolfo Halffter had expressed it:

> For us, the composer was also an intellectual who should take his place alongside other intellectuals in the cultural life of the country during the agitated history through which we lived.[100]

Halffter and others like him, such as Padre Otaño, felt that history, literature, and aesthetics should form the foundation of a composer's education. They decried the tendency of talented young people to go to the conservatory simply to acquire a set of mechanical skills without exposure to the broader world of ideas that would inform and inspire their work.[101]

---

[97] Gemma Pérez Zalduondo, "Formulación, fracaso y despertar de la conciencia crítica en la música española durante el franquismo (1936–1958)," in *Music and Dictatorship in Europe and Latin America*, ed. Roberto Illiano and Massimiliano Sala (Turnhout: Brepols, 2009), 451.

[98] Marco, "Los años cuarenta," 407.

[99] Ibid., 400.

[100] Casares, *Música y músicos*, 38

[101] Marco, "Los años cuarenta,"409.

One of the great ironies of the Franco era was that, in spite of its strident anti-intellectualism, it produced a new generation of composers who were in many respects far more intellectual than most of their predecessors, and far more attuned to developments beyond the Pyrenees. The regime did not actively suppress this activity precisely because it dovetailed conveniently with Franco's desire for international rehabilitation, for acceptance by the West and the economic assistance that acceptance would bring along with it. And like abstract art, atonal and electronic music did not have the subversive and revolutionary potential of other types of music, especially musical theater. In other words, it was pretty safe. Thus, Stravinsky was welcomed during his return visit to Spain in 1955, and works by Bartók and Hindemith were once more taught in music conservatories. Concerts occasionally featured works by the Second Viennese School, as well as by Messiaen, Dallapiccola, and Petrassi. Spain was readmitted to the International Society for Contemporary Music (ISCM) in 1955, and the music of Catalan dodecaphonist Joaquim Homs (1906–2003) represented Spain at the Stockholm Festival the following year.[102]

The seeds sown in the 1950s would germinate in the 1960s, as we shall see in Act III, but the outcome was neither a victory for the traditionalists nor the avant-garde but rather for a new kind of music.

---

[102] Pérez Zalduondo, "Formulación, fracaso y despertar de la conciencia crítica en la música española durante el franquismo (1936–1958)," 467–68.

5

ACT II
Scene ii
Navarro
1932–60

The first four decades of Torroba's life witnessed his rise from lower-middle-class obscurity and a lackluster academic career to the pinnacle of musical stardom in Madrid. *Luisa Fernanda*, his first major hit, placed him in the front rank of zarzuela composers past and present; in addition, his position as impresario at the Calderón gave him an unprecedented platform from which to launch future successes.

Indeed, Torroba's music dominated the 1932–33 season at the Calderón. Two of the premieres were his own zarzuelas, **Azabache** (August 18, 1932), set in Andalusia, and **Xuanón** (March 2, 1933), set in Asturias. Three of his previous zarzuelas were revived and added to the repertory along with works by Vives[1] and Chapí. Among the revivals was *Luisa Fernanda*, frequently billed as one of the two performances each night. Seldom did a week pass when at least one of Torroba's zarzuelas was not on the stage. He recalled this epoch with some fondness, and pride, many years later:

> I remember that *La Caramba* earned me a lot of money. *La Chulapona* and *Maravilla* were performed two hundred times, one after the other, at the Teatro Fontalba. I started out as an impresario at the Teatro del Centro, today the Teatro Calderón. With scarcely 4,000 pesetas you could mount a work and maintain the enterprise. I spent nine years as impresario at the Centro and later went to the Teatro de la Zarzuela. At the highpoint of *Luisa Fernanda*, I had three companies.[2]

---

[1] Torroba felt a special affinity with Vives, based in part on personal acquaintance. In Valera, "Federico Moreno Torroba," 21, he was asked if he knew Vives well: "Well, yes, because when he was sick in bed, he entrusted me with orchestrating the intermedio of *Talismán*, which was the last work he composed."

[2] Colmenero, "Lírico Moreno Torroba." It remains unclear in exactly what sense he had three distinct companies, or what their respective names and venues were. Perhaps they were three different companies at the Calderón itself.

As an impresario, he had the opportunity to assess many voices. He later cited among his favorites: "Emilio Sagi-Barba, Felisa Herrero, and Matilde Vázquez. Felisa premiered the roles of *La Chulapona*, *La Marchenera*, *Matilde*, and *La Caramba*. Sagi-Barba appeared in...*La Pastorela*."[3] Plácido Domingo placed his own mother, Pepita Embil Domingo, in this select group. His parents had met while singing Torroba's zarzuela *Sor Navarra* in 1938, and she was evidently among the favorite sopranos not only of Torroba but also Sorozábal, Guerrero, and others. In fact, according to Plácido, Torroba used to say that "she *was* Luisa Fernanda."[4] Plácido's father also earned the composer's encomiums. Torroba told Plácido, Jr., that "no-one had ever sung the lines 'Ay mi morena, morena clara...' [from *Luisa Fernanda*] so well and meaningfully as my father."[5]

So successful was Torroba as an impresario, so impressively had he advanced the cause of Spanish musical theater, that in 1933 the Junta de la Música y Teatros Líricos presented him one of two annual awards for best impresario (the other went to Luis Calvo in Barcelona). This honor netted him the handsome sum of 25,000 *pesetas*.[6]

Since Adolfo Salazar was a member of the Junta at that time, he might have been among those who approved the award. Yet, his attitude toward the zarzuela would remain ambivalent. On occasion, he seemed to approve of it, at least the best examples. For instance, he declared that "In his zarzuelas, Barbieri brought about that creation of the Madrilenian style developed so delightfully by Bretón, Chapí, Chueca, the Valverdes, and other lesser talents."[7] No scent of snobbery there. And he thought very highly of Vives's work, so much so that he was actually pleased with the public's negative response to *Talismán* (1932) because it confirmed his elitist view of the superiority of Vives and inferiority of the public. As Sánchez Sánchez has written on this subject, the *zarzuelistas* themselves felt little rapport with the Junta, its aims and overreaching power, which extended into the cultural marketplace that the zarzuela composers already dominated. After the lurch to the right in 1933, the Junta became "a mere consultative organ within the Ministry, presided over by the sub-secretary of Public Instruction and Fine Arts."[8]

---

[3] Cortés-Cavanillas, "El maestro Moreno Torroba," 47.

[4] Pablo Zinger, "Son of Zarzuela," *Opera News* (July 1997). There is a famous chorus of returning expatriates in Caballero's beloved zarzuela *Gigantes y cabezudos*; however, though Plácido's family left Spain in 1946 with Torroba's company, the Domingo family remained expatriates. They felt comfortable in Mexico and stayed on, forming a zarzuela company in Guadalajara. Plácido's parents actually fell in love during the 1938 production of *Sor Navarra*. "There is a moment in *Sor Navarra* when the soprano declares her love for the baritone, and after three months of performing the piece together, my father and mother got married." See Plácido Domingo, *My First Forty Years* (New York: Alfred A. Knopf, 1983), 7.

[5] Plácido Domingo, liner notes for *Luisa Fernanda* (Auvidis Valois, V 4759, 1995), 28.

[6] Suárez-Pajares, "Moreno Torroba, Federico," *Diccionario de la zarzuela: España e Hispanoamérica*.

[7] Adolfo Salazar, *Music in Our Time*, trans. Isabel Pope (New York: W. W. Norton, 1946), 305.

[8] Víctor Sánchez Sánchez, "Un zarzuelista en la Junta Nacional de Música. *Talismán* de Vives, como modelo para el Teatro Lírico Nacional," in *Música y cultura en la Edad de Plata, 1915–1939*, ed. María Nagore, Leticia Sánchez de Andrés, and Elena Torres (Madrid: ICCMU, 2009), 545.

However, disdain for the genre is also evident in the writings of some of the most eminent Spanish musicologists of recent history, including Federico Sopeña, who not only deemed zarzuela inferior to Italian opera but also felt that it deflected Spain's best composers of musical theater from creating an indigenous brand of opera, i.e., *ópera española*, on a level comparable to that of other national traditions, especially Italian.[9] As we have seen, however, others, including Salazar, thought that Spanish opera was a doomed enterprise. On this point, he and Torroba were *en rapport*, and Torroba chose not to chase the chimera of opera but rather to pursue zarzuela with adamantine resolve.

Thus, Torroba never allowed his organizational efforts to impede his creative work as a composer. In fact, this same year of 1933 witnessed the premiere of a work many—including Torroba himself—regard as one of his very best, if not very best known: *La chulapona*. As we noted earlier, it remains one of the ironies of Torroba's career in musical theater that his most popular work, *Luisa Fernanda*, was not necessarily his personal favorite. Apparently those laurels went to *La chulapona* and *Monte Carmelo* (1939).[10]

> *Luisa Fernanda* is good because the people love it, and I write for the people. For myself, *La Chulapona* pleases me a great deal. It seems to me to be a very direct work, very characteristic. But musically, *Monte Carmelo* is my favorite.[11]

Like a protective parent, Torroba was saddened to see the extraordinary success of one offspring eclipse the achievements of her siblings:

> Of course, I am grateful for the success of *Luisa Fernanda*, but understandably I lament the fact that other beloved daughters are now forgotten: *La Chulapona*, which is finally being done more; *Monte Carmelo*, a work of which I am very fond; *La Caramba*, which enjoyed enormous success and was presented two hundred times to full houses; and many others, [which,] for diverse reasons, such as problems with the cast, the inertia and convenience of those choosing repertoire, etc. [are rarely seen.][12]

[9] Federico Sopeña, *Historia de la música española contemporánea* (Madrid: Ediciones Rialp, 1958), 20–21.

[10] One of many interviews in which Torroba made this disclosure was "Las 15 mil representaciones de la zarzuela 'Luisa Fernanda,'" *El Comercio* (Buenos Aires), February 1, 1981. Another is Mallo, "Los noventa jovenes años."

[11] Imbuluzqueta, "El compositor Federico Moreno Torroba."

[12] J. L. García del Busto, "Moreno Torroba estrena dos piezas 'para ser cantadas por el pueblo,'" *El País*, November 6, 1981. According to Federico, Jr., "*La Caramaba* takes place in the era of Goya. La Caramba was a happy, informal, and not very serious rich woman from Granada, who moved in the circles of Madrid nobility, and with Goya. She introduced a new fashion among her royal friends by wearing a big ribbon on her head." This is from the manuscript of an undated talk Federico, Jr., gave in the United States, possibly in San Diego. The manuscript is in the family archive in Navarra.

Still, it was precisely this acceptance of the public's judgment, his willingness to cater to their tastes, which was central to his success. Federico, Jr., later gave an illustration of Torroba's sensitivity and receptivity to the audience's preferences in this regard. Concerning his addition of some crowd-pleasing vocal fireworks to one of the numbers in *La Caramba*,

> There was a song for contralto that ended very softly, fading out perfectly, and the public gave it polite applause. Torroba then said, "They don't like it." He revised the final eight measures or so...to make the ending more Italianate, more dramatic.... This time the audience reacted very favorably. The Spanish public likes to leave the theater raving about the soprano's high notes![13]

In fact, Torroba shared the audience's love of high notes, sometimes to the consternation of the singers themselves. Soprano María Dolores Travesedo recalls a few occasions when Torroba was conducting, and as she hit a concluding high note, he would stretch out his arms and push her to hold it until she thought she would choke! One such instance occurred at the end of the ever-popular "Mazurka of the Parasols" in *Luisa Fernanda*.[14]

The disparity between the success of *Luisa Fernanda* and his other zarzuelas provoked from Torroba the rueful observation that though he had composed over seventy works for the stage, only a small handful, i.e., *Luisa Fernanda* and two or three others, had any staying power.[15] Torroba knew the history of the zarzuela as well as anyone, and he noted that even during the genre's heyday, the public rejected a great number of works. The silver lining of this cloud was the proof it offered of the public's passionate engagement with zarzuela. Torroba cited Bretón's *La verbena de la paloma* and Vives's *Bohemios* as examples of works that were initially received with indifference but later became "models of the genre." He also mentioned Luna, Guerrero, and Sorozábal as important composers of zarzuela.[16] Unfailingly modest, he went on to say that "Neither do I want to deny my failures: I have had them, some of them noisy; neither do I want to deny the attacks of the press and, on occasion, a great embarrassment." He noted that even *Luisa Fernanda* had gotten some bad notices, which were no indication of its future (successful) trajectory.[17]

---

[13] Interview with William Krause, Madrid, July 18, 1988.

[14] From an interview with William Krause, Madrid, June 6–11, 2010.

[15] Mallo, "Los noventa jovenes años."

[16] Torroba once praised Jacinto Guerrero, composer of *El huésped del sevillano*, saying that "he was a very critical man, but I admired him for his great sense of theater, being able to triumph with a zarzuela like *Los gavilanes* or a *revista* like *La blanca doble*." See Mallo, "Los noventa jovenes años."

[17] Torroba states this in an undated manuscript in the family archive entitled "Aventuras y desventuras de la zarzuela como género." It was the text of a lecture, but when and where he gave it remain unknown. He cites as seminal works Chapí's *revoltosa* and Giménez's *La tempranica*, and he

Proof of such inexplicable vicissitudes is at hand with *La chulapona*: after its premiere, it would wait thirty-five years before another production in Madrid.[18] Again, Torroba realized that he was not alone in this regard:

> Chapí wrote 160 works, and only 3 endure. It's a national disgrace, and I don't understand it. A foreign author premieres three works *total*, and all three endure. Is it due to the good judgment of the composer? To some idiosyncrasy of the foreign public? The fact is that, there, a composer writes four or five works and becomes a millionaire. In Spain, we live, but we don't make grand fortunes writing music.[19]

One senses that Torroba was idealizing the situation foreign composers endured. Few would ever make a million dollars, though some writers of Broadway musicals did quite well, and it was no doubt those composers he was primarily referring to. It is not clear why this issue of relative incomes bothered him as much as it seems to have. He made a considerable amount of money from his music, lived very comfortably as a result, and otherwise rarely expressed frustration or disappointment with his financial lot in life. In fact, he was basically a contented man. True, he was quite convinced that though *Luisa Fernanda* had made him a lot of money, "any American composer in my situation would be a multimillionaire." Still, he could truthfully say with satisfaction that "I live well." And he did.[20]

This complaint about money was merely one element in a larger complex of grievances filed under the general heading of "The Zarzuela Doesn't Get Enough Respect," especially from the government. He always felt that the Spanish government should do more to protect and promote the zarzuela as a priceless and uniquely Spanish art form. Just as the Roman senator Cato ended every speech, regardless of its theme, with the injunction "Carthage must be destroyed,"[21]

emphasizes the influence of Viennese operetta in *La Generala* of Vives and *El trust de los tenorios* of Serrano. He notes that Vives's *Doña Fracisquita* was inspired by *La discreta enamorada* of Lope de Vega, and goes on to state his belief that this zarzuela "established a model from which the genre evolved, serving as a springboard for future creations."

[18] This observation appears in "La zarzuela nacional," *Cambio* 16/405 (September 9, 1979), 52. *La chulapona* was revived by the Centro Cultural de la Villa de Madrid in 1979, as part of a zarzuela festival. This article remarked that the work was a "virtual novelty" because so much time had elapsed since its last production. However, Gómez Marco, program notes, 33–37, summarizes a more impressive history of recording. A piano roll of the Mazurka from Act I appeared already in 1934. Two 78s from 1936 offer two excerpts, including "Ese pañuelito blanco." The Pasodoble was recorded in 1955 for Phillips Iberica on the Alhambra label, and in 1974, Plácido Domingo recorded the Romanza for Columbia. Ataulfo Argenta recorded the whole zarzuela for Columbia between 1954 and 1957, and that remained the only complete recording until 1988, at which time a DVD of the Teatro de la Zarzuela production that year became available from Spanish Television.

[19] Imbuluzqueta, "El compositor Federico Moreno."

[20] San Martín, "Federico Moreno Torroba."

[21] "Carthago delenda est." This is the *locus classicus* of the passive-periphrastic construction that every student of Latin learns.

so, too, Torroba rarely passed up an opportunity to castigate the government for doing too little on behalf of the zarzuela. We will take up this doleful state of affairs further on, and again in Act III, Scene ii.

In any case, in regards to the difference between the public's and Torroba's assessments of his works, conductor and noted interpreter of Torroba's works Miguel Roa has sided with the composer, saying of *Luisa Fernanda*, "it is not his best work, though not far off that mark. I maintain that his best work is *La Chulapona*, largely because it had the best libretto Torroba ever worked with. It is a bon-bon." He further insisted that our *compositor madrileño* contributed "great modernity" to the zarzuela.[22] Not everyone has shared this opinion, however. Critic Fernando Pérez Ollo asserted that,

> Though some pages of *Luisa Fernanda* stand out in the history of the genre and would be essential in any anthology, [in the case of] *La Chulapona*, no. Among the reasons are that the story is simple and hackneyed, the humor lacks impact, and the atmosphere of the work exudes a *casticismo madrilenista* undeniably derived from earlier models. The libretto has little of interest and too many characters...who are irrelevant to the drama. However, Torroba's music makes us forget all this and saves the work.[23]

This is a minority opinion, not one shared by us but offered here for the sake of "fair and balanced" coverage. Ruiz de la Serna agreed that pacing was a problem in the drama, that the action in the second act is too drawn out, "loaded with an excess of incidents," in contrast to the outer acts, which exhibit brisker movement.[24] One thing is certain: the public loved the work. At the premiere, the audience applauded so heartily and for such a long time that the composer "had to remind them that they would miss the last streetcar, though they had already missed it."[25] We will examine this important work in some detail in the following scene.

Colón Calling

As early as July 1932, the Teatro Colón in Buenos Aires had extended an invitation to Torroba and the Teatro Lírico Nacional to perform in Argentina. In 1934 Torroba accepted the offer and took his zarzuela troupe there for four months, staging *Luisa Fernanda*, Giménez's *La tempranica*, and Vives's *Doña Francisquita*.

---

[22] Nerea Alejos, "Baluarte acoge una 'monumental' version de la zarzuela con 'La chulapona,'" *Diario de Navarra*, November 24, 2005, 92.

[23] Fernando Pérez Ollo, "Madrileñismo a tope y coro lírico Nuevo," *Diario de Navarra*, November 30, 2005, 80.

[24] Ruiz de la Serna Chulapona 1988, 31.

[25] Ibid., 29.

Torroba's zarzuelas marked the first performance of the genre at the Colón, before then exclusively an opera house.[26] This would be but the first of over thirty trips he would eventually make to Buenos Aires; in fact, he went again already the following year.[27]

Shortly after his arrival, Torroba demonstrated an aptitude for using the press to his own advantage, issuing a statement to the Argentine public concerning his company and its artistic aims—as well as difficulties. One can read between the lines to tease out his feelings about the current political situation in Spain.

> It is difficult [in Spain] to form zarzuela companies. Right away the intervention of the unions leaves them without musicians, choristers, and nearly without artists, because many are union members. Moreover, everyone is demanding larger and larger salaries, and to raise the curtain on a production now costs about 5,000 *pesetas*. It is been relatively easy for us to put together a cast only because [we can draw on] the three companies we have already created in Spain.[28]

He then ventured to explain something of the cultural significance of the zarzuela, at the same time ingratiating himself to this public by appealing to the Hispanic heritage he and they shared:

> I want to offer to the Argentine public an embrace of *hispanidad*, to initiate the fraternity that will exist between us during my brief stay in the Argentine capital.... I have come with a few works that are authentically Spanish, which have a *castizo* spirit and are not operas because they cannot be. Spain is not disposed to the production of lyric drama in the fashion of Italy or Germany.... All of the attempts at Spanish opera are mediocre and lack national personality. The zarzuela inspires Spain, and it is the true Spanish tradition of lyric theater. First and foremost, I want the *porteño* public, while accepting the modest expression that the zarzuela possesses in its technique, to experience the national spirit of our theater, inspired by the grace and humor of our national songs.[29]

---

[26] *Diario de Navarra*, September 13, 1982.

[27] In "'La zarzuela está vivita y coleando,'" he said that his 1975 visit to the famous port city was his thirty-second trip there, since the 1934 premiere. See "El reputado músico habla de sus obras y de la temporada del Colón," *La Razón* (Buenos Aires), November 29, 1935, for confirmation of his journey there the following year.

[28] "Un mensaje del maestro Torroba dirigido al público argentino," *La Razón* (Buenos Aires), October 23, 1934. It may be a mere quibble, but we note that in the Colmenero piece quoted above, from 1979, he said that in the 1930s one could produce a zarzuela for "scarcely" 4,000 *pesetas*. Yet, at that time he complained of the burden that 5,000 *pesetas* imposed. It seems he sometimes idealized the past, or complained about the present, for dramatic effect.

[29] Ibid.

In tandem with some excellent renditions, this strategy seems to have paid off. The critical reception of *Luisa Fernanda* was universally positive, inspiring a river of encomiastic prose to match the Río de la Plata itself. A few excerpts here suffice to prove the point.

> His talent, culture, and good taste give rise to a series of pages notable for their freshness, vivacity, and flavor.... [Torroba], an inspired musician and expert on Hispanic folklore, uses elements of popular origin, transforming and stylizing them with secure mastery, and succeeds in constructing a score with a vigorous melodic line.[30]
>
> Color and emotion alternate with the discretion of good taste. The writing is beautiful, and the instrumentation reveals a secure mastery of the orchestra.[31]
>
> [I]n his inspired music, so full of popular feeling, [Torroba] has written pages full of exquisite flavor, purely and genuinely *madrileñas*.[32]
>
> The music is as *castizo* as the text...and it is accessible to all without descending to vulgarity.[33]
>
> In their melody and rhythm, Maestro Torroba's musical numbers are nourished by popular music, in accordance with the region and epoch in which the events are taking place. Thus, the numbers proceed from the fresh airs of Madrid to the agile rhythms of the traditional *cerandero* of Extremaduara.... There are numerous colorful pages in the score, rich in expression and descriptive in a painterly way.[34]

In short, Torroba and his music were a hit, and this foray initiated an ongoing love affair between him and Buenos Aires. In addition to his 1935 return, other South American capitals became a regular part of his touring schedule. *Luisa Fernanda* remained hugely popular in Latin America and, according to its author, "crossed the Atlantic thirty-five times" between 1934 and 1979.[35]

The Critic

In Madrid, Torroba customarily kept abreast of musical activities around him. As a music critic, his "Vida Musical" column appeared in *Informaciones* from the

[30] "El acento típico y castizo de Madrid vibra en 'Luisa Fernanda,'" *Noticias Gráficas* (Buenos Aires), October 28, 1934.

[31] "'Luisa Fernanda' fue el estreno inaugural," *La Nación* (Buenos Aires), October 28, 1934.

[32] "Se darán por última vez 'Doña Francisquita' y 'Luisa Fernanda,'" *El Diario* (Buenos Aires), November 12, 1934.

[33] "'Luisa Fernanda' en el Colón," *El Mundo* (Buenos Aires), October 29, 1934.

[34] "'Luisa Fernanda' tuvo éxito," *Crítica* (Buenos Aires), October 28, 1934.

[35] Colmenero, "Lírico Moreno Torroba."

mid-1920s to the early 1930s.[36] His concert reviews tended to be descriptive, though not superficial. Generally speaking, he was very kindhearted and generous, a potentially fatal flaw in a reviewer seeking to attract an avid readership. In fact, according to Federico, Jr., he only once wrote a negative review (of a symphony concert)—which subsequently attracted the enthusiastic encomiums of several readers! He concluded that being a newspaper critic was not his line of work and gave it up.[37]

More important by far is what his reviews, positive or negative, tell us of his own tastes and inclinations. For instance, on January 1, 1925, Torroba gave an overview of the concerts presented by Madrid's two main orchestras, the Sociedad Filarmónica and Orquesta Sinfónica, in 1924. Not surprisingly, he was very pleased with the Sociedad's performances of Ravel's *Alborada del gracioso* and Falla's *El retablo de Maese Pedro*, praising them as "reflections of the spiritual purification of the people."[38] Of special interest in this review is his singling out of "the very personal Russian composer Sr. Strawinsky [*sic*], who passed through the Teatro Real with his incomparable muse." Torroba does not state which work was done, but his admiration for Stravinsky, the High Priest of Musical Modernism at that time, reveals a commendable openness to widely divergent styles of composition. He was definitely not among the reactionary *españolistas* who condemned the art of Picasso or the influence of Debussy and Stravinsky on Spanish composers, as happened with the Spanish production of Falla's *El sombrero de tres picos*, for instance, on which Falla collaborated with Diaghilev and Picasso.[39]

One other review makes clear his support for local composers other than Falla, who were attempting to renovate Spanish music with elements of Impressionism and neoclassicism. In particular, he was impressed with Turina, who, though he was readily influenced by "this or that school or simply by this or that system," nonetheless always "conserves an eminently personal style."[40]

Of greater importance is the early documentation of Torroba's life-long campaign to rally state support for Spain's theaters and performance organizations. Throughout his public life Torroba urged the government—regardless of its ideological bias—to increase support for Spain's cultural institutions. In the review of 1924 concerts cited above, he took the opportunity to goad the government into providing more support for both orchestras, if not to subsidize them completely then at least to help lift the tremendous economic burden on them, which ticket sales alone could not ameliorate. This was necessary to permit the orchestras to compete with "the most base of [unspecified] public concerts,"

[36] A survey of the reviews from this period indicates that his contributions decreased in length and frequency ca. 1930 and ceased altogether with the advent of the Second Republic, in 1931.

[37] This is according to Federico, Jr., in an interview with William Krause, Madrid, July 18, 1988.

[38] Federico Moreno Torroba, "El año musical," *Informaciones*, January 1, 1925, 7.

[39] See Hess, *Modernism*, 130–60, for an in-depth reception history of this ballet.

[40] Federico Moreno Torroba, "La vida musical," *Informaciones*, January 24, 1925, 4.

saying that orchestral programs were on the same level of cultural importance as museums and conferences. He wanted to "raise a voice of alarm" in order to find a "remedy" for the uneven playing field on which organizations like these had to compete in the cultural arena, given the immense difficulties under which they labored and the equally immense benefit they provided the public.[41]

Torroba's customary argument contrasted the quality of Spain's musical life with that of France and Germany. He believed Spain's cultural institutions could rival those of northern Europe only if they were to enjoy similar state support. Torroba accurately contended that state support was particularly lacking in the areas of music and theater. As Suárez-Pajares has pointed out, composer Óscar Esplá, the head of Junta in the 1930s, was directing a third of its budget of 1,224,000 *pesetas* to the Teatro Lírico Nacional (directed at that time by Torroba), but this was only a fourth of what Vienna spent on its theaters.[42] Moreover, the project never gained much altitude because serious composers were not committed to it. *Zarzuelistas* had a different aesthetic orientation, and other composers "thought it absurd to write an opera when for all practical purposes there was no possibility that it would be presented even one time."[43] This was largely the consequence of public apathy and the lack of suitable venues. Federico, Jr., later observed that:

> Unhappily, in Spain the zarzuela does not get the aid it deserves, as does the operetta in Austria or the musical vaudeville in France. A permanent theater throughout the year would be necessary, but as old General Franco never went to the theater, it never received help; now our Socialist government goes to the theater—they go asleep, but at least they go![44]

This does not altogether explain why Broadway musicals, which received no direct state subsidies of any kind, nonetheless sometimes made their authors fortunes of which Torroba could only dream (and obviously did). His son had an answer for that conundrum: people in the United States can afford ticket prices on Broadway but similar prices in Spain would be impossible for most to afford, hence the need for government support.[45] We have additional explanations for the disparity between Broadway and the Grand Way (Gran Vía) and will offer them in Act III, Scene ii.

State support for musical theater may not have been readily forthcoming, but as a result of Torroba's manifold activities and notable successes, his stature in

[41] Torroba, "El año musical."

[42] Suárez-Pajares, "El periodo de Entreguerras."

[43] Sánchez Sánchez, "Un zarzuelista en la Junta Nacional de Música," 538. The zarzuelista in question was Vives.

[44] This is from the manuscript cited above of an undated talk Federico, Jr., gave in the United States, possibly in San Diego.

[45] This is according to Federico, Jr., in an interview with William Krause, Madrid, July 18, 1988.

Madrid grew rapidly. Recognized as a successful critic, impresario, and composer, he was elected to the Real Academia de Bellas Artes de San Fernando in 1934. On February 21, 1935, he was formally installed as a member. At the age of forty-three, he was the youngest person ever to be elected to the Academy. While there should be no doubt that Torroba had fully earned this recognition, it and his appointment that same year to the Junta Nacional de Música y Teatros Líricos y Dramáticos were connected to a conservative shift in the Republic, as a result of the elections in 1933 that put the right wing in power.[46]

Discurso

At his installation, Torroba delivered a lecture on the meaning of *casticismo* relative to music.[47] His "discourse" before the Academy provides us with the most valuable and enduring insights into his creative philosophy. Although he never mentions Miguel de Unamuno by name, it is clear that the famous philosopher's writings have left a profound imprint here, that Torroba is attempting to translate Unamuno's ideas about tradition and history into the context of music, which otherwise held little interest for Unamuno (as it did for the rest of the Generation of 98).[48] Indeed, Unamuno did not think that music played any central role in Spanish culture and identity: "Music, the most algebraic art, is German, French,

---

[46] Emilio Casares Rodicio, "La música española hasta 1939, o la restauración musical," *España en la música de Occidente*, 319. Other members of this reconstituted and renamed Junta included Serafín Álvarez Quintero, Eduardo Marquina, Turina, and Alberto Romea. Its formation was announced in *El Sol* on July 30, 1935. It, in turn, was superseded in 1938 by the Consejo Central de la Música, whose membership no longer included Torroba, now waiting out the war in Navarra. See "Disposiciones legales," 261–62. However, the winds shifted again with the formation of a Junta Nacional de Teatros y Conciertos in that same year. Torroba was appointed a member of this committee, along with Manuel Machado and José María Pemán, but he cannot have been very active, given the time frame and logistics. When this metamorphosed into the Consejo Nacional de Teatros a year later, he did not remain a member of it.

[47] Federico Moreno Torroba, *Discurso leído por el Señor Don Federico Moreno Torroba en el acto de su recepción pública y contestación del Señor Don Ángel María Castell el día 21 de febrero de 1935* (Madrid: Real Academia de Bellas Artes de San Fernando, 1935).

[48] Unamuno was, in fact, indifferent to music, as was the rest of the Generation of 98, and they paid scant attention to Spanish composers in their writings. See Federico Sopeña Ibañez, *Historia de la música española contemporánea* (Madrid: Rialp, 1958), 73–80. In Sopeña's view, the relationship of the Generation of 98 to music could be summed up in one word: "nada" (nothing). To be sure, Unamuno *did* take an interest in zarzuela as a form of dramatic literature. But he was critical of its mass appeal and disconnection from the "genuine instincts of the common people." See his essay "La regeneración del teatro español," in *Obras completas*, 4 vols., ed. Manuel García Blanco (Barcelona: Vergara, 1958), iii, 339. Encabo, *Música y nacionalismos en España*, 19, notes Unamuno's acerbic sentiments about popular culture in general and the zarzuela in particular, in a letter to Eugenio Noel of December 1911: "the evocations of flamenco, bullfights, pornography, and the género chico, it's all the same: it is a plague, and a plague of dementia."

or Italian," not Spanish.[49] It would seem at first glance that this view was completely contradictory to Torroba's, but that may not be so. Torroba is not so much making a case for the importance of music to Spanish national identity as he is the necessity of imparting that same identity to his own compositions. Unamuno had nothing to say about that sort of reverse engineering. Salazar shared Unamuno's feeling about the status of music in Spanish society, noting the "popular basis and nonintellectual quality" of it, that it rarely proceeds from "highly cultivated intellects [or] refined tastes."[50] All of this speaks to Unamuno's ambivalence about Spain's place in a world dominated by science and technology, a world in which Spain had yet to play an important role. Here he was in opposition to Ortega y Gasset and others, like Salazar, who felt that Spain had to modernize. Instead, Unamuno declared, "If it were impossible for one nation to produce both a Descartes and a St. John of the Cross, I would choose the latter."[51]

To be sure, Torroba contradicts himself at times and makes questionable forays into anthropology and musicology, in which he had no specialized training. Yet, this snapshot of his thinking is no less revelatory for all that, particularly insofar as his views did not change substantially over time. The discourse is too long to include in its entirety here. Rather, we focus our critical commentary on the key concepts he presents and develops (page numbers in parentheses refer to the published *Discurso*).

Not surprisingly, he moves quickly to valorize "*lo castizo*," which he understands to represent tradition purified over long periods of time, "a vigorous synthesis that endures, despite all vicissitudes, thus constituting the firm roots of a single trunk" (p. 12). Shifting metaphors, he declares that tradition is the "very basis on which rests the culture of any given people, as their racial traits manifest in life, in customs, politics, and art, thereby forming the solid foundation of all cultural expression and, by extension, civilization itself" (p. 12). For emphasis, he reiterates this point: "Tradition...is something very alive, very imminent and subtle" (p. 12).

Here is a distillation of Unamuno's concept of the "tradición eterna," a timeless cultural inheritance that is present in the everyday life of the people. This everyday life, rarely treated in history books, is what Unamuno calls "intra-history," and it is the ground from which the eternal tradition arises.

> This intra-historical life, silent and continuous like the bottom of the
> ocean itself, is the substance of progress, the true tradition, the eternal

---

[49] Unamuno, *En torno al casticismo*, ed. Rebaté, 141.

[50] Salazar, *Music in Our Time*, 304. In this sense, he appears to agree with Ortega y Gasset, who described Spaniards as being, like the Russians, a "pueblo" race, i.e., their songs and dances are "popular and anonymous" rather than "erudite and personal." See Ortega y Gasset, *Invertebrate Spain*, 70–71.

[51] Cited in Hess, *Modernism*, 47. From an article in *ABC*, September 12, 1909, cited and translated in Martin Nozick, *Miguel de Unamuno* (New York: Twayne Publishers, 1971), 195.

tradition, not the false tradition some seek in the buried past of books and papers, monuments, and stones.

...It was not the Restoration of 1875 that renewed Spanish history; it was the millions of people who went on doing what they had done before...their same labors, the same songs with which they continued plowing the fields. A wave is not different water; rather, it is an undulation that runs through the same sea.

In short, "tradition is the substance of history,...as its sediment, as the revelation of the intra-historical, of the unconscious in history."[52]

Thus, Unamuno's—and by extension Torroba's—conception of tradition is synchronic rather than diachronic, a cultural heritage not from an earlier time but present in every time, i.e., now, not yesterday. Unamuno had made this point unmistakable in his essay, declaring that Spaniards must seek the eternal tradition "in the living present and not in the dead past."[53]

Yet, Torroba sees this tradition as something more than merely desirable or inevitable; it is absolutely vital to the survival of a people. For victory goes "not to the strongest, but rather to the most cultured. Tradition confers a 'personality' on a society," which enables it "to survive the greatest misfortune and calamities....A country without a personality is a country in plain decadence," on its way to extinction (p. 13). New York Senator Daniel Patrick Moynihan once observed that "the central conservative truth is that it is culture, not politics, that determines the success of society." Torroba agreed with this assessment of culture and politics in his *Discurso*, and to that extent he was solidly in the conservative camp. However, though he prided himself on being apolitical, on never getting immersed in politics, his repeated goading of the government to support the arts suggests that he might tacitly have agreed with the other half of Moynihan's formulation, i.e., "The central liberal truth is that politics can change a culture and save it from itself."[54]

Having staked out the centrality of tradition to his argument, Torroba roams further afield, sometimes treading shaky ground. For instance, he asserts that "the most primitive peoples sing and dance but not for pleasure or entertainment, because the lives our remote ancestors led were so extremely hard that we must assume it left them little time or energy for such diversions" (p. 14). This sweeping generalization is untenable. It is safe to say that in most traditional cultures,

---

[52] Unamuno, *En torno al casticismo*, ed. Rebaté, 144.

[53] Ibid. And yet, on other occasions, Torroba seemed to espouse a linear view of music history. For instance, in García, "'Lo único que no se repite,' regarding whether history repeats itself, he said: "Yes, in a few different colors, it repeats itself; the only thing that does not repeat itself is music," as its stylistic evolution continues. But he is referring here to art music, not the "eternal tradition" of folk music.

[54] Cited in an article by Tim Rutten, "How We Arrived at Our 'Tea' Time," *Los Angeles Times*, October 24, 2010, E1.

music and dance have always played a central role in the ceremonial life of the community. Social and religious rituals were and are viewed as vital to the group's survival, and hence music in particular is not merely a form of entertainment. But Torroba had no empirical basis whatsoever for stating that "primitive" peoples derived no pleasure from singing and dancing. Being members of the same species as Torroba himself, it seems inconceivable that they would not do so.[55]

In any case, he goes on to assert that song and poetry found physical expression in dance. Transmitted across generations, song, poetry, and then dance are the basis of all popular art, which, "enlarged, developed, and modified by the liturgy, provided the birthplace for theater" (p. 15). Again, what basis exists for positing this sequence of events? He does not say. However, we seem to have moved beyond the time of primitive peoples and into the Middle Ages, though he does not state as much. Certainly there was a close connection between vernacular and sacred music in the European Middle Ages, which found expression in morality plays and liturgical dramas, the distant antecedents of opera and zarzuela. But he next elides into an even less sustainable argument, one resting as it does on an insecure historical foundation.

Torroba now proclaims, without citing any authority for his statement—though he says it is "well demonstrated"—that "all of our popular music" proceeds from the Arabic tradition.

> All of our musical folklore, from north to south, east to west, with the already mentioned exception [of the Basque region], is of an Arabic origin. This tradition is of supreme importance, because it makes our music totally, absolutely, and definitely distinct from the music of all other European countries. (p. 15)

Flying ever closer to the sun on waxen wings, he finds that,

> Indeed, the most beautiful legacy, the richest heritage that the Arabs left us was their music: secular music, perfect music, the essence and quintessence of all music, and technical knowledge acquired precisely through the traditional transmission from numerous remote oriental civilizations, of which we have no other record. (p. 16)

These assertions are questionable on several counts. Though one can readily sympathize with his enthusiasm for Arabic music and its imprint on Spanish

---

[55] J. Anderson Thomson, Jr., observes that music, dance, and ritual stimulate the production of hormones directly related to pleasure (dopamine) and the formation of communal bonds (oxytocin). This was as true of our distant antecedents as it is of us today. "For our ancestors, singing and dancing, music and movement, were all one." See J. Anderson Thomson, Jr., with Clare Aukofer, *Why We Believe in God(s): A Concise Guide to the Science of Faith* (Charlottesville, Virginia: Pitchstone Publishing, 2011), 95.

culture, does it really constitute a "richer heritage" than the decorative arts and architecture, than, say, the Alhambra in Granada or the Great Mosque in Córdoba? Absolutely not. And exactly what is it about Arabic music that Torroba finds so compelling, anyway? Its modality? Rhythms? Texture? Texts? Melodies? Vocal production? Instrumentation? He does not specify. One could cite a tendency toward melodic embellishment, complex rhythmic elaboration and metrical freedom, the augmented-second interval in the so-called Andalusian scale, and the nasally vocal production of flamenco singing. However, the guitar is a chordal instrument, unlike the *oud*, which had not been played in Spain for centuries. And the whole notion of harmony and chord progressions, as realized on the guitar, has nothing whatsoever to do with Arabic music. Neither does the resulting homophonic texture of simultaneous guitar playing and singing find any precedent in Arabic music. The basic texture seems to be heterophonic, or variant versions of the same melody played simultaneously. Specific melodies are difficult to identify because Arabic music, as it was practiced during the Middle Ages, was primarily an oral tradition. We have no way of knowing whether this or that tune traces its ancestry back to that distant past.

Finally, on what basis does he assert that the remnants of Arabic music in Spain constitute the only record of music from "numerous remote oriental civilizations"? Which ones, exactly, and how does he know no other record survives? Just guessing that he might mean other parts of the Muslim world in the Middle Ages, e.g., Iran, Central Asia, and parts of India and China, it is a fact that we have documentation and artifacts concerning music completely independent of what one can find in the Iberian Peninsula (though in all fairness, at the time he gave this speech, that history was not yet well known). In short, what he has conjured up here is nothing but ethnomusicological smoke and mirrors.

What matters most about his remarks is not their historical or musicological accuracy, but rather what they reveal about Torroba's stance toward the Muslim occupation. During the heyday of Romanticism, authors, painters, and composers reveled in the exotic heritage of Arabic Spain. A steady stream of writers, artists, and musicians tramped through the Alhambra in search of inspiration, of the real Spain. Indeed, Albéniz himself declared on his deathbed that the Moorish-Gypsy south was the "real" Spain, whose essence and spirit he had always tried to capture in his music.[56] But there was increasing dissent over this view in the late 1800s. The Generation of 98, including Unamuno and Azorín, focused not on Andalusia but rather on Castile as the spiritual heartland of the nation, from which Spain drew its strength and inspiration, from which national renewal would come. The most potent expression in music of this Castile-centered vision of Spanish identity is Granados's *Goyescas*, which celebrates Madrid in the time of Goya, of the *majos* and *majas*. Granados felt far less attraction to Andalusia, and evocations of it in his music are relatively rare.

[56] Clark, *Portrait of a Romantic*, 264.

Nationalist sentiment in the early twentieth century veered increasingly toward Castile and away from Andalusia as the source of Spanish identity, particularly in the neo-classical works of Manuel de Falla, such as *El retablo de maese Pedro* and the harpsichord concerto. This turning away from the Romantic fixation on Andalusia among intellectuals and artists had at least something to do with race, religion, and colonial politics. After all, the Arabs and their Moorish allies were racially other, and they were definitely not Catholic. The right wing in particular held that genuine Spaniards were Catholic and non-Semitic, non-African. Right-wing ideologues were predictably reluctant to embrace Semitic Muslims (note that Moroccans are not Arabs or Semites) as the ultimate progenitors of the nation's culture. Right-wing nationalists chose to view Moroccans as Spain's colonial subjects, not its former overlords.[57] This attitude certainly prevailed among the forces of Franco, even now gathering their strength and awaiting the moment to strike, to impose their vision of Catholic and Castilian Spain on the country, a vision not of Moorish conquest but of Spanish reconquest. (How ironic that Franco's shock troops and personal guard during the Civil War were made up primarily of—Moroccans!).[58]

Another important figure in this discourse was Pedrell, who was quite convinced that the principal influence on Spanish music was *Byzantine* and that Arabs and Moors had left almost no imprint.[59] In other words, he (and others) were at the opposite end of the spectrum of opinion from Torroba on this point. But that is all these were: opinions. They were the product of competing visions of the country's past and future, rooted in divergent politico-cultural ideologies. They were not based on anything like thorough and dispassionate investigation. And there is one conspicuous omission that makes all of this even more suspect: Gypsies! At no point does Torroba once mention them, though their impact on Spanish music was as great or greater than that of Arabs or any other ethnic or racial group. Of course, the impact of the Jews on virtually every aspect of medieval Iberian culture was also significant, but he is silent about them as well. (These omissions should not be construed as suggestive of racial or religious prejudice. There is no hint of that in the biographical record.)

The ultimate irony in all of this is that there are no evocations of Arab *Al Andalus* in the music of Torroba, though Gypsy-style flamenco does come front and center in several compositions. In fact, the majority of his works for both the stage and

---

[57] I am indebted to Madrid journalist and historian José María Ridao, who shared these insights with me over breakfast in Berlin on May 29, 2010.

[58] As William Krause points out in his dissertation (189), "While Franco was hostile to nineteenth-century French liberalism, Torroba was a great admirer of many foreign composers, particularly Debussy, Ravel, Franck, Bartók and Wagner. Furthermore, his view of Spain was inclusive, in contrast to Franco's divisive policy of subjugating Spain's non-Castilian and culturally diverse regions. Torroba regarded the folklore of every region of Spain with respect and wrote zarzuelas set in Castile or Andalucía with the same conviction as songs in which he set Navarrese and Basque poetry."

[59] See Hess, *Falla and Modernism*, 175. Pedrell expressed these sentiments in his *Cancionero musical popular español* (Barcelona: Boileau, nd), i:76.

guitar celebrate instead Castile and regions farther north, especially Navarra. In other words, there is a striking disjuncture between his passionate evocation of the Arab tradition and the actual source of his inspiration as a composer, which was, in fact, much more in line with Unamuno, Azorín, and the Generation of 98, not to mention Granados.

Thus, Torroba once again lies outside simplistic dichotomies. Though he exalts (and exaggerates) the Arab imprint on Spanish music, in his own works there is a consistent orientation toward Castile and Madrid, largely as a result of his status as a confirmed *madrileño*. Yet, he certainly never rejected Andalusianism, and several of his works for guitar (*Fantasia flamenca*, *Ay, malagueña*) and the stage (such as *La virgen de mayo*, *Azabache*, and *Monte Carmelo*) are rooted in the culture of that region. In short, Torroba charts his own course, and his embrace of the Arabic heritage signals his unwillingness to conform to right-wing dogma—and his willingness to digress from Unamuno.

At least Torroba hereby *does* celebrate some element of foreign influence in Spanish music, no matter how remote in time. He goes on to affirm that Andalusian folklore, exhibiting the greatest Arab influence, has in turn been the most prominent of Spain's regional traditions. Yet, he then appears to back away from the celebration of foreign influence in his subsequent conviction that other regions possess musical traditions just as rich, if less well known. In fact, precisely because they are "more virgin," they are therefore of incalculable interest, because they have not been "contaminated with adulterations of foreign elements" or learned devices that destroy their "spontaneous sincerity, the fragrant freshness, the succulence of the truly popular" (p. 17). We are thus left wondering: is foreign influence good or bad? Is it the bedrock of Spanish folk music, or a form of cultural pollution? He has painted himself into a rhetorical corner here from which he—and we—cannot escape.

In any case, this quest to explore "virgin territory" in Spanish folklore resonates with Unamuno's summons to those living in the present to "bring to light" the eternal tradition of every people, "in order to make conscious what is now unconscious in them."[60] Hence Torroba's insistence that "to find something lost, is…nothing less than to discover ourselves" (p. 18). And he was as good as his word, when it came to composing. As Federico, Jr., has noted, Torroba carefully studied the various regional musics before setting any sort of story there. He knew all of Spain very well.[61] In fact, it was the regional character of zarzuela that set it apart from other styles of operetta: the zarzuela has the same characteristics in terms of form as French and German operetta, but not in terms of content, because it is very Spanish and all the themes are regional and local. It is a very specific kind of genre.[62]

---

[60] Unamuno, *En torno al casticismo*, ed. Rebaté, 147.

[61] This is according to Federico, Jr., in an interview with William Krause, Madrid, July 18, 1988.

[62] Marie Pascal, "Derechos de autor y otros temas actuales," *La Nación* (Buenos Aires), April 30, 1978, 2.

However, we continue to ponder why Torroba celebrates the Arab "contaminations" while disdaining other "foreign adulterations" elsewhere. Perhaps that which was originally Arab has, by virtue of its antiquity, become *castizo*. But does that not imply that more recent influences will, with the passage of time, themselves become "pure" as well? And does he not contradict his earlier openness to foreign influence as long as it did not dilute or occlude "*lo castizo*"?

In the end, all of this is rather academic because Torroba's basic thesis itself is flawed. It is in no way demonstrable that Arab influence is pervasive or palpable throughout Spain. There are many musical traditions, particularly in the north (and not just the Basque country), that exhibit no Arab imprint whatsoever, neither in their scale types, instruments, dances, nor vocal production. The Catalan *sardana* and the Galician *muñeira* are just two examples. Torroba knew this as well as anyone.

The seeming paradox in all of this rhapsodizing about *lo castizo* is that its ultimate goal is to achieve universality. Universalism, i.e., relevance beyond the Iberian Peninsula, was an ongoing preoccupation of Spanish composers in the late nineteenth and early twentieth centuries. Albéniz, for instance, adjured Spanish composers "to make Spanish music with a universal accent."[63] Yet, what he meant by that is something different from what Torroba intended. Albéniz strove to achieve "universality" through the incorporation of modern trends, from France and Germany in particular, into his *españolismo*. In other words, his method was to look *outward*. Torroba says that universality can only be achieved by looking more deeply *inward*. "We must attain universality with that which is purely Spanish, if we want to be recognized as Spanish" (p. 19). This accords perfectly with Unamuno's declaration that the eternal tradition is ultimately "universal and cosmopolitan."[64] Torroba continues, stating that the revival of Spanish music,

> will come when we direct our gaze, with all love and veneration, to that which is ours, enclosing it in the tight circle of its nationalism, which ... is the means I consider most efficacious for achieving its universality. By having studied [this art], ... [w]ith each passing day I am ever more firmly committed to the Spanish, nationalist, traditionalist, and *castizo* course I have charted for my music." (p. 27)

Again, Torroba was no xenophobe and he did not dismiss out of hand any foreign influence. Nonetheless, he stated:

> This does not mean that in an exclusively national culture there is no room for all human aspects, because these traits are not necessarily readily identifiable. There is always some sort of synthesis. But it is only

---

[63] See Clark, *Portrait of a Romantic*, 290.
[64] Unamuno, *En torno al casticismo*, ed. Rebaté, 153.

through the understanding and full realization of our own personality
that we can universalize it. This is done by utilizing the sap of our own
roots, taking foreign ideas only when they are general, fundamental to
the human organism and spirit. (p. 14)

A passage such as this makes it apparent that though Torroba's philosophy echoes
that of Rogelio Villar, he is not as uncompromising, particularly in regard to
French Impressionism. We recall his admiration for Ravel and for Impressionistic
works by Falla, particularly *Noches en los jardines de España*. And this ideological
flexibility is clear enough in his own music, which is not nearly as academic or doctrinaire as his remarks here would suggest.

It comes as no surprise that he regards the zarzuela as the ideal musical vehicle
for achieving this Spanish *risorgimento*. As Roger Alier observed, Torroba "thinks
of the zarzuela as the sole solution to all the ills of Spanish music."[65] Even the
composer himself basically admitted as much: "I believe that the zarzuela is the
most representative kind of national music, not just of one epoch but in all
periods."[66] Yet, once again demonstrating a certain selectiveness about which
foreign influences have or have not had a salubrious effect on Spanish culture,
Torroba states that Italian influence was a sign of decadence and that those
musico-theatrical works steeped in it have been forgotten. "Only those with a typically Spanish color continue to serve as models of our *teatro castizo*" (p. 21). The
Spanish public recognizes as much and responds to zarzuela "with sincerity and
enthusiasm, . . . for the zarzuela is, even now, the most perfect and natural Spanish
medium for the expression of musical *casticismo*" (p. 22). Fair enough, but his derogation of Italian influence too conveniently ignores the immense influence of
Italian opera on even the most "Spanish" of zarzuelas, especially his own! The
impact of Puccini, for instance, is omnipresent in his works of this period—and
nothing to be regretted. In any case, we might ponder another contradiction: how
is it that the public knows enough to respond favorably to works that exude *españolismo castizo*, yet is in the next moment seduced away by ones contaminated by
foreign influence? Is the public fickle and changeable, or is Torroba simply prone
to cherry picking his facts to support his conclusions, regardless of resulting
contradictions?

Torroba is nonetheless aware that the rejection of foreign influence can lead
directly to a suffocating xenophobia, which he warns against. Rather, he proposes
to "universalize our personality" by remaining open to those international trends
that do not necessarily threaten the national character of Spanish culture (p. 14).
This, too, was Unamuno's stance in *En torno al casticismo*. Whatever the case,
Unamuno himself forthrightly addressed the issue of hybridity and the harm that
a belief in racial—and thereby cultural—purity has caused throughout history.

---

[65] Roger Alier Aixalà et al., *El libro de la zarzuela* (Madrid: Daimon, 1982), 83.

[66] Gómez Ortiz, "Moreno Torroba."

Though he maintains that something *castizo* is pure, "without the admixture of foreign elements," he warns against an "ancient prejudice" contained in that expression:

> Thousands of errors and injuries have resulted from believing that the races we call pure are superior to mixed races. In fact, it has been proven in the course of animal husbandry as well as human history that [whatever disadvantages] racial intermixing may produce, it is a source of new vigor and progress.[67]

Therefore, hybridity is not only inevitable but also beneficial. Yet, it is not easy to reconcile the quest for "purity" with an embrace of hybridity. At what point does the hybrid become "pure"? With the passage of a certain amount of time? But if the eternal tradition is something in the present and not in the past, why would it require centuries to become "pure"? One could be excused for thinking that both Unamuno and Torroba were chasing philosophical miasmas here, but we are out of our depth in such philosophical matters and leave parsing them to wiser heads. Alier, however, experiences no such hesitation and is not especially forgiving in this regard:

> This accumulation of contradictions illustrates the absurdity of the extreme positions that inform beliefs about "national music." This attitude is insupportable unless we renounce all critical sense and adopt a comforting position in which it is affirmed (although at times not believed) that everything Spanish is inherently better, or at least equal to, anything that a collection of persons constituting "the foreign" can offer us.[68]

Torroba's lyrico-poetic effusions concerning *españolismo castizo* triggered the desired response in his conservative Academia audience, and in journalist Ángel María Castell, who spoke immediately afterward and whose remarks were published with the *Discurso*. He hailed Torroba's lecture as "one of his most inspired scores, without music paper." It was a "virile and patriotic hymn to the tradition of Spanish lyric art," (p. 27) exhibiting a "salubrious *españolismo*, so necessary at all times, and essential when a sectarian and iconoclastic spirit invades all the orders of social life, and the concept of patriotism, as well as morality, descends to the category of rules" (p. 29). Here Castell makes explicit the political content that was slyly implicit in Torroba's words. The country was in the grips of a political environment that threatened the very fabric of Spanish culture and life, of the nation. Again, Alier cuts to the heart of the matter: "the word 'casticismo' is nothing more

---

[67] Unamuno, *En torno al casticismo*, ed. Rebaté, 127.
[68] Alier et al., *El libro de la zarzuela*, 82.

than a way of alluding to the essential characteristics of a nation and of its nation-alism."[69] To be fair, Torroba made no effort whatsoever to conceal his nationalist impulses about music. He declared them quite openly, though their exact relevance to the political environment at the time is not clear from his own remarks.

Navarra Refuge

In any case, these philosophical ruminations constituted the distant rumblings of a tremendous storm that was soon to break over Spain, a cataclysm of violence that Torroba and his fellow *madrileños* could hardly have anticipated. By his own account, Torroba experienced the commencement of hostilities as a sudden and unexpected event:

> [One day,] I went to the Escorial in order to deliver something to [the playwright Carlos] Arniches, and we waited there till the next day. On that very next day the Civil War broke out. I remained in Madrid for four-teen months, naturally very frightened.[70]

Torroba apparently thought it safest to remain in Madrid. He was understand-ably concerned not only for his own safety but for that of his wife and two young children. But he proved to be no safer there than he would have been in most other places. For instance, Óscar Esplá, former President of the Republic's Junta Nacional de Música, was nearly shot by leftists during the early phases of the war due to mistaken identity.[71] Soon it would be Torroba's turn to face the terror.

After fourteen months, the Republicans came to suspect that he had com-posed the Falangist hymn *Cara al sol* (Face to the sun). The actual composer of this hymn was Juan Tellería Arrizabalaga (1895–1949), not Torroba.[72] Through the influence of a journalist, Gisbert, the Republicans were finally convinced of this, and he was released.[73] Torroba described this harrowing experience many

[69] Ibid.

[70] Vicent, "El pentagrama," 14.

[71] This was first reported by Chase in "Spanish Musicians Since the Civil War," 499–500.

[72] See Marco, "Los años cuarenta," 404. We should note here that this incident was not the first time that Torroba had been accused of writing music for the fascists. When *Luisa Fernanda* premiered in Barcelona in 1934, a rumor was circulating that Torroba had composed a hymn for the Juventudes de Acción Popular, the youth wing of CEDA (Confederacion Española de la Derecha Autónoma), the conservative Catholic party headed by José María Gil-Robles. The performance was interrupted by shouts of "¡Viva el fascismo!" answered by "¡Viva la República!" Security forces had to intervene to restore order. It was a huge scandal, and Torroba complained to local authorities, insisting that he had written no such hymn, a fact corroborated by local journalists soon thereafter. See Sánchez Sánchez, "Moreno Torroba," 22.

[73] Federico Moreno Torroba, *El Pais*, November 14, 1981. Also Germán Lopezarias, "Los años pro-hibidos," *Pueblo*, April 21, 197? [Na].

years later, claiming not to have known or been told the reason for his detention:

> I was put in jail for fifteen days, at the Dirección General de Seguridad, but no one did anything to me there. There were no declarations or accusations, or anything. I spent two weeks on a miserable wooden bed, listening at night to the jailers shouting the name of this or that person. Of course, that poor person was not going to respond. No one said to me so much as "to hell with you." Then Gisbert arrived... who at that time was a journalist with *El Heraldo*. He had connections and was able to get me out. I fled immediately for San Sebastián disguised as a Cuban, wearing a casual shirt and a red scarf around my neck. I put those clothes on and left running.[74]

Fearing now for his life, Torroba immediately left Madrid and settled in Santesteban, in the northern province of Navarra, where his wife's family had a home. As Federico, Jr., later noted, "this area was already liberated from communism." He went on to say,

> The war trapped all of us in Madrid, but we were able to escape to Santesteban by way of Valencia, Marseille, and Hendaya. We spent the rest of the war there. My father formed a little zarzuela company and gave concerts with it in the nationalist zone in the north. It was at this time that he composed a zarzuela set in the rural north, *Sor Navarra*, a theme related to the patriotic exaltation of the moment.[75]

Actually, Navarra, a historic bastion of Carlism and resolutely conservative, had fallen into Franco's grip at the outset of the war and remained a safe haven for Torroba and his family. During these years he continued to compose and perform, as circumstances permitted. Four zarzuelas were produced during this time, *Sor Navarra* (1938), *Pepinillo y Garbancito en la isla misteriosa* (1938), *Tú eres ella* (1938), and *El maleficio* (1939). These zarzuelas were performed in northern Spain, away from Madrid. *Pepinillo* premiered at the Teatro Argensola in Zaragoza. The other three works premiered at the Teatro Victoria Eugenia in San Sebastián. Torroba developed a deep rapport with this picturesque part of Spain and later expressed his feelings in one of his compositions: "I am a Navarro first and fore-

---

[74] Vicent, "El pentagrama," 14.

[75] Estévez, "Federico Moreno Torroba," 40. According to a review of a Sevilla production of *Sor Navarra* at the Teatro Cervantes, published in *ABC* (Sevilla) February 2, 1939, 21, the plot deals with Nieves, who enters a convent because of the callous treatment from her sister Merche, whose impending marriage to Rodrigo has fallen through because he is clearly in love with Nieves. The story's ambience is enlived by the *jota navarra*.

most, and a Spaniard by virtue of being a Navarro. / And before seeing Navarra lose its rights, I would rather lose my life." This is from the lyrics of a *zortzico* that Torroba composed.[76] Torroba declared that "Ultimately, I feel like an honorary Navarro."[77] This speaks to the important issue of identity, and how Spaniards in particular have multiple identities, their hierarchy depending on context (e.g., Barcelonesa, Catalana, Española, Europea, etc.). Torroba's identity was neatly arranged: *español*, *madrileño*, *navarro*, in that order. Moreover, he was a member of the Hispanic diaspora, something that surfaced strongly when he was in Latin America. Finally, whether he saw himself this way or not, he increasingly became a citizen of the world, one who traveled widely, got along well with a variety of people, and felt quite at home wherever he went, whether in Peru, Japan, or Russia. He was a living example of his dictum that music that delves deeply into tradition becomes universal. By being, in an uncomplicated way, a Spaniard, he achieved a sort of universality as a human being, one loved and respected wherever he went.

The whole issue of identity is too often reduced to simplistic formulations for political purposes. Philosopher Georgia Warnke makes it clear that each of us possesses multiple identities, for an individual cannot

> possess only one identity, any more than a text can possess only one meaning. Instead, just as we approach texts from within different interpretive wholes and therefore can understand their meaning in different ways, we approach individuals from within different wholes and therefore can understand their identities in different ways.[78]

In other words, the relative strength of these identities will change according to the cultural context in which we find ourselves. As Warnke states, "Our task as individuals is to develop and organize our identities in ways that give our lives the meaning we want for them."[79] Torroba needed no encouragement to do this, as it seems to have come naturally to him.

All of this notwithstanding, Navarra would always hold a special attraction for Torroba. Less than a year before his death he said, "Santesteban is my creative refuge. I like being there for the atmosphere, the tranquility, and a very warm and welcoming house, full of memories."[80] "It is here that music alone flows from me."[81] On another occasion he observed that "I rest by working. When I write in

[76] See "La muerte de Federico Moreno Torroba," *Diario de Navarra*, September 13, 1982, 11. The exact date of this composition is not known.

[77] In García del Busto, "Moreno Torroba estrena dos piezas."

[78] Georgia Warnke, *After Identity: Rethinking Race, Sex, and Gender* (Cambridge: Cambridge University Press, 2007), 232–33.

[79] Ibid., 225.

[80] Ignacio Elizalde, "Proyectaba un poema sinfónico sobre Navarra," *Diario de Navarra*, November 23, 1982.

[81] "Federico Moreno Torroba," *Diario de Navarra*, February 27, 1994, 34.

Santesteban, I often work until 3 a.m. And I'm happy because, what's more, if I need to try something out at the piano, I don't disturb the neighbors."[82]

As one journalist noted, "His children married *Navarros*, and his grandchildren were born in that region of Spain." Yet, even in this article, sentimentality toward Navarra always had a political component, which Torroba never openly expressed but certainly understood and apparently accepted. This journalist went on to complain that there were many people who intended to "sovietize" Navarra. He defiantly reminded his readers that "the *Navarro* is loyal to his rights and will sacrifice his life for them, but he does not seek independence from the Fatherland."[83] This patriotic theme cropped up in another *El Alcázar* article, which joked that under Franco there were four seasons, and now, under democracy, "there is only one: summer."[84] Torroba's effusions about Navarra wisely skirted the political and remained strictly sentimental in tenor.

The experiment of the Second Republic had afforded Torroba many professional opportunities. Such was his stature that he received La Orden de la República in 1935. But with the Republic's demise, he and his countrymen were forced to adapt—not to an entirely new ideology, but to the consolidation of conservative forces that had been present in Spanish society for decades.[85] Generalísimo Francisco Franco, the leader of the fascist forces, interpreted his success as "a victory over liberals and internationalists."[86] In his view, the Civil War was to rid Spain of Freemasons, Jews, regionalists, anticlerics, and communists, as well as to "liquidate the nineteenth century, which should never have existed."[87] The essence of Spain's culture, he argued, was in Castile, the birthplace of the empire. The Spaniard's character was formed before the Enlightenment, and owed nothing to Europe. Thus, Franco's brand of nationalism stressed restoration, retrogression. Spain's glorious past would somehow be the model for its tenuous future.[88]

Postwar Realities

With the end of the Civil War in March of 1939, Torroba made plans to re-enter Madrid's musical life. His first production enjoyed tremendous initial success but

---

[82] Imbuluzqueta, "El compositor Federico Moreno Torroba."

[83] Fernando López and L. de Tejada, "La Nacional y homenaje navarro a Moreno Torroba," *El Alcázar*, November 8, 1981, 32.

[84] Antonio D. Olano, "¡Viva Navarra! Homenaje a Moreno Torroba," *El Alcázar*, November 3, 1981.

[85] Tomás Marco, *Historia de la música española*, 159.

[86] Javier Jiménez Campo, "Rasgos básicos de la ideologia entre 1939–45," *Revista de Estudios Políticos*, n15 (1980): 85.

[87] Ibid., 87.

[88] Raymond Carr, *History of Spain: 1808–1975*, Oxford History of Modern Spain, 2d ed. (Oxford: Claredon Press, 1982) 601.

later ran afoul of the censors when subsequent productions were attempted. Perhaps modeled after Juan Valera's 1874 novel *Pepita Jiménez*, the zarzuela **Monte Carmelo** (1939) told the story of a woman and a priest falling in love with one another.[89] The libretto was by the redoubtable duo of Romero and Fernández-Shaw. Apparently a work in preparation as early as 1932, for whatever reason its final appearance was delayed for seven years.[90] Premiering at the Calderón on October 17 and starring Luis Sagi-Vela, it was a huge hit with both the critics and the public.[91] Regino Sainz de la Maza enthused that it "reanimated and revived the greatest glories of the zarzuela," praising Torroba's "fresh and graceful flow of melody" and "rich orchestration."[92] The work was still going strong in December and traveled to Barcelona in 1940.

How bitter a pill it was for the authors, then, when Franco's censors declared the work's libretto sacrilegious and prevented its repetition for a number of years. This was a situation made all the more disappointing to our composer because, as we have seen, he considered this to be his finest work. The tangled performance history of this zarzuela and the repeated jousting with censors that the authors had to undertake give us insight into Torroba's understandable frustrations with the situation now prevailing in a new cultural climate, dominated first and foremost by the concerns of the Catholic Church.

There is a file in the government archives in Alcalá de Henares containing correspondence between the authors and censors regarding *Monte Carmelo*, and it sheds a great deal of light on the whole affair.[93] It was apparently submitted on September 11, 1939, and approved September 27, 1939, on condition of certain excisions in Act II. These pertained to the nature of the love interest, just the sort of thing the priestly censors would not endorse. Were those changes made? Despite Romero's later assertions to the contrary (see below), apparently they were not, or this work would not have experienced repeated difficulties in getting permission from the censors. The authors attempted to revive *Monte Carmelo* for a production in the fall of 1940, but when they made application on September 11, to the Subsecretaría de Prensa y Propaganda del Ministerio de la Gobernación, the petition was denied.

Upon yet another application, in late 1944, censor P. Constancio de Aldeaseca laid bare his objections in a response of January 3, 1945. These included "certain

[89] Albéniz's opera *Pepita Jiménez* (1896) was based on this same novel but generated no such controversy during that earlier epoch. See Clark, *Portrait of a Romantic*, 136–61.

[90] Torroba makes mention of this work already in "El reputado músico habla de sus obras y de la temporada del Colón," *La Razón* (Buenos Aires), November 29, 1935. The earliest notice of it, however, occurs in September 18, 1932, in *Blanco y Negro*, which speculates that Faustino Arregui will be starring in *Monte Carmelo*. It predicts that this will be "a success equal to *Luisa Fernanda*."

[91] See "Notas teatrales," *ABC*, October 20, 1939, 19, which describes it as "*the* lyric event of the year."

[92] Regino Sainz de la Maza, "Informaciones teatrales," *ABC*, October 18, 1939, 15.

[93] Archivo General de la Administración, 73/08155 97/39.

sentences uttered by Sr. Arzobispo de Granada [that] reduce his figure to a level of vulgarity, indecorous with his station and dignity," as well as the love of Esperanza and Juan María for one another, which would be "scandalous." Even if that were changed, he was convinced that this was still a work suitable only for adults, not children.

Federico Romero wrote to the censor on October 29, 1947, stating that the original production at the Calderón had been cleared in advance with the censors; however, with the reorganization of the government department of Cinematography and Theater (Cinematografía y Teatro), they would have to renew permission. The new bureaucratic arrangements proved less sympathetic to this work. Thus, Romero's petition did not have the desired effect, and permission was denied, yet again, because of the impermissible love interest. The censor on this occasion was R. P. Fr. Mauricio de Begoña. His report of November 13, 1947, states that "the theme of Esperanza's love for the priest Juan María should be excised. This character should be a student or seminarian."

Since the authors deemed this premise vital to the entire work, they decided to withdraw it, though not without protest. Romero refers to a movie he has recently seen, *La Fe* (1947), which he deems far worse in regard to priestly *amor* and yet which won the first Premio Nacional and critical praise. He believed that it was time to reassess *Monte Carmelo*. However, the official response was what one sees above, that the priest should be some other type of character. Another response from the censors, dated December 3, 1947, gives the exact pages where changes must be made (i.e., 124, 128, and 141). Obviously, this did not go over well with the authors, who gave up again. Torroba was quick to recognize the new political and social reality in Spain. By avoiding further controversy, his career was not seriously hampered by this confrontation.

Already in 1935 Torroba had said that he was planning to write a number of film scores, which included *Lola Triana* (story by José María Pemán) and *El capitán Veneno* (story by Antonio de Alarcón), as well as a filmic version of *Luisa Fernanda*. All of these were supposedly under contract with Ediciones Cinematográficas Españolas.[94] No doubt the war interfered with these plans, but when that conflict subsided Torroba composed twelve film scores between 1939 and 1966. Outstanding among them is *La canción de Aixa* (1939), directed by Florián Rey and starring Imperio Argentina in the title role. The action takes place in a Muslim milieu in which a fragile truce between two warring families depends on the marriage of a young man from one family to a woman from the other; however, the young man has been having a dalliance with Aixa. In order to stave off a resumption of hostilities, Aixa takes up with the young man's cousin, who is charmed by her singing. This Romeo-and-Juliet-type story had some resonance in the context of the Spanish Civil War, when it was made. It was actually a

[94] He makes reference to these projects in "El reputado músico habla de sus obras y de la temporada del Colón."

collaboration between Spanish and German film companies and was shot in Germany. A much later German collaboration was *El enigma de los Cornell* (*Hotel der toten Gäste* in its West German release) of 1965, directed by Eberhard Itzenplitz. Torroba's music is notable for its jazzy character, completely divorced from his normal Spanish idiom and earlier film scores.

In any case, Torroba's musical style did not change at all as a result of Franco's ascendancy and the right-wing ideology now gripping the country. After all, a *pasodoble* under the Republic was the same as one under Franco. But librettos were another matter and were closely scrutinized for antiregime or anticlerical sentiments. Thus, *Monte Carmelo* was not the only zarzuela by Torroba that ran afoul of the censors. For instance, though *Azabache* was revived during the Franco era, the censors insisted that certain changes had to be made. The action takes place harmlessly enough among Gypsies in Granada and deals with two young lovers whose relationship exacerbates a conflict between their respective families. The old Gypsy Azabache first complicates and then resolves the conflict. The file on this work indicates submission of a new version of the book, by Antonio Quintero and Pascual Guillén, on May 21, 1949.[95] The text, utilizing Andalusian dialect, came through largely unscathed, though on page 40, the censor did not approve of the expression "as there is a God" ("como hay Dió"). Apparently the suggestion that there might not be a God was too much. Perhaps such an offhand reference to the Supreme Being gave offense, though it is very common to invoke the deity in Spanish. The censor's summary of the work is interesting:

> A light work with an insubstantial argument, characterized by a certain atmosphere of disrespect for religion typical of the period during which it was written [i.e., the Republic in the 1930s]. There are several "filler" scenes introduced with no other objective than to provoke hilarity [with] irreverent situations. This irreverence, which at times borders on ridicule and contempt, is the dominant note of the work.

After suggesting a few changes here and there, he granted permission, despite his obvious disregard for the quality of the work as a whole. *Azabache* was revived in 1942 in Buenos Aires and 1952 in Madrid, both times under a new title, *Boda gitana* (Gypsy wedding), though with the original libretto by Pascual Guillén.[96] It is interesting to see what the censors redlined in the text. For example, on page 2, Piti asks for one favor: that the Guardia Civil would leave them alone ("Que nos

[95] Archivo General de la Administración, (3)46 73/8862 83/49. A historic recording of this work, made in 1933 and conducted by Torroba, has been reissued on the Blue Moon label, 7544. See Zueras Navarro, "Sus obras menos conocidas: Más sobre Moreno Torroba."

[96] Archivo General de la Administración, 7(3)46 73/8961 54/51. "Boda Gitana, a comedy in three acts based on the book of the zarzuela entitled 'Azabache,' premiered at the Teatro Calderón in Madrid, August 18, 1932." The title was changed to avoid rights and royalties problems with the original cast. This is explained in a letter by the authors dated March 5, 1952.

quiten la guardia siví"). Of course, the Civil Guard was a federal police force that enforced the government's will. So that passage had to come out. Another example of disapproval appears on page 6, where Paz says, "But God is present everywhere" ("Pero Dios está en toas partes"), to which Piti responds, "Ay, look, like the radio!" ("Ay, mira, como la radio!"). That had to come out, too. Comparisons of the deity to something as mundane as a radio were insufficiently respectful. Perhaps the whiff of pantheism present in this observation also caused concern.

La Caramba, with a text by Luis Fernández Ardavín, premiered in 1942 at the Teatro de la Zarzuela. Its file proves that it cleared the censors with very few changes.[97] However, according to Federico, Jr., some priests nonetheless considered it immoral. During confession, people in Bilbao and Pamplona were asked if they had seen the zarzuela and told that it was a mortal sin to do so. The main reason for this was that at the end of the drama, La Caramba enters a convent, and the libretto comments, "A nun can never be a woman with a happy life."[98]

Of course, Torroba was not alone in experiencing these problems. Alonso's La calesera, premiered in 1925 and popular during the Second Republic, was interwoven with Republican themes, "political exaltations of the moment." At the end of the first act is a scene in which the characters take out a flag and sing 'Libertad, libertad." Franco's censors demanded that, in subsequent productions of the zarzuela, the word "liberty" be taken out.[99]

The issue of censorship in Spain during the Franco era is important in relation to the cultural life of the time. There were two types of censors: the first consisted of members of the Falange, who wanted to repress ideas dangerous to the state. They scrutinized press and other publications. The second type was comprised of priests, who wanted to defend against immorality and anticlericalism. They scrutinized entertainment.

According to Rafael Abella, permission to mount a musical comedy in 1944 required submission of the following to censors for review, at least fifteen days in advance:

1. Libretto in duplicate;
2. Drawings for costumes, also in duplicate, on 18 x 22 cm paper, showing the color of the fabric;
3. Set designs;
4. Nominal relationship of the artists;

[97] Archivo General de la Administración, (3)46 73/08210 2957/42.

[98] Interview with William Krause, Madrid, July 18, 1988. The work was favorably reviewed in "Informaciones y noticias teatrales," ABC, January 13, 1944, 16.

[99] Ibid. It is worth noting that the Republican government also censored theatrical productions. See Berta Muñoz Cáliz, El teatro crítico español durante el franquismo, visto por sus censores (Madrid: Fundación Universitaria Española, 2005), chapter 1, n3, at http://www.bertamuñoz.es/censura/cap1_1.html (accessed August 16, 2011).

5. Page providing the route that the tour will take and localities it will travel through.[100]

The censors would then visit the dress rehearsal to make sure everything was in order. They were nearly all Jesuit priests, and they were looking for anything that could be interpreted as contradictory to the teachings of the Church, especially regarding sex and family life. Sex was only for procreation. Interestingly, they took almost no interest in the music itself, only texts.

As the Civil War drew to a close and the eventual victor became apparent, the facile distinction between loyalty and conformity in the actions of noncombatant citizens was blurred and is now irretrievably lost to subsequent historians. Two scant pieces fall into this ideological no man's land. The climate of censorship, repression, and dictatorial control we have discussed is the necessary context for considering Torroba's composition of *Himno del trabajo* (Hymn of work) in 1938 and the Air Force hymn, *Sobre campos y trincheras* (Over fields and trenches) in 1939.

The message of *Himno del trabajo* seems harmless enough: workers putting their trades and skills to use in creating a new nation, etc.—until we get to the bit about "I am imperial Spain."[101] Such songs were an important part of the new regime's cultural program, for they helped to establish that "the authentic Spain, the authentic Spanish tradition, is one.... the production of *cancioneros* [song collections] was intended to serve this idea."[102]

The modern Spanish Air Force (Ejército del Aire) was formally established shortly after the war, on October 7, 1939. Our composer set the text of a hymn for it as well. It was eventually replaced by a new hymn in 1967, and is now known as the "old" Air Force Hymn, *Himno antiguo del Ejército del Aire*.[103] The tenor of

---

[100] Rafael Abella, *La vida cotidiana bajo el régimen de Franco* (Madrid: Ediciones Temas de Hoy, 1984/1996), 116. These exact stipulations were promulgated in the press. See "Informaciones y noticias teatrales," *ABC*, January 13, 1944, 16.

[101] The text is by Falangist Tomás Borrás (1891–1976). Borrás was a playwright, journalist, and theater critic, who had written approvingly of the 1915 production of *El amor brujo* in which Torroba performed (see *La Tribuna*, April 16, 1915; cited in Gallego, *El amor brujo*, 263). We know next to nothing about his relationship with Torroba. However, the innocuous march Torroba composed is catchy but generic and utterly uncharacteristic of him.

[102] Pérez Zalduondo, "Formulación, fracaso y despertar de la conciencia crítica en la música española durante el franquismo (1936–1958)," 457–58.

[103] The text is by Agustín de Foxá (1906–59), author of the lyrics for the Falangist hymn *Cara al sol*. This Air Force hymn quickly became popular not only with the Ejército del Aire but also with the Escuadrilla Azúl (Blue Squadron, i.e., volunteer pilots equivalent to the Blue Division) fighting in Russia. Torroba later collaborated with Foxá on a lyric comedy in two acts and seven scenes entitled *Baile en Capitanía*, which premiered at the Teatro de la Zarzuela on September 16, 1960. This was a musical version of a comic drama by Foxá that had premiered at the Teatro Español in Madrid on April 22, 1944. Its action takes place during the Carlist wars in the 1860s. The scenic direction was by Cayetano Luca de Tena, a prominent figure in the theater around 1960. See García Carretero, *Historia del Teatro de la Zarzuela*, iii, 41.

Trinchera's text resembles that of the previous *himno*. In this case it speaks of the courage and skill of Spain's pilots as they protect their great nation.

It should not surprise us if Torroba preferred a Franco victory to one by the "communists." He had flourished under the Second Republic and had never openly expressed any antagonism toward it, yet his treatment at the hands of that government once the war started, his arrest and detention on suspicion of having composed just this sort of hymn, certainly persuaded him that his existence would be precarious if the left triumphed. By taking refuge in the Nationalist stronghold of Navarra during the latter part of the war, he and his family were protected by Franco's forces. Writing these songs in the immediate wake of said salvation, i.e., 1938–39, was the least he could offer as repayment. And, in fact, he could afford to do no less. Recall that during the 1940s, the restaging of his beloved *Monte Carmelo* was blocked by Franco's censors; others of his works were also criticized. Torroba's professional survival depended on his cooperation with the regime, and turning down these assignments (if that is what they were) would have jeopardized that survival. As Stanley G. Payne notes, "anyone who hoped to find a place in the 'new Spain' had to affiliate himself with the 'Crusade.'"[104] It is obvious that Torroba put very little of himself in these marches; he clearly tossed them off in order to fulfill an apparent obligation.

This, at least, is the opinion of Pepe and Celín Romero, who knew Torroba intimately. Members of the Romero family had fought on the Republican side, and, in a mirror image of Torroba's ordeal, Celedonio (the *pater familias*), had been imprisoned by Franco's forces after the fall of Málaga in 1937. Because he had given some concerts for the International Red Cross, he was suspected of being in league with the leftists. It was only after some friends persuaded the authorities that he was just a harmless, apolitical guitarist that he was spared. Yet, Celedonio would later give benefit concerts for the same official labor unions, or *sindicatos*, that Torroba's *Himno del trabajo* extols.[105]

It is nearly impossible for us now to understand the chaotic and dangerous circumstances that Spaniards like Torroba and Celedonio Romero endured during and just after the war. We must not rush to judgment, as only those who have lived in a police state can really understand what it is like. Both men did what they thought was necessary to stay alive and remain professionally active. In any case, rather than clarifying Torroba's political allegiances, these songs actually add to the ambiguity of his stance. Federico, Jr., tells us that during the Civil War, Torroba taught him and his sister Mariana to sing both the Republican and Francoist

[104] Stanley G. Payne, *Falange: A History of Spanish Fascism* (Stanford, California: Stanford University Press, 1961), 201. Was Torroba a member of the Falange? According to Payne, "a law of October 1, 1938, declared that anyone who had been jailed for political reasons in Republican territory would automatically become a member" of the Falange. We do not yet know if this included Torroba, but if it did, it would not have been an act of volition on his part.

[105] Interview with Celín and Pepe Romero, September 5, 2010.

hymns, so that they would be well prepared should they find themselves trapped in one area or the other. This suggests a high degree of political ambivalence, of using music as a shield against reprisals rather than as a declaration of personal affiliation. Faced with a Franco triumph, Torroba apparently did what he had instructed his children to do: make the winner's music. Everyone knows that he who pays the piper calls the tune. All we can say for certain now is that, if they contributed to his survival, these forgettable ditties were a small price to pay for the beautiful music he would produce as a result of his survival.

One should note that during the 1950s Torroba less frequently titled his stage works zarzuelas, preferring instead such nomenclature as *comedia musical, comedia lírica, sainete,* or even *espectáculo.* The reasons for this are not entirely clear, but there does not seem to have been any political motivation for it, as no stigma was attached to the word zarzuela.

Indeed, as a composer of stage works and guitar music, Torroba posed no challenge to the regime, fiascos such as *Monte Carmelo* notwithstanding. He continued on his chosen path and relied as much on noninterference as patronage. As an internationally renowned composer and conductor, he was not dependent on the government for his success. Resuming his role as impresario at both the Teatro de la Zarzuela and Teatro Calderón, he staged sixteen zarzuelas between 1940 and 1945, the two most successful being *Maravilla* (1941) and *La Caramba* (1942).[106] *La ilustre moza,* based on Lope de Vega's play *La moza de cántaro,* premiered during the 1942–43 season, and the end of the decade witnessed the production of *El cantar del organillo,* on April 16, 1949, at the Teatro de la Zarzuela. In addition, the works of other zarzuelists, both contemporary and traditional, were regularly performed. To be sure, these productions were modest in comparison to those of the prewar years. Spain was in the process of recovering from the Civil War, and resources for its cultural institutions were scarce.

Return to the Americas

Recognizing the limitations of the new Spain, Torroba began to expand his network abroad in search of new audiences for his touring company. In 1946, he formed a zarzuela company that toured the Americas for two seasons, with assistance from the Franco government. Productions were mounted in Cuba,

---

[106] Historic recordings of these works, conducted by Torroba, have been reissued on the Blue Moon label, 7526. See Zueras Navarro, "Sus obras menos conocidas: Más sobre Moreno Torroba." *Maravilla* premiered at the Teatro Fontalba on April 12, 1941, and the critics compared his lyricism favorably to Puccini's. See García Carretero, *Historia del Teatro de la Zarzuela,* ii, 96. A program for *Maravilla* is in the Navarra archive, and it contains excerpts from the local press, all encomiastic: *ABC,* Miguel Ródenas; *Arriba,* Antonio de Obregón; *Hoja official del Lunes,* Víctor Ruiz Albéniz; *Informaciones,* Antonio de las Heras; *Ya,* Jorge de la Cueva; *El Alcázar,* Emilio Morales de Acevedo; *Madrid,* J. Montero Alonso; *GOL,* Raimundo de los Reyes.

Puerto Rico, and Mexico. This arrangement would prove beneficial not only to Torroba but to the host countries, for as Sturman points out, "During the 1940s Latin Americans struggled with economic problems and began to rely once again on imported productions to complete their theatrical seasons."[107]

While in Mexico in 1947, Torroba composed the zarzuela *El orgullo de Jalisco* (The Pride of Jalisco).[108] This work deserves mention, as the plot and music are based on Mexican themes from the region of Jalisco, and it illustrates Torroba's interest in folk and popular music outside of Spain. In fact, we can judge from numerous collections found in his personal archive in Navarra that Torroba retained an interest in Mexican folk music throughout the rest of his life. This zarzuela is significant for another reason: it is a vivid demonstration of Torroba's uncanny ability to acquire and absorb almost any type of music and turn it to his own purposes. His capacity to mimic other styles of music was already on display not only in earlier regional zarzuelas, such as *Xuanón* and *Azabache*, but also in *Polonesa*, which premiered at the Teatro Fontalba in Madrid in late January of 1944. *Polonesa*, loosely based on the life and music of Chopin and set in Warsaw and Paris of the 1830s, consists almost entirely of evocations of Chopin's style, composed by Torroba. There is scarcely a hint of his trademark Hispanism anywhere in the score.[109]

We know as yet little about the performance history of *El orgullo de Jalisco*, but others of his works, including *Luisa Fernanda*, *La chulapona*, *La ilustre moza*, *Maravilla*, and *La Caramba*, were presented at the Teatro Arbeu in Mexico City (*La Caramba* premiered on January 3, 1947, and *La chulapona* two weeks later). Their grueling schedule included two presentations a day and three on Sunday, for a total of fifteen performances a week with no days off. This continued until March 16, followed by a tour of the provinces; Torroba and his company departed Mexico in July—without the Domingo family, which had decided to remain there.[110]

While the critics and general public greeted these productions with genuine enthusiasm, some members of the Spanish expatriate community and Mexican government were hostile. After the Spanish Civil War, many left-wing exiles had settled in Mexico, and some former Republicans did not welcome him. From

---

[107] Sturman, Zarzuela, 42.

[108] For whatever reason, Torroba later recalled that the year was 1948, though that was incorrect. See A. C., "Federico Moreno Torroba, gloria musical de España," *La Voz de Aviles*, November 24, 1976. Perhaps at the end of a long life it became increasingly difficult to remember such precise details.

[109] A program for *Polonesa* is in the Navarra archive. On January 26, 1944, an open rehearsal was held as a benefit for the families who were victims of a recent building collapse in the calle de Maldonado (see *ABC*, January 16, 1944, for more on this). Torroba conducted an orchestra of forty musicians. In the program, Torroba says of his music: "'Does it use music by Chopin?' This is what people have been asking me for some time about the work, and I always answer, 'Little, very little. A few recollections, a few reminiscences, which are necessary in a work about Chopin.'"

[110] For an excellent summary of this tour, see Xavier A. Torresarpi, "Plácido Domingo en México," *Pro Ópera* (May–June 2011): 38–39.

their perspective, Torroba's government-sponsored tour was little more than propaganda. Articles appeared in *La Nación*, organ of the leftist Partido Acción Nacional (National Action Party), demanding that he and his company leave the country. Communist refugees expressed their indignation by putting up posters that said "Death to Franco, Moreno Torroba, leave" (Muera Franco Fuera Moreno Torroba).[111] Some argued that by encouraging the dissemination of the traditional zarzuela, Franco was misrepresenting Spanish music, ignoring the works of Falla, Gerhard, and other progressives. However, this was imputing to the dictator too much sensitivity to and interest in music.

In fact, Torroba's own feelings about Franco were at best ambivalent. He once described the Caudillo as *"un cero a la izquierda"* ("a zero to the left," i.e., an ignoramus) when it came to music,[112] and the allegation was not unfounded. "They say that he liked *Marina* [by Arrieta], but that is not certain. He didn't have an ear for music. Maybe he liked military marches, but not much else." One cause for this ambivalence may have had to do with the treatment he received from Franco upon his return from the American tour. He had apparently lost money and asked Franco to compensate him for his losses, feeling that the regime had benefited from his success and should not mind expressing some monetary gratitude. Franco demurred, and Torroba apparently never forgave him.[113]

One reason Franco declined to help Torroba was that the composer had been photographed receiving a bear hug from Indalecio de Prieto, the socialist leader and former minister of finance in the Republican government. It was a spontaneous gesture of affection and reconciliation on Prieto's part, not one initiated by our composer. But the photo appeared in the press and got back to the Spanish government.[114] In fact, Torroba had several friends in the expatriate community, among them Rodolfo Halffter, a Republican who had emigrated to Mexico, and Segovia, who spent a number of years abroad. As mentioned earlier, he maintained friendships with such disparate personalities as Rafael Alberti, a member of the Spanish communist party who returned from exile in 1975, and José María Pemán, a poet, dramatist and friend of the Franco regime.[115] Franco did not appreciate such evenhandedness, however.

---

[111] This information appears in a fascinating article by Ana Cecilia Terrazas, "Pepita Embil, su marido y la compañia de Moreno Torroba enfrentaron a un México republicano que acusó de franquista a la zarzuela," *Edición México*, September 3, 1994.

[112] "Para esto de la música Franco era un cero a la izquierda. Dicen que le gustaba *Marina* [zarzuela by Arrieta]. No es cierto. No tenía oído. Tal vez le gustaran las marchas militares, pero ni eso." Quoted in Vicent, "El pentagrama," 14.

[113] This is according to the composer's grandsons, Jacobo and Tristan, in a conversation with the authors, June 25, 2011, in Madrid.

[114] Ibid.

[115] José María Pemán was the librettist of Torroba's unpublished songs *Arenitas de mi amor* and *Lola la de Triana*, both ca. 1945.

In Madrid, Torroba also had detractors. Pablo Sorozábal, a distinguished zarzu-elist in his own right, became Torroba's rival in postwar Spain. The rivalry was of a personal nature, involving lingering sentiments about the Civil War and the dis-ruption of the 1936 premiere of Sorozábal's *La tabernera del puerto*. It appears that some Falangists formed a claque at the Fuencarral and interrupted the performance, because they thought that Sorozábal was a leftist. Sorozábal remained convinced that Torroba had orchestrated the whole affair, but available documentation in government archives does not support this claim, and the librettists themselves disputed it.[116] Nonetheless, Sorozábal's suspicions poisoned relations between the two composers for the rest of their lives.

In any case, Torroba and Sorozábal mixed about as well as oil and water. Torroba described his relations with Sorozábal as "bad, because he has a very special character. We have never been friends. He is very solitary."[117] Sorozábal was very opinionated and bitter, believing that Franco had "sold Spain to the U.S.," of which it was now a "vassal state." Like Torroba, he thought the zarzuela was losing cultural ground due to the lack of government support. And he held the similarly self-contradictory view that "politics have nothing to do with art." But he also thought that the public's lack of money for tickets and its interest in sports were partly responsible. He did not share Torroba's nationalist ideology, however, saying that "to belong to a nation is horrible, and there should not be nations or flags or borders." It is easy to see why they did not get along. Sorozábal confirmed that the censors were not interested in the "notes on the page but rather the words in the libretto."[118] He was certainly in a position to know, claiming that one of the censors objected to the fact that one of the fisherman characters in *La tabernera del puerto* was wearing a red shirt! When the work was produced in Madrid after the war, Sorozábal was forbidden to conduct it because the regime believed he was a "red." He denied any such thing, saying that he hated politics and never belonged to a political party.

Torroba certainly did not share Sorozábal's assessment of the United States, which he liked visiting, especially New York, where he enjoyed attending

[116] In correspondence between Sorozábal and librettist Jesus María de Arozamena, Sorozábal accused Torroba and journalist Manuel Merino of instigating the disruption of the premiere of *La tabernera* in 1936. On that occasion, fascist censors stopped the performance. To date, there has been no independent research to prove this allegation. The file on this work in the Archivo General de la Administración, (3)46 73/8397 819/40, makes no mention of Torroba or this incident. The censors had virtually no objections to anything in the libretto, except for a bit of dialogue on p. 16, in which Simpson expresses his disbelief in God. Those few lines were the only excisions the censors made. That the libretto's authors did not support Sorozábal's claims is apparent in Federico Romero, *Cinco cartas boca arriba de F. Romero y Guillermo Fernández Shaw* (Madrid: Repoker, 1950). In any case, *La tabernera del puerto* was staged repeatedly during the Franco era and remains one of the staples of the repertoire.

[117] María Luz García, "'Lo único que no se repite es la música,'" *Última Hora*, April 23, 1982.

[118] This material comes from an interview with Pablo Sorozábal by William Krause, Madrid, July 27, 1988.

American musical theater.[119] The vitality of Broadway left a strong impression on him, and its influence appears in the increasing frequency with which he subtitled his stage works as *comedias musicales*. More international in their character, the *comedias* relied less on regional ambience and music. The impact of Gershwin on Torroba's final stage work, the opera *El poeta* (1980), is something we will note in Act III, Scene ii. In any event, upon his return to Madrid in mid-1947, Torroba produced three more stage works before 1950.

Throughout the 1950s, Torroba continued to prosper as an impresario in Madrid and in worldwide tours with his company. This was a very productive period, one in which he premiered five theater works for the Teatro de la Zarzuela, as well as eleven others for production elsewhere in Madrid. However, these were not as well received as previous works. An exception was *María Manuela*, his most popular zarzuela of the decade. It premiered at the Teatro de la Zarzuela on February 1, 1957, though it was first produced in Buenos Aires in March of 1955, by the company of Faustino Garcia.[120] In three acts, this work marked the end of Torroba's twenty-five-year collaboration with Guillermo Fernández Shaw. Conspicuous in this zarzuela is the influence of Broadway, especially in the rich and imaginative orchestration as well as the occasional harmonic or rhythmic nuance of a jazzy nature. Also of some importance is the production of *La chulapona* at the Greenwich News Theater in New York during the 1958–59 season. Translated into English, the production reached a previously untapped audience.[121]

Torroba's demanding schedule as impresario and conductor did not afford the time or inspiration for large-scale works for the guitar. Works produced during the 1940s and 1950s were not as ambitious as his prewar compositions. Large groupings of miniatures in the books *Guitarra española I–VIII* were published during 1956–60, but they did not reach a wide audience, except for the ever-popular **Romance de los pinos**, which Torroba reused in other works. Another well-known work from this period is **Madroños** (published in 1954, though possibly composed as early as 1929).[122] Despite the lull in Torroba's output, Segovia continued to present his music to a worldwide audience. As Segovia's students adopted his repertory, earlier works such as *Sonatina, Suite castellana, Piezas características,* and *Nocturno* were passed on to a new generation of performers.

However, this period was not as unproductive for the guitar as it might appear. In 1953, Torroba finished the first draft of the guitar solo, *Sonata fantasía.* This

---

[119] We recall that Torroba toured Latin America often, but he also found time to visit New York. He traveled there on behalf of the SGAE to pursue agreements with BMI and ASCAP in 1950. Though he did not become vice president of the Sociedad until 1957, he was already acting in some sort of official capacity by the late 1940s.

[120] García Carretero, *Historia del Teatro de la Zarzuela*, iii, 18.

[121] The information in this paragraph comes from an untitled press clipping in the Navarra archive, dated May 31, 1982.

[122] We are grateful to Spanish musicologist Leopoldo Neri for information concerning the genesis and premiere of this work.

work was dedicated to Segovia.[123] It is not certain if Segovia ever received it in this form, as it was not published until 1975 (and subsequently in 1990 and 2002). Its importance lies in the fact that it contains much of the thematic material for one of his finest works, **Diálogos entre guitarra y orquesta** (1977). (This will be discussed in Act III, Scene iii.) The 1940s and 50s appear to have been a period of reflection and preparation for the remarkable outpouring of music that occurred during the last two decades of Torroba's life.

During the 1950s, Spain's isolation began to abate as new international factors came into play. As part of its overall Cold War strategy, the United States made major economic and military investments in Spain, beginning with a treaty in 1953. While many Spaniards resented foreign support, which served to strengthen Franco's position, there was also the expectation that there would be a welcome influx of currency and ideas. Torroba's "espectáculo lírico" *Bienvenido Mister Dólar* (1954) is a light-hearted satire on the public's expectations. With fantasies of new wealth, characters vie for everything from luxury goods to soccer stars. Its title was clearly a nod in the direction of the landmark film *¡Bienvenido Mr. Marshall!* (1952), which was a poignant satire of the Franco regime's embrace of the United States[124] However, there is nothing of political satire in Torroba's charming little work, which is set in the Caribbean.[125] The lyrics for one of the numbers, a playful "Fantasia Afro-Cubana," give us some idea of the work's tropical-erotic languor (the scenic indications in the script at this point call for hammocks strung between palm trees).

Table II:ii:1: Lyrics to "Mi noche tropical" from *Bienvenido Mr. Dólar*

Mi noche tropical	My tropical night
Caricia y flor	Caricia and flower
Noche sensual	Sensual night
De loco amor.	Of love insane.
La noche tropical	The tropical night
Que me besó	That kissed me
La flor del mal	The flower of evil
Nos embriago.	Intoxicated us.
Besar	Kissing
Y en otros labios poner	And on another's lips

(continued)

---

[123] This score is found in the Navarra archive.

[124] See Julio Arce's excellent analysis of this classic film, "Irony, *esperpento*, and Parody in the Music of *¡Bienvenido Mister Marshall!*" in *Diagonal: The Journal of the Center for Iberian and Latin American Music* 7 (2011), available online at http://cilam.ucr.edu/diagonal/issues/2011/index.html.

[125] The file in the Archivo General de la Administración, (3)46 73/9096 6/54, raises no objections but states that the work was suitable for audiences 16 and older. The text for this "Fantasia Lírica en Dos Actos" was by P. Llabres and Fernando Egea, and the work premiered on January 22, 1954, presented by the Hispano-Argentina company.

Table II:ii:1: Continued

Calor	To place warmth
Calor de dulce ilusión	The warmth of sweet dreams
Y alli beber	And there to drink
Con angustiosa ambición	With anguished ambition
Toda una loca pasión.	All of a crazy passion.
Noche de mi amor.	Night of my love.
Luna, sombra y flor...	Moon, shadow, and flower
En que mi carne morena	In which my dark flesh
En que mi carne morena	In which my dark flesh
Supo del beso mejor.	Knew the best kiss.
Vuelve a dejar	Return to leave
Sobre mi boca la hiel	On my mouth the bitterness
De aquellos labios	Of those lips
Que a mi saben a miel...	That to me tasted of honey...
Besar...	Kissing...
Besar...	Kissing...
Besar...	Kissing...

This sort of entertainment was the polar opposite of what other Spanish composers were attempting to accomplish at this time. Cristobal Halffter coined the term "Generation of 51" to designate his contemporaries, many of whom had completed their conservatory training in 1951. In a broader sense, the term connotes the group of composers born around 1930 who initiated the resurgence of the international avant-garde in Spain in the late 1950s and early 1960s. Along with Halffter, outstanding musicians such as Alberto Blancafort (1928–), Luís de Pablo, and Juan Hidalgo (1927–) were part of this heterogeneous group. These composers sought to assimilate the achievements of Stravinsky and Bartók, serialism, aleatory, and electronic music. They felt an urgency to make up for lost time and consequently passed very quickly through these techniques before settling on more personalized styles of their own.[126] Torroba had little in common with these composers, and they increasingly viewed him as an anachronism. All that notwithstanding, the old maestro still had a few musical aces up his sleeve and was poised to compose some of his finest works in the two decades ahead.

[126] Tomás Marco, *Historia de la música española*, 208.

1. Madrid's symbol is a bear eating fruit off of a *madroño* tree.

2. The Puerta de Alcalá is one of the many gates built in Madrid during the reign of Carlos III, in the 1700s.

3. The Puerta del Sol ca. 1890. It was and remains the heart of Madrid's commercial and social life.

4. Right off the Puerta del Sol is calle de la Montera, 3, where Torroba was born.

5. José Moreno Ballesteros was an accomplished church and theater musician and composer.
Courtesy of Federico Moreno-Torroba Larregla

6. Moreno Ballesteros worked at the church of San Millán y San Cayetano in Madrid.

7. Torroba at age 2, dressed as Turiddu from Mascagni's *Cavalleria rusticana*.
Courtesy of Federico Moreno-Torroba Larregla

8. Young Torroba tries his hand as a toreador. He counted many famous bullfighters among his friends.
Courtesy of Federico Moreno-Torroba Larregla

9. A notable *madrileña* institution was the *tertulia*, gatherings at cafés where people could discuss politics and the arts. The Café de Levante, shown here, was popular with writers and journalists, and it displayed paintings by Leonardo Alenza.
Courtesy of Museo de Historia, Madrid

10. Founded in 1850, the Teatro Real closed for many years just after the production of Torroba's 1925 *La virgen de mayo*.

11. Torroba married Pilar Larregla at the Baroque Church of San José, just off the Gran Vía, in 1926.

12. The distinctive cover art for *Azabache*, Torroba's 1932 zarzuela set in Granada.
Courtesy of Federico Moreno-Torroba Larregla

13. Torroba in the 1930s.
Courtesy of Federico Moreno-Torroba Larregla

14. Torroba (front row, fourth from right) and the cast at a banquet celebrating the successful 1932 premiere of *Luisa Fernanda* in Madrid.
Courtesy of Federico Moreno-Torroba Larregla

15. Torroba reveled in the bucolic serenity of Santesteban, in Navarra. It provided a safe haven during the Civil War and an ideal environment for creative work thereafter.

16. Street dancers perform the *jota navarra* during the 2006 Festival of San Fermín in Santesteban. The sights and sounds of Spanish music and dance inform Torroba's music.

17. Torroba conducting the famous "Marzurka de las sombrillas" from *Luisa Fernanda*, at the Teatro de la Zarzuela (date unknown).

18. Torroba at a production of *Xuanón* in Buenos Aires, ca. 1960.
Courtesy of Federico Moreno-Torroba Larregla

19. Argentine guitarist Irma Costanzo with Torroba, whose *Homenaje a la seguidilla* for guitar and orchestra she performed in Buenos Aires in 1975, with the composer conducting.
Courtesy of Irma Costanzo

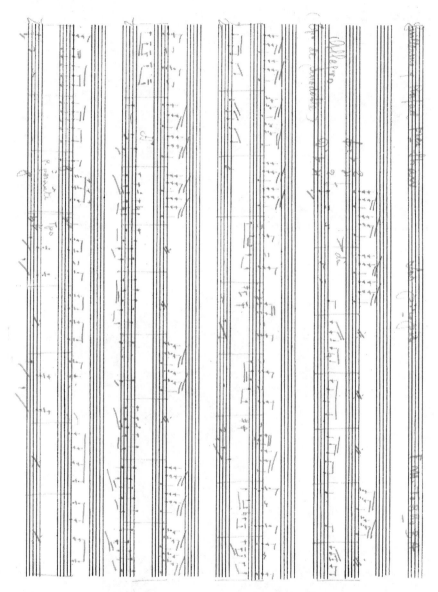

20. A sample of Torroba's music script, which was somewhat idiosyncratic yet perfectly legible.

Courtesy of Federico Moreno-Torroba Larregla

21. The *art nouveau* façade of the Sociedad General de Autores y Editores in Madrid, of which Torroba was president 1974–82.

22. The Real Academia de Bellas Artes de San Fernando is one of the most venerable cultural institutions in Spain. Torroba was admitted as a member in 1935 and became director in 1978.

23. Torroba receives the Medalla de Oro de las Bellas Artes from King Juan Carlos and Queen Sofia in 1980, in recognition of his contributions to Spanish culture.
Courtesy of Federico Moreno-Torroba Larregla

24. After the death of his wife in 1977, Torroba continued to find joy in his children and grandchildren. Standing from left to right: Federico, Jr., and his wife, Carmen Macicior, and their son Tristán in his arms. Sitting from left to right: Daughter Mariana's son Lucio Arrieta Moreno-Torroba, Federico, Sr., Pilar Arrieta Moreno-Torroba (Mariana's daughter), and Federico, Jr.'s other son, Jacobo Moreno-Torroba.
Courtesy of Federico Moreno-Torroba Larregla

25. Torroba in 1980, with fellow composers Ernesto Halffter (second from right) and Joaquín Rodrigo (third from right), along with the conductor Enrique García Asensio (far left). Rodrigo's wife, Victoria, is on the far right.

Courtesy of Manuel Halffter

26. From right to left: Pepe Romero; Torroba's daughter, Mariana; Torroba; and Pepe's future wife, Carissa. Torroba developed a close relationship with the Romero family, which recorded four of his concertos: *Diálogos* (Pepe); *Homenaje a la seguidilla* and *Tonada concertante* (Ángel), and *Concierto ibérico* (Quartet).
Courtesy of the Romero family

27. Torroba's funeral service took place at the Iglesia de la Concepción on September 14, 1982. He had performed there many times.

EXCMO. SR.
D. FEDERICO MORENO-TORROBA BALLESTEROS
COMPOSITOR
★ 3 MARZO 1891   † 12 SEPTIEMBRE 1982
D. E. P.

28. Torroba's tomb, in the Sacramental de San Justo, is utterly modest and inconspicuous, befitting his humility but not his stature as one of Spain's greatest musicians.

29. Federico, Jr., is a successful conductor and composer in his own right, and he and
his wife, Carmen, maintain the family archive in Santesteban.

6

ACT II
Scene iii
Major Works of the Period 1932–56

The principal works of this period are remarkable in one key respect: they seem utterly disconnected from the historical events that accompanied their genesis. One could easily imagine Torroba writing the same pieces exactly the same way even if the Civil War had never taken place and the Republic had continued peaceably on its course, with Franco becoming little more than a footnote to history. In short, Torroba's music for the stage and guitar exhibited no conspicuous change in style, much less any sudden shift toward a nationalist aesthetic in order to conform to the new sociocultural order after the war. It is in this sense that Torroba genuinely was, as he always insisted, *apolitical*.

It is true, however, that his most important works from this period are those written for the stage; it is equally as true that this outpouring of lyric theater represented the final florescence of his creativity in that arena. In the final period of his long career, the guitar comes front and center, particularly in concertos for one or more guitars, works in which he reveals a gift for orchestral writing already obvious to zarzuela *habitués* but not concert audiences of that time familiar only with his guitar solos. We survey several stage works here, representing the decade 1932 to 1942, from *Azabache* to *La Caramba*. Despite the devastation of the Civil War, the public's appetite for zarzuela continued unabated during this time, and in response, Torroba brought forth some of his finest inspirations in the aftermath of that conflict.

It is beyond the scope of this book to survey all, most, or even very many of his seventy stage works in depth, that is, present a synopsis of every act and several musical examples from each. In addition to *Luisa Fernanda* and *La marchenera*, Torroba composed about a half dozen zarzuelas that have had any real staying power.[1] We deem two of these—*La chulapona* and *Monte Carmelo*—genuine masterpieces

---

[1] We look at five of those half-dozen here; the book will conclude with a brief treatment of one other zarzuela, *Maravilla* (1941).

and lavish the most attention on them here. After all, the composer himself thought these his finest zarzuelas. The others we examine here are truly lovely works, and though they are rarely staged in their entirety, they offer particular numbers of interest, numbers that have retained their popularity in zarzuela anthologies and that give us a clear idea of Torroba's stylistic breadth, imagination, and skill. We offer abbreviated descriptions of them, including a plot summary and one or two musical inspirations.

Stage Works

Azabache

The action of the three-act zarzuela *Azabache* is set in present-day Granada and commences in a church, during a Gypsy wedding. The emphasis on Gypsy culture in this work extends to the text, which is thoroughly and expertly rendered in Gypsy Andalusian dialect. The music is in a similar vein and repeatedly evokes the songs and dances of this group and region. The two Gypsies getting married, Juan Ortega and La Golosina, have been living together for thirty years and have grown children. In fact, at precisely this moment of matrimonial celebration, their daughter María Paz expresses her desire to marry a refined young man named José Moreno, who is an engineer. They reject this otherwise desirable union because of a longstanding conflict with José's family. María Paz rebels against her parents' wishes and declares her intention to go on loving José; in fact, when José appears on the scene, the young lovers set off to elope. However, a wealthy Gypsy named Azabache interrupts their escape.

Love triangles are a staple of Torroba's zarzuelas, and predictably, Azabache loves María Paz as well, though he has told no one of his feelings. The plot thickens when he reappears after the wedding, seriously wounded and claiming that José was the assailant. María Paz nurses Azabache back to health, which only intensifies his feelings for her. Meanwhile, José's sister comes to speak with the two, insisting on José's innocence. Azabache agrees to pay for José's release from jail, because only in this way can he know for sure whom María Paz truly loves. In reality, she feels a certain grateful affection for Azabache, but as he fears, she is still in love with José. Seeing that his suit is hopeless, Azabache confesses that it was not José who injured him after all: his wounds were self-inflicted! In a rather predictable display of noble resignation reminiscent of Vidal, he relinquishes Paz to José and departs with a disreputable Gypsy named Cinizo, both of them in search of redemption and happiness. María Paz gives him a carnation to remember her by, and the curtain descends.

Among the memorable numbers in this work is a *bulerías* sung by María Paz in Act II (no. 8), which expands upon themes presented in the Preludio. During Azabache's convalescence, she sings him a song to lift his spirits. Her lively number

Ex. II:iii:1 *Azabache*, Act II, no. 8, "Granaina de la Alhambra de Graná," mm. 24–41

tells a famous legend of Boabdil, the last Moorish king of Granada, whose falling tears caused red carnations to sprout from the ground (hence the significance of María Paz's parting gift to Azabache). In a clever shift of rhythm, the number breaks into a *zapateado* at rehearsal 4, before returning to the *bulerías*. The overall form is AA'BA'' (see ex. II:iii:1).

Xuanón

A lyric comedy in two acts, *Xuanón* is set in an imaginary mining town, Sama de Laviana, in the northern region of Asturias, around 1880. Mining is one of the mainstays of the Asturian economy, and given the large number of poor laborers there, it is not surprising that issues of class come to the fore in this drama. However, unlike the text for *Azabache*, José Ramos Martín's libretto makes little attempt to utilize the dialect of ordinary Asturian folk, save for a few expressions here and there; instead, the language is largely *madrileño*, in order to make it comprehensible to the Madrid audiences for which it was ultimately intended. Its use of a more widely comprehensible variety of Spanish may help explain its subsequent success in Barcelona and even in Mexico (1947).

To be sure, the Asturian audiences who soon embraced the work expressed no objections to the libretto. Still, the zarzuela could not completely avoid controversy, and a claque of protestors attempted a boycott of the Calderón premiere, without anything like the success of the work they were protesting (it is not yet clear just what they found offensive about the *Xuanón*, though it probably pertained to labor strife in Asturias).[2]

The zarzuela commences with a pilgrimage in honor of the Virgen de los Paxarinos. Xuanón, an angry and arrogant young miner, gets into a vehement dispute with Manolín over who will dance with a local girl, Rosina. She wisely agrees to dance with both men, but Xuanón haughtily rejects her offer. The elderly Sabina now confronts Xuanón and asks that he stop singing offensive songs (*coplas*) every night in the local *chigre*, an Asturian bar that serves cider (*sidra*). His outpourings are upsetting the widow Belarma, who lives across from the *chigre*. Predictably, Xuanón responds that he is afraid of no one, least of all a woman.

At this point, a group of girls assembles to make an offering to the Virgin. Among them is Oliva, who laments the fact that her former *novio* (fiancé), Pichín, is no longer interested in her. He went off to Cuba before they could get married and made a fortune there. He has since returned but has made himself unavailable to her. He soon appears, finely attired, but remains aloof. Oliva is consoled by her friend Pin, who is also hurt by Belarma's indifference to him. He plans to leave the village for Cuba as soon as possible, to start a new life. Everyone is startled to discover two old people, Sabina and Manín, kissing. Belarma enters to defend the former; interestingly, Xuanón does the same for the latter. However, as Belarma departs, she and Xuanón have a heated exchange. The real nature of their relationship remains, for now, something of a mystery to us, though we recognize that such extreme repulsion often conceals extreme attraction. Oliva now appears with a newborn baby boy who has been abandoned at the altar of the Virgin. No one has any idea whose it is, but Belarma takes charge of it, while a celebratory Asturian dance brings the act to a close.

Act II begins in the little plaza of the village. As the miners sing their coarse songs in the *chigre*, a group of young women, led by Oliva, reprimands them for

---

[2] See Víctor Sánchez-Sánchez, "Xuanón," *Diccionario de la zarzuela: España e Hispanoamérica*, ed. Emilio Casares Rodicio (Madrid: ICCMU, 2002), 951. The following plot summary is indebted to this scholar's excellent entry.

Ex. II:iii:2 *Xuanón*, Act II, no. 6, "Corazón de la seducción," mm. 97–102

their behavior. This confrontation sets up one of the most delightful numbers of the work, "Corazón de la seducción" (Heart of seduction) (see ex. II:iii:2). It pits choruses of miners and women against one another while exuding an Asturian fragrance in its lively foursquare ostinatos and drone. In fact, one finds these devices throughout the entire score, in which Torroba frequently uses measure-repetition signs to save time writing out the same notes and rhythms.

The miners continue to entertain themselves and to celebrate with Pin his impending departure for Cuba. Pin's "En el camino de Mieres" (On Mieres Road) (Act II, no. 7) was such a hit that it had to repeated three times at the premiere. In a nod toward the community workers' choirs (*orfeónes*) popular in the Asturias region, Torroba provides a cappella male-choir accompaniment, singing *bocca chiusa* (closed mouth).[3]

Pachín arrives at the *chigre*, and in an ensuing exchange with Oliva, we learn that he did not make a fortune in Cuba after all. He has simply been putting on airs in the hopes of marrying a woman of means. This confession paves the way for their reconciliation. It now becomes apparent that Xuanón is enamored of Belarma. He also resorts to dissimulation, with no more success than Pachín. He pretends to be the father of the baby boy and offers to help Belarma in caring for him. She graciously

[3] See Víctor Sánchez-Sánchez, "Xuanón," *Diccionario de la zarzuela*, ii, 951. For more on the *orfeón* in Spain during the 1800s, see Clark, "The Iberian World," as well as the entry by María Nagore Ferrer on "Coros, I. 1–10: España," in Emilio Casares Rodicio, ed., *Diccionario de la música española e latino-americana* (Madrid: Sociedad General de Autores y Editores, 1999).

accepts his offer, but Manín spoils this plan by announcing that the real mother has been found. Xuanón is forced to admit that he simply wanted to be united with Belarma. In his lovely romanza, "En los cuentos de aldea no hay que fiar" (One can't trust village stories) (Act II, No. 12), he asks for forgiveness and love. The concluding chorus exults in Belarma's success in capturing Xuanón.

La chulapona

La chulapona is set in Madrid at the end of the nineteenth century. As Julián García León points out, it is an example of costumbrismo, i.e., a presentation of local manners and customs, but one that, instead of focusing on the present, "is nostalgic and seeks to perpetuate a longed-for past."[4] Predictably, the authors and composer idealize and romanticize that past. In this sense, La chulapona resembles Vives's Doña Francisquita, and in fact, both works retell Vega's La discreta enamorada, itself a retelling of the third story of the third day of Boccaccio's Decameron, in which a self-determining woman sets out to satisfy her romantic longings, rather than remaining a passive object of desire.[5]

The word chulapona is not easy to translate, but in the context of this drama, it refers to a streetwise, self-possessed woman in tune with and exercising some influence on the daily lives of the ordinary people who inhabit her ordinary world.[6] Indeed, unlike La marchenera and Luisa Fernanda, this is a story of working-class people who are not at odds with the government or wealthy overlords. Rather, the plot focuses on complicated personal relationships, which ultimately result in an illegitimate child. This zarzuela is especially steeped in casticismo, regionalism, and social mores, making it hard to export beyond Spain and Spanish-speaking areas, though not impossible.[7] The success of its 1995 production at the Edinburgh Festival is proof that zarzuela can reach across cultural and linguistic boundaries, if given a proper chance.[8]

However, the music speaks a more universal language. The music of the 1890s was full of habaneras, schottisches, pasodobles, and mazurkas, and though this was all anachronistic by the era in which Torroba composed his score, these numbers retained their popular appeal well into the twentieth century.[9] The second act

---

[4] Julián García León, "'La Chulapona', alegoría y homenaje a la zarzuela decimonónica," La Chulapona, program notes for the production at the Teatro de la Zarzuela, Madrid, February 6 to March 7, 2004 (Madrid: Teatro de la Zarzuela, 2003), 14.

[5] Ibid., 15.

[6] Manuel Alvar Ezquerra, Diccionario de madrileñismos: Voces patrimoniales y populares de la Comunidad de Madrid (Madrid: Ediciones La Librería, 2011), 118, define a chulapón or chulapona simply as a member of Madrid's lower classes.

[7] R. Alier, X. Aviñoa, F. X. Mata, Diccionario de la zarzuela (Madrid: Damión, 1986), 222.

[8] See Webber, Zarzuela, 178. We recall that it was also successfully produced at the Greenwich News Theater in New York during the 1958–59 season.

[9] Sánchez Sánchez, La Chulapona, program notes, 2004, 24.

revolves around an afternoon at the bullfights, providing an opportunity for festive *guajiras* and *pasacalles*.[10] The highlight of this act is a presentation of *bulerías*, *tanguillo*, *peteneras*, and a *zapateado*,[11] all flamenco genres and accompanied by guitar and orchestra. This memorable moment recalls the second scene of Bretón's *La verbena de la paloma*. The influence of earlier *zarzueleros* is also apparent in the *guajiras* of Juan de Dios, another in a long line of Cuban *guajiras* and which resembles the one in *La revoltosa* by Chapí (No. 3). The *chotis*, in fashion after 1880, was most famously evoked in Chueca's *La Gran Vía*. Likewise, the habanera was popular everywhere and appeared in *La gallina ciega* of Caballero, not to mention Arrieta's *Marina* and Caballero's *Los sobrinos del capitán Grant*.[12] Enrique Franco finds that the orchestral introduction, with its use of the bolero rhythm, resembles Caballero's *El dúo de la Africana* (a work invoked in the opening scene). The *zapateado* follows in the footsteps of Giménez, while the mazurka is indebted to Chueca. The *chotis* ("No puedo"), *pasacalle* ("Como soy"), and *jota* remind one of Caballero, as does the habanera ("Ese pañuelito blanco").[13] None of this is meant to suggest that Torroba's music lacks originality, only that the composer's distinctive style exhibits obvious continuity with a long line of antecedents.

This persistent emphasis on musical realism finds a parallel in the text. *La chulapona*'s action takes place in the barrio Latino during the final decade of the nineteenth century. The denizens of that district spoke a *chulo* (low-class) dialect, full of colloquial expressions that librettists López Silva and Arniches employed to realistic advantage.[14] This approximation of the local argot virtually requires the listener/reader to use a glossary, to look up terms like *bimba* (a type of hat), *curiana* (cockroach), *chambra* (type of shirt), *filfa* (lie), *guinda*, or *langosta* (police).[15] These expressions are not familiar even to most speakers of Castilian, especially outside of their immediate context, and would be utterly mysterious to English speakers with anything less than an advanced degree in *madrileño* dialects.

The radical application of unusual social conventions imposed by bourgeois morality provokes in the protagonists of *La chulapona* (unlike *Doña Francisquita*) a true psychological tragedy, which does not accord with this type of zarzuela because it becomes a rather sorrowful *sainete*. The happy music of the final *pasacalle*, featuring

[10] The Spanish-Cuban *guajira* is characterized by its strong hemiola. *Pasacalles* are street songs, sung by young men to their beloved, who listen from their window above the street.

[11] The *bulerías* is a lively flamenco song and dance that employs a *compás*, or meter, of twelve beats with accents on 12, 3, 6, 8, and 10. This produces a hemiola effect (*sesquiáltera* in Spanish). The Andalusian dance *peteneras* is characterized by the alternation of 3/8 and 3/4 meters. The *zapateado* is a dance is quick 6/8 meter, with accents shifting between the first and second beats of the triplets.

[12] Ibid., 25-26.

[13] Franco, *La Chulapona*, program notes, 1988, 14–15.

[14] Hernández Girbal, *La Chulapona*, program notes, 1988, 19.

[15] García León, *La Chulapona*, program notes, 2004, 16.

Ex. II:iii:3 *La chulapona*, Act I, no. 1-A, Introducción, mm. 1–4

the *organillo*, adds a touch of irony to the bitter outcome.[16] "In this case the love tri-angle dissolves to form a square: Señor Antonio, a victim of self-deception, offers him-self as a sacrifice, blinded by his dream."[17] In fact, this is a work in which love, virtue, and trust do not carry the day.[18]

The spirited introduction announces its Spanish pedigree with the rhythms of the *seguidillas*, and, as was the case with *La marchenera*, makes effective use of orchestral color, including triangle, castanets, tambourine, and pizzicato strings. This is one of Torroba's most arresting and distinctive orchestral creations (see ex. II:iii:3).

The action commences in the laundry establishment of the *chulapona*, Manuela. The year is 1893. In the opening scene, the laundry girls are hard at work, but not so much so that they cannot sing a song, in this case a number from Caballero's *El dúo de la Africana*, "No cantes más *la Africana*" (Stop singing *la Africana*), led by the lovely young Rosario. Torroba blends the music of the introduction with this chorus, providing a smooth transition from the one to the other. A young man nicknamed Cravat (El Chalina), after his stylish necktie, soon appears at the door, and he and the girls sing and dance a mazurka, "Las chicas de Madrí" (The girls of Madrid) (Act I, no. 1-B), accompanied by an *organillo*, or barrel organ (see ex. II:iii:4). This is a charming evocation of café music from that epoch.

The plot soon thickens as Manuela's ne'er-do-well father, Don Epifanio, barges in. He is an alcoholic who has run up a considerable debt to Rosario's mother, Venustiana, who pursues him for repayment. The Don hides from her behind some petticoats, while El Chalina persuades her to look elsewhere. Finally, we are introduced to *la chulapona* herself, as Manuela sings a lovely *chotis*, "Crei que no

---

[16] Ibid.

[17] Ibid., 17.

[18] Javier Suárez-Pajares, "Chulapona, La," *Diccionario de la zarzuela: España e Hispanoamérica*, ed. Emilio Casares Rodicio (Madrid: ICCMU, 2002), 488.

Ex. II:iii:4 *La chulapona*, Act I, no. 1-B, "Las chicas de Madrí," mm. 1–4

Ex. II:iii:5 *La chulapona*, Act I, no. 2-B, "Como soy chulapona," mm. 33–36

venia" (I thought he would not come). Her love of being a true *madrileña* is clear in her memorable *pasacalle* "Como soy chulapona" (As I am the chulapona), which celebrates her status as the leading lady of plebian Madrid (see ex. II:iii:5).

Though Manuela is always the object of male attention, whether on the street or in the laundry, and though she appreciates it, she is intent upon her boyfriend, José María. Now the love triangle is complete, because Rosario is jealous of Manuela and covets José María for herself. Their trio, "¿Se puede pasar, paloma?" (May one pass, dove?) (Act I, no. 3), makes these feelings clear to all. Rosario now resorts to sowing seeds of doubt in Manuela's mind about her beau's faithfulness, but before that process reaches fruition, Manuela's down-and-out brother, Juan de Dios, arrives, begging for financial assistance (like father, like son). At just this moment, however, Venustiana returns with the police in hopes of finding and arresting Don Epifanio. General hilarity ensues, but Manuela reveals her innate nobility by pawning her embroidered *mantón*, or shawl, to secure her father's release. While Manuela is distracted, Rosario tearfully expresses her love to José María, who embraces her as they sing the famous habanera "Ese pañuelito blanco" (That little white handkerchief) (Act I, no. 5). The gentle, playfully amorous character of this number establishes, if nothing else, the immaturity of the lovers, a certain insouciance that will have grave implications further on (see ex. II:iii:6).

However, Manuela soon discovers them and proudly dismisses her boyfriend, declaring that, for all she cares, he can marry Rosario instead, if he wants. Thus ends the first act.

Ex. II:iii:6 *La chulapona*, Act I, no. 5, "Ese pañuelito blanco," mm. 5–12

Act II commences with the sort of outdoor setting typical of the zarzuela at this point in the drama, in this case a small plaza in the Morería neighborhood. The orchestra renders a lively *seguidillas* to accompany large groups of people making their way to the local *corrida*, or bullfight (Act II, no. 6). The impecunious Juan de Dios sings a rather coarsely comical *guajira*, "En la Habana hay una casa" (There is a house in Havana), to persuade passers-by to give him some money for the bullfight. Don Epifanio is more in need of a drink than a bullfight and steals Juan's guitar to sell for liquor. Number 7 is an extended *pasacalle* and concludes the first scene of Act II. In it, we learn that José María is now engaged to Rosario, as Manuela is too proud to take him back, and he is too proud to beg forgiveness! *La chulapona* herself appears in order to buy her shawl back from the moneylender, but Rosario is wearing it as she accompanies José María to the *corrida*. Manuela pays the debt and reclaims her *mantón*, giving Rosario a scolding for good measure. This number is further evidence of Torroba's masterful ability to maintain musical interest while advancing the drama, through the use of arioso, recitative, and melodrama. Ronald Crichton thought the entire zarzuela gave evidence of a "real opera composer's ability to present situations in music."[19]

A seductive *nocturno* in the orchestra establishes the ambience of scene 2, on a pleasantly warm evening in Madrid at the Café de Naranjeros in the plaza de la Cebada, an establishment owned by one Señor Antonio, who is also an admirer of *la chulapona*. The voice of a flamenco singer and the sound of two guitars emanate

---

[19] Ronald Crichton,"*La Chulapona*: Edinburgh Festival," *Financial Times*, August 19, 1989, 19.

Ex. II:iii:7 *La chulapona*, Act II, no. 8, "Tienes razón, amigo," mm. 10–14

from the café, amid shouts of "olé." This scene centers, however, on the feckless José María, who arrives after a week's absence, trying to sort out his feelings for the two women. He sings a *romanza*, "Tienes razón, amigo" (You're right, friend) (Act II, no. 8), which is one of the lyric highpoints of the drama. The minor key and meandering melodic line convey a sense of his confusion, though there is no doubting his passion as it eventually ascends to high G. Torroba cleverly interweaves the café performance with this song of José María, who echoes the plaintive "¡Ay!" of the flamenco singer within (see ex. II:iii:7).

The third and final scene of this act (no. 9) is one of the musically most memorable in all of Torroba's works. For, we are now treated to a performance within a performance, a potpourri of flamenco numbers staged within the café. As mentioned above, the *palos* represented include *bulerías*, *tanguillo*, *peteneras*, and *zapateado*.

Manuela encounters José María, and the crowd watches them in silence as they are soon reconciled with one another, in the course of a lovely habanera, "Digale uste' a ese sujeto" (Tell him about that). Señor Antonio is not pleased with this outcome, as he still has his sights set on her. In the following act, his fortunes will change. The second act concludes with an ingenious recapitulation of previous themes, including the introduction to Act I, the aforementioned habanera, and "Ese pañuelito blanco."

The concluding act begins with a reprise of the introduction to Act I. The setting is the Viveros de la Villa, a forested locale on the banks of the Manzanares River.

Ex. II:iii:8 La chulapona, Act III, no. 11-B, "¡Ay, madrileña chulapa!" mm. 56–62

Venustiana has eloped with the organ grinder, so that situation has now been resolved. Manuela is about to marry José María, and the wedding party is posing for a photograph. The ensemble sings and dances a *chotis*, "¡Ay, madrileña chulapa!" (no. 11-B), which extols the charms of an everyday gal from Madrid (see ex. II:iii:8).

Rosario longs to take Manuela's place at José María's side and pleads with him to return to her, claiming she is carrying his child! José María, however, is committed to Manuela and refuses her request. Rosario resigns herself to her fate and makes her peace with Manuela, wishing her well. She admits that she had acted out of jealousy but is now reconciled to the situation. She also informs Manuela that she is pregnant with José María's baby. Their duo is one of most touching moments in this zarzuela.

The drama concludes with Manuela abandoning José María for Antonio, the café owner. Noble in both spirit and deed, Manuela does not wish to see the baby grow up without its father. And yet, the situation is not uniformly grim. Though she does not love Antonio and will spend many long nights yearning for the man she truly loves, José María has proven himself unreliable, and we are safe to assume (or rationalize) that she is probably better off without him.

Webber speculates that the reason this work is not as popular as *Luisa Fernanda* is that it does not have the same wealth of memorable tunes. After all, the librettists allowed for just one *romanza*, the kind of solo song that audiences and critics held as a crucial benchmark in assessing a zarzuela. And yet, in the words of Webber, "*La chulapona's* dazzling mixture of popular song, catchy dance and orchestral wizardry has enthralled audience at home and abroad."[20] Anyone who views the DVD of the 1988 production will be left with no doubts about that. This zarzuela is a magnificent achievement.

Monte Carmelo

However, the zarzuela that Torroba considered to be his finest is *Monte Carmelo*, though it has been almost completely eclipsed by *Luisa Fernanda*. This occlusion has resulted not so much from audience preferences, however, as from the fact that *Monte Carmelo* ran afoul of Franco's censors and could not gain a proper footing on the stage after its initial production. A revival of this captivating work is long overdue.

Featuring a libretto by the redoubtable duo of Romero and Fernández-Shaw, the zarzuela's action takes place in Granada during the middle of the nineteenth century. Act I commences in a little salon in the house of the marqués del Avellano, whose residence is known as the "Casa del Emperador" (The emperor's house). Esperanza, the eldest of the daughters of marqués Don Sancho, sadly contemplates the Albaicín (Gypsy quarter) from an enclosed balcony. She is melancholy because she is smitten with someone she cannot have, and her ruminations speak of death from unrequited love: "I die because I do not die." This is a quote from St. Teresa of Ávila, whose writings she has been reading, though Esperanza's love is profane, not sacred.

Esperanza's doleful meditation is interrupted by the entrance of her grandmother, Mamá Dolores, the widowed countess of Monte Carmelo and widowed marquesa of Avellano y del Alminar. Though advanced in years, she possesses a youthfully cheerful disposition that is contagious. She is accompanied by Currito, her coachman (*cochero*), and Angustias, her handmaiden (*doncella*), who is carrying some cakes. Also in her train are Miguel, the butler of the marqués; María Cleofe, a Gypsy apprentice of the handmaiden; a female cook; a female servant (*criada*); and a waiter (*mozo de comedor*).

Mamá Dolores announces the arrival at Granada of her nephew, Manrique, Count of Monte Carmelo and Royal Guard of the Vatican, who intends to marry one of her two granddaughters. For this purpose, she has invited Manrique to have chocolate, along with don Alonso, Archbishop of Granada, and don Lope, captain general. Serafina, the wet nurse (*nodriza*), now appears. She is a neatly dressed, poised, and very talkative Gypsy woman. She is also the mother of María Cleofé and of Joselito, assistant to Manrique. She quickly enters into a spirited conversation with Mamá Dolores.

[20] Webber, *Zarzuela*, 178.

One of the finest numbers of the work is Manrique's impassioned aria "Granada mía" (My Granada), which he sings in the company of Joselito as they make their way to the party. He exults in the beauties of the city, finding charm in both its "mud and gold," its bells and towers, and above all, the Alhambra, with its myrtle and cypress trees, waterfalls, and soaring breezes. His "beautiful Granada is a Gypsy girl, with the body of an odalisque and the soul of a guitar." The number's chromatic and modal inflections, as well as its animated rhythms in the style of the *seguidillas*, strongly convey the Spanish ambiance of the story and Manrique's passionate nature (see ex. II:iii:9).

Back at the party, various other guests now arrive, including the marqués don Sancho, a compulsive gambler who has squandered the family fortune, and Luis Doncel, assistant to the captain general. A little later, Manrique and Joselito, as well as don Lope and don Alonso, arrive. After serving chocolate, Esperanza and Rafaela are presented by their grandmother. Esperanza has a lovely voice and is asked to entertain the guests with a song. In her habanera, "Madre de mis amores"

Ex. II:iii:9 Monte Carmelo, Act 1, no. 3, "Granada mía," mm. 57–65

(Mother of my loves) (Act I, no. 4), we learn that she is weary of the routine of her life but has no alternative, save one that is unavailable. She feels herself to be "a little sailboat adrift in the middle of the ocean." The solo calls for a voice of operatic agility and grace, especially in the concluding cadenza, which ascends to high F. This provided the audience with just the kind of vocal athletics it craved (see ex. II:iii:10).

Act II presents a change of locale, to the country estate (*carmen*) of Mamá Dolores, called Monte Carmelo. Esperanza and Rafaela sing stories of love from the Albaicín, accompanied by Gypsy girls with clapping and dancing. This is the sort of song and dance audiences expected and enjoyed at this point in the drama. Don Lope warns don Sancho that if he does not liquidate his debts soon, he will lose all of his possessions. Meanwhile, Joselito finds a woman's garter (*liga*), and he and his male companions speculate as to its owner. This serendipity gives rise to Manrique's "Una liga de mujer" (Act II, no. 7), a strophic song with a *zambra*-like rhythm, every measure of which exudes an Andalusian fragrance (see ex. II:iii:11).

Luis Doncel declares his love for Rafaela, as his passion has been aroused by believing that the garter belongs to her. Mamá Dolores enters, surrounded by young women who are wondering who will snare the highly desirable Manrique. Rafaela and Luis discuss the garter, and it is clear that she reciprocates his feelings for her. We now learn the exact nature of poor Esperanza's predicament, as she is in love with Juan María, secretary of the Archbishop. Discouraged by the impossibility of her love, she tells Manrique that she will marry him instead.

The final act opens at night on the streets of the Albaicín, which Torroba evokes in a gorgeous *Nocturno* for orchestra. This is one of the finest orchestral numbers that Torroba ever wrote for the stage, and given its length, almost seven minutes, it would be suitable as a concert excerpt. As dawn breaks, a crowd of Gypsies appears at the door of a monastery. Madre Martirio only allows Serafina to enter to see her nephew, a chaplain. Esperanza and Manrique now appear, seeking to speak with the Mother Superior and Juan María, respectively. In a very poignant exchange, Esperanza and Juan María express their feelings for one another in a

Ex. II:iii:10 Monte Carmelo, Act I, no. 4, "Madre de mis amores," mm. 96–99

Ex. II:iii:11 *Monte Carmelo*, Act II, no. 7, "Una liga de mujer," mm. 8–13

love duet of remarkably poetic intensity. In the end, however, Juan María declares that "his kingdom is not of this world" and makes clear his intention to dedicate his life to God. Manrique now informs Juan María that he has been appointed as the canon of Guadix (a small city in the province of Granada), which will take him away from Esperanza. The third scene takes us back to Monte Carmelo, where several loose dramatic threads are tied up, with the exception of one big strand. Luis agrees to marry Rafaela, while Manrique offers to pay off don Sancho's debts. Mamá Dolores now offers Esperanza's hand to Manrique, but he refuses, saying that he intends to become a monk. Manrique gives the garter to Luis, and Mamá Dolores recognizes it not as Rafaela's but rather her own! It served its purpose in bringing Luis and Rafaela together.

The play concludes with a high-spirited ensemble number, "Guarda, guarda" (Keep, keep) (Act III, no. 13), whose lively tempo and rapid declamation provide an upbeat and hopeful conclusion to this tale of thwarted *amor* (see ex. II:iii:12).

The ending cannot be entirely happy, because Esperanza will never be united with Juan María. Of course, such a thing would have been scandalous and absolutely impermissible during the Franco era. As it was, the very idea that she was in love with him, and he with her, was too much for the censors.

This plot bears a remarkable similarity to *Luisa Fernanda*, *La chulapona*, and *Azabache* in that there is a classic love triangle, though with a curious twist in this case: the religious convictions of the two men make them unavailable to the woman (Esperanza's name, "hope," like Paloma's in *La marchenera*, "dove,"

Ex. II:iii:12 *Monte Carmelo*, Act III, no. 13, "Guarda, guarda," mm. 52–60

ultimately represents a cruel irony). In all cases, there is a noble renunciation of a claim, in *Luisa Fernanda* on Vidal's part, in *Azabache* on the old Gypsy's part, or in *La chulapona*, on Manuela's part. In this case, Juan María remains true to his duty, and Manrique joins him in seeking God's favor. Esperanza does not press her advantage but will seek companionship elsewhere. As in *Luisa Fernanda* and *La chulapona*, the ending is less than satisfying, or even just. But it provided role models of self-sacrifice and virtue that no doubt resonated with the audience's own values. As was the case with French *opéra-comique*, there was a moral to these stories that transcended the exigencies of humor and romance.

However, lest some be tempted to see this as a result of the Catholic Church's dominance during the Franco era, we recall that the Jesuit censors had serious reservations about this work. Moreover, we know from contemporary press accounts that the authors had been working on *Monte Carmelo* as early as 1932, during the Second Republic. In short, the religious overtones owe no debt to the social policies of Franco's regime.

La Caramba

La Caramba was the sobriquet of a real-life singer, María Antonia Fernández (1751–87), who rose from obscurity in Andalusia to the heights of musical celebrity in Madrid. In this little drama, however, fame is not enough to satisfy her longings, as the man she loves has chosen another. Heartbroken, she enters a convent. The drama opens in a tavern in Motril, a small town near Málaga, in which dancers, singers, and guitarists are entertaining the clientele of El Zurdo, the proprietor of the establishment. Among the guests on this occasion is Fabián, Baron of Moncada, a young soldier moving to Madrid. The beautiful and talented María Antonia soon enters and is persuaded to perform a lovely *romanza*.

Fabián is enchanted by María Antonia and convinces her to follow him to Madrid, where there are "diamonds and palaces, fiestas and receptions." The glittering appeal of the capital, as described by Fabián, is irresistible, and María Antonia declares that she will seek her fortune in Madrid. However, her boyfriend, Máximo, appears and reproaches her for performing in the tavern, as he has forbidden her to sing in public. She reminds him of her parents' poverty and the necessity of her earning money to support them. Máximo proposes marriage, but María Antonia refuses his offer and instead resolves to follow Fabián to Madrid. In frustration and disgust, Máximo leaves her for good.

Scene two opens in a *botilleria* (ice-cream parlor) connected to the Teatro Príncipe in Madrid. Fabián is conversing with Ramón de la Cruz, celebrated composer of *sainetes*. Fabián has just returned from France, and though he earlier did not want to marry María Antonia, now that she is famous, he desires her with all his heart and is seeking her out at the theater, where she is performing. Manuela arrives with her husband, the French ambassador, and de Gaston, his secretary. Manuela is smitten with Fabián and jealous of María Antonia.

In the second act, Goya is working in his studio, painting portraits of both "La Caramba" and Manuela, who pose for him. María Teresa Cayetana, the XIII Duchess of Alba, immortalized in several Goya paintings, soon enters with her entourage, and she sings a spirited *romanza*, "Me llaman la Duquesa Cayetana" (They call me Duchess Cayetana). Thereafter, Fabián's father, Don Pedro, arrives from Aragon (home region of Goya as well), determined to put an end to his son's infatuation with La Caramba. He wants the help of his friend Goya, who promises to arrange a meeting with María Antonia. Fabián finally appears, and Manuela invites him to a masked ball. He accepts her invitation but remains transfixed by the portrait of La Caramba. He now sings his own *romanza*, "Tus besos no me tientan" (Your kisses do not tempt me), a love song to María Antonia, the object of his adoration. Finally, María Antonia herself arrives, singing a memorable *romanza*, "Soy María Antonia" (I am María Antonia).[21] In the presence only of Goya, Don Pedro tells her to forget his son, which she roundly refuses to do.

The setting of the final act is the park of El Prado de San Fermín, during carnival season. La Caramba and her friends are having lunch. She is very sad because she cannot forget Fabián, her only true love. Fabián passes by, and she runs after him. They sing a rapturous but forlorn duo, as she recalls her promise to forsake him. They part, and she enters the nearby convent of the Capuchinos de San Antonio del Prado, to don the veil and free herself from earthly temptations—and

[21] Such "Yo soy" (I am) arias are staples of the zarzuela repertoire and serve to introduce or flesh out a character.

Ex. II:iii:13 *La Caramba*, Act III, no. 13, "Gloria a Dios en las alturas," mm. 82–89

pleasures. As she and her carnival companions enter the church, they hear a choir of young boys singing the Gloria (curiously, in Spanish, not Latin). Such an evocation of liturgical music may be an exception in Torroba's stage works but nonetheless provides convincing evidence of his thorough familiarity with this style—which is not surprising, given his extensive experience as a church organist (see ex. II:iii:13).

The music of *La Caramba* is conceived in the manner of the *tonadilla*, a light eighteenth-century song form germane to the epoch in which the drama takes place (not to be confused with the *tonadilla escénica*, a musical skit). It is safe to say that this work represents Torroba's own "Goyescas," though unlike Granados, he makes no use of historical music from that period. Rather, the music is at home in Andalusia and Madrid ca. 1900 and features the mazurkas and *romanzas* that audiences relished.

Spain's cultural life suffered greatly both during and after the Civil War. While many composers found post-war Spain stifling, the environment was still conducive to Torroba's writing zarzuelas. The popularity of *La Caramba* and his other works from the 1940s has been cited as an indication of Spain's "sentimentality and conservatism" after the Civil War.[22] In retrospect, the success of these zarzuelas may tell us something about the transformation that was taking place in Spain. Clinging to the faded glory of the Romantic zarzuela was, in a way, an acknowledgement of the *género grande*'s growing irrelevance in the age of television

[22] Donald Thompson, *Doña Francisquita*, 143.

and cinema. Unlike virtually every other zarzuela composer, however, Torroba had an ace up his sleeve, one that would allow him to survive the declining fortunes of his beloved zarzuela: his beloved guitar.

Guitar Works

Torroba was much more prolific in his composition of guitar music during this period than one might at first expect. Though he wrote almost nothing for the instrument during the 1940s, he composed a very substantial three-movement *Sonata-Fantasía* in the early 1950s. As Angel Gilardino points out, it is "the largest and most extended piece he ever dedicated to his favourite instrument."[23] The first movement is skillfully cast in sonata form, while the last is a rondo. These are predictable choices, but rather than the normal slow movement in between, Torroba offers a brief intermezzo.

After this major work, Torroba composed numerous short numbers for the "Guitarra Española" series in the late 1950s, published by Ediciones Musicales in Madrid. These delightfully evoke a variety of regions and regional styles, e.g., "Bolero menoquín," "Aire Vasco," "Ronda," "Sevillana," "Segoviana," "Trianera," and "Ay, malagueña." Curiously, these have received relatively less attention from guitarists than the other works we examine, and they remain outside the standard repertoire, though there are a few excellent recordings.[24] One significant exception to this obscurity is "Romance de los pinos," later reincarnated under the title "Montemayor" in *Castillos de España*; it also forms the basis for the slow movement of *Diálogos entre guitarra y orquesta*, as well as the song "Caminando por el monte" from the *Romancillos*. We begin our brief survey of his guitar music from this era, however, with a stand-alone work, *Madroños*, an evergreen concert favorite among guitarists and audiences alike.

Madroños

This spirited work first appeared in print in 1954, published by Schott in Segovia's guitar series, though recent research suggests that an earlier version was composed and premiered as early as 1929.[25] During an after-dinner

---

[23] Taken from the notes by Angelo Gilardino for the most recent edition (Ancona, Italy: Bèrben Edizioni Musicali, 2002). He estimates that the work was composed in the early 1950s, but not later than 1953.

[24] Maximilian Mangold, *Spanische Gitarrenmusik*, Musicaphon M56833, 2000.

[25] In e-mail correspondence with the authors during December 2011, Spanish musicologist Leopoldo Neri revealed that numerous reviews from around 1930 clarify that the work was premiered by Regino Sainz de la Maza. Neri found a manuscript version of the work in the Sainz de la Maza family archive dating from 1929 but not identical to the final version published in 1954. We include and discuss here that final version.

conversation with Segovia in January 1975, on the night before a master class in which I was to play (at the North Carolina School of the Arts, where I was a senior), I asked the legendary guitarist what the title *Madroños* meant. Having never traveled farther east than Winston–Salem, North Carolina, I had absolutely no idea, other than that it clearly had something to do with Spain.[26] Much to my surprise, Segovia did not have a ready answer; in fact, he was not quite sure. He speculated that it might refer to the *pregones* (song-like calls) of peanut vendors on the streets of Madrid, or perhaps to the little fabric balls attached to the skirts of dancers. Neither of these explanations is necessarily incorrect. *Madroños* is eminently lyrical and could easily suggest the hustle and bustle of the Puerta del Sol, for example (though today the peanut vendors have been replaced by women selling lottery tickets); its lively rhythms could likewise suggest the animated movements of a dancer's skirt, and anything attached to it.

Still, having given this quandary more thought over the intervening thirty-seven years, I remain unsatisfied with either description. Instead, I choose to invoke Ockham's razor by selecting the simplest and least imaginative explanation: the title refers to the many *madroños* trees that dotted the urban landscape of Torroba's Madrid. One might object that this piece evinces absolutely no connection to a large plant; however, the titles of Torroba's guitar pieces are often evocative and fanciful, and have no connection whatsoever to the music itself. Increasingly, Torroba's titles seem more designed to conjure up appealing images, regardless of their inherent relevance to the music. This may well have served a commercial purpose, and it certainly dovetailed with the tourist industry on which the Spanish economy became increasingly dependent during this period. A Minnesotan like me or a Californian like Bill could savor the arboreal splendors of Spain, not to mention its castles and other monuments, without leaving the comfort of his practice room. Sheet music costing only a few dollars became a sort of magic carpet, whisking one to exotic locales in faraway places. But Torroba could just have easily named this piece *Calles* (streets) or *Cafés*, without a total collapse of credibility. The piece is ultimately not about anything at all except itself—and the Spanish folklore from which it undeniably draws its inspiration.

As with almost all of his music, its national pedigree is on display from the first measure, regardless of the title's meaning or relevance. The rhythm strongly suggests the Castilian *seguidillas* in its triple meter and insistent repetition of a quarter-eighth-eighth motive (see ex. II:iii:14). In this respect, then, the title makes perfect sense, as it connects the music with Madrid. As in so many of his pieces, the form is ABA, though as we have noted elsewhere, Torroba has a knack for

[26] The master class and the conversation that preceded it took place in January 1975, at the North Carolina School of the Performing Arts, the conservatory of the University of North Carolina.

Ex. II:iii:14 Madroños, mm. 1–4

thematic development, which is on display in the sequencing of his main theme within the B section.

Romance de los pinos

The other guitar work from this period that has had considerable staying power is also inspired by vegetation, this time pine trees. But before we get too carried away with romancing the pines, we must recognize that no single work better demonstrates the interchangeability of title and music in Torroba's guitar works than this one. As we noted above, this same music reappears in quite different contexts in later compositions, with quite different associations. Again, it is the music itself that speaks to us, regardless of any programmatic associations the title may suggest. And titular affection for our arboreal friends is about the only thing these two works have in common, as they are of completely contrasting characters. Whereas *Madroños* is lively and passionate, "Romance of the Pines" is dreamily meditative and serene (see ex. II:iii:15).

Though it is in the same ternary form (ABA) as *Madroños*, there is nothing especially Spanish about this work, except for the Phrygian cadence of the B section. One occasionally hears it said that this piece conveys a sort of reverie induced by viewing evergreen loveliness swaying gently in the breeze. Since it was composed in Navarra, where there is an abundance of beautiful pines, that could well be the case. Again, however, the character of the piece speaks for itself; appreciating it does not require a title at all.

Ex. II:iii:15 Romance de los pinos, mm. 1–3

If these little gems demonstrated nothing else about Torroba's style, their opposing natures would surely provide evidence of his emotional and psychological range and versatility. Yet, despite their disparate affects, each one is memorable for its lyricism. The old *zarzuelero* was never at a loss for a beautiful melody, regardless of the genre or medium for which he was composing.

ACT III

1960–1982

May songs of love replace the chants of war.
[¡A los cánticos de guerra sustituyan los de amor!]

Luisa Fernanda, Act III

7

ACT III
Scene i
1975
The Beginning

On July 1, 2006, I was walking briskly from my *pensión* in downtown Madrid to the Teatro Real for a new production of *Luisa Fernanda*, starring Plácido Domingo. As usual, I was a bit behind schedule, but hoped I would have just enough time to get there before the curtain rose on Act I. As I rounded a corner onto the Gran Vía, however, I realized that my space-time calculations were way off. For there in front of me churned a vast and seemingly unnavigable sea of humanity—and judging from their extravagant dress and rainbow banners, a very *gay* sea at that.

It quickly dawned on me that this was the Gay Pride Parade; indeed, Madrid has one of the largest gay communities in Europe, centered in the nearby *barrio* named after *zarzuelero* Federico Chueca, composer of *La Gran Vía*. So, the size of the event was entirely predictable, but it was the irony of the situation I found truly overwhelming: the performance of a *zarzuela grande*, a relic from the era of the Second Republic, with its musical message of love and reconciliation, was taking place at the same time as a public celebration of homosexuality absolutely unthinkable during Franco's reign. A year earlier, Spain had become one of the first countries in Europe to legalize gay marriage (another being the Netherlands). I could not help imagining that the old *Caudillo* must have been rolling over in his grave at the sight. That image brought a broad smile to my face, even as I took my seat at the Teatro Real just in time for a deeply moving performance.

On November 20, 1975, Generalísimo Francisco Franco passed into eternity, taking with him an epoch in Spanish history so complex and controversial that historians will continue mulling it over for a very long time to come. But this end was actually a beginning, the initiation of a new period in the nation's annals that would witness, paradoxically, the emergence of the Spain for which many of Franco's opponents had fought so desperately during the Civil War almost forty years earlier, and which Franco himself would have forestalled indefinitely, had he and his followers been able to do so. In the end, they were not: they had absolutely and positively lost the larger conflict that had rent the country since Napoleon's 1808 invasion. Spain would be a democratic nation fully incorporated into modern Europe in every facet of its national being: economic, legal, military, diplomatic, and cultural. And yet, the extremists on the left also lost. Spain would never be a "workers' paradise," experience the dubious blessings of a "dictatorship of the proletariat," or become an anarchist utopia. Who won this larger civil war, then—not the one from 1936 to 1939 but rather the one that lasted from 1808 to 1975? Who won the ultimate battle for Spain's soul and future? Reality won. Pragmatism won. Moderation won. Reason won. Spain won.

The transition would not be immediate, painless, or without some moments of crisis, but considering the magnitude of the transformation Franco's passing would now facilitate, it remains one of the more remarkable such transitions in European history, on a par with the Velvet Revolution in Czechoslovakia fourteen years later. Europe was gradually moving to the middle, with the collapse of dictatorial regimes on both the extreme left and right. To be sure, the Cold War continued apace throughout the 1970s, and the fall of the Berlin Wall was still well over a decade away. Spain remained allied with the West against the Soviet Union. And yet, the last gasp of fascism in southern Europe presaged the death throes of communism in Eastern Europe, though few realized it at the time. The remaining battle lines between East and West, the sad legacy of World War II, would dissolve sooner than most then dared to hope.

The principal reason that the transition after Franco's death went so smoothly was that it was not as sudden as it appeared. The metamorphosis from dictatorship to democracy had been taking place gradually and at many levels since at least 1960, and it was greatly aided by the steady improvement in Spain's economy that occurred over that period. Carolyn Boyd aptly sums up the economic achievements of this era and the reasons for it:

> Opus Dei ministers advocated controlled economic modernization that would raise living standards without raising expectations for political change. Between 1957 and 1964 they stabilized the *peseta*, lifted import restrictions and limits on foreign investment, authorized collective bargaining (within the official syndicalist structure), and laid the groundwork for rationalized state economic investment and planning.... With these reforms in place, the stage was set for the "Spanish miracle." The rapid economic growth of 1960–73, when Spain's GDP rose at an average annual rate of 7.2 percent, transformed Spain's agrarian economy into an industrial one. By 1975 only 29 percent of the active population earned their living in agriculture, 70 percent of the population lived in cities, and per capita income had risen from $300 to $2,246 a year.[1]

[1] Boyd, "History, Politics, and Culture, 1936–1975," 99.

According to Vincent and Stradling, this impressive rate of growth was matched by no other country except Japan.[2] It was driven to a large extent by tourism, which in turn stimulated economic modernization and liberalization, promoted and overseen by Opus Dei. This somewhat secretive group has been the focus of a lot of attention in recent history, partly as a result of Dan Brown's 2003 novel *The Da Vinci Code* and the 2006 movie based on it, and much of that attention has been negative. It is not our purpose to examine the group's nature or history, but its conservative, orthodox teachings and the comfortable relationship of its founder, St. Josemaría Escrivá de Balaguer (1902–75), with the Franco regime are well known.

Thus, it may strike some as more than a little ironic that Opus Dei played a leading role in the rapid development of a modern, industrial economy in Spain, and that it also sought to address deficiencies in the educational system by modernizing curricula in philosophy, history, and science. Opus Dei technocrats in Franco's cabinet realized that a modern economy requires an educated workforce, and they were "firmly committed to professionalism, education and technological development."[3] Thus, education's share of the budget doubled between 1962 and 1976, and in 1970, free and compulsory schooling between the ages of 6 and 14 became law. Of course, as Spain became more industrialized and urban, it also experienced the growing strength of labor unions and demands for greater political freedom. Strikes occurred with increasing frequency, and young people in particular were less content with the status quo.[4]

The regime's survival depended on its alliance with the West, whence came economic and financial assistance and foreign exchange, mostly from tourism. This also mandated a certain degree of liberalization, if for no other reason than to maintain appearances. That is what the Western powers required from the regime before they would do business with it. The paradigm Franco and his Opus Dei technocrats adopted would not shock the politburo in China today: retain tight control of political life while liberalizing the economy and—gradually, where possible—culture. Montero Díaz has summed this up perfectly:

> The dominant characteristic of *franquismo* was the permanent control of political life by executive power, without any more restrictions than its own self-control. The pressure of this power over the people diminished as the years passed, but it never lacked the resources, legal or material, to make itself effective with the necessary intensity. The basic transformations of the regime were produced in economic and social areas from the

---

[2] Mary Vincent and R. A. Stradling, *Cultural Atlas of Spain and Portugal* (New York: Facts on File, 1995), 163.

[3] Ibid., 173.

[4] Ibid., 166. "Between 1964 and 1974 Spain experienced about 5,000 strikes; 1975, the last year of Franco's rule, saw a further 3,156 stoppages. Furthermore, 45 percent of strikes staged after 1967 were political in nature, as against a mere 4 percent of those called from 1963–67."

60s on. The result of this was the increase, until they were numerically dominant, of the modern middle class: technicians, specialized workers, liberal professionals, civil servants, bank employees, salespeople, etc. The parallel extension of professional education, secondary and university, and the opening up to the outside world initiated by the regime, introduced cultural innovations and political aspirations...that the regime could not liquidate and with which it had to coexist during its final years.[5]

Of course, this is a Faustian Pact, as the Chinese are finding out: sooner or later, dictatorship and liberalization prove incompatible. To paraphrase Abraham Lincoln's 1858 House Divided speech, the Spanish nation would have to become all one thing or all the other.[6] The difference between Spain then and China today is that Spain was run by a *caudillo*, not a party of faceless bureaucrats. Once he was gone, the future of Spain would depend on his handpicked successor—who turned out to be a closet reformer, i.e., Juan Carlos I.

In the 1960s, Franco's regime waged a charm offensive to maintain the support and confidence of the United States and Western Europe. This project was largely cultural, to show that despite the dictatorship, Spain was a modern country and sufficiently tolerant to merit continued assistance. Thus, the liberalization of culture "lent a patina of credibility to the regime."[7] After all, a too-rigid, too-brutal dictatorship would have made it politically difficult for democratic regimes to lend it aid. Franco's Spain had to put its best foot forward on the international stage if it was to continue on its upward trajectory, and to conceal as best it could its continued opposition to regionalist forces, labor unrest, and political dissent, especially among students and intellectuals—who nonetheless led the way toward reform. As Montero Díaz notes, the "incorporation into Spanish society of generations that had not participated in the Civil War made it increasingly difficult to maintain the political and social myths of the previous years, and resistance to the regime grew steadily."[8]

Already in the 1950s, the regime had begun to sanction and promote avant-garde art. The Instituto de Cultura Hispánica (ICH) was established in 1951 and in that same year organized the first Bienal Hispanoamericana de Arte (BHA). It helped convince Franco's government of the "urgent need to be receptive to certain artistic tendencies that were in vogue in Paris and New York during those years."[9] The ICH thus played a crucial role in overcoming Spain's isolation, and

---

[5] Montero Díaz, "El Franquismo," 639.

[6] For a deeply insightful study of this and other Lincoln speeches, see John Channing Briggs, *Lincoln's Speeches Reconsidered* (Baltimore: Johns Hopkins University Press, 2005).

[7] Marzo, *Art modern i franquisme*, 12.

[8] See Montero Díaz, "El Franquismo," 659.

[9] Marzo, *Art modern i franquisme*, 16.

especially in drawing closer to the United States, by promoting modern art as a kind of propaganda. After all, what other means did Spain have to make its presence felt in the world? It could not do so in sports, industry, or science but only in the cultural arena. This was obvious even to Franco, who otherwise disdained the arts. Culture thereby became an "arm of the state."[10] This makes it much easier to understand why a surrealist like Salvador Dalí

> had no difficulty in returning to Spain when he wished, and giving his approval to the Franco regime. His gripping depiction of *The Crucifixion* (1954) was another example of the way in which he was able to appeal at one and the same time to his commercial instincts, to the official religious ideology of the regime, and to his subdued erotic preferences.[11]

The cultural, political, and economic facets of Spain's situation in the 1960s were tightly interwoven, and any development in the one affected the other two. As Montero Díaz believes, "It could be asserted that the change that prepared Spanish society for political openness was cultural; but that could not take place—or only with great difficulty—without the creation of a new articulation of the economy," chiefly through the Stabilization Plan of 1959.[12]

The 1960s witnessed recovery and rediscovery of the culture of exile, for instance, the films of Luis Buñuel, who had fled with so many others to Mexico. The gradual liberalization in publishing fostered the rebirth of Ortega y Gasset's *Revista de Occidente*. And now the works of expatriate composers like Rodolfo Halffter and Roberto Gerhard could be published in Spain itself.[13] As Juan Pablo Fusi notes, the "established" culture of the Franco era—not the "official" culture—was liberal. "On the one hand, critical culture was radicalized; on the other, it was regionalized."[14] In the 1960s, essayists, economists, sociologists, and historians tried to project a new vision of Andalusia, focusing on economic and social problems and not on the stereotypical images, i.e., Gypsies, bullfights, flamenco, Holy Week, promulgated *ad nauseam* in the media to promote tourism. Though Franco and the avant-garde made for very strange bedfellows, the artistic avant-garde's aesthetic goals meshed perfectly with the regime's *realpolitik*. As Luis Marzo observes,

> Spain's abstract expressionists were not only palatable to Franco's regime, they unwittingly served its interests. Franco's state wanted art that could be exported as proof of the regime's spiritual values, but that did not

---

[10] Ibid., 48–49.

[11] Kamen, *The Disinherited*, 311.

[12] Ibid., 651.

[13] Fusi, *Un siglo de España*, 132–33.

[14] Ibid.

carry any overt political criticism. Abstract expressionism was perfectly suited to this purpose.[15]

There was a concomitant increase in the number of professorships and universities, easing of restrictions on foreign travel, and a dramatic increase in tourism, which boosted local economies.[16] Political liberalization followed as well, partly resulting from pressure exerted by Spain's new allies. In 1966, the *Ley de Prensa e Imprenta* superseded the earlier Press Law of 1938 and relaxed press censorship, allowing for greater freedom of expression and a livelier, more multifaceted political dialogue. In 1967, Spaniards were able to vote freely for 108 representatives to the Cortes, even though the government determined the other 457. In that same year, legislation promoted religious freedom. Although Roman Catholicism would no longer be the official state religion, this development was fully in keeping with the reforms of Vatican II (1962–65) and its endorsement of religious tolerance. Still, Spain remained a long way from complete freedom of the press. Even with the passage of the Press Law, censorship did not cease. As several Spanish scholars have noted, "The existence of priests, ex-priests and ex-seminarians in the organs of censorship should not surprise us if we bear in mind that the head of Ordenación Editorial was, during the first nine years of the *Ley de Prensa*, Faustino Sánchez Marín, a former seminarian from Extremadura who had abandoned his vocation in the final stages of preparation."[17] The old guard was not quite ready to run up the white flag.

In 1969, Franco designated as his successor Juan Carlos de Borbón (1938–), grandson of Alfonso XIII. He thought this young man sufficiently conservative and dedicated to authoritarianism that the regime would be safe with him. Instead, King Juan Carlos was dedicated to the opposite of autocracy, and thus the old dictator's determination to restore the aristocracy would have unforeseen and unintended consequences. With Franco's exit, the attendant ideology of *franquismo* was finally bereft of any residual *raison d'etre*. Moreover, "during the final years of the Franco regime, the vast majority of Spaniards saw it as normal that the political future of the country should be similar to the present of other European countries.... [young people] could not conceive of a future which was not similar to their neighbors.'"[18]

Thus, dictatorship in Spain ended with a whimper, not a bang. The first free and fair general elections since 1936 were held nineteen months after Franco's death, on June 15, 1977, and brought a significant number of socialists into the Cortes.

---

[15] Marzo, "The Spectacle of Spain's Amnesia," 93.

[16] See Montero Díaz, "El Franquismo," 658.

[17] Georgina Cisquella, José Luis Erviti, and José Antonio Sorollo, *La represión cultural en el franquismo: diez años de censura de libros durante la ley de prensa (1966–1976)* (Barcelona: Editorial Anagrama, 2002), 45.

[18] Juliá, "History, Politics, Culture, 1975–1996," 106.

On February 23, 1981, members of the Guardia Civil, commanded by Lieutenant-Colonel Antonio Tejero, attempted a coup and seized control of the Cortes in the parliamentary chamber. In a further show of force, the army sent tanks into the streets of Valencia.[19]

Juan Carlos, confirmed as a constitutional monarch by the Constitution of 1978, went on national television to defend that constitution by denouncing the coup, reminding the soldiers of their loyalty oath, and compelling the conspirators to back down. The siege ended only a day after it had begun. The king had made it clear that he would not be silenced except by force, something the rebels had neither the means nor the will to accomplish. Juan Carlos earned almost universal praise for his coura-geous and principled defense of democracy, even from the leader of the Spanish Communist Party, Santiago Carrillo. And the young king boldly and unequivocally continued to support Spain's fledgling democracy, stating a few years later that,

> The democratic process in Spain is a historically irreversible fact. National sovereignty is in the hands of our people, and no one will dare to take it away. National reconciliation is a reality.[20]

In 1982, in the same year as Torroba's death, Felipe González was elected Spain's first socialist prime minister since the days of the Second Republic. All of these developments had far-reaching implications for Spanish culture. The 1978 Constitution heralded a new era of press freedom. The Ministry of Culture recov-ered and promoted the cultural legacy suppressed by Franco, celebrating the work of exiled artists and intellectuals. The socialist government was determined to build on these advances and bring the resources of the government to bear on promoting the arts, "especially in those areas where private initiative was likely to be lacking." As E. Ramón Arango notes,

> The Socialist government announced in November 1982 that Felipe González intended to double the budget available to the arts, and in August 1983 Minister of Culture Javier Solana stated his intention to remedy "Spain's profoundly unfair distribution of cultural goods" by introducing art and music education into Spanish schools "on the same level as mathematics."[21]

Also significant was the Spanish Historic Heritage Act of 1985, which sought to "renovate theatres and auditoriums, and subsidize artistic expression."[22]

---

[19] Vincent and Stradling, *Cultural Atlas of Spain and Portugal*, 167.

[20] Juan Carlos de Borbón, "Un mensaje del Rey," *Diario 16* (Madrid), September 1984, and repro-duced in Sinova Garrido, ed., *Un siglo en 100 artículos*, 449.

[21] Arango, *Spain: From Repression to Renewal*, 212.

[22] "Cultural Policy in Spain," 4.

The sad irony here is that, after decades of complaining about the lack of government support for the arts, under both the left and right, Torroba finally got his wish—but too late for him to be able to witness and appreciate it.

The Musical Parallel

The liberalization we noted in other sectors of society also prevailed in the country's musical life. We have already observed that Franco and his coterie were not aficionados of the arts and devoted relatively little attention to music per se. The censors were mostly priests whose chief preoccupation was with texts and what those texts said about religion.

By the mid-1960s, composers within Spain such as Luis de Pablo had long since abandoned *nacionalismo casticista* in favor of the international avant-garde. The composers of the Generation of 51 formed ensembles and institutes devoted to the performance of avant-garde music. As society gradually liberalized, Torroba clearly had the opportunity to change with the times, but he instead continued to refine the aesthetic he had always pursued. The contrast between Torroba and this new generation of composers is illustrated by considering the initial concert by *Zaj*, a group founded by composer Ramón Barce in 1964. The first work on the program was John Cage's *4'33"* (1962). This was later followed by Cage's *Variations III* (1963) for prepared piano.[23] During the 1960s, another major influence on Spanish composers, especially Tomás Marco (1942–), was Darmstadt and Karlheinz Stockhausen. At this same time, Torroba had not yet written his last zarzuela or guitar suite *Castillos de España*. In the age of hip-hop, such distinctions may seem trivial, but at the time, these two radically different approaches to composition demarcated radically different worldviews.

In fact, one must say that, despite the flowering of the Spanish avant-garde in the 1960s, the outside world continued to focus on the older, traditionalist compositions of Torroba and Rodrigo, especially those guitar works composed for Segovia. These provided the musical equivalent of the tourism on which the Spanish economy became increasingly dependent in the 1960s, with their appealing and accessible evocations of Spanish monuments and places, songs, and dances. William Krause has dubbed this sort of thing *casticismo comercial*,[24] to emphasize its commercial viability and abandonment of controversial philosophical baggage. The world could get plenty of atonal music from other sources, but it

---

[23] Ángel Medina, "Primeras oleadas vanguardistas en el área de Madrid," in *España en la música de Occidente: Actas del Congreso Internacional celebrado en Salamanca 29 de octubre–5 de noviembre de 1985*, 2 vols., ed. Emilio Casares Rodicio, Ismael Fernández de la Cuesta, and José López-Calo (Madrid: Ministerio de Cultura, 1987), ii, 386–87.

[24] See William Craig Krause, "*Casticismo* before and after 1939," *Diagonal: Journal of the Center for Iberian and Latin American Music* 7 (2011), http://cilam.ucr.edu/diagonal/issues/2011/Krause.pdf.

wanted its Spanish music to sound, well, Spanish. Nonetheless, it was the atonal works of Torroba's contemporaries that served as window-dressing for an otherwise conservative nationalist regime. There is considerable irony in that fact.

The inability of the Spanish avant-garde to displace the traditionalists at home resulted largely from a lack of domestic enthusiasm for experimental music. As Lorenç Barber has pointed out,

> There is no sector of Spanish culture more mistreated, or better said, less taken into account than the musical. The Spanish bourgeoisie, including the most cultured and informed among them, has been and in large measure continues to be estranged from the problematic of musical sound.[25]

In part, this was because the Franco era did not represent a clear break with the past but rather sought to "sacralize and banalize it." Falla's music became less "a point of departure" and more an "indisputable dogma." Spanish music could not escape from this dead end of stale neoclassicism except by "leaping into the void," a void into which the public was largely unwilling to follow. Frederic Mompou saw this clearly enough, lamenting that "except in rare cases, Spanish composers have resisted the strong current that has carried along the majority of European composers."[26]

However, the reformers soldiered on. Pablo continued to be a leader of the Spanish avant-garde and served as president of the Juventudes Musicales (JJMM) in Madrid from 1959 to 1963. This group began in 1952 in Madrid, and it opened a chapter in Barcelona the following year. The JJMM consisted of a group of young composers determined to transform the Spanish musical landscape. Pablo organized the Festival de Música Joven Española (June 1960) to provide exposure to these young Spanish composers. Another group with which he was associated was the Grupo Nueva Música (New Music Group). Their first concert took place already in March 9, 1958, at the Real Conservatorio. The program of this concert boldly declared: "We are not 'nationalists.' [Yet], we feel ourselves to be as irrevocably Spanish as we are passionately European."[27] To be sure, this was not a completely novel sentiment in the history of Spanish music, as we have seen. The interesting point here is that this rather defiant break with the past, as they saw it, occurred not only under the noses of but also with the official approbation of the very nationalistic Franco regime. And more was to come.

Already in 1959, in the series "Aula de Música" (Music Classroom) at the Ateneo in Madrid, György Ligeti gave classes on electronic music. This series also featured Spanish serialists talking about their music. Cristóbal Halffter confessed that his

---

[25] Lorenç Barber, "40 años de creación musical en España," *Tiempo de historia* 6/62 (January 1980): 199.

[26] Ibid., 201.

[27] Ibid., 203.

"greatest aspiration was to Latinize serialism." How he would go about that was not entirely clear from his remarks, but at this remove in time, it is safe to say that the project never got off the ground.[28] The Aula de Música also sponsored lectures on serial and postserial music, on Schoenberg, Webern, Messiaen, Stockhausen, Berio, and other stalwarts of contemporary music.[29] All of this represented, on a musical level, the sort of integration with Europe that Franco and his technocrats were attempting at the economic level; hence, these events met with no interference from the regime.

Indeed, another such festival, Música Abierta (Open Music), was organized in Barcelona by composer Juan Hidalgo in 1960 and brought over two stalwarts of the American avant-garde, John Cage and David Tudor, who gave concerts in Barcelona and Madrid. These efforts did not enjoy much in the way of state or public support, but neither were they prohibited.[30] One of the major steps forward was the government's hosting of the Festival of Music of the Americas and Spain, held in Madrid in 1964 and sponsored by the Organization of American States and the Institute for Hispanic Culture. This joint venture showcased the newest music of the United States, Latin America, and Spain at an event designed to enhance inter-American relations. During the Cold War, avant-garde music sent abroad by the United States, especially that employing serial techniques, was meant to extol freedom, anti-Communism, and scientific exploration. For Spain, the prominence of Spanish serial works can be read as Spain's attempt to enter the European cultural milieu once more. The cooperation of the United States and Spain during this festival allows us to question the myriad uses of music, from promoting freedom to fascism.[31]

If one compares this to the way that avant-garde music was suppressed in the Soviet Union, denounced as decadent and formalistic, insufficiently relevant to the proletariat, one can see why atonal music became a useful ace-in-the-hole in Cold War poker. It did not matter whether the Franco regime liked it. All that mattered was that it made them *look* better than the Bolsheviks. And just as abstract painting posed no iconographic threat to either the Church or the regime, so atonal music was safely apolitical. It deployed no hymns or songs associated with any oppositional political movement, and its disdain for folklore made it mute in matters of regional separatism. It made no attempt and had no real ability to mobilize the masses or inspire insurrection. The relative indifference of the Spanish public to that sort of thing made it harmless enough.

[28]   Ibid., 204.

[29]   See Medina, "Primeras oleadas vanguardistas en el área de Madrid," 372–77, for more on the activities of the Aula de Música.

[30]   Ibid., 205.

[31]   For an in-depth look at this festival and its historical moment, see Alyson Payne, "The 1964 Festival of Music of the Americas and Spain: A Critical Examination of Ibero-American Musical Relations in the Context of Cold War Politics" (PhD diss., University of California, Riverside, 2012).

In fact, at the same time the regime capitalized on and claimed as its own the triumphs of the musical avant-garde, it was benefiting from the overseas success of progressive Spanish artists. It projected this renovated image outward to reha-bilitate its reputation and to stimulate the tourist industry, which would in turn help to stabilize and legitimize the regime.

Yet, we must avoid lapsing into an artificial dichotomy here, in which the only two sides of the musical coin are the traditionalist (and increasingly anachro-nistic) guitar pieces of Torroba and Rodrigo on the one hand, and the avant-garde creations of Pablo and Hidalgo on the other. For the truly defining event in Spanish music in this historic moment would come from neither of them but rather from the release of Paco de Lucia's incendiary flamenco-fusion masterpiece *Entre dos aguas* (19753).[32] In this work, Paco[33] (1947–2014) redefined not only flamenco guitar but flamenco itself as an art form, generating a novel image of Spain at once old and new, captivatingly hip, and irresistibly seductive. *Entre dos aguas* repre-sented his radical reinterpretation of a traditional, if marginally important, *palo* (genre) called a *rumba gitana*, an Afro-Cuban import that had gained currency earlier in the century. Paco sailed the *rumba gitana*, and flamenco along with it, to a whole new world by including electric bass and an assortment of Afro-Cuban percussion in his ensemble, e.g., conga drums, *güiro*, and bongos. Aside from his super virtuosity and blinding speed, especially his *picados* (scale runs), his innova-tive harmonic vocabulary drew heavily from Latin pop (especially bossa nova) and jazz. The steady, downbeat-oriented duple meter of the rumba had obvious appeal because of its danceability and similarity to the prevailing meter of rock and salsa.

Moreover, Paco's shoulder-length hair, black turtleneck sweater, and scarab necklace constituted a sartorial obituary for the Franco era, as he now boldly defined what it meant to be "cool"—Spanish style.[34] In short, Paco had set off a thermonuclear explosion of flamenco fire and phalangeal pyrotechnics that for-ever altered the cultural landscape of Spain. No wonder a pack of right-wing thugs once confronted him on the street and beat him up.[35] They knew that the radical break with the past his art represented slammed the door shut on the *Caudillo*'s vision for Spain more resoundingly than any number of laws could do—or any

---

[32] An excellent study of Paco's life and career up to the early 1990s is available in Juan José Téllez, *Paco de Lucia: Retrato de familia con guitarra*, series: Señales de vida (Sevilla: Qüásyeditorial, 1994).

[33] He was born Francisco Gustavo Sánchez Gómez, in Algeciras, Andalusia. He adopted the stage name of Paco de Lucia, in honor of his mother, Lucia Gomes. We hereafter refer to him simply as Paco.

[34] There are several clips available on YouTube of Paco performing *Entre dos aguas*. I accessed the clip at http://www.youtube.com/watch?v=2oyhlad64-s on January 30, 2011.

[35] Donn E. Pohren, *Lives and Legends of Flamenco: A Biographical History* (Madrid: Society of Spanish Studies, 1988), 339. "On one occasion Paco innocently made some remark to a reporter that was printed out of context, and Paco was beaten up on the streets of Madrid by a gang of far-right thugs." Paco made his home in the Yucatan Peninsula for many years.

number of abstract paintings and serialist string quartets. The erudite ruminations of Salazar and other intellectuals notwithstanding, there was now a new
pecking order in Spanish music, and its first principle was simple enough: roll
over, Beethoven.

From this point on, it was Paco and his emulators—of which there was soon to
be a small army—who came to dominate Spanish music at home and abroad. The
commoditization of *Nuevo Flamenco*, a fusion of traditional flamenco[36] with rock,
jazz, and Latin pop, created a market for *rumbas gitanas* so great that virtually
every number the Gipsy Kings has recorded is some variant of it. The *rumba gitana*
has become a centerpiece of the international soundscape from Stockholm to
Sacramento, from São Paulo to Singapore. Whatever the arbiters of taste may
think of it, this development symbolized Spain's (re)entry into the global culture
at large, fulfilling Unamuno's long-ago vision of a Spain at once ancient and
modern, thoroughly *en rapport* with the outside world without losing its sense of
uniqueness and individuality, its collective being, or *ser*.

[36] See Fusi, *Un siglo de España*, 137. There is some irony in the fact that *Nuevo Flamenco* was made
possible by the revival of traditional flamenco that had been taking place since the 1950s, especially
with the I Concurso de Cante Jondo de Córdoba in 1956, reinforced by festivals, recordings, *tablaos*
(flamenco cafés), competitions, and great performers such as dancers Antonio Gades and Carmen
Amaya, as well as guitarists Niño Ricardo, Mario Escudero, and Sabicas. However, because Franco had
promoted it for nationalist purposes, young people tended to associate flamenco with the regime, and
were consequently indifferent to it—until Paco.

8

ACT III
Scene ii
Español
1960–82

Public support for the zarzuela was beginning to wane in the 1960s, continuing a trend noticeable already in the previous decade. As we saw in Act II, Scene ii, Torroba always maintained that the zarzuela needed and deserved government subsidy, and that the lack of it was the principal cause for the genre's troubles. He was fond of noting that musical theater in France, Austria, and other European nations enjoyed much higher levels of state support. Moreover, his extensive travels in Latin America convinced him that even in Argentina, Chile, and Puerto Rico, music societies, universities, and other organizations lent considerably more financial assistance to the zarzuela than it received in Spain, a situation he found more than a little ironic.[1] The obvious remedy was a government subvention to support a Teatro de la Zarzuela, which he thought would benefit Spain more than a Teatro de la Ópera, an idea some others were promoting.[2]

In his view, the lack of necessary financial assistance resulted in a sort of "vicious circle. Composers don't write zarzuela because there are no companies to mount them....And mounting them is very difficult if the companies can't count on a subvention." He himself often had to produce zarzuelas outside of Spain because of such difficulties, something that benefited the government despite its neglect: "One must remember that the zarzuela is a great ambassador in America."[3]

---

[1] Moreno Torroba, "Aventuras y desventuras."

[2] Valera, "Federico Moreno Torroba," 21.

[3] "Moreno Torroba: 'No dejaré que la zarzuela muera," *El Mercurio* (Santiago, Chile), September 14, 1979. Np, na. Torroba made these remarks to the press during a trip to Chile at invitation of the Spanish Embassy and zarzuela impresario Faustino García. He conducted *Luisa Fernanda* as part of a week-long festival at the Teatro Carlos Cariola.

This chain of causation took different forms in different interviews. For instance, in another article he opined that,

> [T]here are no premieres today because there are no stable companies; there are no stable companies because there are no singers; there are no singers because there are no authors; there are no authors because it is not possible to make a living doing that.[4]

As a result, it was "now impossible to launch a season longer than four months. There are no permanent companies, and no guarantee of continued employment for the performers."[5]

Clearly, due to the decreasing number of new productions, and declining revenues, singers of the first rank were not keen to sing zarzuela, and young singers coming up through the ranks steered clear of it as well. The absence of trained performers made producing zarzuelas more difficult, and more expensive, as experienced professionals could demand higher fees.[6] This required charging more for tickets, which then reduced audiences even further. He expatiated on this problem with more than a hint of exasperation:

> Undoubtedly the current difficult moment of the zarzuela is not due solely to economics but also to the scarcity of singers, actors, and choristers. The gradual disappearance of lyric companies has produced a natural alienation and disillusion among those artists, as well as writers and composers. The Spanish lyric theater needs a cultural and even...patriotic vision, and not just with the standard repertory but with new works, these being especially difficult to realize because of never-ending economic difficulties. I say repertory and new works because zarzuela "anthologies" present us with a non-genre. The basis of our zarzuela is and always will be the libretto...but if the book "goes nowhere" (as we say in theatrical argot ["no marcha" in Spanish])...there is no zarzuela.[7]

His reference to "zarzuela anthologies" was a shot across the bow of the Antología de la Zarzuela, the brainchild of José Tamayo (see below). When asked if the zarzuela had been abandoned in general, he responded:

> For all practical purposes, it is in the hands of professionals who support it as best they can, but there is a shortage of official help, especially in terms

[4] Aguado, "Lo que dice el maestro Torroba."

[5] Mengual, "Federico Moreno Torroba: 'El género de zarzuela está enfermo,' *Levante*, June 6, 1981. Np.

[6] Opera has also been afflicted with this problem of escalating fees for superstars. See Norman Lebrecht, *Who Killed Classical Music? Maestros, Managers, Corporate Politics* (Secaucus, NJ: Carol Publishing Group, 1997).

[7] Moreno Torroba, "Aventuras y desventuras."

of musical research and paying grants to singers so that they can complete their training and dedicate themselves entirely to singing, instead of having to supplement their artistic activities with other kinds of work.[8]

Torroba himself had not abandoned zarzuela in principle, insisting that he and others could write "magnificent works, with possibilities for export," but not without state support for the companies that would produce them.[9] The only other real disincentive was the lack of satisfactory librettos, not of time, reflection, and inspiration.[10] He received many librettos but was not happy with any of them.[11] For all these reasons, Torroba's 1966 zarzuela *Ella* would be his last. In fact, his pessimism about the zarzuela's future extended to classical music in general: "I see that composers of the *género lírico* have no future. And in general classical composers have a difficult future."[12] Torroba still felt he had a future ahead of him, but it would be trying, and brief.

As a consequence of all this, journalist Lola Aguado remarked in 1981 that "the truth is that our lyric theater is such a phenomenal desert that a premiere [the opera *El poeta*], though it be by a composer who performed his military service in 1912, is a real event!"[13] Two years earlier, another journalist had concurred that "no important zarzuelas have been composed in the last thirty years. It appears that the constituent elements of the genre, nationalism and regionalism [*costumbrismo*], frighten off modern composers."[14]

This state of affairs did not perturb José Tamayo, organizer of the famous Antología de la Zarzuela, which presented staged excerpts from various classic works. "The repertoire we have is sufficient to make us proud of a genre that is so representative of Spain, as the opera is of Italy, as the operetta is of Vienna, or as the musical comedy is of Broadway."[15] The patriotic tone of his reflections was quite deliberate. He organized an Antología de la Zarzuela in 1979 that took place over a period of ten days, in Madrid's Plaza de Toros. The press reported that it was a "spectacle of nationalist nostalgia," during which the Spanish flag was prominently displayed. Tamayo proudly declared that "The Spanish flag is Spain!"[16] That sort of patriotic rhetoric may seem overheated today, but we recall that this was only four years after the death of Franco. The embers of right-wing nationalism

---

[8] Alonso, "Homenaje en el Ayuntamiento," 3.

[9] García, "'Lo único que no se repite.'"

[10] Ibero, "Moreno Torroba."

[11] Mateo Cladera, "El maestro Torroba dirigira su 'Luisa Fernanda,'" *Baleares*, April 23, 1982.

[12] Colmenero, "Lírico Moreno Torroba."

[13] Aguado, "Lo que dice el maestro Torroba."

[14] "La zarzuela nacional," *Cambio* 16/405 (September 9, 1979), 52.

[15] Actually, Torroba went one step further than Tamayo, averring that "the stage works of Chapí, Bretón, and Jiménez exhibit *more* quality than Viennese operetta" [italics added]. Mengual. "Federico Moreno Torroba."

[16] "La zarzuela nacional," 53.

still glowed with some intensity, stirred by Tamayo and others (though not Torroba). The zarzuela was their musical emblem of choice.

When asked about an earlier "anthology" by Tamayo's company, in 1971, Torroba was ambivalent, not for political but rather aesthetic reasons: "It is fine, but it is not zarzuela, properly speaking" but rather a collection of excerpts from various works that appeal to the public's curiosity or nostalgia.[17]

Yet, even the nationalist regime had never been especially sympathetic to the zarzuela's declining health. When asked which regime, socialist or Francoist, had been more supportive of zarzuela, Torroba answered, with mild disgust, that neither was particularly helpful.[18] On one occasion, speaking at an event in his honor, he made a concrete proposal (pun intended): "If it were possible to reduce just one kilometer of highway in some national project and dedicate those funds instead to promoting the zarzuela, many people would be grateful."[19] And he did at times advance rather specific proposals, such as the following:

> My idea is that the state should not contract with a company for a period of less than three months. They should establish themselves in provinces like Madrid and Barcelona, a minimum of two companies that present a complete season, with the appropriate months off for vacation. With this kind of continuity it would be possible to increase the current repertoire because the company would have more time to rehearse and consequently be able to premiere two new works every year, preferably on commission, presented by the author and approved by a competent board of directors.[20]

Perhaps Torroba could have been more effective had he gotten politically involved, to change the government's treatment of the arts. But that would have been contrary to his nature. Did he ever get involved in politics? "Absolutely never," he affirmed. He was never tempted by politics because it seemed to him "a very complicated thing, which, in the final analysis, just messes up the world. I have always thought that being a politician consists in making promises; but of course, the promises very seldom become reality. In any case, I have had and continue to have very good friends who are politicians."[21]

---

[17] C., "Moreno Torroba ha cumplido ochenta años," *La Vanguardia*, March 17, 1971.

[18] See Jaze, "Maestro Moreno Torroba, más de medio siglo al servicio de la música española," *Diario de Avisos*, May 19, 1982. When asked by the interviewer in which of the two periods, the dictatorship or democracy, more attention was devoted to zarzuela, he responded: "In neither very well. Music in general and zarzuela in particular supported themselves."

[19] Alonso, "Homenaje en el Ayuntamiento," 3. Alonso was a well-known local author. The mayor also spoke at this event. His name was José María Aroca Ruiz-Funes, and he was a leftist from a leftist family. He was also the first democratically elected mayor of Murcia since the end of the Franco regime. Yet, there he was, praising Torroba to the skies: "He has disseminated a bit of the Spanish soul."

[20] Amelia Hernández, "La ópera levanta cabeza," *Arriba*, October 11, 1977, 25.

[21] San Martín, "Federico Moreno Torroba."

We now know that such a response is a bit too simple, as his music, and that of his contemporaries, cannot be fully extricated from its social and political context. But direct involvement and active participation were not for him. Serving on an administrative commission and holding an office within the party apparatus were two very different things in his view. Besides, though he noticed that all Spanish governments had expressed the best of intentions in regards to supporting the arts, they never had the resources, though in the post-Franco period, he had "great hopes in the present moment because the king and queen are great lovers of music."[22]

At times, the zarzuela's sorry state seemed to reach crisis proportions in the imaginations of those who loved it. Asked by a journalist in 1972 when the "crisis" had begun, Torroba responded "about twelve years ago. But look, they have been talking about a crisis of the zarzuela for centuries. I believe that what the zarzuela needs in times like these is state support in the form of a subvention."[23]

On other occasions, however, he insisted that there was no crisis in the genre itself, only that companies could not exist on ticket sales alone—nowhere in the world, for that matter. Companies needed government subventions to facilitate "renovation of the traditional repertoire with new works."[24] Unlike Tamayo, he was not content to see the genre rest on its laurels. But what seems to have made Torroba especially bitter was not the government's apathy toward the genre but the "fire in the rear" that it took from specialists who should have known better. They were also responsible for the decline of the zarzuela, because they prejudiced the public against it:

> [T]he zarzuela has its obstinate detractors, especially in the writings of certain music lovers, musicologists, and commentators.... Can you imagine that, in his day, a maestro of the stature of Felipe Pedrell, guru of Spanish music pedagogy, was a detractor of the zarzuela? His judgements concerning the genre are inconceivable.[25]

Indeed, though Torroba was "well aware that many music lovers look down their noses at the zarzuela,...the truth is that creating a zarzuela is much harder than writing symphonic music."[26] Of course, much depends on the quality of one's work. Though it is clearly a case of comparing apples and oranges, still, it is not clear which work in the history of the zarzuela required greater effort to create than Beethoven's Ninth Symphony. But having written in both symphonic music and operetta, Torroba was in a position to know. And the bitter result of this kind

---

22 Gómez Ortiz, "Moreno Torroba," 15.

23 Maso, "Teatro Victoria: Presentación de 'Luisa Fernanda' en la temporada de zarzuela."

24 "La muerte de Federico Moreno Torroba," 11.

25 Moreno Torroba, "Aventuras y desventuras."

26 "Moreno Torroba: 'No dejaré que la zarzuela muera.'"

of prejudice was that "a mediocre symphony gets more attention and respect than a successful zarzuela."[27] In any case, he thought that Spain's legacy as a musical nation was completely bound up with the zarzuela:

> The zarzuela is something we Spaniards have that is truly our own. Our musical tradition is less prominent [in relation to other European countries, which] have many more important symphonic works than we do. But when a zarzuela appears, *there* is Spain.[28] [emphasis added]

However, Torroba also held contemporary composers responsible for the zarzuela's decline, accusing some of them of suffering from "creative impotence." Their writing did not possess the necessary "grace, charm, melodic spontaneity— romantic, jovial, or dramatic—that the genre requires." A "lack of inspiration" was the result of composers' focusing on "pure technique based on elements of absolute simplicity," rather than on "genuine musical content."[29] Yet, there were young composers capable of writing zarzuela. A year before his death, Torroba cited at least two emerging talents equal to the task:

> But of course, there are young composers of melodic music who could dedicate themselves to the zarzuela. I really believe it. Which ones? I don't know, perhaps Manuel Alejandro or Juan Carlos Calderón, for example. I am certain they could write very successful zarzuelas.[30]

But the fact that these distinguished contemporary musicians have not found their way into the annals of the zarzuela tells us something of the genre's demise— and of Torroba's stubborn refusal to give up on it totally. Federico, Jr., carries on in that spirit, having declared that "the zarzuela will never die because it is something that belongs to us, that we Spaniards alone possess, and with whose music we strongly identify."[31] Yet, the public was partly responsible for the genre's troubles as well:

> The zarzuela reaches the public very directly, all sorts of public. The Spanish public is very demanding and rejects works that do not possess all the conditions for success. The foreign public is easier or more understanding, or more cultured.[32]

---

[27] Diez-Crespo, "Moreno Torroba," 27.

[28] "Moreno Torroba: 'No dejaré que la zarzuela muera.'"

[29] Moreno Torroba, "Aventuras y desventuras."

[30] Berasategui, "Moreno Torroba," ix.

[31] Montse Chivite, "Moreno-Torroba: 'Navarra mantiene su afición a la zarzuela,'" *Diario de Navarra*, November 15, 1994, 40.

[32] Imbuluzqueta, "El compositor Federico Moreno Torroba."

Torroba's view concerning the necessity of government support merits serious consideration, but one wonders if there are not other factors that made a continuation of the zarzuela tradition unlikely, with or without subsidy. One of the chief reasons for decreasing public enthusiasm was certainly connected with the ascendancy of cinema and television. After all, admission to the movies cost much less than theater tickets, and movie theaters claimed an increasing share of the market. For instance, Torroba regretted that the Teatro de Novedades in Barcelona had been converted into a movie theater, as it had once witnessed four hundred performances of *Luisa Fernanda* and thus held a special relationship with the genre and his own compositions.[33] But such conversions were often the only way venues like the Novedades could survive at all (it became a theater again in 1992 but closed its doors for good in 2006). Torroba's old Teatro Calderón had to find a corporate sponsor to survive and is now the Teatro Caser Calderón de Madrid.

Of course, people could watch a zarzuela on television virtually for free, even if the experience was not the same as seeing one live. Torroba himself worked on television adaptations of zarzuelas. During the mid-1960s, he helped persuade Spanish Television (TVE) to produce zarzuelas for broadcast. It was hoped that presenting the zarzuela in a contemporary medium—television—would stimulate the public's interest. Twelve zarzuelas appeared on television and vinyl recordings, including *Maruxa*, *El huésped del Sevillano*, *Los bohemios*, and *Las golondrinas*.[34] The series was called Antología Lírica and extended from 1968 to 1972.[35] While Juan Orduña was the chief producer, Torroba was closely involved, serving as conductor and impresario for the duration of the project. The television productions received a warm reception at the time but ultimately did not achieve their desired effect. The LP recordings, on the other hand, attracted a great deal of interest, and CDs of them are still on the market.[36]

Perhaps Torroba proved to be his own worst enemy by helping establish the zarzuela on television, but he would have argued that public exposure to zarzuela there could result in a greater appetite for live performance. Indeed, though television might serve to popularize the music, he naturally believed that zarzuela was something that had to be experienced live, in the theater.[37] Torroba's actual concern was not so much that people would become habituated to watching zarzuela on television as that they might simply never have the *opportunity* to see it in the theater, "the way God demands."[38]

[33] Valera, "Federico Moreno Torroba," 21.

[34] A. C. "Federico Moreno Torroba."

[35] Rioja, "Federico Moreno Torroba," 28.

[36] In 2004, Suevia Films released a boxed set of seven DVDs, including *La revoltosa*, *Bohemios*, *Las golondrinas*, *La canción del olvido*, *El huésped del Sevillano*, and *El caserío*.

[37] Torroba expressed this opinion in Ángeles Maso, "Teatro Victoria: Presentación de 'Luisa Fernanda' en la temporada de zarzuela," *La Vanguardia*, June 10, 1972.

[38] Rioja, "Federico Moreno Torroba," 28.

Yet, there was something more fundamental at work here. We recall that Torroba was a big fan of Broadway and attended productions there whenever he was in New York. Among his favorite musicals was *42nd Street*;[39] when asked which musical he would like to have written himself, he cited *Brigadoon*![40] All of this begs a question: Broadway received no government support whatsoever, yet it was in a kind of golden age at just the time the zarzuela was going under.[41] It also faced competition from cinema and television, yet it more than held its own. And production expenses for many Broadway musicals were much greater than those for zarzuelas. We recall that Federico, Jr., attributed the musical's success to the ability of New Yorkers to pay much higher ticket prices than the Spanish public could afford. The lavish productions and expensive promotion of Broadway musicals assured the popularity of many works—and the resulting fortunes of some composers.

However, one hastens to point out that Broadway musicals exhibited much greater musical diversity than the zarzuela. Musicals embraced a wide variety of styles, from evocations of jazz and mambo in *West Side Story*, to quasi-Scottish music in *Brigadoon*, and eventually to rock in *Hair*, *Grease*, and *Jesus Christ Superstar*; the latter was another musical that impressed Torroba.[42] The musical has always displayed a remarkable ability to adapt to contemporary taste, to changes in musical fashion. Can we imagine a jazz zarzuela? A rock zarzuela? Hip-hop, anyone? No, and the mere suggestion sounds absurd. The cause of this apparent absurdity is precisely the connection of the zarzuela with *casticismo*, with Torroba's own insistence that the zarzuela reflect the life, customs, and music of the Spanish people, that it be a mirror of *traditional* Spanish society and culture. As he insisted over and over, "This very Spanish genre must have, above all else, a popular character...that reflects the life of a particular region, especially of Madrid and Andalusia."[43]

---

[39] *42nd Street* is a musical from 1933 with a book by Michael Stewart and Mark Bramble, lyrics by Al Dubin and music by Harry Warren. The 1980 revival won a Tony Award, and this is apparently the production Torroba saw. He made this remark in San Martín, "Federico Moreno Torroba," and also in Vicent, "El pentagrama," 14: "The other day, in New York, I saw a fantastic musical called *42nd Street*....I liked the whole thing."

[40] Alfredo Mañas, "Querido Maestro:" *Autores: Revista de información de la S.G.A.E.*, n3 (October 1982): 24. "I would have liked to have written something like *Brigadoon*, which I think is one of the best musical comedies of all times!"

[41] In a conversation with Walter Clark, September 23, 2010, Broadway-musical scholar William Everett expressed the opinion that the decline of the zarzuela took place at the same time that musicals in the style of Rudolf Friml and Sigmund Romberg were going out of style. The difference, of course, is that Broadway found something to replace them with, and the zarzuela did nothing comparable. We hasten to point out that the vast majority of US theaters, other than those on Broadway, are nonprofit organizations and qualify for tax-deductible donations, as well as grants from federal, state, and local governments.

[42] San Martín, "Federico Moreno Torroba." He also liked *Annie* (1977), but not *Evita* (1979). He was not certain, however, that *Annie* and *42nd Street* (a 1933 movie that became the 1980 show) would endure. That "remained to be seen."

[43] Cladera, "El maestro Torroba."

To be sure, we also prefer the traditional zarzuela and understand anyone else's attachment to it. The works of Torroba and his predecessors possess a charm and magic all their own. And yet, one must play devil's advocate here and ask just how many schottisches, *pasodobles*, waltzes, *jotas*, habaneras, and *zapateados* audiences will continue to enjoy before they start looking elsewhere for entertainment, for something reflecting contemporary tastes and times. Because of the zarzuela's inability to adjust to a rapidly changing musical environment—or better said, the unwillingness of zarzuela composers to think outside the box they had created for themselves—the genre was essentially doomed to an existence in intensive care, permanently connected to government life-support—when it could get even that.

After all, why *not* a jazz, rock, or hip-hop zarzuela?! That is a legitimate question. The waltz, habanera, and schottische had all come from elsewhere, and the Pucciniesque quality of so much of Torroba's own writing was in no way autochthonous to Spain. If the zarzuela could absorb foreign styles and influences in the late nineteenth and early twentieth centuries, why could it not continue to do so in the last decades of the 1900s? If it could reflect the popular culture and society of Madrid in the 1860s or 1920s, why not Madrid in the 1960s or 70s, when young people especially were coming under the spell of rock and other African American musical fashions?

In short, the zarzuela became a thing of the past because authors and composers ceased to be able to think of it any other way. These thoughts crossed Torroba's mind, but he felt that modern life was not conducive to the zarzuela, that it did not offer suitable subject matter, precisely because culture had become so international, because the cityscapes and soundscapes of England, Spain, the United States, and other countries were becoming homogenized and undifferentiated, resulting in a loss of *casticismo*. On one occasion he lamented that "the music that [young Spanish musicians] are making now, above all in contemporary music, could just as easily be Russian or Belgian as Spanish."[44] He elaborated on this later:

> Music today is international, like life itself. If you walk down a street in London, you will see people dressed the same way they are here. And down a street in the United States, the same. But people continue to have problems, passions, and affairs. Today's affairs would have been very serious in another epoch. Now, no. Thus, when these affairs are portrayed on stage, there is no impact. Music is an extension of romanticism, and today there is too little romanticism.

In this same interview Torroba averred that the theater was an instinct. "An instinct... contact with the public.... It cannot be explained.... In matters of art,

[44] "'Si sale mal "El poeta" es culpa mía,'" *El Imparcial*, May 21, 1980.

nothing can be explained.[45] Given his instinctive approach to the theater, it is not surprising that he occasionally contradicted his views of the compatibility of modern life with the zarzuela, at least in regard to subject matter. Once, when asked if he would put the text of *Luisa Fernanda* to the same music today that he had forty years earlier, he responded, "with the same book, yes. But today I would prefer not to work with traditional books but rather with stories that reflect the problems of our own time."[46]

The question persists, however, as to what sort of music he would write in setting such librettos. Certainly not the same type of music as before. Would it have been possible to compose a zarzuela about our own time without resorting to music that reflected the popular fashions of that time? Probably not, but he never went down that path. Again, however, he was aware of the need for renovation, even if he could not be the agent for it:

> The most important thing is that the zarzuela evolve. The jokes that made people laugh thirty years ago are no longer funny. And music itself has progressed a great deal, especially in regard to harmony.[47]

Torroba once noted that "theatrical impresarios appear more inclined towards modern [popular] music" than zarzuelas, another factor contributing to the genre's eclipse.[48] It is odd that he did not perceive the opportunity here to obey that old adage: "If ya can't beat 'em, join 'em!" He was not unalterably opposed to popular music, as his preferences in Broadway musicals strongly suggest. For instance, he spoke approvingly of the Beatles, saying that they "make music of quality."[49] Indeed, he was aware that some popular-music groups were using his melodies in their songs. In particular, during the 1970s, Pequeña Compañía had successfully recorded a pop version of the famous "Habanera del Saboyano," from the first act of *Luisa Fernanda*, and he saw this as completely benign.[50] After all, were not other groups "doing the same thing with Beethoven?" he asked rhetorically. In fact, they were.[51]

---

[45] Aguado, "Lo que dice el maestro Torroba."

[46] Maso, "Teatro Victoria."

[47] "Moreno Torroba: 'No dejaré que la zarzuela muera.'"

[48] Berasategui, "Moreno Torroba," ix.

[49] Gómez Ortiz, "Moreno Torroba," 15. "The Beatles make music. Light music of quality has not gone overboard."

[50] San Martín, "Federico Moreno Torroba."

[51] Perhaps he was referring to "A Fifth of Beethoven," the disco arrangement by Walter Murphy and the Big Apple Band of 1976, immortalized in the 1977 film *Saturday Night Fever*. He also cited the example of Rodrigo, who was making lots of money off of popular arrangements of his *Concierto de Aranjuez* by Miles Davis and Chick Corea. See Mallo, "Los noventa jovenes años."

However, when pressed on the dominance of pop, the most he could marshal was ambivalence. Interviewed on this very topic and when asked about his reaction to popular music, he was generous: "The phenomenon of the pop-music invasion since a few years ago is frankly odd. Truthfully, I can tell you up front that there are many [songs] that I like, that have originality and force." But his interrogator pressed on:

> Truly, Maestro Torroba, do the efforts and sacrifices of a conservatory musician have any value in the face of this massive international expansion of pop, folk, or underground music, to cite three examples? Don't composers with real training and who have made sacrifices in their struggles feel somewhat cheated?

Torroba responded thoughtfully:

> That is a difficult question to answer, but I can tell you with complete assuredness that a true composer never feels cheated, in spite of the pop invasion. That which is authentic endures, whether in music, literature, or art. And, yes, the efforts expended during the years in the conservatory have their compensation, believe me.[52]

One must give Torroba his due: for a man of his years and conservative temperament, he was admirably fair and remarkably open-minded. Yet, his view of popular music also poses a lack of imagination, an inability to conceive how the "pop invasion" could be turned to the zarzuela's advantage. And it is true that on other occasions he was less favorably disposed. Only months before he passed away, he responded to a query about whether he liked the "music of today, of the young people." He conceded that young people "were with rock," but that it did not make "beautiful things, because the only way to do that is to write a beautiful melody, and that is what rock lacks."[53]

In any case, he was not a complete pessimist regarding the future of the genre, as he noted interest among young people in the audience, some even with long hair. Asked if the zarzuela arouses the same emotion today as before, he responded, "Well, yes. The same as before, because it is the greatest musical representation of Spain."[54] He reiterated his faith in the younger generation even more forcefully in another interview. When a journalist suggested that young people continued to demonstrate apathy toward the zarzuela, Torroba averred, "Who says such barbarities? The boys and girls of today are discovering rock *and* the zarzuela. As a

[52] Rioja, "Federico Moreno Torroba," 28.
[53] Cladera, "El maestro Torroba."
[54] Maso, "Teatro Victoria."

result, we require the funds to present zarzuelas in a dignified manner: orchestra, choruses, decoration, costumes."[55]

Indeed, it is hardly impossible to like both rock and zarzuela at the same time. But, again we ask, why did it not occur to him or anyone else to combine these two? It could have made for a momentous change in the zarzuela's fortunes, literally and figuratively, thus obviating the need for government support. Alas, the historical moment has now passed and will not return. Despite all that, Torroba found plenty of other things to occupy his time.

Sociedad de Autores de España

Torroba was not confined to composition. Freed from the responsibilities of being a full-time impresario, and of writing continuously for the stage, Torroba would take on daunting responsibilities in cultural administration, first as vice-president and then president of the Sociedad General de Autores de España, and as director of the Real Academia de Bellas Artes de San Fernando.

The Sociedad General de Autores de España (SGAE), which protects the copyright interests of Spanish authors, both literary and musical, had long been an important facet of Torroba's professional life. After serving as vice-president for seventeen years, Torroba was elected president in 1974. During his presidency, Torroba took important steps to integrate Spanish law and practice with that of other nations. By doing so, he helped ensure the payment of Spanish artists who were not always compensated for performances of their works abroad. Torroba was also instrumental in sorting out a scandal involving fraudulent royalty payments to members of the society.[56] As a highly esteemed citizen of his country, Torroba served as a diplomat in cultural exchanges with several nations. While president of the SGAE, he signed a cultural exchange agreement with the VAAP, a Soviet society of artists and writers, in July of 1982.

Torroba was the perfect choice for this position because he knew the history of the SGAE and had played an important role in its genesis. His description of its early years bears the stamp of personal authority:

> The Society facilitated, in exchange for the rights to rent, copies of materials without which the author would have to bear the costs and, today, the copying of a zarzuela or a symphonic work. The SAE [Sociedad de Autores y Editores] was at its outset a circle of authors that,...got together mornings to chat about incidents in their respective work. The

---

[55] Arazo, "Moreno Torroba."

[56] Juan José Alonso Millán, "Homenaje," *Autores: Revista de información de la S.G.A.E.*, n3 (October 1982): 4; *Diario* (Valencia) June 8, 1981; Jaze, "Maestro Moreno Torroba."

administration was very basic. And thus we come to 1932, the year in which Federico Romero founded the SGAE.[57]

Though he had already been vice-president, the presidency was a big step up:

> In the period that I was vice-president, my mission was limited to complying with the agreements reached by the counsel and the president. In my term as president, I have had the difficult assignment of enacting all the administrative proceedings in regard to recordings, cassettes, video-cassettes, etc. New recording techniques have compelled us to give an entirely new spin to administration, to make it more modern and agile. We have had to discipline some members who were abusing the terms of their contracts, arrogating to themselves rights they don't actually have, and that has been a very difficult task. Today we can say that the SGAE is at the same level as any equivalent organization anywhere in the world.[58]

In 1975, he told the press that the SGAE had eight thousand members, and that of those, only thirty could live off of their royalties. He cited a singer named Arbez, who accompanied himself on the guitar, as the top earner, having made eight million *pesetas*; interestingly, he was followed by Rodrigo, above all for his *Concierto de Aranjuez*.[59] So, this new job of Torroba's was a great responsibility, affecting thousands of creative artists and requiring the management of large sums of money. Clearly, all of this had an enormous impact on the country's cultural life.

In the 1970s and early 80s, the SGAE struggled through a period of political transition and technological change. The country was moving from dictatorship to democracy, even as technology introduced new formats, such as cassettes and videotapes, which required adjustments in the SGAE's policies regarding replication and copyright. One journalist credited Torroba with representing a "progressive spirit of reform, a man with drive and optimism, who does not waste any of the time remaining to him in this life."[60]

His travel itinerary alone gave some evidence of his immense energy. He traveled extensively in western Europe on SGAE business, as well as to Russia and Japan. How many hours a day did he work (in 1980)? "Between five and eight. In the morning I work in my office at the SGAE. In the afternoon, at home, I work at the piano composing, or I do other things. Apart from all that, travel, meetings, and meals."[61] He also made time to attend a wide variety of concerts: "I listen to all

---

[57] Federico Moreno Torroba, "Una llamada a la colaboración de todos," *Autores: Revista de información de la S.G.A.E.*, special fiftieth-anniversary issue (1982): 43–44.

[58] Jaze, "Maestro Moreno Torroba."

[59] "Moreno Torroba, el más famoso compositor."

[60] María, "La empecinada juventud."

[61] Ibid.

kinds of music, including those that I don't like, in order to understand what not to do."[62] Concerning his eating habits, one interviewer learned the following: "His breakfast is frugal: coffee and cookies (*galletas*, which could also mean biscuits or crackers)....At mid-day, it is his custom to have a beer. Rarely is he able to eat lunch at home."[63] Given the rather hectic pace he had to maintain, did Torroba ever think of retiring? "When they retire me!"[64] In the event, only death would accomplish that feat.[65]

Yet, there must have been times when he thought of hanging it up, as he had to confront some bitter controversies. For instance, we alluded above to the fact that some members were not reporting performances so that they would not have to share royalties with the SGAE. This was a clear violation of their agreement as members, and Torroba had to address the issue by affirming the SGAE's position and taking disciplinary action against the offenders, who did not take these measures lying down.[66] Torroba never lost his cool, which the press noted:

> ...the artistic has prevailed over the administrative. The prudence and silence of the SGAE and its president have been well noted in the face of the attacks it has been enduring over the past two years as a consequence of its financial reorganization, which was necessary not because of anything the administration did but was rather due to a series of irregularities on the part of a certain number of members, who wanted to increase their earnings. This gave rise to a series of attacks on television, radio, and in the press, attacks that verged on personal threats. Thus the counsel of the administration came to the conclusion that it should make a formal declaration vindicating the president, protecting him against all malicious acts.[67]

---

[62] Gómez Ortiz, "Moreno Torroba," 15.

[63] "Diecisiete presuntos estafadores en la Sociedad de Autores," clipping from a Valencia newspaper, May 11, 1981 [Na], on the occasion of his trip there to clarify SGAE affairs. Torroba's favorite dishes were "stewed potatoes, lentils with pork sausage, and homemade paella." See San Martín, "Federico Moreno Torroba."

[64] María, "La empecinada juventud."

[65] In another interview, the journalist summarized his work routine thus: He gets up every day at 8. If a thought occurred to him while lying in bed, he writes it down before leaving the house and looks it over again before leaving. He goes to the SGAE and works till 2 p.m., goes home, eats lunch, takes a nap ("pequeña siesta"). Then he works till supper. He reviews his work one more time, then goes to bed. When he's resting, when vacation arrives, he works more. "In Navarra, in my home in Sanesteban, I work ten hours a day and never get tired. For me, work is recreation." See Sagi-Vela, "Moreno Torroba, nonagenario," 23. Even when in Madrid, though, he would sometimes work until the wee hours, if he was obsessed with a particular project. "This agrees with him, because he was a night owl as a youth [*noctámbulo*], and if he goes to bed too early, he gets a headache." From Gómez Ortiz, "Moreno Torroba," 15.

[66] And journalist Luis Diez came to the defense of the workers affected by this affair in his article "Víctimas, los trabajadores," *El Socialista*, n181 (November 26–December 2, 1980): 37.

[67] "Exaltación, homenaje y desagravio a Moreno Torroba," *El Imparcial*, July 4, 1980.

Concerning the responsibilities he had taken on at the SGAE, he relied on his unfailing sense of humor and capacity for self-reflection: "Yes, I recognize that I must be something of a masochist, because it causes me a lot of headaches; however, I do like it. The composer is a very strange being. He always believes that his work is not sufficiently accepted, rewarded, or promoted."[68] His philosophical frame of mind and stoic ability to endure hardship stood him in good stead in a variety of life situations that would have tested the mettle of even the strongest spirits.

In 1981, he traveled to Valencia to clarify his mission at the SGAE, and to explain the sometimes drastic measures he had found it necessary to take. He also took the opportunity to express his admiration for Valencian José Serrano (1873–1941), who had been a leading composer of zarzuela and a friend of his:

> I have come to reaffirm our commitment to pursuing the struggle within the Society to restructure it completely; although I consider that the norms have been concluded and clarified, there are eighteen sentences against individuals implicated.... Beyond that, I have come to express my very special interest in the SGAE's memorial to maestro Serrano. I myself went to his *tertulia* at the café Castilla; many early mornings I accompanied him to his home, after the *tertulia*, and he would play the piano for us. We are preparing to place a commemorative plaque on the house where he lived for so many years.[69]

Denouncing those who had committed fraud earned Torroba a long campaign of threats. "At one point I felt it necessary to hire bodyguards. That is always disagreeable. They have called me a thief and I don't know what else. But I will defend honorably and energetically the interests of the Society over which I preside."[70] All of this makes it clear why one commentator cast Torroba's job in a dramatic light:

> The SGAE is "his battle." His titanic struggle is to give it a definite order, to bring it up to date. He sends his fleet forth to battle against [those] who navigate the stormy ocean of audiovisual falsification. The modern pirates do not have a patch over the left eye or a wooden leg. They do not rob, but they nonetheless devalue intellectual property. They are eager to bring to market their tapes and videos with stolen music and images.[71]

[68] Mallo, "Los noventa jovenes años."
[69] "Diecisiete presuntos estafadores en la Sociedad de Autores."
[70] San Martín, "Federico Moreno Torroba."
[71] Olano, "¡Viva Navarra!"

Sixty of the two hundred authors sanctioned by the SGAE were deprived of their voting and attendance rights at Juntas Generales of the SGAE. They appealed for reinstatement. Apparently some recording artists were selling pirated copies of their recordings without going through the SGAE. This is the sort of thing Torroba had to deal with.[72] Movie producers were also up in arms over rights issues, especially in Catalonia and the Balearic Islands.[73]

Torroba remained fair and firm in the face of opposition. "I consider that to be a natural reaction of those who are opposed to reform or the abolition of a system of distributing profits that…has given way to a resolution providing various expedients with serious sanctions."[74] He was determined to take corrective action, but he was never vindictive or reactionary. And his leadership style had a positive effect. By his death, the SGAE's membership had increased to thirty thousand.

Real Academia de Bellas Artes de San Fernando

In 1978, Torroba was elected director of the Real Academia de Bellas Artes de San Fernando. First elected to the academy in 1934 as its youngest member, he was now its oldest. It was clearly a deeply meaningful occasion for him, a validation of his many years of work there, his many contributions to its intellectual and cultural life, and to his stature as an "elder statesman" in the cultural life of the nation. Yet, he was never one to get carried away with praise or lapse into complacency:

> I am surprised and moved by the results of the vote and accede to my new post with the intention to work, because there is a lot of work to do at the Academia. The labor of the Academia is transcendental, but already it can be even more so.[75]

And he found a way to combine his activities as composer and administrator. His Three Preludes for Organ were premiered at a mass at the chapel of San Antonio de la Florida, one customarily celebrated by the Academia for the souls of Goya and other departed members (the chapel is adorned with very distinctive frescoes by Goya). The press took favorable notice of this premiere, only a few months before the composer would join Goya in eternity:

[72] "Solicitan la suspensión de la junta general de la Sociedad de Autores," *El País*, March 9, 1978, 27.

[73] "Los cineastas lo tienen muy negro," *Mundo Diario*, April 21, 1978.

[74] L. M., "Moreno Torroba habla claro," *Ya, Hoja del Lunes*, October 3, 1977.

[75] "Moreno Torroba, director de la Academia de Bellas Artes," *La Vanguardia*, May 10, 1978, 19.

They are brief fragments, inspired, emotive, with a clearly Spanish character, new evidence of the enviable fecundity of an artist whose many years do not seem to weigh him down.[76]

A special issue of the Academia's journal was published in his honor after his death. Those contributing noted his punctuality in chairing meetings and his careful attention to his duties. He presided over a period of "revitalization" and played a major role in the restoration of the Academia's headquarters on the calle de Alcalá, a restoration he would not live to see completed. His seemingly inexhaustible reserves of energy and will were a source of astonishment, as Ramón González de Amezúa remarked:

> On numerous occasions he would appear at 5 p.m. for a meeting after arriving that very morning from Buenos Aires or New York—and all without giving the slightest indication of pressure or haste, as if it were the most natural thing in the world.[77]

Above all else, he was exacting and judicious in all of his negotiations,[78] skills he had no doubt honed during his many years working as an impresario and conductor.

The Conductor

Indeed, Torroba seemed to grow more energetic and productive with each passing year, to have found some elixir of life in work itself. He was increasingly active as a conductor during this time in his life. He conducted the Buenos Aires Symphony Orchestra, the television orchestra of Montevideo, the municipal orchestras of both Lima and São Paulo, and ensembles in Uruguay, Peru, and Chile, leading them in programs of Spanish music.[79] And he was increasingly prolific in the recording studio as conductor and producer. Under his direction, over three hundred works of various composers were recorded, including twenty complete zarzuelas. Recording labels included Columbia, RCA, SEECO, Capitol, and Decca in the Americas, and Hispavox, Iberia, and La Voz de su Amo in Spain. As he himself explained, "When I begin to conduct, the baton is converted into an extension of

[76] The information in this paragraph comes from an untitled press clipping in the Navarra archive, dated May 31, 1982. The event to which it refers was also reported in "Música para la Academia de Bellas Artes en la festividad de San Fernando," *El País*, May 31, 1982.

[77] Ramón González de Amezúa, "Un hombre extraordinario," *Academia: Boletín de la Real Academia de Bellas Artes de San Fernando*, n55 (second semester 1982): 20–21.

[78] Antonio Fernández-Cid, "Evocación del Maestro Moreno Torroba,"*Academia: Boletín de la Real Academia de Bellas Artes de San Fernando*, n55 (second semester 1982): 34.

[79] See "'La zarzuela está vivita y coleando,'" 56.

my very being."[80] And that "being" maintained a grueling schedule of conducting appearances at home and in Latin America.

As we have seen, during these years there was apparently more enthusiasm and support for the zarzuela in Latin America, at least among the creole elite, than in the country of its origin. And Torroba's works were evergreen favorites with audiences there. At one memorable performance in Lima, the audience demonstrated its remarkable familiarity with and love for *Luisa Fernanda*:

> Maestro Moreno Torroba had to repeat the immortal Mazurka [de las sombrillas] three times. The public sang with real spirit the parts of the chorus, men, women, and everyone. The ovation heard in the Municipal Hall was tremendous. Someone shouted: Long live Spain and long live Peru!"[81]

Here is proof positive of what Torroba claimed, that the zarzuela was a cultural ambassador *par excellence* and helped to cement the cultural and historical ties between the mother country and its former colonies, at least among the creole population. It definitely served a useful public-relations purpose.

In 1980, a year before he turned 90 years old, he conducted *Luisa Fernanda* in Montevideo, with an all-Uruguayan cast, at the Ciclo Lírico del Sodre.[82] One critic marveled at the sight of the aged master in front of the orchestra and singers:

> Maestro Torroba...belied his 89 years with a firm baton...and his ability to extract the best from our instrumentalists (the orchestra was enchanted with the Spanish composer, and that was apparent in several respects), dexterously accompanying the voices and tastefully rendering the purely instrumental passages, like the interlude with the mazurka.[83]

This mirrored a production two years earlier, at the Teatro Municipal in San Juan, Puerto Rico, which enjoyed a prolonged ovation. Torroba always knew that the show must go on, regardless of how he was feeling:

> The Spanish composer, who, despite suffering from a bad cold, did not miss a single rehearsal, said to the public that although he was not a

[80] Arazo, "Moreno Torroba: 90 años de vitalidad," *Las Provincias* (Valencia), June 6, 1981.

[81] F. M., "La representación 10 mil de *Luisa Fernanda*," clipping in Navarra archive, newspaper unknown (Lima). Plácido Domingo's mother may have had something to do with starting what apparently became a tradition at performances of *Luisa Fernanda* in Latin America. In Domingo's notes for *Luisa Fernanda* (Auvidis Valois, V 4759, 1995), 28, he states: "I will never forget how, in every performance, my mother encouraged the public to join in the 'Mazurka of the Parasols'. The number had to be repeated four or five times."

[82] Carlos Gasset, "La alegría de hacer musica," *El Día* (Montevideo), November 15, 1980, 18.

[83] Ibid.

sentimental type, he was deeply moved by the enthusiasm of the public that packed the hall, which dates back to the early 1800s, when Puerto Rico was still Spanish. "The zarzuela is sick but it can recover," said Moreno Torroba in commenting on the state of the genre in Spain and in the Spanish-speaking world.[84]

In addition to conducting *Luisa Fernanda* innumerable times, he led the Orquesta Filarmónica de Buenos Aires in his *Homenaje a la seguidilla*, with Irma Constanzo as guitar soloist (see below for more on this work). His manner of rehearsal struck one observer as both illustrative and endearing:

> The composer, with pencil in hand, directed with short gestures... using onomatopoeia, "tik, tiki-tiki-tiki ti"; singing, "tirará rirarí tararirará"; and later solfège, "Sol Mi Sol (a breath) Fa La Sol Mi Sol."[85]

This sort of preparation had its intended effect, and the audience sent him back to Spain "on waves of ancient affection."[86]

In July of 1974, our composer was in the spotlight at the Festival Federico Moreno Torroba, held in Miami and attended by 8,500 people. The festival featured both *Luisa Fernanda* and *La chulapona*, in addition to two symposia, one about his guitar music and the other, about his zarzuelas. The event was sponsored by the Ministerio de Asuntos Exteriores de España, Sociedad Pro-Arte Grateli, and the Miami-based *Diario de las Americas*, which reported extensively on the festival. Officials present included the governors of Florida and Puerto Rico, as well as the mayor of Miami.[87]

To be sure, Torroba was not first and foremost a conductor, and not even one of the leading Spanish conductors of his time. But once on the podium, he brought special qualities to the task.

> Torroba was not a great orchestral conductor, but when he descended into the pit, using a small baton and measured gestures to convey the flowing and expressive musical phrases, a particular *castizo* character made an impression.[88]

---

[84] "Aclaman delirantemente a Moreno Torroba," *Diario de la Americas* (Puerto Rico), April 18, 1978.

[85] Pompeyo Camps, "Moreno Torroba e Irma Constanzo armaron una tempestad de rasguidos y humoradas," *La Opinión* (Buenos Aires), June 28, 1975, 13.

[86] Pedro Massa, "Éxito de Moreno Torroba en Buenos Aires," *ABC*, June 1, 1975, 54.

[87] See María Elena Saavedra, "Festival Federico Moreno Torroba anuncia la Sociedad Pro Arte Grateli," *Diario de las Americas*, June 6, 1974, and Mercedes Hernández-Amaro, "Termina con dos valiosas conferencias que sobre zarzuela y guitarra dicta el maestro," *Diario Las Americas*, July 27, 1974, 10.

[88] Antonio Fernández-Cid, "Moreno Torroba, centenario," *Música clásica, ABC* 3/78 (February 27, 1991), 1–3.

While he certainly knew his business and had clear ideas about what he wanted in a performance, he exhibited a *laissez-faire* attitude toward the singers. Baritone Antonio Lagar noted that "I could sing completely free. He followed me; he was very flexible and let me do my own interpretation."[89] Ángel Romero asserts that Torroba was very enthusiastic and conducted with emotion, but that at times, his absorption in the music could cause him to get carried away. For instance, while conducting a recording of the Castelnuovo-Tedesco concerto, "every time I played the cadenza, Torroba would say something like 'bravo' or 'estás tocando como un rey' [you're playing like a king], or he would make noise with his baton and wreck the recording. It took ten takes to get through the cadenza, as the recording engineers repeatedly had to ask him to be quiet."

Torroba remained in demand as a conductor and was always on the go. While some people find travel exhausting, Torroba seemed to derive renewed vigor from it. In fact, as Pepe Romero recalls, he was able to put almost any available spare time to good use:

> Some of the most beautiful compositions...came to him at the most unusual moments. I remember one time riding on a DC-10 airplane, and I was at the time quite scared of that particular aircraft. It got very turbulent. I was sitting next to him, and he was saying, "Oh, don't worry. This is the best airplane." Then, all of a sudden, he became very quiet and needed a pen right away. So, I gave him my pen. He wrote the ending for the *Diálogos*. He changed the complete ending. Another time, we were having breakfast about 7:00 in the morning at a pancake house. Actually, my parents, my two brothers, and I were all with him and his daughter, and he, Torroba, was a man who liked most everything in life, except pancakes. He hated them. He could not understand how anyone could eat those little things that tasted like pages in a notebook. As he was sitting there complaining about how terrible they tasted, again he got inspired and wrote a beautiful, beautiful piece.[90]

His evident wanderlust found an outlet in the numerous tours he undertook, directing zarzuelas and also conducting orchestras in the standard literature. Latin America was always a favorite destination. On March 12, 1965, he premiered his zarzuela *Rosaura* at the Teatro Colón in Bogotá, Colombia. Particularly popular was *Luisa Fernanda*, which was done, yet again, in Buenos Aires on June 17, 1975, at the Colón, with the composer conducting.

Beginning in 1970, government administration of Spain's musical institutions underwent further modification. The Secretaria Técnica, which had regulated the

---

[89] Interview with William Krause, Madrid, June 6–11, 2010.

[90] Bill Dávila, "Pepe Romero Reminisces about Federico Moreno Torroba," *Soundboard* (summer 1983): 144–45.

Orquesta National and the Teatro Zarzuela, was abolished, and the Comisaria de la Música was resurrected at least in name if not in practice. At this juncture, Torroba assumed the titles of Comisario del Teatro Zarzuela and Director de la Compañía Lirica Nacional, the resident company at the Teatro Zarzuela.

Torroba always wanted the security of government support, and yet, he had a bit of the gambler in him, and he knew when to hold 'em and when to fold 'em. He had a sort of Zen attitude toward administration in general and composing and directing zarzuelas in particular:

> The secret is to administer the moment.... like the bullfighter who with-draws just in time and, even more so, the gambler who quits while ahead. If I had had two or three consecutive successes and then withdrawn in that moment, without getting involved in more failures, I could have been rich. The secret is to know when to gather in the harvest at its height and then retire with that.[91]

Thus, recognizing the moribund state of the zarzuela, Torroba's attention as a composer now shifted almost exclusively to the guitar, the only musical crop yielding much of a harvest during this period. As he himself expressed it,

> In Europe in general, it is difficult to write lyric theater, and therefore I have decided to compose for the guitar. They still compose operettas in Spain and France, though poorly, because there are no resources. Everyone hopes that the state will provide the necessary support, but even then, the performers are not there. Voice teachers encourage their students... but they dedicate themselves instead to opera. If they wanted to sing zarzuela, where would they work?[92]

Guitar to the Rescue

Of course, none of his administrative or conducting activities could satisfy his need to compose. Whatever the reasons were for the "crisis" in which he saw musical the-ater mired,[93] he adapted to the reality by increasing his attention to guitar composi-tion. Unlike the zarzuela, the classical guitar experienced something of a boom in the 1960s with the growing fame of Andrés Segovia and the emergence of guitarists who studied with or were deeply influenced by him, including the Anglo-Australian John Williams, Californian Christopher Parkening, and Italian Oscar Ghiglia. Other guitar virtuosos, such as the Englishman Julian Bream, Spaniard Narciso Yepes, and

---

[91] Centeno, "Moreno Torroba."

[92] "Moreno Torroba, el más famoso compositor actual."

[93] Gómez Ortiz, "Moreno Torroba," 15.

Venezuelan Alirio Díaz, also contributed greatly this renaissance of the classical guitar and its repertoire. Torroba's music rode to new heights of celebrity on this wave of popularity. Most important at this juncture was the association he established with the Romero family of guitarists, consisting of father Celedonio and his three sons, Celín, Pepe, and Ángel. Together they formed the first guitar quartet in history to achieve any degree of celebrity. As Segovia aged, Torroba's most challenging works would be written for and/or recorded for the first time by the Romeros, especially Pepe and Ángel. Torroba's relationship with the Romeros would eventually supersede that which he had enjoyed for decades with Segovia.

The year 1960 was pivotal in this respect. In December of 1960 Torroba wrote to Segovia[94] to say that he had finished his *Concierto de Castilla*.[95] This was to be the first of ten concertos for one, two, or four guitars and orchestra. These works appeared in rapid succession. The following year he again wrote to Segovia to inform him of the completion of a concerto, "Diálogos," an early version of **Diálogos entre guitarra y orquesta** (Dialogues between guitar and orchestra). Segovia did not premiere the concerto, and it languished for another decade. Perhaps it was due to Torroba's deepening relationships with guitarists Narciso Yepes, Irma Costanzo, Michael Lorimer, and the Romero family that Segovia did not premiere *Diálogos*.[96] It is also true, however, that late in his career he no longer had the technical facility to execute this supremely challenging work. John Duarte reports playing Pepe Romero's superlative recording of *Diálogos* for the aged maestro, who, "whilst commenting on the masterly performance,... took out his handkerchief and mopped his eyes. It was a moving moment."[97]

Homenaje a la seguidilla (1962), a guitar concerto, was first heard in Paris, with Narciso Yepes. It would also wait until 1975 for its formal premiere at the Teatro Colón in Buenos Aires, with the composer conducting and Irma Costanzo as soloist. Costanzo was a native of Buenos Aires who had studied with Yepes and Uruguayan Abel Carlevaro. In fact, Yepes recorded the work in 1976. After substantial revisions, it was recorded again in 1981, with the composer conducting the English Chamber Orchestra and Ángel Romero playing guitar. As Federico Sopeña said of this work:

> [In the case of Moreno Torroba,] without subjecting himself to any fad, faithful to himself and secure within that faith, his "Homenaje a la segui-

---

[94] Quotations from letters between Torroba and Segovia were provided to William Krause by Mrs. Andrés Segovia, via Alberto López Poveda, on July 18, 1990, in Madrid. These letters remain unpublished and in her private possession.

[95] Federico Moreno Torroba, unpublished letter from Torroba to Segovia, December, 1960.

[96] Santos Martín Pancorbo, interview with William Krause, Madrid, July 12, 1990.

[97] John W. Duante, *Andrés Segovia, As I Knew Him* (Pacific, Missouri: Mel Bay Publications, 1998), 99. He also held Ángel in very high regard. Ángel himself reports that Segovia once greeted him at Carnegie Hall and kissed his hands. Ángel Romero, interview with Walter Clark, September 20, 2011.

dilla" is like an autobiographical anthology, which one listens to with pleasure. I believe that the hour has arrived in which our programming will open more and more to the works of our composers who, dispersed by the Civil War—an entire generation—die twice, because the first death was that of incurable nostalgia.[98]

Local critics also sang the praises of Costanzo and the new work, describing it as "abounding in attractive and playful ideas, nobly conceived and realized, with a modernism that does not resort to absurdity and cacophony to establish itself as modern."[99]

However, not all critics were as generous in their assessment of Torroba's guitar concertos. *New York Times* critic Donal Henahan provided one such instance in his review of the *Fantasía flamenca*, which premiered November 28, 1976, at Carnegie Hall:

> Cross-breeding is an old and honorable practice in musical composition, which, in more ways than one, might be called the science of mixing strains. Schubert's use of a folk song in the last movement of his "Trout" Quintet comes invariably to mind, but such hybridization has been practiced by important composers in every era. It cannot be argued, therefore, against Federico Moreno Torroba's "Fantasia Flamenca" that his attempt to mate the symphony orchestra with the flamenco guitar was a doomed project. But the work, . . . failed in just about every way possible. Mario Escudero, the flamenco guitarist, played his part fluently while the American Symphony Orchestra under Antonio de Almeida's direction gave a sympathetic account of material so feeble that it needed all the sympathy it could get. The score, in three movements, made intermittent attempts to weave the guitar's figurations into the musical fabric, but all too often it fell back on the sterile device of letting the solo instrument and the orchestra alternate in rudimentary fashion.[100]

In truth, Torroba did write some genuine masterpieces for guitar and orchestra, but the *Fantasía flamenca* was not one of them.

This period also saw a renewed interest in composing for the solo guitar. Correspondence between Torroba and Segovia from 1963 refers to a work "sobre ambiente manchego" (with the ambience of La Mancha).[101] This assortment of

---

[98] Federico Sopeña, "Dos Guitarras: Torroba y Bacarisse," *Hoja del Lunes*, February 23, 1976, np.

[99] R. T., "Irma Costanzo—Moreno-Torroba," *Buenos Aires Musical*, September 1975, 3.

[100] Donal Henahan, "The American Symphony Teams Up with Guitarist," *The New York Times*, November 29, 1976.

[101] According to Santos Martín Pancorbo, interview with William Krause, Madrid, July 12, 1990. In a letter from Torroba to Segovia dated July 25, 1963, it is clear that Segovia had requested a work with a Manchegan theme. This letter is in the Fundación-Museo Andrés Segovia in Linares.

short pieces, *Aires de la Mancha*, was given to Segovia, who in turn gave them to the guitarist John Williams. *Aires de la Mancha* was published in 1966 along with *Once obras para la guitarra* (Eleven works for guitar).

A letter dated July 13, 1968, from Torroba to Segovia reveals that another suite, **Castillos de España** (Castles of Spain), was finished three years before its publication.[102] In this letter, Torroba asks Segovia to supply the appropriate fingering for the movements and arrange them in order. Segovia attached great importance to this and every other work Torroba supplied. Segovia biographer John Duarte reports the following incident in connection with *Castillos*:

> One day, shortly after he had received the score of Torroba's *Castles of Spain*, he showed me a deep pile of music he had earmarked for attention; he said that because Torroba had placed him first, all those years ago, he would always give top priority to anything that he wrote for him. The pile of other scores would have to wait until Torroba's castles were explored. His loyalty to Torroba was not just a simple *quid pro quo*, it was warmed with a real affection.[103]

This work frequently appeared on Segovia's subsequent recital programs and remains the most successful of Torroba's solo works after the Civil War. Neoclassical in form and *castizo* in inspiration, each movement constitutes an impression of a particular castle in Spain, such as the Alcázar de Segovia, Torija, etc. He later composed **Puertas de Madrid** (1976) along the same lines, as a set of pieces inspired by the capital's many arched gates (see Scene iii for more on these two suites).

After over fifty years of collaboration with Segovia, Torroba wrote to him on August 4, 1972, saying, "Thanks to you, my name has circulated throughout almost the entire world. My interest in the guitar I also owe to you... our friendship gives me confidence."[104]

One commentator describes Torroba's guitar music in the following general terms:

> The pieces that he composes are like brief sketches of well-defined color and can be considered worthy successors to the pleasing tradition of salon music; moreover, his compositional technique is traditional and never goes outside the bounds of the tonal system—something that would be pointless, given his aesthetic orientation.[105]

---

[102] Santos Martín Pancorbo, interview with William Krause, Madrid, July 12, 1990. In a letter dated August 14, 1963, Torroba informs Segovia that he has begun working on *Castillos de España*. This letter is in the Fundación-Museo Andrés Segovia in Linares.

[103] Duarte, *Andrés Segovia*, 98.

[104] Ibid., dated August 4, 1972.

[105] Anon., program notes, Orquesta Nacional de España, Madrid, November 1979, premiere of *Concierto ibérico*.

Torroba himself obviously derived inspiration from far earlier sources as well. He once observed that "the vihuela composers…generally took popular themes, presented in a simple form, suggestive and full of color."[106] This view is understandable assuming that most of his exposure to this repertoire came from Segovia's transcriptions of the *pavanas* of Luis Milán, the *Fantasía X* of Alonso Mudarra, or Luys de Narváez's variations on "Conde Claros" and "Guardame la vacas." But a large portion of the vihuela repertoire has no relation to "popular themes" and adheres instead to an international High Renaissance style. Being an art for the nobility, vihuela music often consisted of intabulations of chansons (Josquin's *Mille regretz*, by Narváez, for example) or church music (Enríquez Valderrábano's intablation of a *Motete Jubilate*). The musicological accuracy of his observation is not so important, however. What matters is that he saw in that earliest guitar repertoire a connection to the "eternal tradition" of vernacular music in which his own works were grounded.[107]

Where Torroba broke important ground was in writing for multiple guitars and orchestra. In fact, acting on the suggestion of Joaquín Rodrigo, Torroba contacted the Romeros in the early 1970s.[108] Torroba had been impressed with the success of Rodrigo's *Concierto andaluz* (1967) for four guitars and orchestra, composed for the Romero quartet, and he was interested in writing for this medium, too. Among the first works written for the Romeros were *Estampas* (1975) and *Ráfagas* (1976**). Concierto ibérico** (1976) remains the most popular of these collaborative ventures. The Romeros premiered it in Vancouver on November 19, 1976, and it went on to receive several subsequent performances in North America.

Its Spanish premiere took place on November 17, 1979, at the Teatro Real, where it again received critical acclaim.[109] One critic commented that the concerto's "structure is well defined and the work is very accessible, as the public demonstrated with repeated manifestations of its enthusiasm."[110] We note that this preference for formal clarity was a trait of musical aesthetics during the Franco era and the neoclassicism embraced by most of the composers of the epoch in Spain, all of whom were influenced to some extent by Falla's example. Torroba himself shed valuable light on the *Concierto ibérico* in a 1980 interview, just after the work was recorded by the Romeros on the Philips label, with Neville Mariner leading the Orchestra of St. Martin-in-the-Fields:

---

[106] In the undated ms. for the lecture "Mensajes musicales de la guitarra de hoy."

[107] For whatever reason, his lecture leaps right over the Baroque guitar, as if it never existed, and makes straight for Sor and the Classical period. He would have found plenty of grist for his Unamuno mill in the works of Gaspar Sanz, for instance, especially the famous *Canarios*.

[108] Federico Moreno Torroba, "Llega a Madrid el 'Concierto ibérico', de Moreno Torroba," *Ya*, November 16, 1979, 50.

[109] Anontio Iglesias, "Los Romero y Theo Alcantara, en un estreno de Moreno Torroba," *Informaciones*, November 19, 1979.

[110] Ibid.

I particularly like to compose for orchestra and guitar, but even more so for four guitars. . . . So many Spanish composers like myself have written concertos for guitar and orchestra because the music embodies the characteristics of the traditional Spanish sound. It is full of life, both gay and happy. It represents Spain.

The composer went on to assert that this rendition of the *Concierto ibérico* was the best he had heard and that he was "tremendously satisfied" with it.[111]

The Romeros themselves were deeply convinced of the merit of Torroba's concerto.

"People were very enthusiastic when they heard it," said Celedonio Romero. "'Ibérico' is a jewel of a piece for the soloists. It represents different parts of Spain, Castile and the Basque country, and for example in the last movement some of the rhythms come from Andalusia. This concerto delves deep into the 'feeling' of Spain."

Pepe, the soloist for this recording, explained: "Torroba is a very nationalistic composer. He is a man who has never left the roots of traditional Spanish music. Because he has written so much music for the voice, he writes for the guitar in a way that makes use of actually the most difficult thing to do with it—the legato—to make the guitar sing."

Torroba chipped in: "'Ibérico' is traditional Spanish music. Listen to its modulations, cadenzas, cadences, rhythms, and neo-classical harmonies. I have illustrated the harmonic evolution which has taken place in Spanish music during my own lifetime."[112]

An astute observer of contemporary Spanish music, musicologist and composer Enrique Franco, offered this praise:

Those staves, intended for those who play them today, the Romeros, obey the premises of simplicity, *españolismo*, popular traits and suitable instrumentation typical of Moreno Torroba, spontaneous composer, of a fluid vein.[113]

One other work in this vein was the **Nocturnos**, for two guitars and orchestra, which did not premiere until well after the composer's passing. This fascinating

---

[111] *Music Week*, December 6, 1980 (British publication; no author or title available).

[112] *Classical Topics*, n12 (December 1979): 3.

[113] Enrique Franco, "Composiciones de Moreno Torroba y Strawinsky," *El País*, November 20, 1979, 35.

work was inspired by Goya's paintings of warlocks and witches. Federico, Jr., placed this work in its proper context:

> In the *Nocturnos* we hear three pieces...with a Spanish flavor, inspired by Castilian folklore, without a definite tonality and exhibiting the influence of other composers. The work contains many Debussian moments...in [their] harmonies and details of [their] impressionist style. But always within [his] *castellanismo* or *españolismo*. "Witches" is a slightly sarcastic jota in a Castilian style. One hears that in the solo bassoon and it is developed throughout.[114]

Yet, among the finest of all of Torroba's compositions is *Diálogos entre guitarra y orquesta* (1977). The origins of this work are found in the solo *Sonata-Fantasía* (1953), in which the thematic material for the concerto's second and fourth movements is first heard, and *Romance de los pinos* (1956), which provides the thematic material for the third movement. The 1961 concerto version that Torroba mentioned to Segovia is not extant. Among the five remaining manuscripts, an incomplete guitar part is dated 1957.[115] The only complete scores are dated 1976 and 1978. Two undated reductions are also in the Navarra archive. In any case, Michael Lorimer premiered *Diálogos* in Edmonton in the fall of 1977, and Pepe Romero recorded it in 1978.

Critical reaction to *Diálogos* has almost always been favorable. Commenting on a rendition by Eduardo Fernández with the Orquesta Sinfónica Municipal in Montevideo in 1980, with the composer conducting, a critic wrote the following:

> [*Diálogos*] does not make concessions nor does it exhibit any *españolismo* [clichéd Spanishisms], possessing nonetheless an unmistakable Iberian accent....the piece demonstrates the international level of the young Uruguayan guitarist Eduardo Fernández, who handled the composition with complete mastery and notable technique and sound.[116]

Of course, it is not surprising that an Uruguayan reviewer would form a favorable impression of a work performed by one the country's finest performers (a student of the noted Uruguayan pedagogue Abel Carlevaro). But other critics concurred. Spanish journalist Antonio Fernández-Cid offered a positive assessment as well, again resorting to the term *españolismo*, which can have both negative and positive connotations depending on context:

---

[114] Elisa Ramos, "Homenaje a Federico Moreno Torroba," *Tribuna de Salamanca*, May 6, 2002, 12. In this same article, one F. Colas remarks that the third movement contains hints of the *Rite of Spring*, with impressionism and elements of flamenco in the first movement, while the second is more atonal.

[115] These scores are in the Navarra archive.

[116] Gasset, "La alegría de hacer música," 18.

Lyric *españolismo*, dominance of melody, triumph of the "cantabile," marked knowledge in the genial writing for the soloist, enviably youthful spirit, fluid ingenuity, and grace are his signature traits.[117]

Diálogos is indeed a remarkable work and will receive detailed examination in Scene iii, along with the *Concierto ibérico*.

Ballet

Inasmuch as zarzuela customarily includes dance numbers, it may be said that Torroba wrote dance music throughout his career. However, it was not until the last two decades of his life that he composed expressly for ballet.[118] It is one of the curiosities of Torroba's career as a composer that, despite his obvious religiosity, he composed so little sacred music. When he finally did get around to composing works with a biblical theme, he wrote ballets rather than choral music. Falla was the first Spanish composer to write ballet scores of any significance, and clearly Torroba followed in his footsteps, so to speak—but only to an extent. Nothing like *El amor brujo* would flow from his pen, though he knew that work very well and admired it.

Yet, it would be incorrect to say that Torroba took no interest in sacred works outside the theater. He once told the story of a devotional piece he composed that had a transatlantic career. He had written an Ave Maria for the nuns of a convent in Santesteban.

> Years later, when I was in Mexico, my zarzuela company and I went to church. You already know that Mexicans are a people of the theater, and that they don't go to mass, but they make the sign of the cross before every performance. So, we went to the church and [to my surprise] heard them singing my Ave Maria! A nun from Navarra had moved there [taking the music with her], and they sang it everyday.[119]

However, his main thrust was definitely not liturgical music. In the early 1960s, Torroba began a fruitful collaboration with choreographer Luis Pérez Dávila (known professionally as Luisillo), a leading classical and flamenco dancer of that time. Luisillo (1927–2007) was born in Mexico City and later studied and performed with the renowned flamenco dancer Carmen Amaya (1913–63); by the 1960s, he had his own company, the Teatro de la Danza. Together, Luisillo and

---

[117] Antonio Fernández-Cid, "'Diálogos', un nuevo concierto para guitarra, de Moreno Torroba," *ABC*, March 3, 1982, 52.

[118] A possible exception is a piece for José Greco, 1957. Its exact nature is uncertain.

[119] Mallo, "Los noventa jovenes años."

Torroba created a ballet that represents one of our composer's most significant sacred works. It was based on a parable in Luke 14:16–24, in which Jesus tells of a man who invited some people to supper. When they declined, he invited the poor, maimed, lame, and blind to dine in their stead. As there was still room at the table, yet others were compelled to attend. This story was reinterpreted in the context of the conversion of Gypsies to Catholicism.

El convite was first performed September 26, 1965, in Pomezia (a municipality in the province of Rome), in conjunction with a pilgrimage of about four thousand Gypsies from around the world to Rome.[120] It also coincided with the Pope's birthday. Paul VI celebrated mass at 5 p.m., and this was followed by the coronation of the Madonna of the Gypsies and a procession. Then the ballet was performed. The project was instigated by Julián Cortés-Cavanillas, the Roman correspondent for the Spanish newspaper *ABC*. He provided logistical assistance to the production and coordinated the biblical story with Torroba's score. The invitation-only performance was broadcast on Italian television (TV-RAI). However, due to inclement weather, the Pope was not able to remain for the ballet. So, he invited the company to perform for him at the Vatican, in Clementine Hall, adjoining the Sistine Chapel; afterwards, Paul VI received the performers and Torroba.[121] This was a singular honor, as no comparable performance had apparently ever taken place in that hall. Torroba stated that *El convite* was the brainchild of Luisillo and Monsignor Bruno Nicolini. The work lasted thirty-five to forty minutes and featured a novel juxtaposition of chant-like melodies with flamenco-like *bulerías* and *zambra*.[122]

On September 6, 1975, another of their biblical ballets was done in Rome, this time at the Basilica de Masensio, in the Roman forum. Sometimes referred to by the contemporary press as *Cristo, luz del mundo* (Christ, light of the world), it was also known as *El hijo pródigo* (The Prodigal Son), as it relates the famous parable found in Luke 15:11–52. Both titles refer to the same work.[123] The idea for this ballet originated with Cortés-Cavanillas, the *ABC* correspondent, and his newspaper predictably reported that the performance was a tremendous success. Torroba's score utilized orchestra and chorus, and *ABC* hailed his music as "full of inspiration and technical mastery." In comparing this work with *El amor brujo*, the reviewer could not help but note that Falla's work was "magic,"

---

[120] According to Luisillo himself, in an interview with Julio Trenas, "Luisllo y el Teatro de la Danza," *ABC*, March 3, 1971, 110–11, 115.

[121] This is according to an article in *ABC* dated September 30, 1965. See also Julián Cortés-Cavanillas, "'Luisillo' ha bailado ante el Papa," *ABC*, May 15, 1969, 26–27, for Luisillo's recollections of this event.

[122] Torroba is quoted in Cifra, "Un ballet flamenco actuará ante Paulo VI en la peregrinación gitana," *La Vanguardia*, September, 18, 1965, 9.

[123] See "Estrena en Roma el ballet 'Cristo, luz del mundo,' con música de Moreno Torroba," *La Vanguardia*, September 9, 1975, 42.

while Torroba's, also a masterpiece, was "religion." A subtle but crucial distinction, to be sure.[124]

Once again in Spain, Luisillo and Torroba continued to produce new ballets, including *El torero, su soledad y su destino* and *Por favor, ¿qué hora es?* The latter was a tragedy whose action takes place during the Spanish Civil War. Both works were broadcast on Spanish Television (TVE).[125] None of the above ballets, however, was their first collaboration. Already in 1964 they had created *Aventuras y desventuras de Don Quijote* (The Adventures and Misadventures of Don Quixote), consisting of well-known scenes from Cervantes's novel. Luisillo played the part of Sancho Panza. This ran from November 4 to 12 at the Teatro de la Zarzuela in Madrid. It was repeated at that venue almost two decades later, October 11, 1982, shortly before the composer's death.[126] It has therefore sometimes been cited by the press as "Torroba's last composition," but this is not true.[127] The confusion stems in part from a shortening of the title, to *Don Quijote*, for its most celebrated production, not in Spain but rather in Helsinki, on October 10, 1970, at the Suomen Kansallisooppera.[128] The Finnish critics received the work with favor, and one commentator, Raoul Af Hällström, approved the way that Luisillo played the "deliciously comic" role of the Don's amiable amanuensis.[129]

These appraisals were echoed in the Madrid press during the 1982 revival:

> For his part, maestro Moreno Torroba has written very substantial music, in which there is no shortage of quotations of the popular folklore of La Mancha, so representative of a region and environment, introducing the novelty of including a chorus in a ballet, which sometimes sings a cappella with the stamp of our best polyphony.[130]
>
> Federico Moreno Torroba's music...offers a kind of symphonic poem, with a neoromantic tint,...descriptive like a landscape, divided in six crucial episodes in the life of Quijote and Sancho.[131]

[124] See Eugenio Montes, "Apoteósico éxito del 'ballet' sobre el hijo pródigo, intrepetado en Roma por Luisillo," *ABC*, September 9, 1975, 30.

[125] According to Luisillo in Antonio de Olano, "'Don Quijote', un 'ballet' de Moreno Torroba," *Autores: Revista de información de la S.G.A.E.*, n3 (October 1982): 19.

[126] Confirmation of its 1964 premiere at the Teatro de la Zarzuela is in García Carretero, *Historia del Teatro de la Zarzuela*, iii, 62, and of the 1982 revival, on page 178.

[127] "Estreno de 'Don Quijote', de Moreno Torroba," *El Alcázar*, October 12, 1982.

[128] According to Santos Martín Pancorbo, in a letter to William Krause, May 15, 1992, Joaquín Sotelo Calvo wrote a narrative text for the premiere that was not used in subsequent versions. However, the earlier scores have not been found, making it impossible to know whether the 1964, 1970, and 1982 performances contained the same music.

[129] In a letter to Torroba from the Spanish Embassy in Helsinki, José María Alonso Gamo sent press excerpts concerning the ballet. He summarized their content as "encomiastic" and "enthusiastically favorable." This letter, as well as a program from the production, is in the Navarra archive.

[130] "Estreno de 'Don Quijote'."

[131] "'El amor brujo' y 'Don Quijote', un lujo de ambientación y expresividad," *Diario de Mallorca*, 1982.

...Moreno Torroba's extensive and ambitious score is the fruit of a master who knows how to orchestrate, who knows and masters the chapter on instrumentation and handling of the voices.[132]

Such a reception makes all the more regrettable the work's continued absence from the stage over the last three decades.[133]

El Poeta

Torroba's last large-scale work for the theater was **El poeta**, loosely based on the life of Spanish poet José de Espronceda (1808–42). This opera, written at the suggestion of Plácido Domingo,[134] was premiered at the Teatro de la Zarzuela on June 19, 1980, with the great Spanish tenor in the title role. The score calls for full orchestra, chorus, ballet, supporting cast, and five leading roles.

Concerning the genesis of the opera, Torroba offered this in 1980:

> Three years ago, in Bilbao, I met our great tenor Plácido Domingo, whom I had not seen since he was three years old. I was great friends with his parents, Pepita Embil and Plácido Domingo, Sr., and our great singer suggested that I write an opera. We agreed that a poet would be the best character, and we thought of Espronceda....When it came time to think of someone who could write the libretto, after considering many names, we settled on José Méndez Herrera...and his magnificent poetic spirit, inspiration, and quality are patent in the book.[135]

Some might consider this work a major departure from Torroba's theater style, insofar as it was quite dissimilar to his zarzuelas. Yet, in his own opinion, "in this work I have not held back traditionalism. Nevertheless, I believe the structure is contemporary with regard to the system of harmony and melody."[136] In this four-act work, Torroba laid a great deal of stress on recitative, seldom resorting to aria in the classical sense. The harmony is often chromatic and features frequent modulations. Much of the score consists of harmonically active and detailed orchestral

---

[132] Antonio Fernández-Cid, "El Nacional Español estrenó 'Don Quijote', de Moreno Torroba," *ABC*, October 9, 1982, 57.

[133] At least it was recorded, in 1982 on the Discos Columbia label, SCE 996, with the Symfonicky Orchestr Hlavního Mesta Prahy FOK.

[134] Hernández, "La ópera levanta cabeza," 25.

[135] Ángel Laborda, "'El poeta', de Méndez Herrera y Moreno Torroba," *ABC*, June 19, 1980, 59. Domingo says that *he* first had the idea of an opera about Goya but that Torroba countered with Espronceda. See Helena Matheopoulos, *Plácido Domingo: My Operatic Roles* (Fort Worth, Texas: Baskerville Publishers, 2000), 207.

[136] Ibid.

writing that accompanies a relatively static melodic line. Méndez Herrera's prosaic libretto is set to through-composed music.

The biographer notes with some sadness that Torroba's final stage work was one of his least successful, and despite the considerable anticipation its premiere aroused, it has not held a place on the stage, something that the composer clearly hoped and expected it would. In brief, yet another opera was laid low by an inferior libretto, and even Domingo himself described the libretto as "very weak and superficial." He went on to declare that this was a "problem with many Spanish librettists in our day. They seldom bother to probe deeply into their subjects and end up barely skimming the surface."[137] As is often true in such cases, however, the composer must share some of the blame with the librettist.

Torroba had wanted to write an opera about Goya, a continuation of his fascination with that artist and his epoch already on display in *La Caramba* of the 1940s and a clear demonstration of his affinity for Granados, who composed the most famous Goyaesque music of all time. Yet, he eventually decided to feature a contemporary of Goya's instead, the poet Espronceda. According to one press account,

> The maestro said that his first idea for his work had Goya as the protagonist, a Goya he could present as a man who fights for his ideas and suffers persecution for it. In the end,…the ideological conflict and main argument switched to Espronceda.[138]

Why did he make this change? The composer explained that,

> I was thinking of something *goyesco*, but in light of the scant success of that theme in North America, we decided to employ a poet [as the main character], someone along the lines of Espronceda, without being him exactly. An imaginary poet with a finale of dramatic action, though without the suicide of Espronceda.[139]

Given the lackluster career of this work, one is inclined to second-guess the composer. It is unclear why he thought a *goyesco* theme would not appeal to North American (meaning US) audiences. Perhaps he was thinking of Granados's opera *Goyescas*, which was not well received by New York critics and did not hold a place on the stage (though it was reported as a great triumph in the Spanish press).[140]

---

[137] Matheopoulos, *Plácido Domingo: My Operatic Roles*, 208.

[138] "El maestro Moreno Torroba será enterrado hoy en la Sacramental de san Justo, de Madrid," *El País*, September 13, 1982, 22.

[139] María López Salas, "Ya no escribe zarzuelas," *Nueva Rioja*, September 14, 1977.

[140] See Clark, *Granados*, 157–61, for a discussion of the Met premiere and its critical reception on both sides of the Atlantic.

In fact, *Goyescas* flopped because of its inferior libretto, which was written to accommodate preexisting music! But at least Goya was known and appreciated by US audiences, for his fascinating art, personality, and times. If Goya would not please, what hope was there that a character modeled on Espronceda—a totally obscure figure beyond Spain—would fare any better? Though Espronceda actually died of diphtheria, a suicide might have given the opera some much-needed dramatic spice. But suicides and other gruesome plot devices were not Torroba's specialty. He always felt that love was the best subject of a novel, opera, or zarzuela, especially impossible love.[141]

One American critic speculated that there may have been some political significance to this choice of theme, as a story dealing with "a liberal-minded poet exiled from Spain during the oppressive reign of Ferdinand VII in the 1820s and 30s obviously had particular relevance for a post-Franco Spanish audience."[142] Perhaps, but this would tell us little about Torroba, who concealed his political views and was more interested in composing a successful stage work than making any declarations about democracy.

Torroba's musical means for doing this harkened to his late-Romantic muse, Puccini. Yet, as one US observer noted,

> Moreno Torroba's music suggested a time warp: the composer seemed to be creating as Giordano might have and in no case were there harmonies which suggested the music of this century. The surprise was the honesty of the writing; most "romantic" music composed in 1980 suggests a febrile Puccini, with the vivid color removed. On first hearing, Moreno Torroba's work sounded real and passionate, with the melodies effective though not quite overwhelming enough. . . . The libretto was weak.[143]

In any case, the composer knew that he had the ideal singer for the lead role, i.e., Plácido Domingo. He felt that the personality of Espronceda could be well portrayed by Plácido, and based on what we know of the work's genesis, Plácido shared that feeling. Torroba clearly hoped that this stroke of casting genius would make a success of the premiere, leading to *El poeta*'s adoption in the repertory and paving the way for others to interpret that role.[144]

The premiere of *El poeta* elicited a wide array of reactions. Some hailed the premiere as a "cultural event of the first order,"[145] while others pronounced it stillborn. At the root of the debate was the public's expectations. Many were hoping

---

[141] Arazo, "Moreno Torroba."

[142] Elizabeth Forbes, "Madrid, *El Poeta*," *Opera News* (September 1980). http://www.tenorissimo.com/domingo/articles/on0980.htm.

[143] Speight Jenkins, "A New Opera for Domingo: Torroba's 'El Poeta' Provides an Ideal Role," *Musical America* (October 1980): 40.

[144] Mallo, "Los noventa jovenes años."

[145] *ABC*, June 25, 1980.

for another *Luisa Fernanda* and left the theater aghast. Others admired Torroba's artistic courage, if not the intrinsic merit of the work itself. Among the greatest admirers of the work was the composer himself:

> I have written a work with great sincerity and enthusiasm...I would prefer that, after my extensive output of zarzuelas and, in another aspect, my dedication to the guitar and especially to works for guitar and orchestra, *El Poeta* be the conclusion of my musical vocation.[146]

But retiring was not in his nature. Even as he claimed this would be his final work, he was thinking of others, especially an opera based on *La Celestina* by Fernando de Rojas (c. 1465–1541). It is not clear if he was aware that Felipe Pedrell wrote an opera on that same text, but given his negative view of Pedrell, he was unlikely to have been influenced by that model in any case (see below for more on this project).

Despite initial setbacks, he was in no mood to give up on *El poeta*:

> I believe that it resulted in a genuine success; however, opera is a kind of musical endeavor that, more than any other, requires revision. For example, we have the works of Verdi, premiered with two titles and fundamental changes; we also have multiple versions of *Madame Butterfly*, by Puccini. And certainly *El Poeta* will be no less a case. That is why I am pushing reworking it, to get a premiere outside Spain, probably in Buenos Aires.[147]

Critic Fernández-Cid could almost always be counted upon to offer moral support to Torroba, and despite universal denunciation of the libretto, he was able to find at least one redeeming virtue in it, i.e., that it used a natural kind of Spanish that every listener could comprehend. However, he agreed with Torroba's assessment: though the opera was "ambitious fruit" and demonstrated the "solid pulse" of the composer, it would undoubtedly require some revision because of the poor libretto.[148] In regards to the music, he noted the twin influences of Puccini and Gershwin in the score, which might strike us as irreconcilable opposites. But in another review, he clarified his meaning, suggesting that his subtlety in his "tone color, harmony, structure, and use of solos and tuttis...approach the aesthetic worlds of Gershwin and Puccini."[149]

---

[146] "Opera en directo: 'El poeta', de Moreno Torroba," *Diario 16*, June 25, 1980.

[147] Berasategui, "Moreno Torroba," ix.

[148] Antonio Fernández-Cid, "'El poeta', de Moreno Torroba, con Plácido Domingo como protagonista," *ABC*, June 21, 1980, 48.

[149] Antonio Fernández-Cid, "Plácido Domingo estreno 'El poeta', de Moreno Torroba," *La Vanguardia*, June 30, 1980, 54.

Fernández-Cid was not the only critic to perceive an American flavor in the score. Others noted a contemporary quality in "echoes" of Bernstein or Gershwin,[150] in addition to the "neoverismo" of Gian Carlo Menotti, especially in the recitatives and handling of the voice.[151] Now, there is nothing wrong with an eclectic approach to composition. One could actually argue that *all* composers are eclectic to one extent or another. It takes away nothing from Torroba to find traces of Bernstein, Gershwin, Puccini, and Menotti in *El poeta*. What does cause concern is when a composer seems to lose his or her voice amid these various influences. The sad fact is that no critic said that any of this actually sounded like the *Torroba* they knew and loved. To that extent, the audience was clearly somewhat bewildered because they brought certain expectations to this opera that were not fulfilled. Indeed, it could be, as one critic believed, that *Luisa Fernanda* continued to be Torroba's greatest enemy, eclipsing his symphonic works and even his other zarzuelas. We have seen that Torroba himself harbored similar reservations about it. Of course, what made that zarzuela so memorable were the wonderful vocal numbers he composed for it. Here, there seemed to be little real singing, at least nothing that stood out.[152] And he knew that he had a distinctive style, once remarking that "when I hear something that is mine, I recognize it. There is always a personal stamp that says to me 'this is by Moreno Torroba.'"[153]

Torroba was aware of the dangers of writing music that did not exhibit his distinctive style. Once he revealed that "When I write music, I try not to listen to much other music during that time so as not to be influenced, so that what flows from pen is my own."[154] This was obviously a successful strategy, but because opera was not really his *métier*, he may have become overly reliant on the example set by his idols, thus not being able to find his own voice. There is no doubt that he found opera to be more challenging to compose than zarzuela. "I like opera but it requires more work, more polish. It is another concept of music. By contrast, I have written zarzuelas in twenty days [a reference to *Luisa Fernanda*]."[155] In addition, he perceived that zarzuelas tended to have long runs, whereas operas might be done a few times at one theater and then fold.[156]

It is true enough that this opera was highly conservative in style, and that it conformed to musical traditions Torroba never renounced or so much as questioned. But it was not an atavistic effort and did reveal modernistic touches in its contrapuntal textures, use of the orchestra to comment on the action, expressive dissonance, and the steady flow of musical and dramatic action, in which a

[150] Haro Tecglen, "Un personaje del Madrid," 22.

[151] "'El poeta', de Federico Moreno Torroba," *El Imparcial*, June 22, 1980.

[152] Ángel del Campo, "Estreno de 'El poeta,'" *Pueblo*, June 25, 1980.

[153] Mallo, "Los noventa jovenes años."

[154] Pascal, "Derechos de autor," 2.

[155] Ibid.

[156] Mengual, "Federico Moreno Torroba."

succession of arias, duos, and trios did not disrupt dramatic continuity.[157] It was a deliberate departure from zarzuela, precisely because opera and zarzuela are two different types of musical theater, regardless of their many commonalities. Torroba knew this, but we recall that he had told the Argentines that Spanish attempts at opera had not been convincing (including his own, of course), and that the zarzuela was the kind of musical theater best suited to the Spanish temperament. Most people do not go to an opera to hear its wonderful counterpoint, orchestration, dissonance, and continuity. They go to hear beautiful melodies sung by beautiful voices. It is easy now to say that he should have heeded his own warning, but Torroba was nothing if not ambitious. Opera possessed a legitimacy that zarzuela did not, and he wanted to leave his mark on that genre before his own grand finale, which was closer at hand than he imagined.

Yet, when asked if his aesthetic had changed in this opera, he was defiant in declaring that he had no intention of departing from his own manner. "It is traditional music." Though the score exhibited a variety of influences, they were "not from contemporary music but rather from music that is really music."[158] So, there! In an interview with Fernández-Cid around the time of the premiere, Torroba had something to say about his (very conservative) preferences in musical theater, even if they did not necessarily pertain to this opera. Among Spanish works, he esteemed Falla's opera La vida breve and the zarzuela Las golondrinas by Usandizaga. Chueca, composer of La Gran Vía, was also high on his list of favorites. Predictably, Puccini (La bohème) and Verdi (especially Otello) occupied secure niches in the pantheon of foreign composers he admired. Torroba fully realized that by writing an opera, he was setting himself up for comparison with these masters. And he had the concomitant humility to admit that "if El poeta does not turn out well, the fault will be mine alone."[159]

Of course, one thing Verdi and Puccini had to work with was good librettos. Torroba understood the crucial importance of the text to the overall effect of a stage work. When asked toward the end of his life if he would still consider writing a zarzuela, he said, "I would need a libretto with the possibility of success, because the music alone cannot totally save a text."[160] The same was certainly true of opera, so it is not easy to comprehend why he settled for the libretto Méndez Herrera provided him. Although praising the maestro's music, most critics were of the opinion that it was put "at the service of a very feeble text, without novelty and

---

[157] Ruiz Coca, "Admirable evolución." This critic also deplored the "mediocre libretto" and noted "jazzy allusions" in the second act.

[158] "'Si sale mal "El poeta" es culpa mía'"

[159] Ibid. and Fernández-Cid, "Moreno Torroba, ante el estreno de 'El Poeta,'" ABC, 1980. Np. In another interview, he expanded the list of preferred zarzueleros: Jiménez, Chueca, Caballero, Bretón and Chapí. He still liked Wagner, too. Most interestingly, he said that his own Luisa Fernanda occupied a position in the history of zarzuela similar to that occupied by La bohème in the history of opera, i.e., one of greatest hits of all time. See Sagi-Vela, "Moreno Torroba, nonagenario," 23.

[160] Berasategui, "Moreno Torroba," ix.

very conventional." The overall result was that this work did not remind them at all of his earlier stage works, for which he was justly famous, and that was difficult to accept.[161]

However, it is hard to gauge the public's true response. Domingo and Torroba, revered as musical heroes in their native country, received thunderous applause. In much of the press, their prestige overshadowed the music they produced. However, a few accounts suggest something less than unanimity in the public's reaction. Because there was great continuity in both music and drama, there were no places where the audience could interrupt with applause. This was, of course, a Wagnerian innovation in the 1800s, one picked up by Verdi in his later works, but it ran counter to what audiences wanted and expected to hear from Torroba, and they were frustrated. Others thought the staging itself was weak.[162] Thus, one critic reported that some in the audience at the premiere expressed their displeasure, occasionally shouting "away with this!" ("*fuera*").[163] Another confirmed that "there were noisy protests by some at the conclusion of the opera."[164] At all events, the premiere of *El poeta* was a major event in the life of its composer.

Ever Onward

Even after nearly seventy years of composing, Torroba felt the urge to continue. As he related to one journalist, "I am not accustomed to dwelling on the past. I always have projects ahead of me, and lots of work. I believe that is the reason why so many years have passed without leaving too much of a mark on me."[165] In fact, at age 90 he disclosed that "Every day I wake up with dreams and renewed spirit.... I am now signing contracts for the next five years.... To me, not working is synonymous with boredom."[166]

Some of his time was spent on composing works, and some on revising earlier ones:

> Look, I devote part of my time to revising my works and correcting details
> that I don't find convincing. I believe that everything is perfectible, and
> my preoccupation is to do as much polishing as possible. I am secure in
> the thought that I have been and continue to be the most severe critic of
> my works[167]

[161] Fernando López, and L. de Tejada, "Estreno de 'El Poeta' de Moreno Torroba," *El Alcázar*, June 21, 1980.

[162] Forbes, "Madrid, *El Poeta*."

[163] López and Tejada, "Estreno de 'El Poeta.'"

[164] Ruiz Coca, "Admirable evolución."

[165] Arazo, "Moreno Torroba."

[166] San Martín, "Federico Moreno Torroba."

[167] Alonso, "Homenaje en el Ayuntamiento," 3.

In fact, he never lost the desire to compose, or to think up new possibilities. Beyond *La Celestina*, there were other peaks to climb. When asked if there was anything he would still like to write, he responded: "An opera based on a classic work of Spanish theater, something comic, something like Verdi's *Falstaff*."[168] Even at the time of his death, he still had ambitious plans for the future. Among these included an anthology of his zarzuelas he was preparing for the following season in Madrid.[169] He always believed that "creative work is a question of training and losing the fear to write. What I do a lot of is correct... I have a very precise concept of the work before I write a single note." Moreover, he confided that he had "suffered... during periods in which I thought I had no more music in me. These periods aren't the result of depression. They're inexplicable."[170]

Certainly one of the reasons for his fecundity as a composer was his penchant for working on various projects simultaneously.

> I like to compose various different works at the same time. They provide contrast and stimulation. Before beginning to work on a composition I imagine it in its entirety, thinking about what has to be, and generally I make this initial approximation of the work in bed. What concerns me most then, and what I dwell on elaborating, is the form, because invention and development proceed rapidly. I write on paper what occurs to me, and then I correct and correct. For some passages I go to the piano, because it is necessary to hear the contrasting sonorities in harmonies and modulations.[171]

Within a year of the premiere of *El poeta* he began work on *La Celestina*. This celebrated literary work was published by Fernando Rojas in 1499. Though it is technically a novel, it is written completely in dialogue and thus works well as a play, too. The score has not been found, and there is no evidence to suggest it was completed. This is a shame, because the plot of *La Celestina* is tragic (with comic elements, which is why Rojas labeled it a "tragicomedia") and ends with the accidental death of one lover and the consequent suicide of the other. This was not the sort of story Torroba was accustomed to telling in his stage works, and it would have been most interesting to see how he handled it. Apparently, work on the opera was interrupted by the piano concerto (see below). After that premiered, he planned to return to his new opera.[172] Completed the same year was *Invenciones* (1980) for woodwind quartet and guitar. At Torroba's death, his son revised and published it as *Interludios* for guitar and string quintet (premiered in Madrid by Agustín Maruri, and later recorded by Paul Boucher).

---

[168] Sagi-Vela, "Moreno Torroba, nonagenario," 23.
[169] Jaze, "Maestro Moreno Torroba." See also Fernández-Cid, "Evocación," 34.
[170] Gómez Ortiz, "Moreno Torroba," 15.
[171] Sagi-Vela, "Moreno Torroba, nonagenario, 23.
[172] Stefani, "Federico Moreno Torroba."

In 1979 he had been commissioned by the Pasdeloup Orchestra in Paris to write a piano concerto, an idea that he said "obsessed" him.[173] *Fantasía castellana* was written for the Uruguayan pianist Humberto Quagliata and premiered in Paris in October of 1980. This was the last major premiere of Torroba's music during his lifetime. The pianist himself had moving insights about Torroba's passionate commitment to this work:

> Such high hopes did he have for the... piano concerto that during my daily visits to the clinic where he died,... we would talk about the interpretation of this or that phrase, of our plans for recording it in London, or to tour Latin America together, presenting his one and only piano concerto, which he himself would conduct.[174]

Unfortunately, he would not live long enough to see the realization of these dreams.

By the end of his life, Torroba had received many of the highest honors bestowed upon creative artists in Spain, or anywhere. In addition to the presidency of the Sociedad General de Autores de España and directorship of the Real Academia de Bellas Artes de San Fernando, he became a corresponding member of the Hispanic Society of America (posthumously, December 6, 1985) and Honorary Member of the Columbus Association, American Friendship International Center (May 1955). Other distinctions included:

1. Encomienda de Alfonso X ("el Sabio"), from el Presidente de la República Española (May 6, 1935)
2. Caballero Gran Cruz de la Orden del Mérito Civil, from Francisco Franco (October 20, 1966)
3. Richard-Strauss-Medaille, Die Gema Gesellschaft für Musikalische Aufführungs- und Mechanische Vervielfältigungsrechte, Munich (October 1974)
4. Academico Correspondiente Real Academia de Bellas Artes de San Jorge, Barcelona (January 22, 1975)
5. Miembro de Honor, El Instituto Paraguayo de Cultura Hispánica (September 18, 1975)
6. Medalla de Plata, Círculo de Bellas Artes de Madrid (February 2, 1980)
7. Cruz Roja Española, Madrid. Homenaje a su extraordinaria labor artística y persistente entusiasmo y jovialidad (May 8, 1982)
8. Medalla de Madrid (May 28, 1982)
9. Honored by Granada in acknowledgement of his work for the city and in commemoration of the fiftieth anniversary of *Luisa Fernanda* (June 6, 1982)

[173] Ibid.

[174] Humberto Quagliata, "Recordando al Maestro Federico Moreno Torroba: 'De un apacible rincón de Madrid... a la inmortalidad,'" *El Diario Español* (Montevideo), October 5, 1982, 10.

Cultural institutions throughout Spain designated 1981, the year of his nine-tieth birthday, as a year of national homage in recognition of Torroba's contribu-tion to Spanish music. The city council of Baracalde (now Barakaldo, in the Basque country) rendered posthumous homage to him in March 1983, and two years later, the Vatican followed suit with the Benemerenti, Pope Paul VI (December 20, 1985). As one visitor to his modest apartment in the barrio de Salamanca reported, the beat-up grand piano in his living room was surrounded by shelves holding all of these various awards.[175] Festivals of Torroba's music were periodically held in several major cities, including Madrid, Barcelona, Burgos, and San Sebastián. On May 4, 1980, King Juan Carlos and Queen Sofía bestowed on Torroba the Medalla de Oro de las Bellas Artes (Gold Medal of Fine Arts) in a ceremony at the Prado. Other recipients on this occasion included Joaquín Rodrigo and filmmaker Carlos Saura.[176]

Perhaps the highest accolade he received, however, was what people said about him as a human being. We recall that he thought the true measure of a man's suc-cess was that he be "recognized for his goodwill, equanimity, and generosity." Here is how others generally perceived him in his final year on earth:

> Of retiring stature, serene of spirit, cordial and humane, at 90 years of age he continues to create music with youthful enthusiasm, with that facility of privileged human beings when they are doing what they were born to do.... feverish from a cold, without giving any sign of fatigue or pain... his ever-proper faculty for work rises from his spirit with sim-plicity and naturalness, without the slightest force, without demon-strating the least weariness.[177]
>
> His speech is fluid and serene, without fluctuations up and down due to emotion. He expresses himself with an authority conferred by knowledge of the material, without petulance but with naturalness.[178]

Such encomiums may strike us as slightly hyperbolic, and yet one journalist after another made similar observations. In short, Torroba was, by his own definition, a success. His energy, spirit, and resistless flow of creative inspiration would have been remarkable in a person at almost any age. That he possessed these traits at a time in life when most people struggle to get the cap off their medication or to feed and dress themselves seemed almost miraculous. When people asked him what hobbies, loves, and dreams he had, his three-syllable rejoinder was ever the same: *trabajar* (to work).[179]

---

[175] Vicent, "El pentagrama," 14. They are now in the family home in Navarra.
[176] Pilar Trenas, "El Rey entregó las medallas de oro de las Bellas Artes," *ABC*, May 30, 1980, 33.
[177] Carmen Llorca, "Federico Moreno Torroba," *Ya*, November 21, 1981.
[178] Gómez Ortiz, "Moreno Torroba," 15.
[179] As related to Arazo, "Moreno Torroba."

In short, no one could say that Torroba left these mortal shores without the appreciation of friends, colleagues, and admirers for his superlative contributions to classical music and Spanish culture. One hastens to point out, however, that thirty years later there is still no monument, statue, metro station, or even simple plaque in the entire metropolis of Madrid that bears the name of this man, recalling the musical glory that he, a *madrileño castizo*, brought to his native city. To be fair, there is a street named after him, and there is the Centro Integrado de Enseñanzas Musicales "Federico Moreno Torroba." This superb institution offers a diverse curriculum and maintains a very high level of instruction and performance. Torroba would be proud to have his name attached to it. However, this is located on the outskirts of the city and far from areas that tourists frequent.[180] Neither are there any monuments either to Albéniz or Granados. Such reticence on Spain's part concerning some of its greatest musicians seems self-effacing. Frankly, it defies comprehension.

Death

We noted at the outset of this book that, when a reviewer asked him if he was afraid of death, Torroba stoically responded that he was now ready for it in a way he had not been before. In fact, he always had a sense of humor about his age. Some years earlier, when asked how old he was, he said that he was counting his age the way they proceed through the countdown when launching a rocket, by going backwards rather than forwards. Thus, though he was now 81 years old, he always told people he was 80. Every year he lost rather than added a year![181] But there is no doubting that he lived a long time. What was his secret? "No secret," he said, "just do a lot of intellectual work and avoid sports. Sporting activity should end at a certain age. Those who are running about, doing little jumps, that is fatal! But above all, the secret is to work, work, and work."[182] A little whisky went a long way, too, as did a genetic propensity for longevity: he liked to remind people that his father lived to age 95. In any case, just a few years before his passing he observed that "I don't feel old. I still don't know what old age is. Work relaxes me."[183]

A passionate devotion to work is a recurring motif in the many interviews he gave toward the end of his life. His work ethic was not only remarkable but also

---

[180] It is located on calle del General Ricardos, 177, in Madrid. There is a calle Moreno Torroba in the municipality of Mahadajonda, about ten miles northwest of the city of Madrid, in the Comunidad de Madrid. In this same Community there are three streets named after Mozart, including one in the city proper of Madrid.

[181] Valera, "Federico Moreno Torroba," 21.

[182] Sagi-Vela, "Moreno Torroba, nonagenario," 22. On another occasion, he offered this advice: "I don't think of my age, I only think of the day I'm living right now. It is the very best method, and I recommend it to everyone." In Arazo, "Moreno Torroba."

[183] Gómez Ortiz, "Moreno Torroba," 15.

admirable. Still, one wonders if this apparent workoholism was at least in part an attempt to stave off feelings of loss and decline, to forestall the demise he claimed not to fear. His wife, Pilar, predeceased him by five years, passing away on June 25, 1977.[184] He felt the absence of Pilar intensely, for although he was happy, he missed being able to share this happiness with her. She had always been a big help to him, giving him affection and understanding, he said. She went with him everywhere, and they were never closer than when he was experiencing difficulties. He continued to miss her right up to the end of his life.[185] Although he loved being among his books and scores, the apartment on Goya Street seemed empty without her.

Torroba felt like the proverbial maple leaf in autumn, as the hues of his career turned most radiant just before he fell forever from the tree of life.

> I believe I am now in one of my best moments, but I don't know. All old people say the same thing. I remember a famous painter who said he was painting better than ever, when in reality all he was producing were idiotic things.[186]

To be sure, he had always enjoyed good health, and even in the spring of 1982, few saw any cause for immediate concern about his ability to carry on. Plácido Domingo reports that only a month or so before Torroba's death, he had invited him on stage to conduct his music at an outdoor concert in Madrid attended by a quarter million people. "The man's energy was still incredible, and he had an enormous success."[187]

Torroba was fond of telling reporters that he never exercised, though earlier in life he had enjoyed bicycling on occasion, recounting with pride a trip he had once made to Santander with three cousins. They left in the snow and took three days to make the journey. Otherwise, he was not much of a sports fan. He liked watching soccer but was not a supporter of any particular team. "I root for the ball," he joked.[188] He was not a smoker, and he imbibed liquor in moderation.

He had always enjoyed good health, without investing too much effort in it. In one interview, he claimed to have been hospitalized only once, in 1978, due to a severe case of indigestion.[189] However, in another account, he related having been

---

[184] Her obituary appeared in *ABC* on June 26, 1977, 45. It reports that she died in the early morning, surrounded by her husband and children, at the age of 85.

[185] San Martín, "Federico Moreno Torroba."

[186] Gómez Ortiz, "Moreno Torroba," 15.

[187] Domingo, *My First Forty Years*, 155.

[188] Cortés-Cavanillas, "El maestro Moreno Torroba," 47.

[189] Franco, "Una figura del nacionalismo musical." Another article confirms that he was once incapacitated by constipation, but says it was during the epoch of Práxedes Mateo Sagasta (1825–1903), Spanish prime minister, when Torroba was a boy. This article says he also broke several bones, which had healed perfectly. It does not say how he broke them, but perhaps that was in the auto accident. See Vicent, "El pentagrama," 13.

in a car accident, in which he sustained some serious injuries, the only permanent one being sad memories of the event.[190] Presumably that required some hospital treatment. In yet another interview, he admitted to having had surgery—when his tonsils were removed in his 70s. He was concerned that he was too old for such an operation, but the doctor reassured him, relating a similar procedure done on the Bishop of Madrid-Alcalá at his same age. Torroba claimed that *this* was the only surgery he had ever undergone.[191] Once again, a counterpoint of self-contradiction spices up the otherwise mundane aspects of his autobiography.

No matter how many times he had actually gone to the hospital, it was the last time that concerns us most here. Torroba's daughter, Mariana, said that one evening she left him at his home, where he was working at the piano, correcting proofs for a future ballet. The next morning, she returned to find him immobilized.[192] The following is the best-available summary of the fatal condition that caused this:

> The composer was 91 years of age when, last August 25, he suffered a cerebral embolism [stroke], accompanied by urinary and pulmonary infections. During his stay at the Clínica Rúber, [he] experienced a noted improvement, which gave rise to hopes for a complete recovery. He was even able to get out of bed. However, on September 7, maestro Torroba suffered a cardiac complication, for which he was admitted to the intensive-care unit.... His condition deteriorated around 2 a.m. last Saturday, and in spite of all medical efforts, it was not possible to prevent his fatal decline, according to Dr. Contador Caballero, who attended the composer during his infirmity.[193]

Federico Moreno Torroba died on Sunday, September 12, 1982, nearly halfway through his ninety-second year. He himself had once declared that if he did not continue to work, he would quickly decline and wind up in the hospital. "Laziness is the common denominator among those who spend life demanding their supposed rights," he indignantly asserted.[194] No complainer, he. Work was the solution to all problems arising from discontent. Alas, though he never gave in to laziness, work proved not to be the vaunted Fountain of Youth, and he was no Ponce de León. As with every other living thing, his time came, and he went. One positive way to look at his departure is that it came later than he expected. Already in 1971, journalists were congratulating him on reaching the ripe old age of eighty.

[190] A. C., "Federico Moreno Torroba."

[191] Gómez-Santos, "Federico Moreno Torroba."

[192] Alberto López Poveda, letter to William Krause, from Linares (Jaén), July 7, 1990. Torroba preferred to compose at the piano.

[193] "Moreno-Torroba será enterrado," 38.

[194] "La muerte," 11.

He was grateful but expressed a certain anxiety nonetheless: "I am afraid that I will not complete the next decade, and that is sad."[195] Fate smiled on him, however, and granted him one more full decade, and a wee bit more.

Critics were prompt and unanimous in declaring that "the people of Madrid identified with the music of Moreno Torroba and made it theirs... he was considered one of the most *castizo* of all composers."[196] Carlos M. Fernández-Shaw, son of Torroba's former collaborator on *Luisa Fernanda* and *La chulapona*, praised the composer's incessant work ethic, his absence of vanity in small things, his patience with the shortcomings of his subordinates, his appreciation of beauty (including of the opposite sex, whatever that was meant to imply), his curiosity about what was happening beyond Spain, his patriotism, his inspiration, and—yes—his unfailingly good appetite![197]

Among the people closest to Torroba in his twilight years was Pepe Romero, who offered his recollections of a creative artist who clearly had a profound impact on his own artistry:

> [During his final illness, when he was having painful kidney problems], he paid no attention whatsoever to his physical suffering. Instead, we stayed up until what must have been no earlier than 3:30 in the morning. He was sitting at the piano. In his house he had two pianos, a very beautiful grand, and an old upright with a few keys that did not work, and quite a bit out of tune, but for some reason that was the piano he used to compose. That is where he felt comfortable.... He was writing a suite for solo, unaccompanied guitar. He was writing, and I was reading it for him, playing it back for him on the guitar. We had a fantastic time. There was not once a sign on his face or in his expression, and not once did he complain of what would have been to most anyone else a very painful evening. This was typical of the way Torroba was.[198]

Torroba's body lay in state at the SGAE starting Sunday, where hundreds came to view it, including Segovia, musicologist Federico Sopeña, US ambassador

[195] C.,"Moreno Torroba."

[196] Santos Martín Pancorbo, letter to William Krause, January 12, 1991.

[197] "Moreno Torroba: un siglo de música española," *Música clásica*, February 27, 1991, 4–5.

[198] Dávila, "Pepe Romero Reminisces," 144–45. Among his final inspirations were six preludes for guitar, dedicated to Andrés Segovia, who was to live another five years. These were probably the pieces with which Pepe was helping him at the end. And there were other demonstrations of his phenomenal powers of concentration, the most notable (and humorous) taking place at the Romero home in Del Mar, California. Torroba was in the bathroom using the facilities, when he urgently called out for "more paper!" Pepe dutifully brought him another roll of toilet paper. Torroba promptly corrected him: "No, not toilet paper—*music* paper!" Torroba's inspiration, like the call of nature, could strike at any time, and it would not be denied. Conversation with Walter Clark, June 10, 2008. Federico, Jr., tells of similar instances, claiming that the "Dúo del Pañuelito" from *La chulapona* experienced a similar genesis. E-mail to William Krause, December 4, 2008.

Carmelo Bernaola, and a representative from the Russian embassy. The King and Queen, long admirers of Torroba, sent their condolences: "We extend to the entire family our most sincere regrets, profoundly lamenting such a notable loss to the world of music."[199]

On Monday the 13th, at 12:45 p.m., a hearse transported Torroba's remains from the SGAE to the Sacramental de San Justo, on the city outskirts, across the Manzanares River, where he was buried. The hearse preceded four other cars full of floral bouquets sent from around Spain and the world. The following day, a funeral service in his memory was held at 1 p.m. in the Concepción church, where he and his father had often played. Those present at the funeral included Minister of Culture Soledad Becerril, Segovia, General Director of Music and Theater Juan Cambreleng, and composer Ernesto Halffter. Also in attendance were composer and musicologist Tomás Marco, Maribel de Falla (the composer's niece), directors of the SGAE, and other dignitaries.

Torroba's "tomb," in the Patio de Santa Gertrudis (sección baja, P-6, nicho 9), is remarkably plain, simply a horizontal niche in the wall to accommodate his casket.[200] This befits his personal modesty, if not his actual status as one of Spain's greatest composers. It bears no epitaph whatsoever, though the words of Pepe Romero could well suffice: "Torroba will live forever through his music, and particularly in the hearts of those who were fortunate to know him."[201] Torroba had sometimes thought of writing his memoirs, and he would have had a lot to say; sadly, he never found the time.[202] Yet, though he always declined to craft any final utterances for posterity, Torroba's own words might have served as a pithy epitaph telling us all we really need to know about his life:

Music is essential for living and for the spirit.[203]

---

[199] "Ya," reprint of an article that appeared in *Ya* on September 14, 1982, regarding the death of Federico Moreno Torroba. In *Autores: Revista de información de la S.G.A.E.*, n3 (October 1982): 35.

[200] I expected Torroba's tomb to be impressive and prominent in the cemetery, but after an hour of fruitless searching, I asked groundskeeper Jesús Cañadillo for assistance. He had actually been present for the burial in 1982 and was able to take me directly to the composer's final resting place, one so inconspicuous that I would never have found it on my own.

[201] Dávila, "Pepe Romero Reminisces," 144.

[202] San Martín, "Federico Moreno Torroba."

[203] This was in response to a question about what music meant to him. Quoted in Colmenero, "Lírico Moreno Torroba." We recall from the interview in Act I, Scene ii, that he would not even speculate about an epitaph.

9

ACT III
Scene iii
Major Works of the Period 1960–82

As stated earlier, Torroba gradually gave up on writing for the stage during the final creative period of his life, largely because of declining public interest in and government support for zarzuela. Instead, he focused increasingly on writing substantial works for guitar and orchestra; thus, this period witnesses the composition of all ten of his guitar concertos. The two most outstanding of these are certainly the solo concerto *Diálogos entre guitarra y orquesta* and *Concierto ibérico*, for guitar quartet and orchestra. In addition to all this, Torroba wrote some of his most important sets of solo-guitar works during this period, especially the two books of *Castillos de España*, as well as *Puertas de Madrid*, selections from both of which we examine here.

However, though Torroba often expressed disbelief in the perennial chimera of Spanish opera, he could not resist one last attempt to conjure a successful one. Such was the prestige that opera possessed, even for a man as dedicated to the zarzuela as Torroba.

Although it was not by any standard a commercial success and has not held a place on the stage or found its way on to a professional recording, still, the attention and care that Torroba lavished on *El poeta* compel us to examine this work, if only in cursory fashion. It may be that history has misjudged this effort and that it has more to offer than people assumed at the time. Thus, this Scene commences with his last major musico-theatrical production.

El poeta is an opera in four acts loosely based on the life of the best-known lyric poet of Spain's brief Romantic movement, from the 1820s to 40s. The historical figure, José de Espronceda y Delgado (1808–42), led the life of a true Romantic. He was born on a roadside as his parents fled the advancing French army during Napoleon's invasion of Spain. At the age of fifteen, he joined a secret society of conspirators and was imprisoned on several occasions. In 1826 he was expelled from Spain by the despotic Fernando VII, fleeing first to Portugal and eventually to France and England, where he was exposed to the Romantic literary movement in those countries.[1] During his travels, he fell in love with Teresa Mancha, the daughter of an exiled Spanish colonel. They returned to Madrid in 1833 as a result of the amnesty granted by Cristina, the new monarch, but their life together was unhappy and soon led to separation. Teresa ended her life in vice and poverty. Espronceda wrote his famous poem *Canto a Teresa, Descanse en Paz* (Song to Teresa, Rest in Peace) in her memory, before succumbing to a fatal throat infection at the age of 34.

José Méndez Herrera, the librettist of *El poeta*, was sharply criticized by critics for the changes he made in Espronceda's biography. They argued that the factual story was already sufficiently laden with tragedy to provide a very dramatic effect.[2] In Herrera's version, Rosaura (Teresa) is presented as a heroine, glossing over the fact that the historical character had left her husband and child in London to return to Madrid with Espronceda and had ended her life as a prostitute. Herrera's Rosaura meets a much more noble fate: just when she is reunited with her beloved poet, José, she is poisoned by a jealous rival, Luisa.

Above and beyond the liberties that Herrera took with history, Torroba's music came as a shock to many listeners. The harmonic vocabulary is in places very chromatic, while continuous modulations often make tonal centers recognizable only at cadences at the end of scenes or acts. This is particularly the case in recitative passages, which comprise most of the score. Torroba described these recitatives as "conversational music," explaining that they "were conceived as if they were part of a drama, without music."[3] Arias are not always clearly demarcated. At times, they seem to be variations on the recitative's textures rather than distinct pieces. In performance, this can become tedious. Only the third act is broken up into scenes (three); the other acts have no scene changes or breaks in the music. It is clear that Torroba believed a modern opera should incorporate the innovations of Wagner in relation to "music drama," with additional inspiration from Wagner-followers Richard Strauss and Conrado del Campo. Keenly aware of the developments in harmony that had taken place since the days of *Luisa Fernanda*, he was at pains to demonstrate his ability to produce a contemporary score beyond the Spanish-nationalist pale that had become his trademark.

Indeed, the very opening measures of Act I waste no time displaying Torroba's expanded harmonic vocabulary. The music that accompanies José and his comrades as they first enter is an outstanding example (see ex. III:iii:1). At m. 23, the solo cello's eleven-note phrase encompasses eight distinct pitches. The ensuing counterpoint, starting at m. 30, provides no clear harmonic context in which to understand the preceding seven measures. Between measures 33 and 40, F may

---

[1] Richard E. Chandler and Kessel Schwartz, *A New History of Spanish Literature* (Baton Rouge: Louisiana State University Press, 1961), 339.

[2] Eduardo Haro Tecglen, "Las víctimas de la fiesta," *El País*, June 21, 1980.

[3] Quoted in Ángel Del Campo, "Estreno de 'El poeta,'" *Pueblo*, June 25, 1980.

Ex. III:iii:1: El poeta, Act I, mm. 23–46

be identified as a predominating pitch in the bass, but any tonal function it may have is muddled by juxtaposition to the C-flat triad in mm. 33–35. If the A in the bass is combined with the upper triad in this passage, an augmented-sixth chord results, but this still does not accommodate the pitches B-flat and F in the bass. These three measures may be interpreted as V flat 9 flat 5 in the key of B-flat, with the pitch B-flat in the bass considered an upper neighbor of A. But this is not what one perceives simply by listening. These extraordinary bars are about as close as Torroba ever came to writing atonality. No doubt, more than a few people in the audience at the premiere silently prayed for the sudden apparition of a *seguidilla* to provide relief. No such respite was in store until Act III.

As the bass descends chromatically after m. 40, any significance F once had is lost by mm. 47–48, where G-major, C-major, and B-minor chords are heard. If considered briefly in G major, these chords could be interpreted as I, IV, and iii. But the bass continues its descent, moving through a B-flat 7 chord and arriving at an A-minor 6 chord at m. 50. Another chromatic contrapuntal passage then occurs over the next four measures, arriving at a G7 flat 6 harmony at m. 55. Subsequent passages do not shed light on this excerpt, making it hard to describe the harmony relative to a particular key. The first unambiguous tonal cadence does not occur until m. 145.

The story begins with a recitative in which José and his friends lament their exile in Portugal and their inability to affect events in Spain under the rule of Fernando VII. The poet describes how his Spanish verse is born of his inner being. The bulk of *El poeta* consists of through-composed accompanied recitative similar to this passage (see ex. III:iii:2). In these extended passages, the vocal line seems less inventive than the orchestral music and is designed mainly to carry the plot while articulating the inflections of the Spanish language. Meanwhile, the orches-

Ex. III:iii:2: El poeta, Act I, mm. 63–68

tral part is full of melodic invention, similar to the instrumental passage previously examined.

Arias appear sparingly in this opera. In his first aria in Act I, José refers to Spain in a personal manner, saying, "Without you I am only an exile who has lost his sky…and longs to hear your songs" (see ex. III:iii:3). The piece is through-composed in the available score but was recast in ternary form for the 1980 premiere. Its harmonies are also rich in color but more predictable and tonal than previously cited passages and exploit the flatted second, third, and sixth scale degrees, a trait characteristic of Torroba's guitar music as well.

The ensuing recitative passage is lengthy, to allow for plot development: José first meets Rosaura, the colonel's daughter, who will become the object of his desire. It becomes clear that both she and her father share José's desire to liberate Spain, and they join the band of expatriates.

Ex. III:iii:3: El poeta, Act I, José's aria "Porque sin ti soy solo un desterrado," mm. 1–8

José's next aria is sung to Rosaura. Through her, José finds relief from his despair. Analysis of the ensuing ten measures reveals a melody that is diatonic, rarely departing from the key of B-flat. However, the accompaniment is often chromatic and unstable, with added-note sonorities and the use of diminished chords on the raised fourth degree of the scale (m. 430). In this passage, as in many parts of *El poeta*, Torroba employs harmonic progressions that are chromatic in their structure but do not follow tight-knit contrapuntal lines. Underlying these contrasting diatonic and chromatic connotations, however, is a very simple scheme: the tonic is established at m. 425, the dominant at m. 429, an episode to V of V at m. 431, and the return to the dominant at m. 432. The tonic occurs first with an A-flat triad superimposed on it at m. 433, coming to a resolution at the end of m. 434.

Soon joining the group on stage is Luisa, a less-refined individual, who unabashedly states that José is the sort of man she likes. She flatters José, saying that she has read his poetry and that it cures her melancholy. She goes on to say that she feels akin to him and also shares his aspirations for the removal of Fernando VII. The mood is abruptly transformed, however, with the arrival of Portuguese officials saying that all Spanish political exiles must leave the country in three days. The group cannot return to Spain and instead chooses to go north to England or France. The final chorus, which includes the band of refugees, speaks of how they will continue to wage their struggle against tyranny.

The opening of Act II again foregrounds chromaticism, with scarcely a trace of the overt Spanishness that usually pervades Torroba's music. In the ensuing recitative, the exiles are in Bordeaux. They are enjoying the fine wines of the region but idly dream of Madrid. Rosaura is not with the group, and it seems apparent that Luisa has taken up with José, despite another man's advances (Regino). Her short passage about her affection for José moves from G-sharp minor to E minor, enriched by a C-sharp in the melody. The numerous added tones make for luxuriant harmony, but the underlying root movement remains clear. Torroba may stray from the ground he cultivated in the zarzuela, but he never loses sight of it completely.

Rosaura's absence is not adequately explained in the libretto. The historical character would have been married in London at this point. Without reference to this awkward fact, José's passionate aria is untainted and engaging. Perhaps to emphasize the disturbing text, "to continue this way would be to die without the light of love," the harmonies, centered in A major, are unsettled, exploiting deceptive cadences and excursions into the flat II and flat VI of A.

Critics of the premiere said that Torroba's work was reminiscent of Puccini. Similarities can be found in the use of orchestral octave doubling supporting the vocal line. The climactic point of the line (m. 401) occurs with a dominant-seventh chord resolving to F major, necessitating the prolongation of the phrase in order to return to the key of A major. This resolution is thwarted by the movement to C-sharp minor each time a more conclusive cadence might be possible. The deceptive cadences also support the text by giving a musical image to the loneliness and longing of which the protagonist sings. This aria foretells José's destiny: Rosaura will return to him only to meet a tragic end and leave him alone once more.

By sheer happenstance, Rosaura and her traveling companion, Mayo, arrive in Bordeaux. José and Rosaura meet again, but their joyous reunion, marked by a recitative and duet, is overshadowed by Luisa's boisterous behavior. To hide her jealousy and disillusionment, she gets drunk with the other men, throwing herself in their arms while cynically mocking love by singing that "love is merely a game, but I will play it!"

Act III opens with a short orchestral introduction followed by an extended passage of recitative. Rosaura and Luisa are now together on stage. They have returned to Madrid as a result of a general amnesty and await the return of José. Rosaura thanks Luisa for reuniting her with José, recalling the chance encounter in Bordeaux without realizing that Luisa had loved José but lost him to Rosaura because of that reunion.

In the name of the Dukes of Osuña, the town crier invites everyone to celebrate the amnesty at the palace. The palace garden provides a perfect backdrop for an exuberant number for chorus and dancers (see ex. III:iii:4). This passage is the only part of the opera to recall Torroba's traditional Spanish idiom. The piece is tonal, with clearly demarcated phrases and form. Marked in the score as a "grand exhibition of popular dances," the castanets, *palmas* (hand-clapping), and folk-dance rhythms are unmistakably Spanish. Even the text at one point says, "Bravo, it is very *castizo*." The closing passage is in a key of three flats; a G-Phrygian quality prevails, with frequent alternation between G major and A-flat major. This music is very reminiscent of Falla's "Danza del molinero" from *El sombrero de tres picos*.

After this diversion, the score returns to recitative, and the inevitable confrontation between Luisa and José draws near. Upon his return, she is the first to see him and implores him to return to her. She cannot accept the fact that José came back to Madrid to see Rosaura, not her. Enraged by the sight of José embracing Rosaura, Luisa sings a bitterly powerful aria, portraying José as a cruel traitor. She swears vengeance: "I will judge him...I will kill without pity." The intense emotion of this text is magnified by the disorienting, harsh harmonies that close the aria.

Act IV is much shorter than the preceding acts. After a brief thirteen-measure orchestral introduction, Luisa and Rosaura again open the act with a long recitative. Rosaura is still unaware of Luisa's involvement with José and graciously shares a cup of coffee with her. When Rosaura leaves the room to get Luisa a glass of water, Luisa poisons Rosaura's coffee. At the moment that Rosaura speaks of her happiness with José, she begins to feel faint. José returns in time only to hold Rosaura as she dies. José cries, "I hold death in my arms," to which Luisa replies, "And I hold it in my soul, and I have judged you, José, with the same poison." The opera ends with an allusion to Espronceda's poem "Canto a Teresa," as José sings an aria lamenting the loss of Rosaura.

Ex. III:iii:4: El poeta, Act III, "Hay que aplaudir con fuerza ¡así!" mm. 141–50

The only recording of *El poeta*'s 1980 premiere differs from the autograph score.[4] Most noticeable is the omission of much of the recitative between Luisa and Rosaura at the beginning of the third and fourth acts. Added for the performance were extended orchestral introductions before each act. A beautiful

---

[4] The recording is not commercial. Both it and the autograph are in the Biblioteca Nacional in Madrid.

intermezzo, based on Luisa's aria at the end of Act II, was placed before Act IV. It is hard to surmise the reason for these changes. The longer introductions make the characters' eventual entries less abrupt, and the new intermezzo is a worthy piece in its own right. However, the omission of the women's recitatives weakens the intensity of their rivalry. As a result, it seems that José spends a disproportionate amount of time on stage.

Torroba's score is a clear departure from any of his earlier stage works. While the libretto portrays the life of a Spanish Romantic poet, for the most part Torroba deliberately eschews references to Spain's musical heritage. In his attempt to establish his modernist credentials, he ventured into terra incognita and understandably lost his footing on occasion. *El poeta*'s distinctive fusion of extensive dissonance and ambiguous tonalities with areas of lushly triadic harmonies and strongly folkloric dance music makes it hard to perceive the opera as an integrated whole.

Guitar Works

Castillos de España

It has often been said that writing or talking about music is like dancing about architecture. Anyone who has undertaken to describe a piece of music can vouch for the veracity of that statement. But what is the status of writing music, not dancing, about architecture? Is that just as forlorn an errand? Torroba had precious few works to serve as models for this task. Mussorgsky was inspired by a painting of the Great Gate of Kiev to include a majestic evocation of it in his *Pictures at an Exhibition*; he also provides a musical portrait of "The Old Castle." In the course of Smetana's symphonic river excursion *The Moldau*, we pass another old castle, which he describes in solemn tones. Vaughan Williams's *London Symphony* commences with the sound of bells emanating from Big Ben. Examples in Spanish music are rare but conspicuous: Albéniz's "Torre Bermeja (Serenata)," from *Douze pièces caractéristiques*, conveys his response to the Moorish "Vermillion Tower" at the Alhambra; that same set of buildings inspired Tárrega's tremulous recollections in *Recuerdos de la Alhambra*. But these are the exceptions that prove the rule: music about architecture is relatively rare and apparently as challenging to contrive as words about music. It may be the easiest thing in the world, however, merely to attach the name of an architectural monument to a composition, whether or not any concrete connection between the title and music actually exists. This is probably the case with *Castillos de España*, the fourteen pieces of which appeared in two books, published eight years apart (eight pieces in 1970 and six more in 1978).

We had occasion earlier to note, for instance, that "Montemayor" from Book I of this suite, started out life years earlier as *Romance de los pinos*. According to

Federico, Jr., Segovia himself requested that "Romance de los pinos" be included in *Castillos de España*, and it became "Montemayor."[5]

How one gets from pine trees to castles is not entirely clear, unless the music had so tenuous a connection with the former that entitling it with the latter presented no hermeneutical hurdle. Make no mistake about it: these are some of Torroba's finest works for solo guitar. But one could just as easily rename them *Palacios*, *Pueblos*, or *Puertos de España* (palaces, villages, or ports) without diminishing our enjoyment of the music itself one iota. We suspect that the evocation of Spanish castles enhanced the collection's marketability more than it shed useful light on the intrinsic nature of the pieces themselves.

Take, for instance, one of the most popular numbers from Book I, "Alcázar de Segovia." Subtitled *Llamada*, or "call," it summons us to behold the splendor of these monuments from Spain's fabled past. *Alcázar* is an Arabic word for fortress, and Segovia's is one of the most picturesque, even fairy-tale-like, castles in Spain. Poised on a cliff overlooking farmland outside the city, its pointed towers thrust confidently, even dreamily, skyward. Certainly the forte dynamics, boldly broad rhythms, and resolute major key of the opening measures could suggest its majestic appearance. Though marked 6/8, the groupings and stresses create two measures of 3/4 alternating with two of 6/8. The resulting hemiola gives this the feeling of Spanish folklore. Moreover, the modal I-ii progression in the first two measures conveys a slightly antique quality to the harmony (see ex. III:iii:5). However, while these attributes plausibly correspond to one's impression of the Alcázar, this piece could just as readily be describing many other castles that adorn the Spanish countryside.

Its form resembles a rondo, ABABCA' coda, but the sections are not symmetrical in length. There are predictable excursions to other keys, including the parallel minor and the supertonic, B minor, which he had highlighted already in the first bar of the A section. In mm. 62–66, the prominence of B-flat adds an Andalusian color to the harmony. In those measures, we find the harmonies A, C, B-flat, A-flat, and E. While A, C, and B-flat imply a Phrygian cadence to A, present

Ex. III:iii:5: *Castillos de España* I, "Alcázar de Segovia," mm. 1–4

[5] In a letter from Torroba to Segovia of August 22, 1969, the composer acknowledges his request but expresses reservations, because of the popularity of *Romance de los pinos* and because he has already used it in *Diálogos*. This letter is in the Fundación-Museo Andrés Segovia in Linares.

also is the tonal cadence, E to A. The mixture of tonality and modality—A major/minor/Phrygian—persisted through the decades as a hallmark of Torroba's style, though it appears with varying degrees of prominence and intensity in the various instances we have noted. In "Alcázar de Segovia," it virtually dictates the harmonic language of the piece.

"Turegano" is a castle in a different town but the same province of Segovia, in Castile. Its appearance, for what that may matter, is less whimsical and poetic than the Alcázar's and more along the lines of what one expects of a castle: its massive, solid walls and parapets are well designed for fending off attackers. Moreover, its precincts contain the church of San Miguel. None of this is readily apparent in the music, however, which again exhibits a folkloric character in its dancelike triple-meter rhythms (see ex. III:iii:6). The form is also rondo, ABACA coda, with the addition of a lively introduction on the dominant (the principal melody begins at m. 10).

As we noted already in the *Suite castellana*, Torroba routinely utilizes those keys that maximize the instrument's resonance, here E major, and he uses pedal notes not only to enhance this effect but also to impart a vernacular quality to the score. The repeating rhythmic pattern of the introductory melody also accomplishes this. Whether intentional or not, the incursion of G-natural in the principal theme (m. 16), as a member of a flat-VI7 chord, gives this moment a bluesy sound. Improbable, perhaps, but not entirely implausible, given Torroba's love affair with Broadway musicals and Gershwin, on display as late as 1980 in *El poeta*. Another conspicuous instance of this lowered-third, blues-scale intimation comes in "Torija." In fact, there are numerous cases in *Castillos* of added-

Ex. III:iii:6: Castillos de España I, "Turegano," mm. 1–17

note harmonies, particularly major chords with an added major seventh, which add a slightly jazzy flavor to the harmony. Yet, in almost every other respect, there is little separating the style of the *Castillos* from Torroba's very first pieces for the guitar a half century earlier. Once he found a formula that worked for him, he stuck with it.

However, there is no doubting the genuineness of emotion in these pieces. Furthermore, there is no empty display of virtuosity for its own sake. Rather, the technique remains subordinate to the composer's expressive purposes. We hasten to point out, though, that *Castillos* requires considerable technique to play well, consummate agility and suppleness in both hands. Two of the movements, "Simancas" and "Zafra," are challenging tremolo studies and worthy successors to Tárrega's *Recuerdos de la Alhambra*. Both convey a hauntingly introspective lyricism that employs the tremolo technique in a deeply moving way. In fact, Torroba's penchant for such introspection dovetails with an expansion of his harmonic materials during this late period, which we will note in the other great collection of musical monuments, *Puertas de Madrid*, from 1976.

Puertas de Madrid

In truth, these works are very much in the same stylistic vein as *Castillos de España* and represent no significant departure. But there is one movement whose chromaticism stands out from his earlier works and reflects an awareness of contemporary trends. This is the harbinger of harmonic procedures noted in *El poeta*, which will become apparent in his concertos.

Torroba wrote a very useful and revealing introduction to this collection of seven "gates."[6] He first provides some history of the famous *puertas*, informing the reader that at one time there were more than twenty gates in the defensive fortifications of the city, and that these bore names indicating the direction in which they pointed or that referred to their appearance. For instance, the Puerta de Toledo originally controlled access to the road leading to "the Arabic kingdom of Toledo." (Since Toledo fell to Christian forces in 1085, the gate presumably predated that reconquest.) The Puerta del Ángel, however, was once decorated with a sculpture of an angel; the sculpture disappeared, but the name stuck. Torroba is quick to emphasize, however, that "these 'Puertas de Madrid,'... do not have and could not have a descriptive concept. Each one of them expresses instead a certain emotional quality arising from the contemplation of these gates, through what they represent or suggest." Here is the key to understanding not only *Puertas* but also *Castillos* (or *Madroños* or *Romance de los pinos*). They are not literal descriptions in sound of the objects in question but rather affective

---

[6] In the edition published in Madrid by Editorial Cadencia, 1976.

responses to them, responses that by definition are subjective, vague, capable of multiple interpretations, and even transferable from one kind of object to another.

Of interest to us here is "Puerta de Moros," or Gate of the Moors, which, like the Puerta de Toledo, led to areas under Moorish control. The texture, rhythm, and harmony of this piece's opening measures provoke our own contemplation and response. The work commences with a single melody line, a technique we previously noted in the "Fandaguillo" from the *Suite castellana*. Yet, this theme is completely different. Rather than exhibiting the Hispanic octosyllabic rhythm, it strongly conveys an "oriental" mood in its metrical ambiguity (though the piece is in 2/4) and rhythmic freedom. This is accomplished primarily by ties across bar lines and the alternation of duplet and triplet groupings. The tonality is D minor, and there is a strong initial affirmation of key in the tonic-dominant leap from D to A; however, the ensuing arrival of G-sharp, G-natural, C-sharp, and B-flat serves to heighten a sense of harmonic otherness, a sort of ambiguity that parallels the meandering quality of the rhythm. The overall gestalt of this melody harkens to Andalusian prototypes, and perhaps liturgical chant, in its opening upward ascent followed by a gradual but inexorable, even fatalistic, descent (see ex. III:iii:7).

All of this would certainly accord with the "Moorish" theme of the gate in question. Yet, the desolate loneliness of this melody, its tone row-like quality and the succession of astringently dissonant chords in ensuing measures (e.g., mm. 11–12), suggests to us an intensely personal character transcending any external object. For all the crowd-pleasing exuberance of his theatrical songs and dances, it is in Torroba's guitar music that we get occasional intimate glimpses into his soul. This strikes us as one such glimpse, and the effect is both captivating and deeply moving.

Ex. III:iii:7: *Puertas de Madrid*, "Puerta de Moros," mm. 1–13

Diálogos entre guitarra y orquesta

The greatest hazard a composer of guitar concertos faces is that the soloist will be drowned out by the orchestra. Maintaining the proper balance—enabling David to at least fend off Goliath—is sufficiently difficult that it may be among the reasons there are not more guitar concertos. After the phenomenal success of Rodrigo's *Concierto de Aranjuez*, one might reasonably have expected a stampede of epigones, but that did not happen. Neither Falla nor Turina ever wrote a guitar concerto, and Torroba himself would wait over twenty years after the *Aranjuez* to tackle this genre in earnest. Perhaps another disincentive has been the nearly universal association of the guitar with a Spanish musical idiom. Any composer not wishing to write a work suggesting sunny Spain would no doubt be put off by that connection and forage for another, less typecast solo instrument. Finally, since the guitar is not covered in most courses on orchestration and instrumentation, an academically trained composer unfamiliar with six strings and nineteen frets has to be quite adventurous to write the most difficult kind of music for them, i.e., a concerto.

Torroba had apparently begun a concerto for Segovia as early as 1929, but the fledgling effort found no favor with its dedicatee. In December 1929, Segovia wrote rather dismissively to Manuel Ponce concerning Torroba's concerto:

> Torroba came to spend 15 days in Britanny with us. Under his arm, he brought a concerto for small orchestra and guitar, very melodic, and *sonatine-like*, but is not worth the first few chords of yours. The theme of the andante is beautiful however, and the development has strokes of genius. But all of it is too easy, and the entire first movement, too easy, understand? Too *horizontal*.... Now he is waiting for me to take the work to Madrid, but I am preparing to turn him down based really on my need for rest.[7]

Perhaps Torroba had to mature a bit before he could tackle a guitar concerto with both confidence and aplomb, but once he got started, there was no stopping him. In addition to being a gifted orchestrator, by the 1960s he had had four decades of experience writing for the guitar. Though he was not himself a guitarist, he was confident of his ability to compose effectively for it, either solo or with orchestra. Naturally, he viewed its Spanish association as entirely positive.

Yet, the ineluctable fact remains that the unamplified classical guitar cannot go *mano a mano* with an orchestral *tutti* any more than a squirrel can retard the forward momentum of a truck. Constructing a concerto as a series of "dialogues"

---

[7] In other words, maybe if I ignore him and his concerto, he and it will go away. Quoted in Alcázar, ed., *The Segovia-Ponce Letters*, 49. We have noted Segovia's derogation of Torroba's music before, in connection with the *Sonatina*.

between the guitar and the orchestra is not only an evocative and appealing idea, it is the best way to prevent road kill.[8] Interestingly, the title suggests nothing of a Spanish character, unlike his other concertos. Rather, it displays a certain sensitivity to the sorts of musically abstract pieces common in the 1960s and 70s, with titles saying more about how the work is put together than what, if anything, it means, e.g., "Forms," "Sequences," "Structures," etc. Of course, all concertos are "dialogues" of a sort, in that they feature dramatic contrasts between the soloist(s) and the orchestra. And on balance, this concerto presents no more such contrasts than any other concerto. Once again, we must resist the temptation to read too much into the title *vis-à-vis* the work's musical content. Despite its sundry modernistic touches, this concerto's Spanish character is unmistakable.

Diálogos premiered in 1977, only a year after the publication of *Puertas de Madrid*. It has four rather than the traditional three movements, and in that respect, at least, it resembles Brahms's Second Piano Concerto. Torroba's orchestra includes the usual complement of strings and woodwinds, in addition to trumpet, percussion, celesta, and harp. This is a distinctive chamber ensemble that provides plenty of tone color to work with; however, it is not so large as to forbid a proper balance between soloist and ensemble.[9]

The first movement is in a modified sonata form. Marked "Allegretto, comodo," it commences with a lighthearted melody in the winds and celesta, which prepares the way for the solo guitar's presentation of yet another component of the principal theme group. Its symmetrical phrasing and descending half-step cadence on E suggest Spanish folklore (see ex. III:iii:8).

The guitarist also introduces a contrasting secondary theme, in triple meter and more reflective in nature. The ensuing development features both orchestra and soloist in presenting brief excursions into various tonal centers, sometimes tritone related, as well as metrical alternation and emphatic repetition of certain motivic ideas. Once again, we assert that Torroba was fully capable of developmental writing, when the occasion demanded. In the recapitulation, the soloist restates and offers contrapuntal variation of the principal theme, while the secondary theme appears in the orchestra. The guitar's restatement of the movement's opening material leads to a coda and quiescent conclusion.

[8] When I was eighteen, I composed a Webernesque Quintet for guitar and four instruments (alto sax, French horn, bassoon, and string bass). The eminent American composer Dominick Argento (1927–) took one look at the score and dismissed it with the remark: "The guitar will never be heard!" Although Argento has written some remarkable music for guitar and voice, I believe that he was wrong about my Quintet. But Jeffrey Van, the virtuoso who had requested the piece from me, took Argento's verdict as definitive and never performed it. Admittedly, this constituted no great loss to Western classical music. Still, the incident strongly confirms that a composer's chief preoccupation in writing a guitar concerto has to do with balance.

[9] This treatment of *Diálogos* is indebted not only to William Krause's dissertation, which offers a far more detailed harmonic analysis of it, but also to John Robinson's program notes for a performance of this work by the Ohio Chamber Orchestra on January 22, 1978, with Dwight Oltman, director, and Michael Lorimer, guitar soloist; the latter had premiered the work a year earlier.

Ex. III:iii:8: Diálogos, 1st mvmt., mm. 33–41

The second movement is marked "Andantino mosso" and exhibits the triple meter typical of Spanish folklore. Again, Torroba makes colorful use of woodwinds and percussion in laying out Spanish rhythms reminiscent of the *seguidillas*, though the jazzy harmonies signal that his musical intent is far from ethnographic (see ex. III:iii:9).

The guitar soon answers with its distinctively folkloric theme, though its quirky chromatic shifts create a scherzo-like comical effect. In fact, solo-guitar passages dominate this movement, as the soloist elaborates on the thematic material presented at the outset; still, occasional interjections from the orchestra continue the impression of a dialogue. Brief phrases from the orchestra, also sometimes derived from the basic theme, provide colorful background for the solo instrument. The theme is reiterated intact by the guitar just before the final cadence.

Torroba inverts the inner movements (again, like the Brahms 2nd), saving the atmospheric Andante for penultimate honors. This captivating essay is an arrangement of *Romance de los pinos*, a solo composed for Segovia in the 1950s (see Act II, Scene iii) that was reincarnated in *Castillos de España*. Torroba's choice of this calmly reflective work as the sum and substance of his slow movement reminds one of Ponce's use of his own song *Estrellita* as the basis for the slow movement of his Violin Concerto. However, the comparison in self-quotation stops there. Ponce's acerbic transformation ran against the character of the original; here, the same dreamy, meditative mood prevails, and everything about the writing enhances rather than contradicts the original.

Ex. III:iii:9: Diálogos, 2nd mvmt., mm. 1–16

The movement is basically a series of variations on this number. It begins with softly distant strokes in the timpani and a sense of hazy nostalgia. Appropriately, the guitar (re)introduces us to this beautifully lyric melody, in its original key of A major. To enhance the atmosphere of hushed enchantment, Torroba uses muted strings to extend the melody, followed by modulatory exchanges between orchestra and soloist. The guitar introduces a contrasting secondary theme, accompanied by *tremolandi* strings. A contrapuntal return of the main theme in the strings and a final utterance by the soloist bring this signature movement to a peaceful close.

The lighthearted Allegro wastes no time shifting into high gear, with its rocketing scales in the winds and syncopated punctuations in the strings. The guitar soon presents a theme in the style of a *bulerías*, utilizing the pedal E we have encountered in earlier pieces. The digital pyrotechnics this movement demands of the soloist constitute the supreme test of a guitarist's agility. Moreover, the difficulty of the passage cited below (see ex. III:iii:10) results not only from the speed called for in the right hand but also from awkward movements in the left. The main reason for this is chromaticism, a sudden shift from A minor to D-flat, an uncomfortable key on the instrument. Here is the *locus classicus* of Torroba's updated style.

The skillful means by which Torroba interweaves the orchestra with the solo guitar provides a kind of exchange in which the soloist remains the focus of attention without simply being abandoned by the ensemble. But the concerto genre demands a cadenza, in which the soloist stands forth unfettered by the orchestra, and this movement presents a memorable one before the forceful and emphatic conclusion of *Diálogos*.[10]

There is a modernistic stylization of folkloric materials in this work that reveals Torroba's determination to find a middle passage between traditional and contemporary idioms. In fact, it reminds one a bit of *El poeta* in its eclecticism: a mélange of impressionistic effects in the orchestra, jazz influences in the added-note sonorities, modality bordering on tonal ambiguity, Turinaesque parallel movement of chords, distant echoes of Stravinsky and Bartók in the percussion and off-kilter rhythms, along with Torroba's trademark lyricism and dance rhythms.[11] In short, this concerto reflects a lifetime of listening and absorbing a wide variety of musics. And yet, it bears the composer's personal stamp and persuades us of its genuineness, even after repeated listenings. *Diálogos* represents an important milestone in his evolution as a creative artist, and this evolutionary trend continued into his final guitar concerto.

Concierto ibérico

We know that Torroba was very impressed with the *Concierto andaluz* for four guitars and orchestra by his friend and compatriot Rodrigo. And he was equally impressed with the performers for whom that concerto was composed: Los

[10] Torroba wrote out the original cadenza, but Pepe Romero revised it by adding some rapid scales. Thus, what one hears on the recording is a Torroba-Romero hybrid. Walter Clark interview with Pepe Romero, September 2, 2011.

[11] These observations are indebted to Eduardo de la Fuente, program notes for *Concierto-Homenaje, Federico Moreno Torroba (1891–1982) (en el aniversario de su muerte)*, Salamanca, May 2002.

Ex. III:iii:10: Diálogos, 4th mvmt., mm. 120–35

Romeros. The Romero family was the first guitar quartet of any significance or notoriety in history. Celedonio, his wife, and three sons (Celín, Pepe, and Ángel) were originally from Málaga, where they lived in poverty during the Civil War and its aftermath. Later, they moved to Sevilla, but because of restrictions placed on Celedonio's performing career by a hostile Franco government, which always suspected his politics, he and his family fled Spain to the United States in 1957.

It was only after this time that the idea of a quartet coalesced into a reality.[12] All of the sons were prodigies who showed early talent, and the Romero Quartet flourished with the freedom and opportunity they found in the United States to pursue their distinctive musical vision.

The classical guitar was undergoing a sort of renascence during the sixties, thanks to Segovia and his followers, including John Williams and Oscar Ghiglia. This created a cultural environment receptive to the Romeros, who settled in Southern California because of their personal contacts there and because it reminded them of Spain. This became their base of worldwide operations as both performers and teachers.[13] In the 1970s, the Romeros developed a very close personal and professional relationship with Torroba: he dedicated the *Tonada concertante* to Celedonio, which was subsequently recorded by Ángel, while Pepe made the first-ever recording of *Diálogos entre guitarra y orquesta*. The *Concierto ibérico* was written expressly for the quartet.[14]

We are indeed fortunate to have Torroba's own commentary, taken from the program notes for the 1979 premiere in Madrid, to guide us in understanding this major composition. It appears from this that Torroba's attraction to the guitar quartet was that "four good guitars can give the sensation of a keyboard."[15] For reasons already mentioned, the fourfold multiplication of the instrument gave it a better than fighting chance against the orchestra, putting it on an equal footing with the piano or violin. And that is no small matter here, because Torroba ups the orchestral ante by employing a full-size ensemble: piccolo, 2 flutes, oboe, 2 B-flat clarinets, two bassoons, two F horns, timpani, assorted percussion, vibraphone, xylophone, harp, and strings.

The concerto itself is in three movements. In Torroba's own words:

> The initial measures of the *Concierto ibérico* constitute an expository preamble in the orchestra and each one of the four guitars, which achieve a sort of serenity in presenting the principal theme, imitative in

---

[12] For insights into this period in the Romero family's history, see Walter Aaron Clark, "The Romeros: Living Legacy of the Spanish Guitar. An Interview with Celín Romero," *Soundboard Magazine: The Journal of the Guitar Foundation of America* 36/2 (2010): 60–64. At one point, the family had to sell Celín's bicycle just to be able to buy bread.

[13] Celedonio taught privately, while Pepe has been on the faculty at the University of Southern California for many years; he also taught at the University of California, San Diego. Celín also taught at UCSD as well as San Diego State University. Among the Romeros' foremost students was Christopher Parkening in the 1960s and, much later, from the 1980s onward, members of the Los Angeles Guitar Quartet, especially William Kanengiser and Scott Tennant. The names of Krause and Clark also appear in the annals of Romero pedagogy (the former at USC, the latter at UCSD), but without distinction.

[14] The Romeros recorded both works on Philips LP 9500749, 1980. There is a wealth of correspondence from Torroba in the Romero family's archive, pertaining mostly to the genesis and performances of his concertos.

[15] Quoted in otherwise anonymous program notes of the Orquesta Nacional de España in Madrid, November 1979.

Ex. III:iii:11: *Concierto ibérico*, 1st mvmt., mm. 1–10

conception and continuing in a classical [sonata] form, with a free development and modulatory instability. The second movement, "Andante," presents a transparent theme. This is soon interrupted by a recitative, which, though distant sounding, nonetheless possesses an Andalusian quality. A concise, picturesque motive pervades the third movement with the intrusion, three quarters of the way through, of a melody inspired by a northern theme, entrusted to a division of the strings that picks up the first guitar, then drawing in the principal theme, ornamented with variations and interrupted by a very virtuosic cadenza in the first guitar.[16] Twenty or so optimistic measures bring the concerto to a close.

We note that the concerto begins with some unusually dissonant orchestral declamations, another nod on the composer's part in the direction of the avant-garde (see ex. III:iii:11). They remind one very much of Carl Orff's description of his own use of dissonance as "klanglisches Reizmittel," or sound spice. Schoenberg sought to liberate dissonance by making it so pervasive in a work that the distinction between it and consonance broke down, i.e., dissonance would become the norm. But for essentially tonal composers like Orff and Torroba, dissonance was a kind of salsa, used to spice things up but never to subvert or even seriously challenge the tonal order of their musical language. The tonal center on A in this movement is never in serious doubt, and the *seguidilla* rhythms and strumming of guitars (or simulated *rasgueo* in the orchestra) establish early on the Iberian imprimatur of this work.

Especially idyllic is the principal theme of the middle movement (see ex. III:iii:12). Torroba was never one for making grand pronouncements about the meaning or import of this or that piece or melody, but we sense here again something intimate and very personal. It is yet further evidence, if such were needed, of his melodic inspiration, which would always trump any superficial concessions to modernism at this stage in his output. This movement presents a kind of wistful reverie reminiscent of the slow movement in *Diálogos* (though the ABA structure features a contrasting theme, marked Allegro moderato, in the B section). What makes this melody special is the artfully imitative way that Torroba has set it in the quartet, over sustained harmonies among *divisi* strings.

The third movement, in A major and marked Allegro moderato, commences with trills in the strings and percussive interjections from the timpani and xylophone that create an introductory sense of anticipation. The quartet is soon busy

---

[16] As was the case in *Diálogos*, Torroba's original cadenza was modified by the Romeros. Walter Clark interview with Pepe Romero, September 2, 2011.

Ex. III:iii:12: Concierto ibérico, 2nd mvmt., mm. 1–8

Ex. III:iii:13: Concierto ibérico, 3rd mvmt., rehearsal 12

Ex. III:iii:13: *Continued*

plucking a lively theme in duple meter. As the composer indicated, a "northern" theme appears (at rehearsal 12); precisely what makes it "northern" is not immediately clear, except perhaps for its complete absence of *andalucismo* in modality and rhythm. According to Pepe Romero, it was inspired by a Basque folk tune.[17] Presented in the quartet, it is supported by *tremolandi* strings (see ex. III:iii:13).

[17] Interview with Walter Clark, September 2, 2011.

This lento section provides a particularly effective touch in that it provides a welcome moment of nostalgia and reflection amid the otherwise effervescently "notey" rhythms.

The coda playfully tweaks the avant-garde nose with its harp glissandi, pointillistic percussive effects, and incongruously dissonant chords before a rousing *rasgueo* finish in true Iberian fashion. In fact, in his late works, Torroba inserted such experimental flourishes as a deliberate nod in the direction of the modernists, as if to say, "Here, you see, I could compose this way, if I wanted to!"[18]

Torroba had one more concerto in him, for piano, but that has not maintained any place in the repertoire, despite the high hopes he held for it. It really is with the *Concierto ibérico* that his career as a composer of instrumental music came to its successful conclusion. And this concert-hall success, in tandem with his renown as a *zarzuelero*, is what makes his legacy completely unique among Spanish composers.

---

[18] This is according to Pepe Romero, in the same September 2, 2011, interview cited above. The opening dissonant chords of *Diálogos* serve the same irreverent function.

FINALE
The Legacy of Torroba

Torroba died fifty years after the premiere of *Luisa Fernanda*, the work on which his reputation as a zarzuela composer principally rests. Eighty years after its premiere, it is still regularly produced, in Spain and abroad; in addition, there are several recordings of it, as well as a DVD featuring Plácido Domingo, Jr., as Vidal (Opus Arte ES0969D, 2006). If this were all he had accomplished, he would still occupy an important place in the history of Spanish music. But it was not only far from being his single contribution, it was perhaps not even his best work—in his own opinion, if not the public's. We believe that there are at least ten of his stage works that merit a continued place in the repertoire; in addition to *Luisa Fernanda*, these include *La marchenera, La chulapona, Azabache, Xuanón, Monte Carmelo, La Caramba, Polonesa, Maravilla,* and *María Manuela.* No doubt there are other gems among his dozens of zarzuelas, but in the absence of recordings and published scores, that is difficult to assess. Is there a public for these other works? A limited one, to be sure, but definitely enough to fill theaters, if the productions were well handled. And the public really is key. Given Spain's recent economic difficulties, it is hard to imagine that the additional government support Torroba consistently demanded will materialize anytime soon.

However, Torroba's zarzuelas will fare only as well as the genre itself does. So, what of the zarzuela today? It is far from dead, and in fact, with regular productions at various theaters in Madrid, especially the Teatro de la Zarzuela, and the increasing publication efforts of the Instituto Complutense de Ciencias Musicales (ICCMU) in Madrid, the future looks reasonably bright for the genre. A trip to the recordings section of El Corte Inglés, the huge department store on the Puerta del Sol (near Torroba's birthplace), will reveal an entire row devoted to zarzuela, including numerous DVDs. This is a good sign. Christopher Webber aptly sums up the current situation:

Although many older Spaniards in particular still take enormous pride in zarzuela, it no longer has the social or cultural dynamism of a contemporary art form; indeed, the Forty Plus generation tend to use zarzuela as a pejorative adjective implying "old-fashioned" or "establishment." Their offspring have no such reservations, and the Teatro de la Zarzuela's work with schoolchildren helps foster knowledge of their musical heritage in an energetic and practical way [as Torroba predicted it would]. Madrid may never again have thirty theatres playing zarzuela on any given night, as it did in the early 1900s; but there's no sense of a conservative tradition being preserved in aspic, here or in the rest of the country.[1]

Thus, it seems safe to say that the future of Torroba's stage works is assured, and may grow brighter with time.

What about the guitar music? In 1980, Graham Wade reported that "Torroba's music fell from favour among many recitalists in the 1970's, though in the twenty years before this, his work was an integral part of the aspirant's repertoire."[2] That may well have been the case then, at the high-water mark of the postwar avant-garde, but times have changed in Torroba's favor. In his estimation, "The compositions of Torroba are undemanding on the listener, very rhythmic, concise, with imaginative titles, and closely linked with the dances of Spanish folk music though without being too dependent on flamenco motifs."[3] Although there is a faint whiff of criticism here, it is these very qualities that endear his music to most concert audiences. The swelling number of excellent recordings of his guitar music now available, including by such artists as the Romeros, David Russell, Maximilian Mangold, and Ana Vidovic,[4] demonstrates that Torroba's approach to writing for the guitar has found lasting favor with performers and audiences alike, even after the departure of his great champion, Segovia.

Comparing Torroba with his fellow *zarzueleros*, it is clear that he inherited and brought to great heights a very rich heritage of Spanish musical theater, including not only the *géneros chico* and *grande* but also *revista* and opera. And it is equally clear that his luminous output represented the beautiful sunset, rather than sunrise, of that tradition. But there is one thing that separates Torroba from every other zarzuela composer, from Barbieri through Chapí, Chueca, Bretón, Caballero, Giménez, Serrano, Vives, and Sorozábal: he alone gained a permanent footing in the concert hall as well as the theater. It is not true that these other composers never wrote works for orchestra or chamber ensemble or soloists. But it is hard even for a specialist to point to a single such work that remains in the standard repertoire. Not one.[5] And the reverse is also

---

[1] Webber, *Zarzuela*, 8.

[2] Graham Wade, *The Traditions of the Classical Guitar* (London: Calder, 1980), 154.

[3] Ibid., 153.

[4] For example, *Music of Moreno Torroba*, David Russell, guitar, Telarc CD-80451, 1996; *Federico Moreno Torroba (1891–1982), Guitar Music*, vol. 1, Ana Vidovic, guitar, Naxos 8.557902, 2007. We cited Mangold's album earlier.

[5] And there may well be good reasons for this neglect. For instance, on November 7, 1890, during his London years, Albéniz organized a concert at St. James's Hall that featured orchestral works by Chapí and Bretón, conducted by the latter. On the program were Bretón's own Second Symphony in E-flat and his serenade *En la Alhambra*, as well as Chapí's "Moorish fantasy" *La corte de Granada*. George

true, i.e., that of all the great Spanish composers of instrumental music, from Albéniz through Sarasate, Tárrega, Granados, Falla, Turina, Mompou, Rodrigo, and Pablo, not one composed a zarzuela that takes its place alongside even Torroba's less-celebrated works.

Thus, in assessing Torroba's legacy, this is the most salient fact: he scaled these two quite different mountain peaks, when his best contemporaries found it impossible to ascend more than one. In the final analysis, writing a great zarzuela requires a different skill set from writing a solo suite, a concerto or even a ballet. Torroba exhibited the ingenuity and versatility to survive and thrive in both arenas, and to remain relevant, popular, and innovative for six decades. His sheer longevity, the persistence of his creative imagination over such a long period of time, puts him in an elite class of composers, such as Monteverdi and Verdi—or Rodrigo. And even a casual glance at his works list will reveal that his output was far more varied and prodigious than those familiar only with his stage and guitar works would dare imagine. His oeuvre entices attention not only from musicologists but also from singers, pianists, guitarists, orchestral and choral conductors. There are many opportunities for the revival of numerous works of interest.

How did he do it? Aside from remaining healthy into old age, the main reason for his musical fecundity would seem to be that he early on developed a very clear idea of what he was about as a composer, the type of music he wanted to write, and how that music should be written. And he never strayed very far from those early principles. He knew what he was, what he stood for, and he remained comfortable with himself to the end. He did not go through a tortuous stylistic evolution full of perpetual experimentation and radical changes of course. He never once ceased believing in the desirability of writing music firmly rooted in national traditions, i.e., the variegated Spanish soundscape that he loved so much.

Indeed, as we meditate on Torroba's unflagging devotion to Spain's music, the word *love* keeps coming to mind, reminding us of a favorite Shakespeare sonnet: "...love is not love which alters when it alteration findes, or bends with the remover to remove. O no, it is an ever fixed marke, that lookes on tempests and is never shaken; it is the star to every wandering barke, whose worths unknowne, although his higth be taken."[6] Whether there really is an "eternal tradition" in Spanish culture or anywhere else hardly matters. Torroba believed there was such a thing, that it was nearly sacred, and he hewed to it throughout his career. This tradition—as he understood it, at least—informed everything he did. If a com-

---

Bernard Shaw (*World*, November 12) railed at the "procrustean torturings" of the "ingeniously horrible" symphony by Bretón, while other critics savaged Chapí's offerings thus: "barbaric, long-drawn-out, and flimsy" (*Figaro*, November 8); "cheap, trashy noise" (*Pall Mall Gazette*, November 8); and "sheer tea-garden blatancy" (*Daily Graphic*, November 10). Albéniz's own works were received more warmly. See Clark, *Albéniz*, 78–79, for more on this affair. One hastens to add that these reviews were far from fair or accurate, and in fact, several zarzuelists, including Barbieri and Bretón, wrote beautiful sacred music.

  [6] Sonnet 116, in *The Royal Shakespeare Theatre Edition of The Sonnets of William Shakespeare* (New York: Paddington Press, 1974).

poser wants to remain productive over a long period of time, it is hard to overstate the value of such an attitude in achieving that goal. It imparts both creative inspiration and consistency to a composer's output, by eliminating self-doubt and fruitless detours. This is not to say that such an approach is the only way, or even the best way. For one thing, it makes it more difficult to adapt to changing tastes and fashions, thus posing the risk of irrelevance and obscurity. It is certainly not the route that many of history's greatest composers followed. But it was Torroba's way, and by almost any measurement or standard of success, it worked for him. As Enrique Franco aptly noted, Torroba "knew how to be what he was, and not an imitation of someone else." Thirty years after his death, his brand is still going strong. And as Torroba himself observed, "time is the master who tells the truth."[7] We have tried to convey that truth in this book, and in our view, it validates what Torroba did and how he did it.

Yet, a legacy such as his has only as much value as people attach to it, and that requires continued promotion. Torroba was fortunate to have an immensely talented and energetic son to carry on the family business, so to speak. Federico Moreno-Torroba Larregla has had a distinguished career in his own right. From his father, he learned orchestration, composition, and conducting; he also pursued private studies in solfège, piano, harmony, and counterpoint, all with Ángel Arias. For years he specialized in popular music and *revistas*, but at age 50 he dedicated himself to making recordings, as well as deepening his knowledge of symphonic music and zarzuela. Displaying his father's entrepreneurial spirit, he established a music-publishing group dedicated to controlling the promotion of his own compositions and those of his father.

Since 1960, he has regularly traveled to the United States, conducting and teaching, particularly in Southern California, where his connections with the Romero family have proven useful. In the 1990s, he was named a professor of music at Grossmont College in San Diego, and he established the San Diego Lyric Association, composed mainly of American performers. He trained them to speak and sing in Spanish well enough to stage *Luisa Fernanda*, which the Spanish press found to be "something incredible!"[8] In addition, he has received critical acclaim for conducting stints in Los Angeles and Miami; in the latter, in 1991, he received the Golden Key to the City from the mayor and was appointed to the Order of Gonzalo Roig.

Of course, he has remained active as a conductor in Spain. He formed the zarzuela group "Moreno-Torroba Lyric Company," which toured throughout the country to enthusiastic notices. In 1999, he revised *Luisa Fernanda* for a production at the Teatro de la Zarzuela; his critical edition of that score was published in 2011 by ICCMU (he has also published a critical edition of *La chulapona*). From 1996 to 2005, his own company collaborated with the Compañía MusiArte in

---

[7] Franco, *La Chulapona*, program notes, 1988, 13. Torroba is quoted on p. 15.

[8] María Elena Saavedra, "Moreno Torroba honra a su padre con la dirección de dos zarzuelas," *Diario Las Americas*, February 2, 1991, 8-A.

presenting a variety of classic zarzuelas, which he reorchestrated. However, he is not confined to lyric theater, and in 1995 he conducted a chamber orchestra in performances of Haydn's *Seven Last Words of Christ* in various locales in Spain (the work was originally commissioned by and composed for Cádiz).

At the same time, he has remained productive as a composer. His works include *Rapsodias españolas nos. 1 and 2* for orchestra, two *Villancicos sinfónicos*, and a *Concierto para 5 saxofones y orquesta*. All of these very original creations premiered at leading venues in the capital city. And he has recently composed a piano concerto entitled *Cuatro piezas para piano y orquesta*. As a champion of the zarzuela and as a creative artist, Federico, Jr., has done all a person could do to perpetuate his father's work.

Considering the enormity of Torroba's contributions to cultural administration in his homeland, in addition to everything else he did, it may seem petty to point out the one area in which he made no mark whatsoever: teaching. For whatever reason, he never showed much interest in pedagogy, though he could have joined the faculty of almost any conservatory in Spain, had he wished. An anecdote told by his son suggests that he may not have had the right temperament for the job. On one occasion, someone presented him with a composition to get his advice. "Maestro," he said, "I have only worked on this for a few months." "It shows!" was the master's laconic reply.[9] One suspects that Torroba was in almost every respect a natural musician; explaining to others how to do what came instinctively to him was no doubt tedious beyond his ability to endure.

We have asserted several times in this story what Torroba said of himself: that his principal strength as a composer was as a tunesmith, a crafter of unforgettable melodies. Writing a beautiful melody is a skill very much undervalued in an age when many serious composers disdain this ancient art. Yet, writing a hit melody is much more difficult than the melody itself may lead one to believe, precisely because a successful melody sounds completely natural and logical, as if it sprang into existence fully formed and required no effort to conceive. Fernando Sor shed useful light on a parallel aspect of instrumental technique: "I have always preferred hearing it said of a performance, 'He appears to be doing nothing, that appears so easy'; than to hear it said, 'Oh! How difficult that must be! for he appears to have given proofs of it.'"[10] In other words, good technique is transparent, and Torroba's compositional technique was at times nearly invisible, so natural did he make it seem. It is hard enough to write a single effective melody; to compose hundreds of them, as Torroba did, is a truly remarkable accomplishment.[11]

---

[9] According to Federico, Jr., in a 2007 interview with William Krause.

[10] Fernando Sor, *Method for the Spanish Guitar*, trans. from the original 1830 French edition by Arnold Merrick (New York: Da Capo Press, 1980), 32. Cited in Clark, "Fernando Sor's Guitar Studies, Lessons, and Exercises," 362–63.

[11] Ángel Romero notes Torroba's "exquisite rhythmic and harmonic sense," which was always indispensable in crafting his melodies. Interview with Walter Clark, September 20, 2011.

Ex. Finale.1 *Maravilla*, Act III, no. 12, "Amor, vida de mi vida," mm. 17–26

After all that we have read and written about this great maestro, we believe we have earned the right to close by choosing a melody not yet discussed but that we feel stands out as one of his greatest, which is why we have saved it for last. It is Rafael's celebrated *romanza* (Act III, no. 12) from *Maravilla*, a zarzuela of 1941. Though the work is rarely staged anymore, "Amor, vida de mi vida" (Love, life of my life) is standard repertoire in zarzuela "anthologies" (see ex. Finale.1). In it, Rafael sings of love and loss: "You said goodbye; my life departed."

If we could save only one melody by Torroba from the proverbial burning house, this might be it. Finely crafted, passionate, and eminently memorable, this number would stand for all time as proof positive that Torroba was among the master melodists of his epoch. In a world fraught with man's inhumanity to man, which Torroba observed firsthand, this music serves as an antidote for the grim realities all around us. That is a legacy worth preserving.

Maravilla is set in the early 1900s and tells the story of a zarzuela soprano who has returned from South America after a long and illustrious career. She is alienated by the new way of life in Madrid and finds it difficult to adjust. Throughout the work are heard excerpts of famous zarzuelas in her repertory, wonderful music but no longer in vogue. In resignation, she finally learns to accept the fact that times have changed.[12]

Times indeed change, but the perennial popularity of Torroba's music does not. His compositions were inspired by the eternal tradition of Spanish culture, and they have now themselves become part of that ever-living heritage. As Pepe Romero put it, Federico Moreno Torroba was nothing more or less than the "soul of Madrid and Spain."[13] Few Spanish composers ever sought or achieved more.

[12] See Webber, Zarzuela, 182, for a pithy summary of the plot. The aging soprano, Manuela, is renowned as "The Marvel" (Maravilla), but the story's love interest centers on her daughter Emilia's relationship with Rafael, a baritone at the Teatro Real. He sings his famous aria in the mistaken belief that Emilia has rejected him.

[13] In a conversation with Walter Clark, January 6, 2011.

Appendix 1

CHRONOLOGY

Year	Torroba's Life	Spanish Music	Spanish History
1891	Born March 3 in Madrid; early education at Santo Ángel de la Guarda and Escolapios de San Antón	Premiere of Barbieri's final zarzuela, *El señor Luis el tumbón*; Albéniz concertizing and composing in London; Granados performing and composing in Barcelona; Pedrell composes the opera *Els Pirineus*	Relatively tranquil period, though there is economic stagnation in rural areas, along with growing politicization of the working class and rise of anarchism; founding of Madrid journal *Blanco y Negro*
1893		Segovia born in Linares; Frederic Mompou born in Barcelona	
1894		Premiere of Bretón's zarzuela *La verbena de la paloma* and Albéniz's zarzuela *San Antonio de la Florida* in Madrid	

Year	Torroba's Life	Spanish Music	Spanish History
1895		Premiere of Albéniz's opera *Henry Clifford* in Barcelona	Publication of Miguel de Unamuno's *En torno al casticismo*; beginning of the war in Cuba
1896		Premiere of Albéniz's *Pepita Jiménez* in Barcelona; Roberto Gerhard born in Barcelona; Regino Sainz de la Maza born in Burgos; Roberto Gerhard born in Valls	First cinema program shown in Madrid and Barcelona
1897		Albéniz composes *La vega*, and his opera *Pepita Jiménez* is produced in Prague	Assassination of Prime Minister Antonio Cánovas del Castillo
1898		Premiere of Granados's opera *María del Carmen* and of Caballero's zarzuela *Gigantes y cabezudos*	Spain defeated in war with United States, loses Cuba, Puerto Rico, Philippines, Wake Island, and Guam
1899		Albéniz composes *Catalonia* for orchestra; Tárrega composes *Recuerdos de la Alhambra* for guitar	
1902	Studies at Real Conservatorio and Liceo Francés		Alfonso XIII ascends to the throne
1905		Turina arrives in Paris; Albéniz's *San Antonio de la Florida* and *Pepita Jiménez* produced in Brussels	

Year	Torroba's Life	Spanish Music	Spanish History
1906			Alfonso XIII marries Victoria Eugenia, granddaughter of Queen Victoria; anarchist plot to assassinate king fails
1907		Falla arrives in Paris	Picasso paints *Les Demoiselles d'Avignon*, initiating cubism
1908		Premiere of Albéniz's piano collection *Iberia*	
1909		Deaths of Albéniz and Tárrega	"Semana Trágica" in Barcelona in July
1911		Premiere of Granados's piano suite *Goyescas*	
1912	Premiere of his first stage work, *Las decididas*; drafted into Spanish army		
1913		Premiere of Falla's opera *La vida breve*, in Nice; Celedonio Romero born in Cienfuegos, Cuba	
1914		With outbreak of World War I, Turina and Falla leave Paris and return to Spain	Spain declares neutrality in First World War, and the public's sympathies are divided; Gaudí creates Parque Güell in Barcelona
1915	Enters army reserves until 1930; performs in Madrid premiere of *El amor brujo*	Falla's ballet *El amor brujo* premieres at Teatro Lara in Madrid	

Year	Torroba's Life	Spanish Music	Spanish History
1916	Studies composition privately with Conrado del Campo	Premiere of Falla's *Noches en los jardines de España*; premiere of Granados's opera *Goyescas* at the Met in New York; death of Granados	
1917			Political crisis arises from general strikes
1919		Premiere of Falla's *El sombrero de tres picos* in London	
1918–20	Premiere of symphonic works *La ajorca de oro* (1918) and *Cuadros* (1919)		"Three Years of Bolshevism" (1918–20), unrest in Barcelona and Andalusia
1920	Begins collaboration with Andrés Segovia, composing *Danza*	Falla's *Hommage, pour le Tombeau de Claude Debussy* for guitar	
1921			Military disaster in Morocco; publication of Ortega y Gasset's *La España invertebrada*; founding of Spanish Communist Party
1922		Concurso de Cante Jondo in Granada	
1923	*Sonatina* composed for Segovia	Death of Felipe Pedrell; premiere of Amadeo Vives's *Doña Francisquita*	Military coup brings General Miguel Primo de Rivera to power

Year	Torroba's Life	Spanish Music	Spanish History
1925	Opera *La virgen de mayo* premieres at Teatro Real; premieres of zarzuelas *La mesonera de Tordesillas* and *La caravana de ambrosio*; Torroba and Pablo Luna given control of Teatro de la Zarzuela by Primo de Rivera; establishment of Teatro Lírico Nacional	Teatro Real closes	
1926–27	Marries María del Pilar Larregla y Nogueras, daughter of Navarrese composer Joaquín Larregla, in 1926; premiere of *La pastorela*; publication of *Suite castellana* and other guitar music in Segovia's Schott series, as well as first recordings of his guitar music, played by Segovia on His Master's Voice	Turina composes *Sevillana* and *Fandanguillo* for guitar; Juan Hidalgo born in Canary Islands (1927)	
1928	Premiere of *La marchenera*; daughter Mariana born		
1929	*Piezas características* for guitar published; composition and premiere of *Madroños*	Ramón Barce born	

Year	Torroba's Life	Spanish Music	Spanish History
1930	Given control of Teatro Calderón by Duque del Infantado	Grupo de los Ocho formed in Madrid; Luis de Pablo born	Fall of Primo de Rivera's regime
1931		Junta Nacional de Música y Teatro Lírico established	Alfonso XIII abdicates; Second Republic declared
1932	Premieres of *Luisa Fernanda* and *Azabache*	Death of Amadeo Vives	
1933	Premiere of *Xuanón*; son Federico, Jr., born		Right wing wins national election; establishment of Falange Española, the Spanish fascist party, by José Antonio Primo de Rivera; right-wing Catholic party Confederatión Española de Derechas Autónomas (CEDA) founded
1934	Premiere of zarzuela *La chulapona*; *Luisa Fernanda* produced at Teatro Colón in Buenos Aires, with Torroba conducting		Revolutionary uprising in Asturias put down by Republican forces under command of General Francisco Franco

Year	Torroba's Life	Spanish Music	Spanish History
1935	Appointed to Junta Nacional de Música y Teatros Líricos y Dramáticos; formally installed as member of the Real Academia de Bellas Artes de San Fernando		
1936		Premiere of Sorozábal's *La tabernera del puerto*; Celín Romero born in Málaga	Outbreak of Spanish Civil War in July; Franco is named General-in-Chief and Chief of State in the Nationalist zone; death of Unamuno
1937			Fall of Málaga and Bilbao to Franco; bombing of Guernica by Germans
1938	Flees Madrid for Navarra; zarzuelas *Sor Navarra* and *Tú eres ella* premiere in San Sebastián, and *Pepinillo y Garbancito en la isla misteriosa* premieres in Zaragoza		Republic cut in two; wartime press law establishes strict censorship in Franco-held territory
1939	Zarzuela *El maleficio* premieres in San Sebastián; he returns to Madrid; *Monte Carmelo* produced in Madrid and later Barcelona, but censors block further productions	Rodrigo composes his *Concierto de Aranjuez* for guitar and orchestra in Paris; premieres following year in Barcelona	End of Civil War on April 1 and beginning of General Francisco Franco's dictatorship; Franco declares Spain's neutrality in World War II

Year	Torroba's Life	Spanish Music	Spanish History
1940	Death of his mother, Rosa	Age of the *canción ligera* and "culture of evasion"	
1941–43	Premieres of zarzuelas *Maravilla* (1941), *La Caramba* (1942), and *La ilustre moza* (1943)	Tomás Marco born in Madrid (1942)	
1944	Premiere of zarzuela *Polonesa*	Pepe Romero born in Málaga	
1946	Premiere of zarzuela *El duende azul* (1946), a collaboration with Rodrigo; tours Latin America with his zarzuela troupe (1946–48)	Ángel Romero born in Málaga; death of Falla	Spain, an international pariah, not admitted to United Nations
1947	*El orgullo de Jalisco* composed and premiered in Mexico City		Spain denied assistance under Marshall Plan
1949		Death of Turina	Spain excluded from NATO
1950	Makes first of several subsequent visits to United States		Reemergence of separatist movements, especially in Basque country; diplomatic relations with United States restored
1951		So-called Generation of 51 launches Spanish postwar avant-garde, led by Luis de Pablo	

Year	Torroba's Life	Spanish Music	Spanish History
1952		Founding of Juventudes Musicales in Madrid	
1953		Death of Campo	Concordat signed with Vatican; bilateral pact with United States
1954	Premiere of zarzuela *¡Bienvenido Mr. Dólar!*		
1955		Spain readmitted to the International Society for Contemporary Music	United States formally recognizes Franco regime
1956	Death of his father, José	I Concurso de Cante Jondo de Córdoba	
1957	Premiere of zarzuela *María Manuela*	Romero family of guitarists flees Spain and resettles in United States	
1958		Grupo Nueva Música performs at Real Conservatorio	Death of Adolfo Salazar
1959			Eisenhower visits Spain; economic stabilization plan announced; Basque separatist group ETA (Euskadi ta Askatasuna) founded
1960	*Concierto de Castilla* for guitar and orchestra premiered	Festival de Música Joven Española organized by Luis de Pablo in Madrid; Festival Música Abierta organized by Juan Hidalgo in Barcelona, features John Cage and David Tudor	Gradual economic expansion due to policies initiated by Franco's Opus Dei technocrats

Year	Torroba's Life	Spanish Music	Spanish History
1963			Death of Carmen Amaya
1964	Premiere of ballet *Don Quixote* in Madrid	Festival of Music of the Americas and Spain in Madrid; Ramón Barce forms new-music group *Zaj*	
1965	Ballet *El convite* premiered in Rome		Death of Guillermo Fernández Shaw
1966	Premiere of his final zarzuela, *Ella*		Press Law relaxes censorship
1969			Franco designates Juan Carlos de Borbón his successor
1970	*Castillos de España* I for guitar published; *Don Quixote* produced in Helsinki	Death of Gerhard	
1974	Becomes president of the Sociedad General de Autores de España (SGAE)		
1975	*Homenaje a la seguidilla* for guitar and orchestra premiered in Buenos Aires; ballet *El hijo pródigo* premiered in Rome	Paco de Lucia records his innovative *Entre dos aguas*	Franco dies; Juan Carlos I declared king; lifting of moral and political censorship
1976	*Las puertas de Madrid* for guitar published; *Concierto ibérico* premiered in Vancouver		Death of Federico Romero

Year	Torroba's Life	Spanish Music	Spanish History
1977	Death of his wife, Pilar; *Diálogos entre guitarra y orquesta* premiered in Edmonton, Canada		Censorship officially abolished; first general elections since 1936 held
1978	*Castillos de España* II published; elected director of the Real Academia de Bellas Artes de San Fernando		Constitutional referendum passed
1979			Basque Autonomous Community established
1980	Premiere of opera *El poeta*, starring Plácido Domingo; receives Medalla de Oro de las Bellas Artes from King and Queen		
1981		Antonio Gades and Carlos Saura collaborate on film version of *Bodas de sangre*, first of a trilogy that will include *Carmen* and *El amor brujo*; death of Sainz de la Maza	Adolfo Suárez resigns as prime minister; attempted *golpe de estado* by Guardia Civil quashed by the king
1982	Revival of *Don Quixote* at Teatro de la Zarzuela; death on September 12		First Socialist government elected since Second Republic; Felipe González prime minister

Appendix 2

WORKS LIST

Abbreviations

Bn: Biblioteca Nacional

Lc: Library of Congress, Washington, DC

Ma: Family archive in Madrid

Na: Family archive in Navarra

Ra: Romero family archive in San Diego, California

SGAE: Sociedad General de Autores de España (Sociedad General de Autores y Editores)

UME: Unión Musical Española

Works are organized first by genre, then chronologically. Each listing provides as much of the following information as is available: title (subtitle) (other composers); acts:scenes; librettist(s); date of comp.; venue/date of prem.; publisher, year of publication; location of ms. Unless otherwise indicated, all premiere venues are in Madrid, and all available mss. are located at the SGAE in Madrid, which holds the copyright.

Stage

BALLET WITH ORCHESTRA

Mosaico sevillano; 1954 (piano vers.); UME, ? (piano vers.); Na

Fantasia de Levante (for José Greco); 1; 1957; Ediciones Musicales (Madrid), 1957; Bn
Te voy a contar un cuento; 16; c. 1965–75; np; Na

El Convite (for Luis Pérez Davila, "Luisillo"), Pomezio (Italy), 25-X-65 (Sala Clementina, Vatican, 1965)

Cristo luz del mundo, also known as *El hijo pródigo* (for Luis Pérez Davila, "Luisillo"), Basilica de Masensio, Rome, 6-IX-75

Los novios (for Luis Pérez Davila, "Luisillo"); 1979 or before; 26-XI-79; np

El embrujo torero (see *El torero, su soledad y su destino*)

El torero, su soledad y su destino, also known as *El embrujo torero* (for Luis Pérez
   Davila, "Luisillo"), Madrid, 1957

Por favor, ¿que ho res? (for Luis Pérez Davila, "Luisillo"), Madrid

El hijo pródigo (see *Cristo luz del mundo*)

BALLET WITH CHORUS

Aventuras y desaventuras de Don Quijote (for Luis Pérez Davila, "Luisillo"); 7; Teatro
   de la Zarzuela, 4-XI-64 (revised as *Don Quijote* and performed Suomen
   Kansallisooppera (Helsinki), 10-X-70; revived Teatro de la Zarzuela, 11-X-
   82); Cantabrian, 1982; Ma

BALLET WITH HARP AND PERCUSSION

Ensueño gitano: Romance de la carne gitana (for Rafael de Córdoba); 1; on poem by
   Julián Cortés-Cavanillas; 1977 or before; 16-XI-77; Jacobo, 1977?; Ma

OPERA

La virgen de mayo; 1; P. Max & F. Luque; 1925; Teatro Real, 14-II-25; UME (vs),
   1925 (Bulerías, Plegaria, Raconto, Duo)

Bromas y veras de Andalucía; 1; ("chamber opera") Rafael Gil; 1956; Ateneo
   Madrileño, 29-IV-56

El poeta; 4; J. Méndez Herrera; 1977-80; Teatro de la Zarzuela, 19-VI-80; Bn

ZARZUELA (AND RELATED GENRES)

Las decididas ("fantasia lírica") (with Jose Moreno Ballesteros) 1:2; T.R.
   Alenza;1912; Teatro Lara, 27-V-12; Velasco, Madrid, 1912

Como los ojos de mi morena; sainete lírico; various libretists; 1919 or before; Teatro
   Apolo, 4-VI-1919

Las fuerzas ocultas; 1; A. Plañiols; 1920 or before; La Latina, 15-VI-20

Cuidado con la pintura, 1, A. Plañiols, A.; 1920, Club Hispania (Sevilla), 21-VII-20

Artistas para fin de fiesta; 1?; R. González del Toro, M. Minura; Lara, 28-XII-20

La mujer de nieve; 2; E. Rosillo; 1923 Teatro Cómico; 8-XII-23

La caravana de ambrosio; 1; García Álvarez; 1925 or before; Teatro de la Zarzuela,
   11-V-25

La mesonera de Tordesillas; 3; R. Sepulveda, J. Manzano; 1925 or before; Teatro de
   la Zarzuela, 30-X-25

La vuelta; 1; F. Luque; 1925; Teatro de la Zarzuela, 10-VI-25; Gráfica Literaria,
   Madrid, 1925

Intriga de amor; 2; F. Luque, A. Plañiols; before 1925; Teatro Tívoli (Barcelona),
   1925

La Mari-blanca; 2; R. González de Toro, R. Hernández Bermúdez; 1926 or before;
   Teatro de la Zarzuela, 9-III-26; Velasco, Madrid, 1926

Colasin, el chico de la cola (referred to as "sainete" in *El Sol* review); 1; Calonge;
   Sepulveda; 1926 or before; Teatro Novedades, 6-V-26; Velasco, 1926

Las musas del Trianon (with Pablo Luna); 3; F. García Pacheco, J. Ramos Martín; 1926 or before; Teatro de la Zarzuela, 20-X-26; Ediciones Harmonia, 1927

La pastorela (with Pablo Luna); 3; F. Luque; 1926 or before; Teatro Novedades, 10-XI-26

Como los ojos de mi morena (with Pablo Luna) 1; F. S. Casares; Teatro de Apolo, 4-VI-27

El fumadero (with Pablo Luna); 1; F. Luque, F. Torres; 1927 or before; Teatro Martín, 7-XII-27

La manola del portillo (with Pablo Luna); 3; E. Carrere, F. García Pacheco; before 1928; Teatro Pavón, 21-I-28

La marchenera; 3; F. Gonzalez del Toro, F. Luque; 1928 or before; Teatro de la Zarzuela, 7-IV-28 (new version, Auditorium de Melillia, 9-VII-68); UME, Casa Latina, 1928

El divo ("revista"); 3; R. González del Toro, A. Fernández Lepina; c1928

Cascabeles; 2; P. Llabrés y Egea, J. Tellaeche; ?; Teatro de Apolo, 20-XII-28

Mi mama política (with Pablo Luna); 1; F. Torres; before 1928; ?, 1928

Los guayabitos ("revista"); 2; R. González del Toro, F. Torres, R. Peña; 7-III-29, Teatro Martín, (Madrid)

El Mascot, pasatiempo grotesco en 1 *acto;* "No se llegó a estrenar en 1929 por prohibirlo la Dirección de Madrid" (SGAE)

María la tempranica (revision of *La tempranica* of Gerónimo Giménez); 1; J. Romea, R. González del Toro; 1930 or before; Teatro Calderón, 1-VI-30; Gráfica Literaria, Madrid, 1930

Baturra del temple; 2; V. Redondo del Castillo; 1930 or before; Teatro Calderón, 26-VIII-30

Una de caballeria; 1; F. Torres, R. González del Toro; 1930; 9-III-31, Teatro Martín

Luisa Fernanda; 3; F. Romero, G. Fernández-Shaw; 1932; Teatro Calderón, 26-III-32; UME, 1932

Azabache ("sainete lírico"); 3; A. Quintero, P. Guillén; 1932 or before; Teatro Calderón, 18-VIII-32; Estampa, 1932

La mujer de aquella noche; 3; M. Gongora, L. Mansano; 1932 or before; Teatro Lara, 14-IX-32; UME, 1932?

El aguaducho; 1; G. Fernández Shaw; 1932 or before; Teatro Cómico, 14-XII-32

Xuanón; 2; J. Ramos Martín; before 1933; Teatro Calderón, 2-III-33; UME, 1933

Por la salud de mi madre ("desparate cómico lírico"); 1; E. Marcen; before 1934; Teatro Victoria Eugenia (San Sebastián), 26-I-34

La chulapona ("comedia lírica"); 3; F. Romero, G. Fernández-Shaw; before 1934; Teatro Calderón, 31-III-34; UME (vs), 1934

Luces de verbena ("sainete") (music by Soutullo, completed by Torroba); 2; F. Serrano Anguita, J. Tellaeche Arrillaga; 1935 or before; Teatro Calderón, 2-V-35

Paloma Moreno; 3; F. Serrano Anguita, J. Tellaeche Arrillaga; 1935 or before; Teatro Colón (Buenos Aires), 7-XI-35

La boda del Señor Bringas; 3 ("sainete"); F. Ramos de Castro, A. C. Carreño; before 1936; Teatro Calderón, 2-V-36; Gráfica Literaria, Madrid, 1936

Sor Navarra; ?; L. Tejedor, L. Muñoz Llorente; 1938; Teatro Victoria Eugenia (San Sebastián), 7-XII-38

Pepinillo y Garbancito en la isla misteriosa ("cuento infantil"); 2; J. Miquelarena y Regueiro; 1938 or before; Teatro Argensola (Zaragoza), 1938

El retablo de Navidad (with Tomás Garbizu); 1938 or before; Jesús María Arozamena; Teatro Victoria Eugenia (San Sebastián), 31-I-38

Tú eres ella; 3; L. Tejedor, L. Muñoz Llorente; (possibly1938 or before; Teatro Victoria Eugenia, San Sebastián); Teatro Calderón, 26-IV-40

Oro de ley; 2; ("sainete") M. Merino, L. Cadela, M. Góngora; 1938; Teatro Circo (Zaragoza); 10-X-38

El maleficio; 3; A. Quintero; 1939 or before; Teatro Victoria Eugenia (San Sebastián), 30-IX-39

Monte Carmelo; 3; F. Romero, G. Fernández-Shaw; 1939; Teatro Calderón, 17-X-39; UME, ?

El que tenga un amor que lo cuide ("sainete"); 3; F. Ramos de Castro, A. Carreo; 1940 or before; Teatro Romea (Murcia), 16-XI-40

Nacimiento (retablo de Pascua) (with Cotarelo and Guridi); Coliseum 4-I-40

Maravilla ("comedia lírica"); 3; A. Quintero, J. M. Arozamena; before 1941; Teatro Fontalba, 12-IV-41

La Caramba; 3; Luis F. Ardavín; before 1942; Teatro de la Zarzuela, 10-IV-42; UME (vs), 1942

Una reja y dos pelmazos; 1; B. Prada, L. Clavo; 1942; Teatro Tívoli (Barcelona), 17-VII-42

Boda gitana; 3; P. Guillén; 1942 or before; Teatro Argentino (Buenos Aires), 31-VII-42

Despeherezada (with José Ballesteros); ?; A. Plañiols; 1942 or before; Teatro Fuencarral, 5-IX-42

La leyenda del castillo; M. Ortega y Lopo; Teatro Fuencarral, 5-IX-42

Un viaje a la fortuna (with Garbizu, Alonso, Guridi); M. Arozamena, J. M. Cavanillas; 31-XII-42; Colegio de Areneros (Madrid)

La luna nueva; 3; A. Plañiols; c. 1942

La ilustre moza; 3; L. Tejedor, L. Muñoz Lorente; before 1943; Teatro Tívoli (Barcelona), 3-III-43

Ayer y hoy; 1; L. Calvo, A. Palacios; 1943 or before; Barcelona, 1-X-33

Pizpireta ("comedia lírica"); 1; A. Cuyas de la Vega; c. 1943

Una noche en Aravaca ("estampa lírica"); 2; A. Cuyas de la Vega; c. 1943

Polonesa; 3; J. M. Arozamena, R. Torrado; before 1944; Teatro Fontalba, 27-I-44; UME, 1944

La niña del cuento ("sainete lírico"); 2; F. Ramos de Castro, A. Carreño; before 1944; Teatro Fontalba, 20-V-44

Baile de trajes; 2; Luis F. Ardavín; 1945 or before; Teatro de la Zarzuela, 6-IV-45

¿Usted gusta? ("lírica dramática") (with A. J. Vela); 2; P. Llabrés y Egea, F. Prada Blasco, F. Vázquez Ochando; 1945; Rojas (Toledo), 3-XI-45

Soy el amo ("sainete"); 1; P. Llabrés y Egea; 1945 or before; Teatro Principal (Zaragoza), 12-IV-45

Lolita Dolores; 3; A. Cuyas de Vega, J. Vega Lástima; 1946 or before; Teatro Calderón, 20-IV-46; UME, 1952

El duende azul (with Joaquín Rodrigo); 2; M. Castell, R. Villaseca Mendiolagoitia; before 1946; Teatro Calderón, 22-V-46

El orgullo de Jalisco; 3; ?; 1947; Teatro Arbeu (Mexico City), 1947

Las laureles (rev. of *Soy el amo*, subtitled "sainete"; 3; L. Tejedor Pérez; before 1947; Teatro Fuencarral, 10-V-47

La niña de polisón; 3; L. Navarro, F. Lapi Medina; 1948 or before; Teatro Calderón (Barcelona), 14-VII-48

La Canción del organillo; 3: L. F. Ardavín; 1949 or before; Teatro de la Zarzuela, 16-IV-49

Hoy y mañana ("revista"); 2; F. Galindo, L. Muñoz Lorente; 1949 or before; Teatro Lope de Vega, 14-X-49

Un día en las carreras ("sainete"); 2; P. Llabrés y Egea, A. Cuadrado Carreo; 1950 or before; Teatro Madrid, 5-V-50

Trio de ases ("revista"); 2; A. Paso Díaz, R. Perelló Róndenas; 1950 or before; Teatro Albéniz, 28-IX-50

La media naranja ("comedia musical"); 2; L. Tejedor, F. Sevilla; 1951 or before; Teatro de la Zarzuela, 24-III-51

Huelga de los maridos ("comedia musical"); 3; L. Tejedor; 1951 or before; Teatro Moderno (Logroño), 5-VIII-51

Pitusa ("comedia musical"); 3; L. Tejedor, L. Fernández de Sevilla; 1951 or before; Teatro Circo (Zaragoza), 11-X-51

El tambor del brunch; 3; F. Prada; 1951 or before; Teatre Borràs (Barcelona), 19-X-51

Hola cuqui ("comedia musical"); 2; L. Tejedor; 1951 or before; Teatro de la Zarzuela, 9-XI-51

La señorita bombón; Arriaga (Bilbao); 9-XII-51

Las matadoras ("comedia musical"); 2; L. Tejedor; 1952; Teatro de la Zarzuela, 12-IV-52

Sierra Morena; 3; L. F. Ardavín; 1952; Teatro de la Zarzuela, 13-XII-52

Bienvenido Mister Dólar ("espectáculo lírico"); 2; P. Llabrés y Egea; before 1954; Teatro de la Zarzuela, 23-I-54

A lo tonto, A lo tonto (revista); 2; L. Navarro; 1954 or before; Teatro Principal (Alicante), 2-X-54

Paka y paka ("sainete") (with D. Montorio Fajo, A. Alguero); 3; C. Paradas Jiménez,F. Torres Danza, M. Jiménez Martínez; 1954 or before; Teatro Madrid, 30-X-54

Olé y olé ("fantasia"); 2; P. Llabrés y Egea, D. Corbi Pujante, F. Rodríguez Clemente; before 1955; Teatro Alcázar, 30-IV-55

La monda ("revista"); 2; L. Navarro; 1955; Teatro Alcázar, 22-VI-55; Ed. Musicales Madrid, 1955

María Manuela; 3; R. Romero, G. Fernández-Shaw; before 1955; Teatro Avenida (Buenos Aires) 12-III-55; Teatro de la Zarzuela, 1-II-57

Una noche en oriente ("farsa musical"); 2; A. Paso Cano, M. Soriano Torres; 1957; Teatro Circo (Zaragoza), 23-XI-57

Un pueblecito español; ?; L. Tejedor; 1958; Teatro Avenida (Buenos Aires) 3-I-59

Baile en Capitanía; 2; A. Foxá; 1960 or before; Teatro de la Zarzuela, 16-IX-60

El cachalote; Teatro Cómico, (Madrid) 15-IV-61

El rey de oros ("comedia musical"); 3; L. Fernández de Sevilla, L. Tejedor; before 1961; Teatro Cómico, 19-IV-61

Nacimiento ("retablo") (with G. Bidaola); ?; J. Arozamena, V. Espino, F. Cotarelo; c. 1961

Colomba ("comedia musical"); 2; J.M. Arozamena; 1961 or before; Teatro Alcázar, 14-XII-61

Historias del paralelo ("revista espectáculo arrevistado") (with son, Moreno Torroba Larregla) 3; J.M. Arozamena; 1964 or before; Teatro Victoria (Barcelona), 9-X-64; Prince (Madrid) 13-V-65

Rosaura; 2; L. Tejedor; before 1965; Teatro Colón (Bogotá), 12-III-65

La Guitarra; 27-VII-65

El mundo quiere reir ("revista espectáculo"); 2; J.M. Arozamena; 1965 or before; Teatro Victoria (Barcelona), 17-IX-65

Una estrella para todos (with M. Rodríguez Moreno Buendía, M. López Quiroga); 3; J. Arozamena, R. León Arias, A. Quintero Ramírez; 1965; Teatro Maravillas, 12-XI-65

El fabuloso mundo del music-hall ("revista espectáculo"); ?; J.M. Arozamena; 1966 or before; Teatro Victoria (Barcelona), 16-IX-66

Ella ("lírico dramático"); 2; J.M. Arozamena; 1966 or before; Teatro Maravillas, 11-X-66

Guitar

Guitar works are arranged by genre, then chronologically, and finally alphabetically. Each listing provides as much of the following information as is available: title (subtitle) (dedicatee); movements (titles or tempo words); date of composition; date of premiere; date of publication; location of ms.

CONCERTO FOR GUITAR SOLO AND ORCHESTRA

Concierto flamenco (ded. Sabicas); 3; before 1959, Ra

Concierto de Castilla, 3 (Adagio-Allegro moderato; Andantino Mosso; Andante-Allegro Moderato); before 1960; 1960; Na

Homenaje a la seguidilla (ded. Narciso Yepes); 3 (Andantino; Andante; Allegro sostenuto); 1960–81; Paris, 1962 (incomplete rendition); Buenos Aires,

28-VI-75 (formal premiere); 1981 (recording of second version); Ediciones Musicales Madrid, 1962 (1981 version unpub.); Ra

Romancillos; 4 (Popular; Amatorio; Cortesano; Festivo); c1975; Na

Fantasía flamenca (ded. Mario Escudero); 3; before 1976; Carnegie Hall (New York), 28-XI-76; Ra

Diálogos entre guitarra y orquesta (ded. Andrés Segovia); 4 (Allegretto mosso; Andantino mosso; Andante; Allegro); 1951–77; Edmonton (Alberta), 1977; Mendaur (Madrid), 1977; Na, Ra (reduction)

Tonada concertante (ded. Celedonio Romero); 3 (Allegro; Adagio; Allegro); c. 1975–80; 1982; Mendaur (Madrid), 1982

Sonatina; 3 (ed. P. G. Blanco; arrangement of solo work from 1923 or before); Opus Tres (Madrid), 1995

Imagen de Castilla (ded. Alexandre Lagoya); 3

CONCERTO FOR GUITAR DUO AND ORCHESTRA

Tres nocturnos; 3 (Hogueras; Sombras; Brujas); before 1970; ?; Ediciones Musicales Madrid, 1970, and Mendaur (Casa Latina), 1975; Na

CONCERTO FOR GUITAR QUARTET AND ORCHESTRA

Concierto ibérico; 3 (Allegretto; Andante-Allegro moderato-Andante; Allegro-Moderato-Allegro); 1976; Vancouver (British Columbia), 19-XI-76; Mendaur (Madrid), 1976; Na and Ra

GUITAR QUARTET

Ráfagas; 4 (Adagio; Allegretto calmo; Allegertto mosso-Allegro; Vivace); before 1976; Cadencia (Madrid), 1976; Na

Sonata-Fantasía II (ded. Los Romeros); 3; before 1976; Mendaur (Casa Latina), 1976; Ra, SGAE

Estampas; 8 (Bailando un fandango charro; Remanso; La ciega; Fiesta en el pueblo; Amanecer; La boda; Camino del Molino; Juegos infantiles); before 1979; Mendaur (Madrid), 1979; Ra

Sonatina trianera; 3; before 1980; Cadencia (Madrid), 1980; Na, Ra (copy)

GUITAR AND CHAMBER ENSEMBLE

Invenciones for guitar and woodwind quartet; 4 (I–IX); 1980; Na

Interludios for guitar and string quintet; 1982 (completed by Federico, Jr., and premiered posthumously); Jacobo (Madrid), after 1982

SINGLE-MOVEMENT SOLOS

Nocturno; before 1926; Schott (Mainz), 1926/1954

Preludio; before 1928; Schott (Mainz), 1928

Serenata burlesca; before 1928; Schott (Mainz), 1928

Burgalesa; before 1928; Schott (Mainz), 1928

Scherzando (originally entitled Scherzo); before 1948; Ricordi Americana, 1948; Ra

Alpujarreña (see also orchestral version); before 1952; Cadencia (Madrid), 1952)
before 1952

Madroños; 1929; Schott (Mainz), 1954; Associated Music Publishers (New York)
1961; UME 1972, 1974, 1977; Jacobo (Madrid), 1987

Guitarra española; before 1956; Ediciones Musicales (Madrid) 1956. v.1. Zapateado;
Capricho; Improvisación; Sevillana; Romancillo. v. 2. Segoviana; Minueto del
majo; Rumor de copla; Aire vasco. v. 3. ¡Ay, Malagueña!; Chisperada; Bolero
menorquín. v. 4. Nana; Sonatina y variación (En mi menor); Preludio;
Añoranza. v. 5. Quien te puso petenera; Cancioncilla; Trianeras; Niña merse.
v. 6. Suite miniatura. Llamada; Trémolo, Vals; Divertimento.

Capricho; before 1956; Ediciones Musicales (Madrid), 1956 (series "Guitarra española"; arr. for two guitars pub. 1962)

Niña merse; before 1956; Ediciones Musicales (Madrid), 1956, 1960 (series
"Guitarra española"; arr. for two guitars pub. 1962), Jasrac Crown (Tokyo),
1968, Casa Latina (Madrid), 1980

Guitarra española; before 1958; Ediciones Musicales (Madrid) 1958. v. 8. Tonada,
also Cadencia (Madrid), 1976; Ronda; Romance de los pinos, also
Cadencia(Madrid), 1976; Lejania; Montaraza.

Cinco obras originales para guitarra: before 1960; Ediciones Musicales (Madrid),
1960 Danza prima; Nocturno No. 2; Ronda festiva, Humorada, Marcha de
cojo; (also Casa Latina, 1968, Jasrac Crown (Tokyo), 1980).

Once obras para la guitarra; 11, before 1966; Cadencia (Madrid), 1966. (Habanera;
Feria Sevillana; Alegría; Sevillana; Castilla te llaman; Copla; Minueto goyesco;
Segoviano; Eres Petenera; Chispero; Tararando); (Eres Petenera; Castilla te
llaman; and Minueto, also pub. separately)

Contradanza; 1968; UME/Associated Music Publishers (New York), 1968

Jota levantina; 1968; UME/Associated Music Publishers (New York), 1968

Fandango corralero; before 1970; Ediciones musicales (Mardid) 1970

En todo la Quintana; before 1970; Ediciones Musicales (Madrid), 1970 (also arr. chorus)

Vieja leyenda; before 1970; UME, 1970; SGAE

Jaranera; before 1970; UME, 1970

Chaconne; Lc (M127.M)

Verbenera; before 1970, UME 1970; Na

THEME AND VARIATIONS

Punteado y taconeo clásico; 2; before 1955; UME, 1955

Sonatina y variación; 2; before 1956; Ediciones Musicales (Madrid), 1956 (series
"Guitarra española"), Cadencia (Madrid), 1976

SONATA

Sonata-Fantasía; 2; 1953; Na (themes utilized in concerto, *Dialogos entre guitarra y
orquesta*); Na; pub. as solo work in *The Andrés Segovia Archive*, ed. Angelo

Gilardino, copyright 1975 by Jacobo Music; assigned 1990 to Konzert Musikverlag; assigned 2002 to Bèrben.

Sonatina; 3 (I; II; III); 1923 or before; 17-XII-23; Ricordi, 1924, 1953, Columbia, 1966; Ediciones Musicales Madrid, 1957 as v. 7 of *Guitarra española*; also arranged for guitar and orchestra; Na

SUITES

Suite castellana; 3 (Fandanguillo; Arada; Danza); before 1920; 1923 (Andrés Segovia, soloist); Schott (Mainz), 1926, 1954, Jacobo, 1987

Piezas características; 6 (Preambulo; Oliveras; Melodía; Los Mayos; Albada; Panorama); before 1931; Schott (Mainz), 1931, Associated Music Publishers (New York), 1959; Na

Madrileñas; 3 (Tirana; Copla; Bolero); before 1953; Música del Sur (Barcelona) Southern Music, 1953 (later version for orch. in *Suite Madrileña*)

Suite miniatura; 4 (Llamada; Trémolo; Vals; Divertimento); before 1957; Ediciones Musicales (Madrid), 1957 (v. 6 of *Guitarra española*); Berben, 1970.

Aires de La Mancha; 5 (Jeringonza; Ya llega el invierno; Coplilla; La Pastora; Seguidilla); before 1966; Cadencia (Madrid), 1966; Na

Alegría malagueña; 1966; Na

Castillos de España I; 8 (Alba de Tormes (Trova); Alcañiz (Festiva); Alcázar de Segovia (Llamada); Manzanares de Real (A la Moca Fermosa); Torija (Elegía); Turegano (Serranilla); Romance de los pinos (Montemayor); Sigüenza); 1968; Cadencia (Madrid), 1970, 1973; Na

Molinera; UME, 1968

Tríptico; 3 (Pinotresca; Romance; Festiva); c. 1973; UME, 1973; Lc

Las puertas de Madrid (ded. Pepe Romero); 7 (Las Puertas de Toledo; Alcalá; San Vicente; Hierro; Moros; Cerrada del Ángel); before 1976; Cadencia (Madrid), 1976; Na, Lc (copy)

Castillos de España II; 6 (Calatrava (Festiva); Javier (Evocación); Olite; Redaba; Simancas (Juglaresca); Zafra (Fantasmas)); before 1978; Cadencia (Madrid) 1978

PRELUDES

Ocho preludios (ded. Andrés Segovia); 8 (Largo; Allegretto; Andante; Allegretto calmo; Andantino; Allegretto vivace; Lento; Allegro no mucho); before 1974; Festival of Granada, 1974 (Regino Sainz de la Maza, soloist); Cantabrian, 1981 (first three mvmts. only); Na, Lc (copy)

Preludios; 6; before 1982; Cantabrian, 1982; Na

Vocal

ACCOMPANIED SONG

(voice and piano; *voice and orchestra; **voice and guitar)

El Pirante (Luis de Oliva), 1913–15

La solterita, Todo está igual, Sueño terrible (Enrique López Morín), 1913–15

Tirana castiza, La postinera (Tomás Rodríguez Alenza), 1913–15

La mora cautiva (Enrique López Morín); Faustino Fuentes (Madrid), 1914

Copla de Antaño (Lope de Vega); 1; 1923; UME, 1923

Himno del trabajo (Canción nacionalsindicalista) (Tomás Borrás); 1; c. 1939–40, Diario de la Falange, II Año Triunfal, (Madrid), 1940

Sobre campos y trincheras (Agustín de Foxá); 1; 1939–40 (hymn of Spanish Air Force until 1967)

**Carita de Bronce* (P. Llabrés y Egea, D. Corbi Pujante); 1952, 1973; Na

Todo corazón; 1; before 1952; UME, 1952

Te juego un beso (P. Guillén); SGAE, 1954

**Barrio sud* (R. Desco Morte); 1; before 1955; Ediciones Musicales (Madrid), 1955

**Guayaba* (R. Desco Morte); 1; before 1955; Ediciones Musicales (Madrid), 1955

Noche de la cestanera (R. Desco Morte); 1; before 1955; Ediciones Musicales (Madrid), 1955

Canciones españolas 1; 7 (Aldapeko; Ron, Ron; Fandango castellano; Aurtxo Txikia; Ay que te quiero; Alalá; Bolero de Valldemosa); before 1956; UME, 1956 (Alalá also recorded voice and orch., Decca, 1955)

Canciones españolas 2; 7 (Jota castellana; Cuando salí Marbella; La enamorada; Quisiera verte; La nana; Aquel sombrero del Monte; Rosinyol); before 1956; UME, 1956

Cholita (R. Desco Morte); 1; before 1956; Ediciones Musicales (Madrid), 1956

Amor que yo soñe (R. Desco Morte, Rodemor); 1; before 1957; Ediciones Musicales (Madrid), 1957

Toda Sevilla; Ediciones Musicales (Madrid), 1957

Viejo tango arrabalero (Rodemor); Ediciones Musicales (Madrid), 1957

**Adios amor* (Rodemor); 1; before 1958; Ediciones Musicales (Madrid), 1958

Madrilenito (pasadoble); Ediciones Musicales (Madrid), 1958

Amor legionario (R. Caldera; R. Jiméniz); 1; before 1960; Ediciones Musicales (Madrid), 1960

***Llegando al pinar*, Milagros; 2; before 1961; Ediciones Musicales DIM (Madrid), 1961

***Siete canciones españoles: Romancillos*; 7 (Me llavarán; Los mozos de Valdefuentes; Serenita cae la nieve; Adonde va la niña; Caminando por el monte; Rosaura; Marbella); before 1961; Ediciones Musicales (Madrid), 1961

**Valle verde* (C. Greco); 1; before 1962; Ediciones Musicales (Madrid), 1962

***Yo tenía tres hermanas*; 6 (Cantando a Mariana ; En este llano; Pilar; Llegando al pinar; Milagros; Caminito de la fuente) Ediciones Musicales DIM (Madrid) 1968

**Sevilla es*… (Rafael de León) (ded. Plácido Domingo); 1; 1981; Ma

Perdón para un toro (F. Rosas Janer); 1; before 1982; Ediciones Musicales Belter, 1982

Arenitas de mi amor (J. M. Pemán); 1; Na

Ay, Micaela (I. Ramón Jiménez); 1; before 1956

Gitana iglesia (J. Simón Veldivieso, J.); 1

Lola de la Triana (J.M. Pemán); 1; c. 1950

Tenerife; 1; Na

*Estrella flamenca (A. López Quiroga, D. Corbi Pujante, I. Román Pérez); 1; before
    1957 (possibly from zarzuela *Olé y olé*)

*Quién es mi marido?; 1; F. Prada, J. Valls; ?; Na (lyrics only)

Choral

En toda la Quintana; Ediciones Musicales (Madrid), 1957

Ha nacido: Canción Navidad sobre un canto austriaco (STB); 1; 1959; Mendaur (Casa
    Latina), 1959; Na

La pastorella (SATB); 1; F. M. Torroba; before 1959; Mendaur (Casa Latina),
    1959

Pastores venid: Villancico (SSAA); 1; F. M. Torroba; before 1959; Mendaur (Casa
    Latina), 1959; Na

Asturias; 1971; Na

Niña merse: Habanera (SATB); 1; M. Tamayo; before 1975; UME, 1975; Na

Desde lejos (TTBB); 1; M. Pérez; before 1981: Pamplona, 1981; np; Na

Sabemos lo que somos (TTBB); 1; before 1981; 1981; np; Na

María y José: Canción de Navidad sobre un canto Austriaco (SSAA); 1; F. M. Torroba;
    np; Na

Ande pa Marimorena: Villancico (SATB); 1; np; SGAE (one of a collection of
    villancicos)

Ayála (SATB); 1; F. M. Torroba; before 1959; np; SGAE (one of a collection of
    villancicos)

Boga, boga (SATB); 1?; F. M. Torroba; before 1959; np; SGAE (one of a collection of
    villancicos)

Cantos seranos (SATB); 1; before 1959; np; SGAE (one of a collection of
    villancicos)

En el monte gorbea; Villancico (SATB); 1; F. M. Torroba; before 1959; np; SGAE (one
    of a collection of villancicos)

España tiene un jardín: Villancico (SATB); 1; F. M. Torroba; 1; before 1959; np; SGAE
    (one of a collection of villancicos by various composers)

Caminando, caminando: Villancico (SSA); 1; F. M. Torroba; np; Na

Piano

CONCERTO

Fantasia castellana; 1; 1979; Paris, October 1980; np; Na

SOLO

À *petits pas: One and Two Step*; 1; before 1913; Casa Dotesio (Madrid), 1913

Danse et flirt; 1; before 1913; Casa Dotesio (Madrid), 1913

El mate: Tango argentino; 1; before 1915; UME, 1915

Mosaico sevillano; 1; before 1954; UME 1954; Na (excerpt from eponymous ballet)

Alegrías de Cádiz: Pasodoble; 1; before 1957; Ediciones Musicales (Madrid), 1957; Bn

Fandango corralero; 1; before 1956; Ediciones Musicales (Madrid), 1957 (also in guitar vers.)

Romance antiguo; 1; before 1957; Ediciones Musicales (Madrid), 1957

Torerias: Pasodoble; 1; before 1957; Ediciones Musicales (Madrid), 1957

Chucares: Pasodoble; 1; before 1958; Ediciones Musicales (Madrid), 1958; Bn

El Tato: Pasodoble; 1; before 1958; Ediciones Musicales (Madrid), 1958

Noche sevillana; 1; 1959; Marks Music (New York), 1959

Alegría de Madrid; 1; before 1969; Ediciones Musicales DIM (Madrid), 1969

Cuadro goyesco; 5; before 1940; np; Na (may be orch. reduction)

Semblanza: Homenaje a Joaquín Turina; 1; after 1948; np; Na

Tres obras para piano; 3 (Copla cordobesa; Copla de Puerta Real; 3rd mvmt. missing); ?; np; Na

[Untitled]; 1; np; Ma

Orchestra

SUITE

Aires vascos; ?; before 1956; Ediciones Musicales (Madrid), 1956

Danzas asturianas; 4 (I; II; III; IV); before 1956; Ediciones Musicales (Madrid), 1956; Na

Sevillanas populares; 4 (1–4); 1956; np; Ma

Zambra mora; Ediciones Musicales (Madrid), 1957

Aires de Andalucía; 3; np; Na (parts only)

Aires de Aragón; 3; np; Na (parts only)

Suite madrileña (arr. M. Salinger); 3 (Tiriana; Copla; Bolero); before 1953; Southern Music (Editorial Musical del Sur), ?; Na

Sonatina trianera; 3 (Allegro; Andante; Allegro) before 1980; Casa Latina (Madrid), 1980; Na

SYMPHONIC POEM

La ajorca de oro; 1; 1918 or before; np; Na

Zoraida; 1; before December 1919 (cited in 1919 program for premiere of *Cuadros*); np; Na

Cuadros; 4 (*La Era* [Goya]; *El Baile de San Antonia de la Florida* [Goya]; *Nuestro Señor Crucificado* [Velasquez]; *Ninfas de Diana soprendidas por los sátiros* [Rubens]); 1919 or before; Teatro Price, 19-XII-19; np; Na

Antequera; 1; 1953; Cantabrian, 1953; Na

Mosaico sevillano; 1; before 1954; UME, 1954 (excerpt from eponymous ballet; also arr. piano)

En la reja sevillana; 1; before 1956; np

Gardens of Granada; 1; before 1953; Marks Music, 1953 (piano red.)

San Fermín: Jota de Navarra; 1; before 1960; Ediciones Musicales (Madrid), 1960

Zambra mora; 1; before 1960; Ediciones Musicales (Madrid), 1960; Na

Eritaña; 1; before 1979; Mendaur (Madrid), 1979

Así es la jota; 1; before 1957; np

Las Hormagas; 1; c. 1920–25 (based on manuscript paper, handwriting, and proximity in archive to other works of same period); np; Na (piano red.)

Alpujarrena; 1; c. 1952; np (may be orch. vers. of eponymous guitar work)

Capricho romántico; ?; np (reference at SGAE)

Danza de humo; 1; np; Na (piano red.)

Iberiana; 4; np; Ma (inc.)

Prelude en Do menor; np; Na (inc.)

FILM

La canción de Axia (1939), dir. Florian Rey; lyrics, Manuel de Góngora

El Pecado de Rogelia Sánchez (1940), dir. Carlo Borghesio and Roberto de Ribón
    Santa Rogelia (1940), dir. Roberto de Ribón

¿Por qué vivir tristes? (1942), dir. Eduardo García Maroto

Schottis (1943), dir. Eduardo García Maroto

Santander, al cuidad en llamas (1944), dir. Luis Marquina

Maravilla (1957), dir. Javier Setó *Rogelia* (1962), dir. Rafael Gil

Usted tiene ojos de mujer fatal (1962), dir. José María Elorrieta

El enigma de los Cornell (1965), dir. Eberhard Itzenplitz (*Hotel der toten Gäste*)

La Pandilla (1965), dir. Enrique López Eguiluz

El mejor tesoro (1966), dir. Gregorio Almendros

Miscellaneous

ACCORDION

Vaya por usted; 1; before 1959; Ediciones Musicales (Madrid), 1959 (also piano, 1957)

FLUTE AND PIANO

Dedicatoria; 1; before 1973; UME, Salabert (Paris), 1973

CHORAL

Zortzico (TTBB?);?

Ave Maria (SSAA?); before 1947

FILM

Mari Luz ojos tristes; Na

GUITAR

Canción y danza (possibly 2nd and 3rd movements of *Suite castellana*); no date, Na

ORCHESTRA

Marcha granadera; 1979; Na
Zorongo; 1960; Na

SOLO SONG

Bayón de Copacabana; 1955; Na
Brasil patria querida; 1963; Na
Mambo; Na

UNKNOWN MEDIUM

Danza castellana; before 1950; Casa Latina (Madrid), 1977, Mendaur (Madrid), 1979
Romance Antiguo; Ediciones Musicales (Madrid), 1957

UNKNOWN GENRE

Por fin la encontre; Na (lyrics only)

BIBLIOGRAPHY

(Several articles cited below are from the family archive in Navarra [Na]. These do not always provide enough information for a complete citation. We have tried to obtain this information from other sources, but in several cases, the citations remain incomplete.)

A. C. "Federico Moreno Torroba, gloria musical de España." *La Voz de Áviles*, November 24, 1976.

"A fin de mes se presentará en el Teatro Colón la Compañía Española de Comedias Musicales que dirige Moreno Torroba." *Correo de Galicia* (Buenos Aires), October 21, 1934.

Abella, Rafael. *La vida cotidiana bajo el régimen de Franco*. Madrid: Ediciones Temas de Hoy, 1984/1996.

"Aclaman delirantemente a Moreno Torroba." *Diario de la Americas*, April 18, 1978.

Adame, Serafín. "Luisillo conmemorará a Falla en Australia." *Pueblo*, May 17, 1976.

Aguado, Lola. "Homenaje a Moreno Torroba." *Diario 16*, May 27, 1978.

———— "Lo que dice el maestro Torroba." *Ya*, 1980 (interview with FMT shortly before premiere of *El Poeta* June 19, 1980) [Na]

Alcázar, Miguel, ed. *The Segovia-Ponce Letters*. Trans. Peter Segal. Columbus, Ohio: Editions Orphée, 1989.

Alejos, Nerea. "Baluarte acoge una 'monumental' version de la zarzuela con 'La chulapona.'" *Diario de Navarra*, November 24, 2005, 92.

Alier, Roger. "*Luisa Fernanda*: A Graceful Score." Liner notes for *Luisa Fernanda*. Auvidis Valois, V 4759, 1995, 26–27.

Alier, Roger, and Xosé Aviñoa. *El libro de la zarzuela*. Madrid: Daimon, 1982.

Alonso, Gonzalo. "Milán se rinde ante 'Luisa Fernanda.'" *La Razón*, June 20, 2003, 69.

Alonso, Serafín. "Homenaje en el Ayuntamiento al maestro Moreno Torroba." *Línea. Diario de la Región Murciana*, March 21, 1981, 3.

Alonso Millán, Juan José. "Homenaje." *Autores: Revista de información de la S.G.A.E.*, n3 (October 1982): 4.

Alvar Ezquerra, Manuel. *Diccionario de madrileñismos: Voces patrimoniales y populares de la Comunidad de Madrid*. Madrid: Ediciones La Librería, 2011.

Álvarez Junco, José. "History, Politics, and Culture, 1875–1936." In *The Cambridge Companion to Modern Spanish Culture*. Ed. David T. Gies, 67–85. Cambridge: Cambridge University Press, 1999.

"Amalia Pardo, Faustino Arregui." *Blanco y Negro*, September 18, 1932.

Amorós, Andrés. "Los espectáculos." *La Edad de Plata de la cultura española (1898–1936). Vol. 2: Letras, ciencia, arte, sociedad y culturas*. Ed. Pedro Laín Entralgo, 783–828. Madrid: Espasa Calpe, 1994.

Ansón, Luis María. "La generación del silencio." *ABC*, March 1, 1973.

Arango, E. Ramón. *Spain: From Repression to Renewal*. Boulder and London: Westview Press, 1985.

Arazo, María Ángeles. "Moreno Torroba: 90 años de vitalidad." *Las Provincias* (Valencia), June 6, 1981.

Arce, Julio. "Irony, *esperpento*, and Parody in the Music of *¡Bienvenido Mister Marshall!*" in *Diagonal: The Journal of the Center for Iberian and Latin American Music* 7 (2011). http://cilam.ucr.edu/diagonal/issues/2011/index.html.

Attademo, Luigi. "El repertorio de Andrés Segovia y las novedades de su archivo." *Roseta*, n1 (October 2008): 69–100.

"Ayer murió el maestro Moreno Torroba, último 'grande' de la zarzuela española." *Diario 16*, September 13, 1982, 50.

Barber, Lorenç. "40 años de creación musical en España." *Tiempo de historia* 6/62 (January 1980): 198–213.

Barce, Ramón. "El folklore urbano y la música de los sainetes líricos del último cuarto del siglo XIX: La explicitación escénica de los bailes." *Actas del XV Congreso de la Sociedad Internacional de Musicología*. In *Revista de Musicología* 16/6 (1993): 3217–25.

———. "La ópera y la zarzuela en el siglo XIX." In *España en la música de Occidente: Actas del Congreso Internacional celebrado en Salamanca 29 de octubre–5 de noviembre de 1985*. 2 vols. Ed. Emilio Casares Rodicio, Ismael Fernández de la Cuesta, and José López-Calo, ii, 145–54. Madrid: Ministerio de Cultura, 1987.

Beevor, Antony. *The Battle for Spain: The Spanish Civil War 1936–1939*. Rev. ed. London: Penguin Books, 2006.

Bentivegna Patricia. "A Study of Three Zarzuelas Madrileñas together with a Historical Outline of the Zarzuela." Master's thesis, Columbia University, 1955.

Berasategui, Blanca. "Moreno Torroba, más que noventa anos de zarzuela." *ABC*, November 14, 1981, 8–9.

B. F. O. "Salamanca recupera la música casticista y castellana de Federico Moreno Torroba." *La Gaceta* (Salamanca), May 7, 2002, 15.

Boyd, Carolyn P. "History, Politics, and Culture, 1936–1975." In *The Cambridge Companion to Modern Spanish Culture*. Ed. David T. Gies, 86–103. Cambridge: Cambridge University Press, 1999.

Boyd, Michael A. "The Works for Guitar and Orchestra of Federico Moreno Torroba and a Peforming Edition of *Romancillos* for Guitar and Orchestra." DMA diss., University of Southern Mississippi, 2005.

Bravo Morata, Federico. *Historia de Madrid*. 12 vols. Madrid: Trigo Ediciones, 2002.

——— *Los nombres de las calles de Madrid*. 2d ed. Madrid: Fenicia, 1984.

Brenan, Gerald. *The Spanish Labyrinth: An Account of the Social and Political Background of the Civil War*. Cambridge: Cambridge University Press, 2001 (reprint).

Briggs, John Channing. *Lincoln's Speeches Reconsidered*. Baltimore: Johns Hopkins University Press, 2005.

Butt, John. *Writers and Politics of Modern Spain*. New York: Holmes and Meier Publishers, 1978.

C. "Moreno Torroba ha cumplido ochenta anos." *La Vanguardia*, March 17, 1971.

"Calderón. 'Luisa Fernanda.'" *ABC*, March 27, 1932, 33.

Camps, Pompeyo. "Moreno Torroba e Irma Costanzo armaron una tempestad de rasguidos y humoradas." *La Opinión* (Buenos Aires), June 28, 1975, 13.

——— "Tuvo éxito Irma Costanzo en obras de Moreno Torroba. *La Opinión* (Buenos Aires), June, 1975.

Carr, Raymond. *Spain: 1808–1975*. 2d ed. Oxford: Clarendon Press, 1982.

Casares Rodicio, Emilio. *Historia gráfica de la zarzuela*. Madrid: ICCMU, 2002.

——— "La música española hasta 1939, o la restauración musical." In *España en la música de Occidente: Actas del Congreso Internacional celebrado en Salamanca 29 de octubre –5 de noviembre de 1985*. 2 vols. Ed. Emilio Casares Rodicio, Ismael Fernández de la Cuesta, and José López-Calo, ii, 261–322. Madrid: Ministerio de Cultura, 1987.

——— "Música y músicos de la Generación del 27." In *La Música en la Generación del 27: Homenaje a Lorca, 1915–1939*. Ed. Emilio Casares Rodicio, 20–34. Madrid: Ministerio de Cultura, 1986.

Casares Rodicio, Emilio, ed. *La Música en la Generación del 27: Homenaje a Lorca, 1915–1939*. Madrid: Ministerio de Cultura, 1986.

Cascudo, Teresa, and María Palacios, eds. *Los señores de la crítica: Periodismo musical e ideología del modernismo en Madrid (1915–1959)*. Sevilla: Editorial Doble J, 2011.

Castell, Ángel María. *Discurso leído por el Señor Don Federico Moreno Torroba en el acto de su recepción pública y contestación del Señor Don Ángel María Castell el día 21 de febrero de 1935*. Madrid: Academia de Bellas Artes de San Fernando, 1935.

———— "Informaciones y noticias teatrales: 'La virgen de mayo.' 'El carillón mágico.'" *ABC*, February 15, 1925, 35.

Centeno, Félix. "Moreno Torroba espera dejar una fortuna a sus hijos." *Pueblo* (before 1966).

Chase, Gilbert. "Spanish Musicians Since the Civil War." *The Musical Times* (July 1939): 499–500.

———— *The Music of Spain*. New York: Dover, 1959.

Chivite, Montse. "Moreno-Torroba: 'Navarra mantiene su afición a la zarzuela.'" *Diario de Navarra*, November 15, 1994, 40.

Christoforidis, Michael. "Igor Stravinsky, Spanish Catholicism and Generalísimo Franco." *Context*, n22 (Spring 2001): 61–67.

Cifra. "Un ballet flamenco actuará ante Paulo VI en la peregrinación gitana." *La Vanguardia*, September, 18, 1965, 9.

Cisquella, Georgina, José Luis Erviti, and José Antonio Sorollo. *La represión cultural en el franquismo: diez años de censura de libros durante la ley de prensa (1966–1976)*. Barcelona: Editorial Anagrama, 2002.

Cladera, Mateo. "El maestro Torroba dirigira su 'Luisa Fernanda.'" *Baleares*, April 23, 1982.

Clark, Walter Aaron. *Enrique Granados: Poet of the Piano*. New York: Oxford University Press, 2006/2011.

———— "Federico Moreno Torroba's Relations with the Franco Regime." *Diagonal: Journal of the Center for Iberian and Latin American Music* 7 (2011), http://cilam.ucr.edu/diagonal/issues/2011/index.html.

———— "Fernando Sor's Guitar Studies, Lessons, and Exercises (Opp. 6, 29, 31 & 35) and the London Pianoforte School." In *Estudios sobre Fernando Sor/Sor Studies*. Ed. Luis Gásser, 359–72. Barcelona: Instituto Complutense de Ciencias Musicales, 2003.

———— *Isaac Albéniz: Portrait of a Romantic*. Oxford: Oxford University Press, 1999/2002.

———— "La España de Albéniz y Granados: Dos pasados, dos futuros. In *Música y cultura en la Edad de Plata, 1915–1939*. Ed. María Nagore, Leticia Sánchez de Andrés, and Elena Torres, 129–41. Madrid: ICCMU, 2009.

———— "The Iberian World: The Philippines, Latin America, and Spain." In *Nineteenth-century Choral Music*. Ed. Donna M. Di Grazia. Series: Studies in Musical Genres, ed. R. Larry Todd. New York: Routledge, 2012.

———— "The Romeros: Living Legacy of the Spanish Guitar. An Interview with Celín Romero." *Soundboard Magazine: The Journal of the Guitar Foundation of America* 36/2 (2010): 60–64.

Clark, Walter Aaron, and William Craig Krause. "Federico Moreno Torroba and Andrés Segovia in the 1920s: Turning Point in Guitar History." *Soundboard Magazine: The Journal of the Guitar Foundation of America* 38/3 (2012): 8–13.

———— "Federico Moreno Torroba's *Monte Carmelo* and Cultural Politics under Franco during the 1940s." In *Music and Francoism*. Ed. Gemma Pérez Zalduondo. Series: Speculum Musicae, 20. Turnhout: Brepols, 2013.

Classical Topics, n12 (December 1979): 1–5.

Coelho, Victor Anand. *The Cambridge Companion to the Guitar*. Cambridge: Cambridge University Press, 2003.

Coldwell, Robert, and Javier Suárez-Pajares. *A. T. Huerta: Life and Works*. San Antonio, Texas: Digital Guitar Archive Editions, 2006.

Colmenero, Marisol. "Lírico Moreno Torroba." *La Hora Leonesa*, August 4, 1979.

"Con 'Luisa Fernanda' triunfó Moreno Torroba en el Colón." *República Ilustrada* (Buenos Aires), October 29, 1934.

"Concedida la Medalla de Oro de Madrid a Moreno Torroba en el cincuentenario del estreno de 'Luisa Fernanda.'" *El País*, March 28, 1982.

Cortés, Francesc. "Reflejos, imagenes y distorsiones en la recepción de las vanguardias musicales en Barcelona (1914–1936)." In *Música y cultura en la Edad de Plata, 1915–1939*. Ed. María Nagore, Leticia Sánchez de Andrés, and Elena Torres, 479–506. Madrid: ICCMU, 2009.

Cortés-Cavanillas, Julián. "El maestro Moreno Torroba, 85 años de juventud." *ABC*, October 12, 1975, 46–48.

———— "'Luisillo' ha bailado ante el Papa." *ABC*, May 15, 1969, 26–27.

Crichton, Ronald. "*La Chulapona*: Edinburgh Festival." *Financial Times*, August 19, 1989, 19.

Crivillí i Bargalló, Josep. *Historia de la música español: el folklore musical*. Madrid: Alianza Música, 1983.

"Cronología de una enfermedad." *El País*, September 13, 1982, 22.

"Cultural Policy in Spain." Madrid: Real Instituto Elcano de Estudios Internacionales y Estratégicos, 2004.

Dahlhaus, Carl. *The Foundations of Music History*. Cambridge: Cambridge University Press, 1983.

———— *Between Romanticism and Modernism*. Berkeley: University of California Press, 1980.

———— *Realism in Nineteenth-Century Music*. Cambridge: Cambridge University Press, 1985.

———— *Esthetics of Music*. Cambridge: Cambridge University Press, 1982.

Danner, Peter. "Federico Moreno Torroba." *Soundboard* 10 (1983): 29–31.

Dávila, Bill. "Pepe Romero Reminisces about Federico Moreno Torroba." *Soundboard* (summer 1983): 144–45.

"De sus manos salieron páginas inolvidables de la música española." *ABC*, September 13, 1982, 38–39, 58–59.

Del Campo, Ángel. "Estreno de 'El poeta.'" *Pueblo*, June 25, 1980.

———— "Orfeón Pamplonés: Homenaje a Moreno Torroba." *Pueblo*, November 11, 1981. Np.

"Diecisiete presuntos estafadores en la Sociedad de Autores." Clipping from a Valencia newspaper, May 11, 1981. [Na]

Diez, Luis. "Víctimas, los trabajadores." *El Socialista*, n181 (November 26–December 2, 1980): 37.

Diez-Crespo, M. "Moreno Torroba: Un gran hombre de teatro." *Autores: Revista de información de la S.G.A.E.*, n3 (October 1982): 26–27.

"Disposiciones legales." *La Música en la Generación del 27: Homenaje a Lorca, 1915–1939*. Ed. Emilio Casares Rodicio, 256–64. Madrid: Ministerio de Cultura, 1986.

"Doble distinción para el pianista Humberto Quagliata." *Montevideo*, December 24, 1980.

Domingo, Plácido. Liner notes for *Luisa Fernanda*. Auvidis Valois, V 4759, 1995, 28.

———— *My First Forty Years*. New York: Alfred A. Knopf, 1983.

Duarte, John. *Andrés Segovia, As I Knew Him*. Pacific, Missouri: Mel Bay Productions, 1998.

E. L.-CH. A. "'El problema de los derechos cinematográficos está virtualmente arreglado.'" Clipping from a Valencia newspaper, 1978.

E. V. S. "El estreno mundial de 'Tres nocturnos' abre el Ciclo Música y Patrimonio del Consorcio 2002." *Tribuna de Salamanca*, May 7, 2002.

"El autor de 'Luisa Fernanda se ha superado al comentar el libro de 'La chulapona.'" *La Razón* (Buenos Aires), November 17, 1934.

"El acento típico y castizo de Madrid vibra en 'Luisa Fernanda.'" *Noticias Gráficas* (Buenos Aires), October 28, 1934.

"'El amor brujo' y 'Don Quijote', un lujo de ambientación y expresividad." *Diario de Mallorca*, 1982.

"El compositor Moreno Torroba fue enterrado ayer en Madrid." *Diario de Barcelona*, September 14, 1982, 15.

"El maestro Moreno Torroba, Presidente de la Sociedad de Autores." *ABC*, February 13, 1974, 81.

"El maestro Moreno Torroba será enterrado hoy en la Sacramental de San Justo, de Madrid." *El País*, September 13, 1982, 22.

"'El poeta', de Federico Moreno Torroba." *El Imparcial*, June 22, 1980.

"'El Poeta': La ópera de Moreno Torroba." *Pueblo*, June 25, 1980.

"El público también opina." *Boletín informativo del Instituto de Cultura Hispánica* 14 (November 1, 1964): 4.

"El reputado músico habla de sus obras y de la temporada del Colón." *La Razón* (Buenos Aires), November 29, 1935.

"El sainete musical de Torroba es un cuadro del Madrid Viejo." *Noticias Gráficas* (Buenos Aires), November 17, 1934.

Elizalde, Ignacio. "Proyectaba un poema sinfónico sobre Navarra." *Diario de Navarra*, November 23, 1982.

Encabo, Enrique. *Música y nacionalismos en España*. Barcelona: Erasmus Ediciones, 2007.

Estévez, María Antonia. "Federico Moreno Torroba: Entre los recuerdos de su padre y de su abuelo, el maestro Larregla." *Diario de Navarra*, February 27, 1994, 40–41.

"Estrena en Roma el ballet 'Cristo, luz del mundo,' con musica de Moreno Torroba." *La Vanguardia*, September 9, 1975, 42.

"Estreno de 'Don Quijote', de Moreno Torroba." *El Alcázar*, October 12, 1982.

"Estreno de Moreno Torroba y homenaje de los navarros." *ABC*, November 4, 1981.

"Exaltación, homenaje y desagravio a Moreno Torroba." *El Imparcial*, July 4, 1980.

Everett, William A., and Paul R. Laird, eds. *The Cambridge Companion to the Musical*, 2d ed. New York: Cambridge University Press, 2008.

F. M. "La representación 10 mil de *Luisa Fernanda*." Newspaper clipping from Lima, Peru.

F. R. C. "Estreno del 'Concierto ibérico', de Moreno Torroba." *Ya*, November 21, 1979.

"Fallece el creador de la zarzuela 'Luisa Fernanda.'" *El Mundo*, September 13, 1982, 5-B.

Falla, Manuel de. *On Music and Musicians*. London: Marion Boyars, 1979.

"Federico Moreno Torroba." *Diario de Navarra*, February 27, 1994, 34.

"Federico Moreno Torroba: Entre los recuerdos de su padre y de su abuelo, el maestro Larregla." *Diario de Navarra*, February 27, 1994, 40.

Fernández-Cid, Antonio. *Cien años de teatro musical en España, (1875–1975)*. Madrid: Real Musical, 1975.

———"'Diálogos', un nuevo concierto para guitarra, de Moreno Torroba." *ABC*, March 3, 1982, 52.

———"El Nacional Español estrenó 'Don Quijote', de Moreno Torroba." *ABC*, October 9, 1982, 57.

———"'El poeta', de Moreno Torroba, con Placido Domingo como protagonista." *ABC*, June 21, 1980, 48.

———"Evocación del Maestro Moreno Torroba." *Academia: Boletín de la Real Academia de Bellas Artes de San Fernando*, n55 (second semester 1982): 31–35.

———"Frühbeck dirigió el homenaje a Moreno Torroba de la Sociedad General de Autores." *ABC*, November 20, 1992, 101.

———"Homenaje del Orfeón Pamplonés a Federico Moreno Torroba, en el Real." *ABC*, November 8, 1981.

———"Juicio crítico." *ABC*, November 14, 1981, 8.

———"La Academia de Bellas Artes, en memoria de Moreno Torroba." *ABC*, October 8, 1982, 79.

———*La década musical de los cuarenta: Discurso del académico... el día 30 noviembre de 1980, con motivo de su recepción y contestación de Regino Sainz de la Maza*. Madrid: Real Academia de Bellas Artes de San Fernando, 1980.

———*La música española en el siglo XX*. Madrid: Fundación Juan March, 1973.

———"La Orquesta Nacional, Theo Alcantara y Los Romero en el Teatro Real." *ABC*, November 18, 1979.

———"Moreno Torroba, ante el estreno de 'El Poeta.'" *ABC*, 1980.

———"Moreno Torroba, centenario." *Música clásica*, ABC 3/78 (February 27, 1991), 1–3.

———"Moreno Torroba: un capítulo de gloria en la lírica de España." *Diario de las Americas*, May 17, 1981.

———*Panorama de la música en España*. Madrid: Dossat, 1949.

———"Plácido Domingo estreno 'El poeta', de Moreno Torroba." *La Vanguardia*, June 30, 1980, 54.

———"Un capítulo esencial en la historia del teatro lírico español." *ABC*, September 13, 1982 (reprinted in *Autores: Revista de información de la S.G.A.E.*, n3 (October 1982): 30–31).

Ferrary, Álvaro, and Antonio Moreno Juste. "La vida cultural: Limitaciones, condicionantes y desarrollo. El Franquismo." In *Historia contemporánea de España, siglo XX*. Ed. Javier Paredes, 836–61. Barcelona: Editorial Ariel, 1998.

Forbes, Elizabeth. "Madrid, *El Poeta*." *Opera News* (September 1980). http://www.tenorissimo. com/domingo/articles/on0980.htm.

Fox, E. Inman. "Spain as Castile: Nationalism and National Identity." In *The Cambridge Companion to Modern Spanish Culture*. Ed. David T. Gies, 21–36. Cambridge: Cambridge University Press, 1999.

Franco, Enrique. "Caluroso homenaje a Moreno Torroba." *El País*, November 8, 1981.

———— "Composiciones de Moreno Torroba y Strawinsky." *El País*, November 20, 1979, 35.

———— "Moreno Torroba o la supervivencia del casticismo." *La Chulapona*. Program notes for the production at the Teatro de la Zarzuela, Madrid, September 14–October 1 and October 11–30, 1988, 6–15. Madrid: Teatro de la Zarzuela, 1988.

———— "Moreno Torroba revisa su estilo." *El País*, June 21, 1980.

———— "Una figura del nacionalismo musical. *Autores: Revista de información de la S.G.A.E.*, n3 (October 1982): 34 (first appeared in *El País*, September 13, 1982, 23).

Franco, Francisco. *Palabras del Caudillo*. Madrid: Ediciones de la Vicesecretaría de Educación Popular, 1953.

Francos Rodríguez, J. *El teatro en España: 1908*. Madrid, np, 1908.

Fremont-Barnes, Gregory. *The Napoleonic Wars: The Peninsular War 1807–1814*. Series: Essential Histories, ed. Robert O'Neill. Oxford: Osprey, 2002.

Fuente, Eduardo de la. Program notes for *Concierto-Homenaje, Federico Moreno Torroba (1891–1982) (en el aniversario de su muerte)*. Salamanca, May 2002.

Fuente, Ismael. "Concedida la Medalla de Oro de Madrid a Moreno Torroba en el cincuentenario del estreno de 'Luisa Fernanda.'" *El País*, March 28, 1982.

———— "Julio Caro Baroja, Cela y Moreno Torroba, nombrados hijos predilectos de Madrid." *El País*, May 29, 1982.

Fuente Ballesteros, Ricardo de la. *Introducción al teatro español del siglo XX (1900–1936)*. Valladolid: Aceña, 1987.

Fusi, Juan Pablo. *Un siglo de España, la cultura*. Madrid: Marcial Pons, Ediciones de Historia, 1999.

"Galardón a un madrileño que siempre ejercio de tal." *El Alcázar*, March 28, 1982.

Gallego, Antonio. *Manuel de Falla y El amor brujo*. Madrid: Alianza Música, 1990.

García, María Luz. "'Lo único que no se repite es la música.'" *Última Hora*, April 23, 1982.

García Carretero, Emilio. *Historia del Teatro de la Zarzuela de Madrid. Tomo Segundo: 1913–1955*. Madrid: Fundación de la Zarzuela Española, 2004.

———— *Historia del Teatro de la Zarzuela de Madrid. Tomo Tercero: 1955–2006*. Madrid: Fundación de la Zarzuela Española, 2006.

García León, Julián. "'La Chulapona', alegoría y homenaje a la zarzuela decimonónica." *La Chulapona*. Program notes for the production at the Teatro de la Zarzuela, Madrid, February 6 to March 7, 2004, 9–18. Madrid: Teatro de la Zarzuela, 2003.

García del Busto, J. L. "Moreno Torroba estrena dos piezas 'para ser cantadas por el pueblo.'" *El País*, November 6, 1981.

Garriga-Márques, Ramón. "Exito del ballet 'Don Quijote', en Helsinki." *ABC*, 1970.

Gásser, Luis, ed. *Estudios sobre Fernando Sor/Sor Studies*. Barcelona: Instituto Complutense de Ciencias Musicales, 2003.

Gasset, Carlos. "La alegría de hacer musica." *El Día* (Montevideo), November 15, 1980, 18.

Gies, David T., ed. *The Cambridge Companion to Modern Spanish Culture*. Cambridge: Cambridge University Press, 1999.

Gil de la Vega, Concha. "Federico Moreno Torroba: un madrileño castizo." *Autores: Revista de información de la S.G.A.E.*, n3 (October 1982): 11–12.

Gómez Amat, Carlos. "*La Chulapona* en su momento." *La Chulapona*. Program notes for the production at the Teatro de la Zarzuela, Madrid, September 14–October 1 and October 11–30, 1988, 20–22. Madrid: Teatro de la Zarzuela, 1988.

———— "*Luisa Fernanda* and Its Time." Liner notes for *Luisa Fernanda*. Auvidis Valois, V 4759, 1995, 23–25.

———— "Tiempo de zarzuela." *Boletín informativo de la Fundación Juan March*, n189 (April 1989): 12.

Gómez Labad, José María. *El Madrid de la zarzuela: Visión regocijada de un pasado en cantables*. Madrid: Juan Piñero G., 1983.

——— *La vida y obra de Pablo Sorozábal*. Madrid: Sociedad de Autores de España, 1987.

Gómez Marco, Concha. "La Chulapona en grabaciones." *La Chulapona*. Program notes for the production at the Teatro de la Zarzuela, Madrid, February 6 to March 7, 2004, 33–39. Madrid: Teatro de la Zarzuela, 2003.

Gómez Ortiz, Manuel. "Moreno Torroba o la zarzuela viva." *Ya*, April 4, 1976, 15.

Gómez-Santos, Marino. "Federico Moreno Torroba." *Tribuna médica*, May 28, 1971.

González de Amezúa, Ramón. "Un hombre extraordinario." *Academia: Boletín de la Real Academia de Bellas Artes de San Fernando*, n55 (second semester 1982): 20–22.

González Esteban, Carlos. *Madrid: Sinopsis de su evolución urbana*. Madrid: Ediciones La Librería, 2001.

Greene, Taylor J. "Julian Bream's *20th Century Guitar*: An Album's Influence on the Modern Guitar Repertoire." Master's thesis, University of California, Riverside, 2011.

Halffter, Ernesto. "Federico Moreno Torroba." *Academia: Boletín de la Real Academia de Bellas Artes de San Fernando*, n55 (second semester 1982): 23–24.

Haro Tecglen, Eduardo. "Las víctimas de la fiesta." *El País*, June 21, 1980.

——— "Un personaje del Madrid de Chueca." *El País*, September 13, 1982, 22.

Harrison, Joseph. "Introduction: The Historical Background to the Crisis of 1898." In *Spain's 1898 Crisis: Regenerationism, Modernism, Post-colonialism*. Ed. Joseph Harrison and Alan Hoyle, 1–8. Manchester: Manchester University Press, 2000.

——— "Tackling National Decadence: Economic Regenerationism in Spain after the Colonial Débâcle." In *Spain's 1898 Crisis: Regenerationism, Modernism, Post-colonialism*. Ed. Joseph Harrison and Alan Hoyle, 55–67. Manchester: Manchester University Press, 2000.

Henahan, Donal. "The American Symphony Teams Up with Guitarist." *The New York Times*, November 29, 1976.

Hernández, Amelia. "La ópera levanta cabeza." *Arriba*, October 11, 1977, 25.

Hernández Girbal, F. "Federico Romero y Guillermo Fernández-Shaw." *La Chulapona*. Program notes for the production at the Teatro de la Zarzuela, Madrid, September 14–October 1 and October 11–30, 1988, 16–19. Madrid: Teatro de la Zarzuela, 1988.

Hernández-Amaro, Mercedes. "Festival Moreno-Torroba." *Diario de la Americas* (Puerto Rico), July 17, 1979.

——— "Termina con dos valiosas conferencias que sobre zarzuela y guitarra dicta el maestro." *Diario Las Americas*, July 27, 1974, 10.

Hess, Carol Ann. *Manuel de Falla and Modernism in Spain, 1898–1936*. Chicago: University of Chicago Press, 2001.

——— *Sacred Passions: The Life and Music of Manuel de Falla*. New York: Oxford University Press, 2005.

"Homenaje a Moreno Torroba en El Escorial." *El Alcázar*, June 24, 1980.

"Hoy, entierro del maestro Moreno Torroba." *Ya, Hoja del Lunes*, September 13, 1982.

"Hoy, funeral por Moreno-Torroba en la Concepción." *ABC*, September 14, 1982, 71.

"Hoy se estrena la ópera 'El poeta.'" *El Imparcial*, June 19, 1980.

"Hoy se estrenó 'La chulapona' en el Colón." *La Fronda* (Buenos Aires), November 16, 1934.

Hughes, Robert. *Goya*. New York: Alfred A. Knopf, 2003.

——— *The Shock of the New*. New York: Alfred A. Knopf, 1996.

Ibero. "Moreno Torroba: A los ochenta anos, firme en la brecha lirica." *Diario de Barcelona*, March 24, 1971.

Iglesias, Antonio. "Larregla Urbieta, Joaquín." *Diccionario de la música española e hispanoamericana*. Ed. Emilio Casares Rodicio. Madrid: ICCMU, 2002.

——— "Los Romero y Theo Alcantara, en un estreno de Moreno Torroba." *Informaciones*, November 19, 1979.

Imbuluzqueta, Gabriel. "El compositor Federico Moreno Torroba será homenajeado el viernes en el Teatro Real, en Madrid." *Diario de Navarra*, November 11, 1981.

"Imposición de las Ordenes de Cisneros." *Arriba*, February 10, 1977.

"Informaciones teatrales en Madrid: Calderón: 'Tu eres ella'. Comedia lírica de Luis Tejedor, Muñoz Llorente y el maestro Moreno Torroba." *ABC*, April 27, 1940, 15.

"Informaciones y noticias teatrales." *ABC*, January 13, 1944, 16.

"Informaciones y noticias teatrales . . . : en el Calderón se presentó ayer tarde la compañía de revistas de Virginia de Matos con *Pitusa* del maestro Moreno Torroba." *ABC*, March 2, 1952, 49.

"Informaciones de música, teatros y cinematografos: El Maestro Moreno Torroba, en Sevilla. Hoy, el estreno de 'Sor Navarra'." *ABC Sevilla*, February 1, 1939, 18.

"Informaciones de música, teatros y cinematografos: Teatro Cervantes: Estreno de 'Sor Navarra'. . . ." *ABC Sevilla*, February 2, 1939, 21.

[Interview with Federico Moreno Torroba]. *Brújula* (Madrid), January 3, 1976.

[Interview with Federico Moreno Torroba]. *Music Week* (Great Britain), December 6, 1980.

[Interview with Federico Moreno Torroba]. *Ritmo* (October 1974) (reproduced in *Autores: Revista de información de la S.G.A.E.*, special fiftieth-anniversary issue (1982): 32–33).

Jaze. "Maestro Moreno Torroba, más de medio siglo al servicio de la música española." *Diario de Avisos*, May 19, 1982.

Jenkins, Speight. "A New Opera for Domingo: Torroba's 'El Poeta' Provides an Ideal Role." *Musical America* (October 1980): 40.

Jiménez Campo, Javier. "Rasgos básicos de la ideologia entre 1939–45." *Revista de Estudios Políticos*, n15 (May–June 1980): 79–117.

Jiménez de Parga, María Victoria. "La zarzuela en Madrid en 1934." *La Chulapona*. Program notes for the production at the Teatro de la Zarzuela, Madrid, September 14–October 1 and October 11–30, 1988, 31–34. Madrid: Teatro de la Zarzuela, 1988.

Juliá, Santos. "History, Politics, Culture, 1975–1996." In *The Cambridge Companion to Modern Spanish Culture*. Ed. David T. Gies, 104–22. Cambridge: Cambridge University Press, 1999.

Jurkevich, Gayana. *In Pursuit of the Natural Sign: Azorín and the Poetics of Ekphrasis*. London: Associated University Presses, 1999.

Kamen, Henry. *The Disinherited: Exile and the Making of Spanish Culture, 1492–1975*. New York: HarperCollins, 2007.

Klotz, Volker. "Aspectos nacionales y esteticos de la zarzuela." *La Chulapona*. Program notes for the production at the Teatro de la Zarzuela, Madrid, September 14–October 1 and October 11–30, 1988, 35–37. Madrid: Teatro de la Zarzuela, 1988.

Krause, William Craig. "*Casticismo* before and after 1939." *Diagonal: Journal of the Center for Iberian and Latin American Music* 7 (2011), http://cilam.ucr.edu/diagonal/issues/2011/index.html.

——— "Moreno Torroba, Federico." *Diccionario de la música española e hispanoamericana*. Ed. Emilio Casares Rodicio. Madrid:

——— "¿Quien fue Federico Moreno Torroba en relación a las circunstancias políticas de su época? Un perfil." Unpublished essay, June 17, 2006.

——— "The Life and Works of Federico Moreno Torroba." PhD diss., Washington University, St. Louis, Missouri, 1993.

L. M. "Moreno Torroba habla claro." *Ya, Hoja del Lunes*, October 3, 1977.

L. de A. "El teatro español: Ante una campaña official." *Informaciones*, June 25, 1926, 1.

"'La chulapona', de Moreno Torroba, se estrenará esta noche en el teatro Colón." *La Nación* (Buenos Aires), November 16, 1934.

"'La Chulapona' se estrenó con exito en el teatro Colón." *Tribuna Libre* (Buenos Aires), November 17, 1934.

"La medalla de honor del Bellas Artes, al Instituto de Humanidades Camón Aznar." *ABC*, November 10, 1981, 40.

"La muerte de Federico Moreno Torroba." *Diario de Navarra*, September 13, 1982, 11–12.

"La zarzuela está de luto con la muerte del maestro Moreno Torroba." *El Noticiero Universal*, September 13, 1982, 35.

"'La zarzuela está vivita y coleando.'" *Revista 7 Días* (Argentina), July 18, 1975, 56.

"La zarzuela nacional." *Cambio* 16/405 (September 9, 1979), 52–53.

"La zarzuela que no queria morir." *Periscopio*, n22 (November 17, 1970): 50–51.

Labajo, Joaquina. *Sin contra la música: Ruinas, sueños y encuentros en la Europa de María Zambrano*. Madrid: Endymion, 2011.

Laborda, Ángel. "Conversación con José Méndez Herrera." *ABC*, May 30, 1980, 27.

———. "'El poeta', de Méndez Herrera y Moreno Torroba." *ABC*, June 19, 1980, 59.

Lafuente Ferrari, Enrique. "Recordando a D. Federico Moreno Torroba." *Academia: Boletín de la Real Academia de Bellas Artes de San Fernando*, n55 (second semester 1982): 13–16.

Lannon, Frances. *The Spanish Civil War: 1936–1939*. Series: Essential Histories, ed. Robert O'Neill. Oxford: Osprey Publishing, 2002.

"Las 15 mil representaciones de la zarzuela 'Luisa Fernanda.'" *El Comercio* (Buenos Aires), February 1, 1981.

Laspeyres, Isabelle. "Joaquín Turina à Paris." *Revue internationale de musique française* 9/26 (June 1988): 61–84.

Lecea, Juan María. "Joaquín Larregla, a los 50 años de su muerte." *Diario de Navarra*, June 25, 1995, 58.

Livermore, Ann. *A Short History of Spanish Music*. New York: Vienna House, 1972.

"Llegaron hoy el maestro Torroba y los artistas que actuarán en el Teatro Colón." *La Razón* (Buenos Aires), October 24, 1934.

"Llegó la compañía española del Colón." *La Nación* (Buenos Aires), October 25, 1934.

Llorca, Carmen. "Federico Moreno Torroba." *Faro del Lunes*, September 27, 1982, 3.

———. "Federico Moreno Torroba." *Ya*, November 21, 1981.

López, Fernando, and L. de Tejada. "Estreno de 'El Poeta' de Moreno Torroba." *El Alcázar*, June 21, 1980.

———. "Estreno del 'Concierto ibérico', de Moreno Torroba." *El Alcázar*, November 24, 1979, 28.

———. "La Nacional y homenaje navarro a Moreno Torroba." *El Alcázar*, November 8, 1981, 32.

López Poveda, Alberto. *Andrés Segovia: vida y obra*. 2 vols. Jaén: Universidad de Jaén, 2009.

———. Letter to William Craig Krause, Linares (Jaén), July 7, 1990.

López Salas, María. "Ya no escribe zarzuelas." *Nueva Rioja*, September 14, 1977.

Lopezarias, Germán. "1936–1939: Los años prohibidos." *Pueblo*, April 21, 197?.

"Los cineastas lo tienen muy negro." *Mundo Diario*, April 21, 1978.

"Los estrenos de *La Chulapona*." *La Chulapona*. Program notes for the production at the Teatro de la Zarzuela, Madrid, September 14–October 1 and October 11–30, 1988, 38–43. Madrid: Teatro de la Zarzuela, 1988.

Luca de Tena, Cayetano. "Pequeña historia del año 1891." *Blanco y negro* 79 (November 1, 1969).

"'Luisa Fernanda' en el Colón." *El Mundo* (Buenos Aires), October 29, 1934.

"'Luisa Fernanda' fue el estreno inaugural." *La Nación* (Buenos Aires), October 28, 1934.

"'Luisa Fernanda' se estrenó con gran éxito en el teatro Colón." *Tribuna Libre* (Buenos Aires), October 28, 1934.

"'Luisa Fernanda' será repuesta en el Colón." *La Nación*, June 15, 1975.

"'Luisa Fernanda' tuvo éxito." *Crítica* (Buenos Aires), October 28, 1934.

Machado y Álvarez, Antonio. *Cantes flamencos*. 4th ed. Madrid: Espasa-Calpe, 1985.

Madariaga, Paquita. "Zarzuela en Miami este fin de semana." *El Nuevo Herald* (Miami), February 1, 1991, 1C.

Mallo, Albino. "Los noventa jovenes años de Moreno Torroba." *Heraldo de Aragón*, December 21, 1980.

Mañas, Alfredo. "Querido Maestro:" *Autores: Revista de información de la S.G.A.E.*, n3 (October 1982): 20–25.

Mangold, Maximilian. *Spanische Gitarrenmusik*. Musicaphon M56833, 2000.

Mantilla, Juan María. "Irma Costanzo estrenara un concerito de Torroba." *Ya*, March 22, 1975.

Marco, Tomás. *Historia de la música española: siglo XX* (Madrid: Editorial Alianza, 1983).

———. "Los años cuarenta." In *España en la música de Occidente: Actas del Congreso Internacional celebrado en Salamanca 29 de octubre–5 de noviembre de 1985*. 2 vols. Ed. Emilio Casares Rodicio, Ismael Fernández de la Cuesta, and José López-Calo, ii, 399–411. Madrid: Ministerio de Cultura, 1987.

———— *Spanish Music in the Twentieth Century.* Trans. Cola Franzen. Cambridge, Massachusetts: Harvard University Press, 1993.

———— "Un músico integral." *Autores: Revista de información de la S.G.A.E.*, n3 (October 1982): 33 (reprint of an article in *Diario 16*, September 13, 1982, 16).

María, Manuel. "La empecinada juventud del maestro Moreno Torroba." *El Comercio* (Gijón), February 13, 1980, 39.

Marín, A. "Homenaje a Moreno Torroba en Miami." *ABC*, August 6, 1974, 69.

Marsillach, Adolfo. "Crónicas barcelonesas: Teatros, mujeres, moralidad y costumbres." *Informaciones*, June 16, 1926, 5.

Marti, Octavi. "'La cuitat cremada' cobró 1.200 pesetas." *Tele/eXpres*, April 21, 1978, 30.

Martín Cámara, Francisco J. Letter to William Craig Krause, Madrid, October 17, 1990.

———— Letter to William Craig Krause, Madrid, December 1, 1990.

———— Letter to William Craig Krause, Madrid, January 12, 1991.

Martínez del Alamo, Josefina. "El el estreno de la ópera 'El Poeta.'" *ABC*, June 22, 1980, 23.

Martínez Garin, Charo. "Federico Moreno Torroba, o la última generación clásica de la música española." *Brújula*, January 23, 1976.

Marzo, Jorge Luis. *Art modern i franquisme: els orígens conservadors de l'avantguarda i de la política artística a l'estat espanyol (Arte moderno y franquismo: Los orígenes conservadores de la vanguardia y de la política artística en España).* Girona : Fundació Espais d'Art Contemporani, 2007.

———— "The Spectacle of Spain's Amnesia: Spanish Cultural Policy from the Dictatorship to Expo '92." Trans. Ian Kennedy. *Alphabet City* 4–5 (1995): 90–95.

Maso, Ángeles. "Teatro Victoria: Presentación de 'Luisa Fernanda' en la temporada de zarzuela." *La Vanguardia*, June 10, 1972.

Massa, Pedro. "Éxito de Moreno Torroba en Buenos Aires." *ABC*, June 1, 1975, 54.

Matheopoulos, Helena. *Plácido Domingo: My Operatic Roles.* Fort Worth, Texas: Baskerville Publishers, 2000.

Medina, Ángel. "Primeras oleadas vanguardistas en el área de Madrid." In *España en la música de Occidente: Actas del Congreso Internacional celebrado en Salamanca 29 de octubre–5 de noviembre de 1985.* 2 vols. Ed. Emilio Casares Rodicio, Ismael Fernández de la Cuesta, and José López-Calo, ii, 369–98. Madrid: Ministerio de Cultura, 1987.

Mengual. "Federico Moreno Torroba: 'El género de zarzuela está enfermo.'" *Levante*, June 6, 1981.

Molla, Juan. "Los autores y el derecho del autor." *Métodos de Información* 8/44 (May 2001): 51–53.

Moncayo, Andrés. "Moreno Torroba, una gloria nacional." *Hoja del Lunes*, January 5, 1976.

Montero Díaz, Julio. "El Franquismo: Planteamiento general." In *Historia contemporánea de España, siglo XX.* Ed. Javier Paredes, 639–61. Barcelona: Editorial Ariel, 1998.

Montes, Eugenio. "Apoteósico éxito del 'ballet' sobre el hijo pródigo, intrepretado en Roma por Luisillo." *ABC*, September 9, 1975, 30.

Montijano Ruiz, Juan José. "Historia del teatro olvidado: La revista (1864–2009)." Tésis doctoral, Univesidad de Granada, 2009.

———— "Panorama (breve y retrospectivo) de un teatro olvidado en España: La revista (1864–2010)." *Signa. Revista de la Asociación Española de Semiótica* 20 (2011): 447–70.

Montsalvatge, Xavier. "Moreno Torroba o la vitalidad." *La Vanguardia*, September 13, 1982.

Morales, Luisa. "Dances in Eighteenth-century Spanish Keyboard Music." *Diagonal: Journal of the Center for Iberian and Latin American Music* 1 (2005), http://cilam.ucr.edu/diagonal/issues/2005/morales.html.

Moreda-Rodríguez, Eva. "Italian Musicians in Francoist Spain, 1939–1945: The Perspective of Music Critics." *Music & Politics* 2/1 (Winter 2008): 1–10.

Moreno, Antonio Martín. *Historia de la música española: Siglo XVIII.* Madrid: Alianza Música, 1985.

Moreno Juste, Antonio. "La Guerra Civil (1936–1939)." In *Historia contemporánea de España, siglo XX.* Ed. Javier Paredes, 520–47. Barcelona: Editorial Ariel, 1998.

"Moreno Torroba, director de la Academia de Bellas Artes." *La Vanguardia*, May 10, 1978, 19.

"Moreno Torroba, el más famoso compositor actual de zarzuela, pasó por Montevideo." *El Día* (Montevideo), June 17, 1975.

"Moreno Torroba: 'Esto es un premio a la amistad.'" *ABC*, May 10, 1978, 37.

"Moreno Torroba, Medalla de Oro del Trabajo." *ABC*, August 2, 1973 (morning edition), 55.

"Moreno Torroba, mucha música en muchos años." *Diario de Mallorca* (Palma de Mallorca). December 10, 1976.

"Moreno Torroba: 'No dejaré que la zarzuela muera.'" *El Mercurio* (Santiago, Chile), September 14, 1979.

"Moreno Torroba nombrado director de la Academia de Bellas Artes." *El País*, May 9, 1978, 35.

"Moreno-Torroba será enterrado hoy en la sacramental de San Justo." *ABC*, September 13, 1982, 38–39 (also in *Autores: Revista de información de la S.G.A.E.*, n3 (October 1982): 32).

"Moreno Torroba trae una compañía de zarzuela." *Crítica* (Buenos Aires), October 23, 1934.

"Moreno Torroba: un siglo de música española." *Música clásica*, February 27, 1991, 4–5.

Moreno Torroba, Federico. "Autocrítica: 'Paloma Moreno.'" *ABC*, February 27, 1936, 15.

—— "Aventuras y desventuras de la zarzuela como género." Undated lecture notes.

—— *Discurso leído por el Señor Don Federico Moreno Torroba en el acto de su recepción pública y contestación del Señor Don Ángel María Castell el día 21 de febrero de 1935*. Madrid: Real Academia de Bellas Artes de San Fernando, 1935.

—— "El año musical." *Informaciones*, January 1, 1925, 7.

—— "La ópera en Apolo: 'La Dolores.'" *Informaciones*, February 17, 1926, 3.

—— "Llega a Madrid el 'Concierto ibérico', de Moreno Torroba." *Ya*, November 16, 1979, 50.

—— "Lo que el magisterio puede hacer por la música." *Boletín de la Sociedad General de Autores de España* (January–March 1970): 3–4.

—— "Mesajes musicales de la guitarra de hoy." Undated lecture notes.

—— "Nuestra ofrenda a Chapí." *Boletín de la Sociedad General de Autores de España* (October–December 1970): 3.

—— "Una llamada a la colaboración de todos." *Autores: Revista de información de la S.G.A.E.*, special fiftieth-anniversary issue (1982): 43–44.

—— "Vida musical." *Informaciones*, January 24, 1925, 4.

—— "Vida musical." *Informaciones*, March 10, 1925, 3.

—— "Vida musical." *Informaciones*, April 3, 1925, 4.

—— "Vida musical." *Informaciones*, April 7, 1925, 6.

—— "Vida musical." *Informaciones*, April 22, 1925, 3.

—— "Vida musical." *Informaciones*, April 27, 1925, 7.

—— "Vida musical." *Informaciones*, October 2, 1925, 3.

—— "Vida musical." *Informaciones*, October 15, 1925, 3.

—— "Vida musical." *Informaciones*, October 27, 1925, 5.

—— "Vida musical." *Informaciones*, November 3, 1925, 5.

—— "Vida musical." *Informaciones*, November 7, 1925, 5.

—— "Vida musical." *Informaciones*, November 16, 1925, 4.

—— "Vida musical." *Informaciones*, December 4, 1925, 4.

—— "Vida musical." *Informaciones*, December 24, 1925, 4.

—— "Vida musical." *Informaciones*, January 5, 1926, 5.

—— "Vida musical." *Informaciones*, January 30, 1926, 4.

—— "Vida musical." *Informaciones*, March 2, 1926, 3.

—— "Vida musical." *Informaciones*, March 8, 1926, 4.

—— "Vida musical." *Informaciones*, March 11, 1926, 4.

—— "Vida musical." *Informaciones*, March 18, 1926, 2.

—— "Vida musical." *Informaciones*, March 26, 1926, 4.

—— "Vida musical." *Informaciones*, March 31, 1926, 6.

—— "Vida musical." *Informaciones*, April 8, 1926, 5.

—— "Vida musical." *Informaciones*, April 14, 1926, 5.

—— "Vida musical." *Informaciones*, October 2, 1926, 6.

—— "Vida musical." *Informaciones*, November 15, 1926, 8.

—— "Vida musical." *Informaciones*, November 29, 1926, 6.

—— "Vida musical." *Informaciones*, December 8, 1926, 4.

—— "Vida musical." *Informaciones*, February 13, 1931, 7.

Moreno-Torroba Larregla, Federico. Interview by William Craig Krause, Madrid, July 18, 1988.

———— "Los vínculos de un músico con Santesteban." *Doneztebeko Sanpedro Bestak* (2006): 7–13.

Moreno-Torroba Larregla, Federico, ed. *Luisa Fernanda*. Comedia lírica en tres actos. Madrid: ICCMU, 2011.

Moser, Wolf. *Francisco Tárrega y la guitarra en España entre 1830 y 1960*. 2d ed. Valencia: Piles Editorial, 2009.

Muñoz Cáliz, Berta. *El teatro crítico español durante el franquismo, visto por sus censores*. Madrid: Fundación Universitaria Española, 2005. http://www.bertamuñoz.es/censura/indice.html.

Muro de Iscar, Francisco. "Una gran labor." *Arriba*, February 10, 1977, 8.

"Música para la Academia de Bellas Artes en la festividad de San Fernando." *El País*, May 31, 1982.

Nadal, Pablo. "Recuerdo del maestro." *El Noticiero Universal*, September 13, 1982, 35.

Nagore, María, Leticia Sánchez de Andrés, and Elena Torres, eds. *Música y cultura en la Edad de Plata, 1915–1939*. Madrid: ICCMU, 2009.

"Necrologías del Excmo. Sr. D. Federico Moreno Torroba." *Academia: Boletín de la Real Academia de Bellas Artes de San Fernando*, n55 (second semester 1982).

Nepomuceno, Miguel Ángel. "Amor, guerra y ambición." *Diario de León*, May 30, 2003, 73.

Neri de Caso, Leopoldo. "La guitarra en el ideario musical de Adolfo Salazar (1915–1939)." In *Música y cultura en la Edad de Plata, 1915–1939*. Ed. María Nagore, Leticia Sánchez de Andrés, and Elena Torres, 297–314. Madrid: ICCMU, 2009.

"Noches del Colón: 'Luisa Fernanda', de M. Torroba." *El Diario* (Buenos Aires), October 28, 1934.

Nogueira, Charo. "Retrato de un compositor: 'Sinó trabajase, seguro que envejecería rápidamente.'" *Diario 16*, September 13, 1982, 50.

"Notas teatrales." *ABC*, October 20, 1939, 19.

Nozick, Martin. *Miguel de Unamuno*. New York: Twayne Publishers, 1971.

Öhrlein, Josef. "La zarzuela y el casticismo madrileño." *La Chulapona*. Program notes for the production at the Teatro de la Zarzuela, Madrid, September 14–October 1 and October 11–30, 1988, 23–30. Madrid: Teatro de la Zarzuela, 1988.

Olano, Antonio D. "50 aniversario de la S.G.A.E." *Heraldo Español*, February 24–March 2, 1982.

———— "'Don Quijote', un 'ballet' de Moreno Torroba." *Autores: Revista de información de la S.G.A.E.*, n3 (October 1982): 18–19.

———— *Homenaje a Federico Moreno Torroba*. Madrid: Sociedad General de Autores de España, 1982.

———— "Moreno Torroba: Entre la inspiración y el trabajo." *Autores: Revista de información de la S.G.A.E.*, n3 (October 1982): 5–10.

———— "¡Viva Navarra! Homenaje a Moreno Torroba." *El Alcázar*, November 3, 1981.

Oliver, Amy A. "The Construction of a Philosophy of History and Life in the Major Essays of Miguel de Unamuno and Leopoldo Zea." PhD diss., University of Massachusetts, 1987.

"Ópera en directo: 'El poeta', de Moreno Torroba." *Diario 16*, June 25, 1980.

Ortega y Gasset, José. *Invertebrate Spain*. Trans. Mildred Adams. New York: W. W. Norton, 1937.

Orwell, George. *Homage to Catalonia*. Intro. Lionel Trilling. Orlando, Florida: Harcourt, 1980.

Pajares, Gema. "Plácido Domingo: 'Cuando canto "Luisa Fernanda" contengo las lágrimas.'" *La Razón*, June 24, 2006, 34–35.

Palacios Garóz, Miguel A. *Introducción a la música popular castellana y leonesa*. Madrid: Artes Gráficas Santiago Rodríguez, 1984.

Pardo Canalís, Enrique. "Don Federico Moreno Torroba." *Academia: Boletín de la Real Academia de Bellas Artes de San Fernando*, n55 (second semester 1982): 7–11.

Pascal, Marie. "Derechos de autor y otros temas actuales." *La Nación* (Buenos Aires), April 30, 1978, 2.

Payne, Alyson. "The 1964 Festival of Music of the Americas and Spain: A Critical Examination of Ibero-American Musical Relations in the Context of Cold War Politics." PhD diss., University of California, Riverside, 2012.

Payne, Stanley G. *Falange: A History of Spanish Fascism*. Stanford, California: Stanford University Press, 1961.

Pedrell, Felipe. *Cancionero musical popular español*. 4 vols. Barcelona: Boileau, nd.

———— *Por nuestra música*. 2d ed. Barcelona: Henrich & Co., 1937.

Pérez Ollo, Fernando. "Madrileñismo a tope y coro lírico nuevo." *Diario de Navarra*, November 30, 2005, 80.

Pérez Zalduondo, Gemma. "Formulación, fracaso y despertar de la conciencia crítica en la música española durante el franquismo (1936–1958)." In *Music and Dictatorship in Europe and Latin America*. Ed. Roberto Illiano and Massimiliano Sala, 449–69. Turnhout, Belgium: Brepols Publishers, 2009.

———"La música en los intercambios culturales entre España y Alemania (1938–1942)." *Cruces de caminos: Intercambios musicales y artísticos en la Europa de la primera mitad del siglo XX*. Ed. Gemma Pérez Zalduondo and María Isabel Cabrera García, 407–49. Granada: Editorial Universidad de Granada, 2010.

Pérez Zalduondo, Gemma, and María Isabel Cabrera García, eds. *Cruces de caminos: Intercambios musicales y artísticos en la Europa de la primera mitad del siglo XX*. Granada: Editorial Universidad de Granada, 2010.

Piquer Sanclemente, Ruth. *Clasicismo moderno, neoclasicismo y retornos en el pensamiento musical español (1915–1939)*. Sevilla: Editorial Doble J, 2010.

"Plácido Domingo es el Espronceda de Moreno Torroba." *Diario 16*, June 18, 1980, 23.

"Plácido Domingo estreno 'El poeta', de Moreno Torroba." *La Vanguardia*, June 21, 1980, 54.

Pohren, Donn E. *Lives and Legends of Flamenco: A Biographical History*. Madrid: Society of Spanish Studies, 1988.

"Presunto fraude de doscientos ochenta millones de pesetas." *Ya*, March 9, 1978.

Prieto, Indalecio de. "Dos infiernos: franquismo y comunismo." *Siempre* (Mexico), September 29, 1954.

Quagliata, Humberto. "Recordando al Maestro Federico Moreno Torroba: 'De un apacible rincón de Madrid…a la inmortalidad.'" *El Diario Español* (Montevideo), October 5, 1982, 10.

R. T. "Irma Costanzo—Moreno-Torroba." *Buenos Aires Musical*, September 1975, 3.

Ramos, Elisa. "Homenaje a Federico Moreno Torroba." *Tribuna de Salamanca*, May 6, 2002, 12.

Radomski, James. *Manuel García (1775–1832): Chronicle of the Life of a* bel canto *Tenor at the Dawn of Romanticism*. New York: Oxford University Press, 2000.

Redondo, M. *Un hombre que se va*. Barcelona: Planeta, 1973.

Remos, Ariel. "Interesantes opiniones de Fernández-Cid sobre la opera 'El Poeta' del Maestro Moreno Torroba." *Diario Las Americas*, August 1, 1980, 11.

Répide, Pedro de. *Las calles de Madrid*. 2d ed. Madrid: Afrodisio de Aguado, 1972.

"Retransmisión, en UHF y en diferido, del estreno de la ópera 'El poeta.'" *El Imparcial*, June 25, 1980.

Ridao, José María. *Contra la historia*. Barcelona: Círculo de Lectores/Galaxia Gutenberg, 2009.

Rincón, José María. *Federico Romero*. Madrid: Sociedad de Autores de España, 1986.

Río López, Ángel del. *Los viejos cafés de Madrid*. 2d ed. Madrid: Ediciones La Librería, 2009.

Rioja, Roberto. "Federico Moreno Torroba: Ochenta y una gloriosas primaveras." *Hilo mundial* (January 1973), 27–28.

Rius, Adrián. *Francisco Tárrega (1852–1909): Biography*. Valencia: Piles, 2006.

Robertson, Geoffrey. *The Case of the Pope: Vatican Accountability for Human Rights Abuse*. London: Penguin, 2010.

Robinson, John. Program notes for performance of Torroba's *Diálogos entre guitarra y orquesta*, Ohio Chamber Orchestra, Dwight Oltman, director, and Michael Lorimer, guitar soloist. January 22, 1978.

Rodrigo, Joaquín. "Federico Moreno Torroba." *Academia: Boletín de la Real Academia de Bellas Artes de San Fernando*, n55 (second semester 1982): 17–19.

Romero, Federico. *Cinco cartas boca arriba de F. Romero y Guillermo Fernández Shaw*. Madrid: Repoker, 1950.

Romero, Federico, and Guillermo Fernández-Shaw. "'Luisa Fernanda.'" *ABC*, March 26, 1932, 16.

Romero, Pepe. "Pepe Romero Reminisces about Federico Moreno Torroba." *Soundboard* 10/2 (1983): 144–45.

Romero de Lecea, Carlos. "En recuerdo de Federico Moreno Torroba." *Academia: Boletín de la Real Academia de Bellas Artes de San Fernando*, n55 (second semester 1982): 25–26.

Rubio, David. "La historia contada a través de la zarzuela." *El Mundo/La Crónica de León*, May 30, 2003, 69.

Ruiz Albéniz, Víctor. "Aquel Madrid." In *Albéniz y su tiempo*. Ed. Enrique Franco, 17–21. Madrid: Fundación Isaac Albéniz, 1990.

Ruiz Coca, Fernando. "Admirable evolución de Moreno Torroba en 'El Poeta.'" *Ya*, June 21, 1980.

—— Program notes for premiere of the *Concierto ibérico*, Orquesta Nacional de España, Madrid, November 1979.

Ruiz de la Serna, Enrique. "Las novedades escénicas del Sabado de Gloria." *La Chulapona*. Program notes for the production at the Teatro de la Zarzuela, Madrid, February 6 to March 7, 2004, 29–32. Madrid: Teatro de la Zarzuela, 2003.

Ruiz Tarazona, Andrés. "Estreno mundial de la opera española 'El poeta', de Federico Moreno Torroba y José Méndez Herrera." *El País*, June 18, 1980, 39.

—— "Garcia Navarro dirigira hoy la ultima representacion de 'El poeta', de Moreno Torroba." *El País*, June 25, 1980, 41.

Saavedra, María Elena. "Festival Federico Moreno Torroba anuncia la Sociedad Pro Arte Grateli." *Diario de las Americas*, June 6, 1974.

—— "Moreno Torroba honra a su padre con la dirección de dos zarzuelas." *Diario Las Americas*, February 2, 1991, 8-A.

Sagi-Vela, Luis. "Moreno Torroba, nonagenario, trabaja diez horas diarias." *Ya Dominical*, November 15, 1981, 22–23.

Sainz de la Maza, Regino. "Contestación a Antonio Fernández-Cid." *La Decada Musical de los Cuarenta. Discurso del académico electo...el día 30 noviembre de 1980, con motivo de su recepción.* Madrid: Real Academia de Bellas Artes de San Fernando, 1980.

—— "Estreno de 'Monte Carmelo', de Federico Romero y Guillermo Fernandez Shaw y el maestro Moreno Torroba." *ABC*, October 18, 1939, 15.

—— "Informaciones teatrales en Madrid: Calderon: 'Tú eres ella.' Comedia lírica de Luis Tejedor, Muñoz Llorente y el maestro Moreno Torroba. *ABC*, April 27, 1940, 18.

Sainz de Robles, Federico Carlos. "Fechas inolvidables para dos Federicos." *Autores: Revista de información de la S.G.A.E.*, n3 (October 1982): 28–29.

—— "Medio siglo de labor fecunda y feliz." *Autores: Revista de información de la S.G.A.E.*, special fiftieth-anniversary issue (1982): 8–31.

Salazar, Adolfo. "El nuevo arte de la guitarra y Andrés Segovia. Obras españolas. El primer concierto del Real. Brahms y Von Holst." *El Sol*, December 20, 1923, 6.

—— *La música de España: La música en la cultura española*. Buenos Aires: Espasa-Calpe, 1953.

—— "La reorganización del teatro lírico nacional y de los conciertos sinfónicos." *El Sol*, April 14, 1931.

—— *Music in Our Time*. Trans. Isabel Pope. New York: W. W. Norton, 1946.

—— [Review of *La virgen de mayo*.] *El Sol*, February 16, 1925.

San Martín, Hebrero. "Federico Moreno Torroba, 90 años de vida y de música." Clipping from unknown periodical, between March 3, 1981, and March 2, 1982. [Na]

Sánchez, Celia. "Intenso encuentro con la musica de Torroba en el Breton." *El Adelanto de Salamanca*, May 7, 2002, 12.

Sánchez Sánchez, Víctor. "Moreno Torroba y la nostalgia de un Madrid idealizado." *La Chulapona*. Program notes for the production at the Teatro de la Zarzuela, Madrid, February 6 to March 7, 2004, 19–28. Madrid: Teatro de la Zarzuela, 2003.

—— "Un zarzuelista en la Junta Nacional de Música. *Talismán* de Vives, como modelo para el Teatro Lírico Nacional." In *Música y cultura en la Edad de Plata, 1915–1939*. Ed. María Nagore, Leticia Sánchez de Andrés, and Elena Torres, 529–48. Madrid: ICCMU, 2009.

—— "Xuanón." *Diccionario de la zarzuela: España e Hispanoamérica*. Ed. Emilio Casares Rodicio. Madrid: ICCMU, 2002.

"Se darán por última vez 'Doña Francisquita' y 'Luisa Fernanda.'" *El Diario* (Buenos Aires), November 12, 1934.

"Se estrenó anoche en el Colón 'Luisa Fernanda', comedia lírica del maestro F. Moreno Torroba." *La Prensa* (Buenos Aires), October 28, 1934.

"Se realizó el homenaje a Torroba." *El Diaro* (Buenos Aires), October 30, 1934.

"Se reprisó 'Marina', vieja obra del maestro Arrieta." *República Ilustrada* (Buenos Aires), November 12, 1934.

Segovia, Andrés. *Andrés Segovia: An Autobiography of the Early Years 1893–1920*. Trans. W. F. O'Brien. New York: Macmillan, 1976.

———— "Breves palabras sobre Torroba." *Academia: Boletín de la Real Academia de Bellas Artes de San Fernando*, n55 (second semester 1982): 27–29.

———— "La guitarra y yo." *Discurso leído por el Excmo. Sr. Don Andrés Segovia Torres con motivo de su recepción pública el día 8 de enero de 1978, y contestación del Excmo. Sr. Don Federico Moreno Torroba*. Madrid: Real Academia de Bellas Artes de San Fernando, 1978.

Serrano Anguila, Francisco, José Tellaeche, and F. Moreno Torroba. "Autocriticia: 'Paloma Moreno.'" *ABC*, February 27, 1936, 15.

Shaw, Donald. *The Generation of 98*. New York: Barnes and Noble, 1975.

"'Si sale mal "El poeta" es culpa mía.'" *El Imparcial*, May 21, 1980.

Sinova Garrido, Justino, ed. *Un siglo en 100 artículos*. Madrid: La Esfera de los Libros, 2002.

"Sociedad General de Autores de España (General Society of Spanish Authors): Worldwide Hommage to Maestro Moreno-Torroba." *Billboard*, November 8, 1980.

"Solicitan la suspensión de la junta general de la Sociedad de Autores." *El País*, March 9, 1978, 27.

Sopeña, Federico. "Dos Guitarras: Torroba y Bacarisse." *Hoja del Lunes*, February 23, 1976.

———— *Historia de la música española contemporánea*. Madrid: Rialp, 1958.

Sorozábal, Pablo. Interview with William Craig Krause, Madrid, July 27, 1988.

Stéfani, Daniel. "Federico Moreno Torroba: La juventud de un compositor de 89 años." *El Día* (Montevideo), October 24, 1980.

Stein, Louise. *Songs of Mortals, Dialogues of the Gods: Music and Theatre in Seventeenth-century Spain*. Oxford: Clarendon Press, 1993.

Sturman, Janet. *Zarzuela: Spanish Operetta, American Stage*. Urbana and Chicago: University of Illinois Press, 2000.

Suárez-Pajares, Javier. "El periodo de entreguerras como ámbito de estudio de la música española." *Mundoclasico.com*, February 21, 2002. http://www.mundoclasico.com/2009/documentos/doc-ver.aspx?id=0011686

————, ed. *Joaquín Rodrigo y la musica española de los años cuarenta*. Valladolid: Universidad de Valladolid/Glares, 2005.

———— "Chulapona, La." *Diccionario de la zarzuela: España e Hispanoamérica*. Ed. Emilio Casares Rodicio. Madrid: ICCMU, 2002.

———— "Luisa Fernanda." *Diccionario de la zarzuela: España e Hispanoamérica*. Ed. Emilio Casares Rodicio. Madrid: ICCMU, 2002.

———— "Moreno Torroba, Federico." *Diccionario de la zarzuela: España e Hispanoamérica*. Ed. Emilio Casares Rodicio. Madrid: ICCMU, 2002.

Subirá, José. *Historia de la música teatral en España*. Madrid: Editorial Labor, 1959.

———— *Historia de la música española e hispano americano*. Madrid: Salvat Editores S. A., 1953.

Tanenbaum, David. "Perspectives on the Classical Guitar in the Twentieth Century." In *The Cambridge Companion to the Guitar*. Ed. Victor Anand Coelho, 182–206. Cambridge: Cambridge University Press, 2003.

Téllez, Juan José. *Paco de Lucia: Retrato de familia con guitarra*. Series: Señales de vida. Sevilla: Qüàsyeditorial, 1994.

Terrazas, Ana Cecilia. "Pepita Embil, su marido y la compañia de Moreno Torroba enfrentaron a un México republicano que acusó de franquista a la zarzuela." *Edición México*, September 3, 1994.

The Royal Shakespeare Theatre Edition of The Sonnets of William Shakespeare. New York: Paddington Press, 1974.

Thomas, Hugh. *The Spanish Civil War*. New York: Simon & Schuster, 1994.

Thompson, Donald P. "*Doña Francisquita*, A Zarzuela by Amadeo Vives." PhD diss., University of Iowa, 1970.

"Tiene aciertos 'La Chulapona.'" *Crítica* (Buenos Aires), November 14, 1934.

Tinnell, Roger D. "Spanish Music and Cultural Identity." In *The Cambridge Companion to Modern Spanish Culture*. Ed. David T. Gies, 287–97. Cambridge: Cambridge University Press, 1999.

Torres Clemente, Elena. "Interrelaciones personales y artísticas entre 'Les Six' y el Grupo de los Ocho de Madrid." In *Cruces de caminos: Intercambios musicales y artísticos en la Europa de la primera mitad del siglo XX*. Ed. Gemma Pérez Zalduondo and María Isabel Cabrera García, 167–213. Granada: Editorial Universidad de Granada, 2010.

Torresarpi, Xavier A. "Plácido Domingo en México." *Pro Ópera* (May–June 2011): 38–44.

Trenas, Julio. "Luisillo y el Teatro de la Danza." *ABC*, March 3, 1971, 110–11, 115.

Trenas, Pilar. "El Rey entregó las medallas de oro de las Bellas Artes." *ABC*, May 30, 1980, 33.

"Triunfo de la zarzuela en Buenos Aires." *ABC*, February 25, 1970.

Turró, Ricardo. "'Luisa Fernanda': una siempreviva de la zarzuela hispana." *Buenos Aires Musical*, July 1, 1975.

"Un ballet flamenco actuará ante Paulo VI en la peregrinacion gitana." *La Vanguardia*, September 18, 1965, 9.

"Un excelente recital de guitarra de la concertista Irma Constanzo." *Mar del Plata* (Argentina), July 9, 1975.

"Un mensaje del maestro Torroba dirigido al público argentino." *La Razón* (Buenos Aires), October 23, 1934.

"Una deficiente 'Doña Francisquita.'" *Crisol* (Buenos Aires), November 6, 1934.

Unamuno, Miguel de. *En torno al casticismo*. Ed. Jean-Claude Rabaté. Madrid: Cátedra, 2005.

———*Essays and Soliloquies*. Trans. Crawford Flitch. New York: Alfred A. Knopf, 1925.

———*Obras completas*. 4 vols. Ed. Manuel García Blanco. Barcelona: Vergara, 1958.

Valencia, Antonio. "'El Poeta.'" *Ya, Hoja del Lunes*, June 30, 1980, 6.

Valera, Augusto. "Federico Moreno Torroba: 'Luisa Fernanda.'" *El Noticiero Universal*, June 8, 1972, 21.

Vall, Alfonso del. "Moreno Torroba, en Bilbao: 'La zarzuela está por los suelos.'" Clipping from unknown periodical, early 1976. [Na]

Vázquez Montalbán, Manuel. *Cancionero general del franquismo: 1939–1975*. Barcelona: Crítica, 2000.

Vicent, Manuel. "El pentagrama de Federico Moreno Torroba." *El País*, November 14, 1981, 13–14.

Vincent, Mary, and R. A. Stradling. *Cultural Atlas of Spain and Portugal*. New York: Facts on File, 1995.

Wade, Graham, ed. *Maestro Segovia*. London: Robson Books, 1986.

———*Segovia: A Celebration of the Man and His Music*. London: Allison & Busby, 1983.

———*The Traditions of the Classical Guitar*. London: Calder, 1980.

Warnke, Georgia. *After Identity: Rethinking Race, Sex, and Gender*. Cambridge: Cambridge University Press, 2007.

Webber, Christopher. *The Zarzuela Companion*. Foreword by Plácido Domingo. Lanham, Maryland: Scarecrow Press, 2002.

"Ya." Reprint of an article that appeared in *Ya* on September 14, 1982, regarding death of Federico Moreno Torroba. *Autores: Revista de información de la S.G.A.E.*, n3 (October 1982): 35.

Zinger, Pablo. "Son of Zarzuela." *Opera News* (July 1997).

Zueras Navarro, Joaquim. "Al respecto de Moreno Torroba." *OpusMusica*, n12 (February 2007). http://www.opusmusica.com/012/moreno.html.

———"Sus obras menos conocidas: Más sobre Moreno Torroba." *OpusMusica*, n30 (November 2008). http://www.opusmusica.com/030/torroba.html.

INDEX

Note: Italicized letter *n* designates footnotes.
Headings which appear periodically throughout the page range are designated with *passim*

CPSIA information can be obtained
at www.ICGtesting.com
Printed in the USA
LVOW12s1205060518
576179LV00002B/8/P